Africa's Development Dynamics 2023

INVESTING IN SUSTAINABLE DEVELOPMENT

This work is published under the responsibility of the Secretary-General of the OECD and the Chairperson of the AUC. The opinions expressed and arguments employed herein do not necessarily reflect the official views of the Member countries of the OECD or its Development Centre or of the member countries of the African Union Commission.

The names of countries and territories used in this joint publication follow the practice of the African Union.

This document, as well as any data and map included herein, are without prejudice to the status of or sovereignty over any territory, to the delimitation of international frontiers and boundaries and to the name of any territory, city or area.

Please cite this publication as:
AUC/OECD (2023), *Africa's Development Dynamics 2023: Investing in Sustainable Development*, AUC, Addis Ababa/OECD Publishing, Paris, https://doi.org/10.1787/3269532b-en.

ISBN 978-92-64-42501-9 (print)
ISBN 978-92-64-41759-5 (PDF)
ISBN 978-92-64-50712-8 (HTML)
ISBN 978-92-64-41655-0 (epub)

Africa's Development Dynamics
ISSN 2790-2765 (print)
ISSN 2790-2773 (online)

African Union Commission
ISBN 978-92-95119-91-8 (print)
ISBN 978-92-95119-92-5 (pdf)

Revised version, April 2024
Details of revisions available at: https://www.oecd.org/about/publishing/Corrigendum-Africa-Development-Dynamics-2023.pdf

Photo credits: © Cover design by Aida Buendia (OECD Development Centre) on the basis of images from Smilewithme, Taparong Siri, Sidhe, Tomiganka/Shutterstock.com.

Corrigenda to OECD publications may be found on line at: www.oecd.org/about/publishing/corrigenda.htm.

Foreword

The annual flagship report *Africa's Development Dynamics* provides the latest information on economic policies on the African continent and in its five regions. It proposes a new narrative assessing Africa's economic, social and institutional performance in light of the targets set by the African Union's Agenda 2063. This 2023 edition explores how Africa can attract investments that offer the best balance between economic, social and environmental objectives.

Africa's Development Dynamics is the product of a collaborative approach. It results from a strong partnership between the African Union Commission's Department of Economic Development, Trade, Tourism, Industry and Minerals and the OECD Development Centre, bringing together a team of academic researchers, economists, statisticians, and experts from Africa and other regions.

The first two chapters explore the current investment landscape in Africa and recommend priority actions, offering lessons from across the continent and beyond. The next five chapters focus respectively on the five regions as defined by the Abuja Treaty: Southern, Central, East, North and West Africa. These chapters tailor policy recommendations to strategic areas in each region, covering natural ecosystems, renewable energy, climate finance and agri-food value chains.

This edition draws on a wide range of data sources to analyse public, private, domestic and foreign sources of investments. These sources are complemented by primary data collected through an AUC/OECD online survey on investment risks, barriers and priorities linked to cross-border investments in African countries. The survey was administered from June to October 2022 to the networks of African business councils and the EU-Africa Business Forum, gathering responses from 58 African and non-African business representatives. Eight in-depth interviews with multinational investors that are members of the OECD Emerging Markets Network (EMnet) were also conducted to supplement the survey results.

The cut-off date for data used in the report was 18 February 2023, except for gross domestic product figures taken from the *IMF World Economic Outlook, April 2023.*

A statistical annex is available online, and its data are updated throughout the year. It contains the latest economic, social and institutional indicators across African countries for which data are comparable. The list of summary tables appears in the last pages of the report. The data are presented by country, region, Regional Economic Communities and other relevant groups of African countries (the categories include resource endowment, levels of income and socio-economic development, geographic access, and language groups). They compare Africa with other world regions and country groups. Additionally, the database offers statistical profiles for different African countries and country groups, comparing key thematic indicators related to investment. This database aims to inform decision makers, advisors, business analysts, private investors, journalists, non-governmental organisations and citizens around the globe who are interested in the development trajectories of African countries.

The full report is published in English, French and Portuguese. An electronic version is also available on line, together with accompanying figures and tables. These, along with the statistical annex, appear on the websites of both the African Union Commission (www.au.int/en/afdd2023) and the OECD Development Centre (https://oe.cd/AFDD-2023).

Acknowledgements

The flagship economic report *Africa's Development Dynamics 2023: Investing in Sustainable Development* (AfDD 2023) was jointly prepared by the African Union Commission (AUC) and the OECD Development Centre. It is published under the aegis of H.E. Moussa Faki Mahamat, AUC President, and H.E. Mathias Cormann, OECD Secretary-General. It was guided by H.E. Albert M. Muchanga, Commissioner for Economic Development, Trade, Tourism, Industry and Minerals of the African Union, and by Ragnheiður Elín Árnadóttir, Director of the OECD Development Centre. The report was supervised by Djamel Ghrib, Director, Department of Economic Development, Trade, Tourism, Industry and Minerals, and by Patrick Ndzana Olomo, Acting Head of the Economic Policy and Sustainable Development Division, Department of Economic Development, Trade, Tourism, Industry and Minerals, along with Federico Bonaglia, Deputy Director of the OECD Development Centre, and Arthur Minsat, Head of the OECD Development Centre's Africa Unit and Senior Economist.

The drafting team of the AUC consisted of Patrick Ndzana Olomo, Acting Head of the Economic Policy and Sustainable Development Division, Rumbidzai Treddah Manhando, Economist, Ndinaye Sekwi Charumbira, Policy Officer (Department of Economic Development, Trade, Tourism, Industry and Minerals), and Yeo Dossina, former Acting Director (Department for Economic Development, Integration and Trade). Regional experts who contributed to the report included Abiodun Egbetokun (De Montfort University and Nigeria's National Centre for Technology Management), Kevin Ibeh (Birkbeck University, University of London), Nabil Jedlane (ENCG Tanger), Nicholas Ngepah (University of Johannesburg) and Bruno Emmanuel Ongo Nkoa (Université de Yaoundé II). The team at the OECD Development Centre, led by Arthur Minsat, Head of the Africa Unit, with Nicolas Friederici, Francesco Napolitano and Elisa Saint Martin, included Bakary Traoré, Keiko Álvarez, Niall Begley, Médina Issa, Sébastien Markley, Ignacio Moreno, Shodai Tonomoto and Anne Weaver. Julia Peppino, Anne-Marie Trang (OECD) and Yamrot Kifle (AUC) gave valuable support to the research, production, logistics and administrative work on the report.

Inputs and data were provided by the OECD Directorate for Financial and Enterprise Affairs, the Network of Foundations Working for Development (netFWD), the International Energy Agency and the OECD Trade and Agriculture Directorate. Chapters 1 and 2 benefited from feedback from Mariya Aleksynska, Nelson Amaya, Pierre de Boisséson, Juan de Laiglesia, Håvard Halland, Alejandra Meneses, Bathylle Missika, Hyeshin Park, Lorenzo Pavone, Jan Rielaender, Henri-Bernard Solignac-Lecomte, Melanie Vilarasau Slade and Ayumi Yuasa (OECD Development Centre); Antonella Noya, Irene Basile and Chiara Petroli (OECD Centre for Entrepreneurship, SMEs, Regions and Cities); Dirk Röttgers (OECD Centre for Tax Policy and Administration); Hélène François, Fatos Koc, Iris Mantovani, Catriona Marshall, Giulio Mazzone, Stephen Thomsen and Martin Wermelinger (OECD Directorate for Financial and Enterprise Affairs); Yasmin Ahmad, Abdoulaye Fabregas, Ida McDonnell and Rachel Morris (OECD Development Co-operation Directorate); David Drysdale and Juliette Schleich (OECD Trade and Agriculture Directorate); Carlos Condé and Alin Horj (OECD Global Relations and Co-operation Directorate); Emma Gordon, Arnaud Rouget, Carlo Starace, Gianluca Tonolo and Daniel Wetzel (International Energy Agency); and Johannes Jütting (PARIS21).

A survey and interviews with private investors supported the original analysis in Chapters 1 and 2. Several African business councils and the EU-Africa Business Forum supported the dissemination of the AUC-OECD Development Centre investor survey from June to October 2022. Interviews, facilitated with support from the staff of the OECD

Emerging Markets Network (EMnet), were conducted with representatives of the AeTrade Group, the African Association of Automotive Manufacturers (AAAM), American Tower, AT&T, Enel Green Power, Eni, Huawei and Mastercard.

The report drew from the following consultations held in 2022 and 2023: the kick-off meeting (March 2022); the high-level consultation event "Mobilizing Investment for Productive Transformation and Quality Jobs" in the framework of Senegal's chairmanship of the African Union in 2022 (May); the joint AUC-DEV high-level working lunch "Strengthening Africa's Regional Production Networks" in the framework of the 21st International Economic Forum on Africa and the OECD Ministerial Meeting 2022 (June); the joint AUC-DEV high-level policy discussion "Enhancing Cross-border Digital Payment Systems for Africa's Regional Trade and Integration" (June 2022); the AUC-OECD Development Centre regional kick-off meeting; the 5th AU Specialized Technical Committee on Finance, Monetary Affairs, Economic Planning and Integration on the theme "Improving Africa's Access to Capital: Debt Management and the Rising Influence of Credit Rating Agencies" (July 2022); the meeting on AfDD 2023 at the Camões Institute; the AfDD 2023 peer review meeting (December 2022); the "AU-OECD/DEV High-level Dialogue on the AfDD 2023 Report" organised back to back with the 36th African Union Summit (February 2023); and the OECD Development Centre Governing Board meeting (April 2023).

Substantive contributions from Anzetse Were (FSD Kenya); Katharina Gugerell, Melinda Kunde and Stefan Weyler (Deutsche Gesellschaft für Internationale Zusammenarbeit [GIZ]); Jeremy Hajdenberg and Samuel Monteiro (Investisseurs & Partenaires), and Rana Roy (consultant) are gratefully acknowledged. The chapters benefited from comments and inputs from the following experts: Barassou Diawara (African Capacity Building Foundation [ACBF]); Ed Brown, Rob Floyd and Charles Odoom (African Center for Economic Transformation [ACET]); Julius Chupezi Tieguhong (African Development Bank [AfDB]); Adenle Ademola (Africa Sustainability Innovation Academy [ASI-Academy]); Eoghan Molloy (Asian Development Bank); Michel Rougeron and Françoise van de Ven (ATIBT); Pamla Gopaul (African Union Development Agency [AUDA-NEPAD]); Jeanne Lätt and Karen Pfundt (Bundesministerium für wirtschaftliche Zusammenarbeit und Entwicklung [BMZ]); Margarida Araújo, Paula Machado and Filipa Sousa (Camões – Instituto da Cooperação e da Língua, I.P.); Richard Eba'a Atyi (Center for International Forestry Research [CIFOR]); Charles Muchunku (consultant); Robert Zougmoré (Consultative Group for International Agricultural Research [CGIAR]); San Bilal and Bruce Byiers (ECDPM); Koffi Simeon (ECOWAS); Colin Bermingham (EIB); Geoffrey Aori Mabea (Energy Regulators Association of East Africa); Anna Hakami, Claire Hunault, Isabelle Magne and Domenico Rosa (European Commission); Kieu Ly Doan and Lisa Roob (GIZ); Matthias Hahl and Tim Heinemann (KfW); Thắng Nguyễn-Quốc (Oxford Economics Asia), Gonçalo Silva Marques (Permanent Delegation of Portugal to the OECD); Giovanni Valensisi (UNCTAD); Rodrigo Deiana (UN DESA); Zoubir Benhamouche, Adam Elhiraika, Sonia Essobmadje, Robert Lisinge and Sheng Zhao (UNECA); Barbara Boreta and Natasha Weisert (UNIDO); Leila Baghdadi (University of Tunis); Andrew Lawrence (University of the Witwatersrand) and Adeel Abbas Syed (World Bank).

The report benefited from external consultations held in 2022 and 2023 at the following meetings: AFD, "L'économie africaine 2022 : vers une relance durable ?"; AUC/UNIDO, "Towards a Commodity-based Greener Industrialization under the AfCFTA" (February 2022); Cameroon's African & Foreign Investment B2B senior management seminar (March 2022); the AUC Fridays of the Commission "Key Actions to Drive Inclusive Growth and Sustainable Development in African Countries" (April 2022); Le Cercle des Économistes, "L'Afrique : partenaire leader" (May 2022); the United Nations Economic Commission for Africa Regional workshop "Scaling-up Private Sector Participation in North Africa" (July 2022); the AUDA-

NEPAD/OECD-DEV High-level Dialogue on Rethinking Development Co-operation at the United Nations General Assembly (September 2022); Innodays: International Conference for Innovation and Entrepreneurship (November 2022); the OECD EMnet's Annual Meeting "Navigating Risk in Emerging Markets: From Crisis to Opportunity?" (December 2022); the African Sports and Creative Institute Business Breakfast "Investing in Africa Sports Industry" (January 2023).

The involvement of the editing, translation and proofreading team was crucial to producing the report on time. The report was edited by Isabelle Delpech (for chapters drafted in French) and Jill Gaston (for chapters drafted in English) and translated by Marika Boiron and the OECD Translation Services. Delphine Grandrieux and Elizabeth Nash supervised the production, and Luminess was responsible for page layout. Aida Buendía and Melodie Descours created the graphic design and the cover, and Irit Perry developed the infographics.

The OECD Development Centre is grateful to the European Commission (DG INTPA), Germany (BMZ/GIZ), Italy (Ministry of Foreign Affairs and International Co-operation) and Portugal (Camões – Instituto da Cooperação e da Língua, I.P., and the Ministry of Foreign Affairs) for their additional support and valuable feedback on this fifth annual edition of *Africa's Development Dynamics*.

Editorial

Investment is key to propel Africa's development, and to attain the African Union's Agenda 2063 and the Sustainable Development Goals. Yet, global crises have widened the African continent's sustainable financing gap. Africa needs an extra USD 1.6 trillion by 2030 – USD 194 billion annually – to achieve the Sustainable Development Goals. The sustainable financing gap can be bridged: it is equivalent to less than 0.2% of the value of global financial assets, or 10.5% of the African-held financial assets.

Since the turn of the 21st century, Africa has boasted the world's second-highest rate of economic growth after developing Asia. Yet despite this strong growth, global investment has shifted focus away from the continent. Greenfield foreign direct investment (FDI) has decreased from 12% of the world's total in 2017 to less than 6% in 2021 – compared to 15% for developing Asia and 10% for Latin America and the Caribbean.

Low sustainable investment is a tragic paradox, when so many opportunities exist. The continent boasts unique assets that should attract more investment to boost transformative and sustainable activities. Take the energy sector. Africa is endowed with 60% of the world's best solar resources, but only 1% of installed solar generation capacity. Africa also has the world's youngest population, with a median age of 19 years. By 2050 25% of the global population will reside in Africa. The world must therefore better invest in African youth now to fully realise its significant opportunities.

Low investor confidence and high cost of capital are holding back investment in Africa more than any other world region. In uncertain times, investors are more attentive to macroeconomic and political risks, like policy predictability and regulatory capacity. Scarce skilled labour and quality infrastructure can hinder investment, notably in technology-driven sectors or where large upfront investment is required. Investors' scepticism results in incongruity: the African continent boasts the world's lowest default rates for infrastructure, yet most projects go unfinanced.

Better policies can turn challenges into opportunities. Our analysis highlights three priorities. First, fit-for-purpose data will support informed investment decisions, better aligning risk perceptions to realities. Too many investors withhold decisions because of insufficient or costly information gathering. Second, African-led partnerships can optimise the impacts of sustainable finance on development and better catalyse investments into local sustainable activities. The deepening and integration of domestic capital markets, the development of local currency bonds and the strengthening of ESG compliance are part of the solution. Third, deepening African integration further, notably by implementing the African Continental Free Trade Area (AfCFTA) and its protocol on investment, will harmonise policies among countries and facilitate value chains development.

The growing partnership between the African Union Commission and the OECD, including through its Development Centre, provides an important venue to inform global narratives on Africa and bring the African continent from the frontier to the heart of global investment. Leveraging our policy dialogue platform on investment and productive transformation in Africa, we are committed to working together to monitor trends and identify good practices on the continent that mobilise greater investment for sustainable development and job creation. We are proud that this joint report, now in its fifth edition, contributes to enhanced global partnerships and an effective policy dialogue that benefits African people.

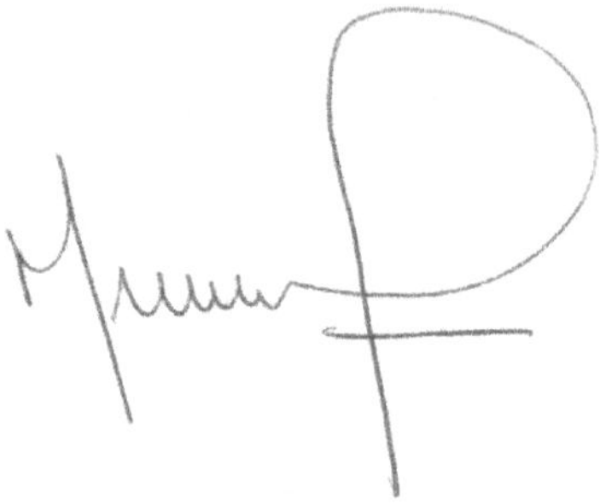

Moussa Faki Mahamat

Chairperson
African Union Commission

Mathias Cormann

Secretary-General
Organisation for Economic Co-operation and Development

Table of contents

Figures

Tables

Boxes

Abbreviations and acronyms

ACEC	Africa Clean Energy Corridor
ACET	African Center for Economic Transformation
AfCFTA	African Continental Free Trade Area
AfDB	African Development Bank
AFSF	Africa Food Security Fund
ASEAN	Association of Southeast Asian Nations
AU	African Union
AUC	African Union Commission
AUDA-NEPAD	African Union Development Agency-New Economic Partnership for Africa's Development
BGFA	Beyond the Grid Fund for Africa
BMZ	Bundesministerium für wirtschaftliche Zusammenarbeit und Entwicklung (Federal Ministry for Economic Co-operation and Development)
CAADP	Comprehensive Africa Agriculture Development Programme
CAAP	Common African Agro-Parks Programme
CAFI	Central African Forest Initiative
CAPEX	Capital expenditure
CFC	Common Fund for Commodities
CFF	Climate Finance Facility
COP	United Nations Conference of the Parties
COSUMAF	Central African Financial Market Supervisory Commission
CRA	Credit rating agency
CSA	Climate-smart agriculture
DFI	Development finance institution
DSSI	Debt Service Suspension Initiative
EAC	East African Community
EAPP	Eastern Africa Power Pool
ECCAS	Economic Community of Central African States
ECOWAP	Economic Community of West Africa Agricultural Policy
ECOWAS	Economic Community of West African States
EFFECT	Equitable Framework and Finance for Extractive-Based Countries in Transition
ESG	Environmental, Social and Governance
EU	European Union
FDI	Foreign direct investment
FiT	Feed-in-Tariff
GDP	Gross domestic product
GFC	Global Climate Fund
GFCF	Gross fixed capital formation
GHG	Greenhouse gas
GIZ	Gesellschaft für Internationale Zusammenarbeit (German Corporation for International Co-operation)
ICT	Information and communications technology
IDA	International Development Association
IEA	International Energy Agency
IFAD	International Fund for Agricultural Development

IFC	International Finance Corporation
IFSWF	International Forum of Sovereign Wealth Funds
IMF	International Monetary Fund
IPA	Investment promotion agency
IPO	Initial public offering
IPP	Independent power producer
ISO	International Organization for Standardization
KPI	Key performance indicator
LAC	Latin America and the Caribbean
NAIP	National agricultural investment plan
NDC	Nationally determined contribution
ODA	Official development assistance
OECD	Organisation for Economic Co-operation and Development
PAAP	Pan-African Auto Pact
PALOP	Países Africanos de Língua Oficial Portuguesa (Portuguese-speaking African countries)
PAPSS	Pan-African Payment and Settlement System
PFI	Policy Framework for Investment
PIDA	Programme for Infrastructure Development in Africa
PPF	Project Preparation Facility
REDD+	Reducing emissions from deforestation and forest degradation
REEESAP	Renewable Energy and Energy Efficiency Strategy and Action Plan
REFiT	Renewable Energy Feed-in Tariff
SADC	Southern African Development Community
SDG	Sustainable Development Goals
SDR	Special Drawing Right
SEFA	Sustainable Energy Fund for Africa
SEZ	Special economic zone
SME	Small and medium-sized enterprise
SWF	Sovereign wealth fund
UN	United Nations
UNCTAD	United Nations Conference on Trade and Development
UNECA	United Nations Economic Commission for Africa
UNIDO	United Nations Industrial Development Organization
WAICSA	West African Initiative for Climate-Smart Agriculture

Executive summary

Africa's sustainable financing gap until 2030 is about USD 1.6 trillion. According to this report's estimates, the continent needs additional financing of about USD 194 billion annually to achieve the Sustainable Development Goals by 2030. This annual sustainable financing gap is equivalent to 7% of Africa's gross domestic product (GDP) and 34% of its investments in 2021. The annual gap equals less than 0.2% of the global and 10.5% of the African-held stock of financial assets.

African economies hold unique assets to close the continent's sustainable financing gap:

- Real GDP growth is estimated to return to the levels before COVID-19, at 3.7% in 2023, the second highest rate in the world after developing Asia (5%) and before Latin America and the Caribbean (1.6%). The growth is estimated at 4.9% in East Africa, 4.3% in Central Africa, 4% in North Africa, 3.8% in West Africa and 1.4% in Southern Africa.
- The proportion of African youth completing an upper-secondary or tertiary education could reach 34% by 2040, up from 23% in 2020 and 18% in 2010. Africa has the world's youngest population, with a median age of 19 years, compared to 30 for Latin America and the Caribbean, 31 for developing Asia and 42 for Europe.
- Natural resources represent key assets for African economies. Natural capital accounts for 19% of Africa's total wealth compared to 7% for Latin America and the Caribbean and 3% for developing Asia. From 2011 to 2020, African forests increased the global carbon stock by 11.6 million kilotons of CO_2-equivalent net emissions, while carbon stocks in forests outside Africa declined by 13 million kilotons.
- Africa's domestic financial resources hold a large potential for sustainable development. Domestic government revenues amounted to USD 466 billion in 2021, equivalent to 17% of GDP, and assets held by African institutional investors amounted to USD 1.8 trillion in 2020, equivalent to 73% of GDP. During the COVID-19 pandemic in 2020-21, intra-Africa foreign direct investment was three times more resilient than foreign direct investment from outside the continent, boosting growth in renewable energies and in information and communications technology.

Despite this potential, global crises are affecting investment in Africa more than in other regions. The average inflation rate for the continent is projected to reach 15.5% in 2023 – the highest level in 27 years – with peaks above 15% in 11 African countries. As of February 2023, 8 African countries were in debt distress (out of 9 globally), and 13 were at a high risk of debt distress (out of 27 globally). Africa's share of global greenfield foreign direct investment has been on a downward trend in recent years, dropping to 6% in 2020-21 (the lowest share in 17 years), while high-income countries in other parts of the world have recorded their highest share ever (61%), compared to 17% for developing Asia and 10% for Latin America and the Caribbean.

The cost of capital in Africa has risen above the levels in other world regions, pricing some African governments out of bond markets while thwarting investments in transformational sectors such as renewable energy. The spread on an average African Eurobond (a measure for the potential cost of sovereign borrowing) reached a 15-year high of about 10 percentage points in September 2022, eclipsing previous peaks. In 2021, the average cost of capital for energy projects was about seven times higher in Africa than in Europe and North America. While experienced investors attain higher average returns in Africa than in other world regions, the lack of reliable information and data is an important barrier to new investments.

To increase resilience to external shocks and improve investor confidence, African policy makers can work with international partners and African civil society to mobilise investments towards Agenda 2063 and sustainable development. The international community must follow through on commitments on debt restructuring and climate finance. African governments, development partners, the private sector and civil society must work closer together to improve Africa's investment landscape. This report proposes three key policy priorities to accelerate sustainable investments on the continent:

- **More and better data will reduce transaction costs, improve sustainability assessments and increase investor confidence.** In 2021, less than a third of African countries (30%) had a fully funded statistical plan, compared to almost half the countries in Latin America and the Caribbean (44%) and in developing Asia (47%). Improved macroeconomic data may help align risk perception with real risks. Partnerships with business associations or academic institutions can allow government agencies to share industry data that inform investors' risk assessments at lower cost. African governments can also facilitate sustainability assessments through disclosure requirements and the provision of training and incentives to smaller firms with limited capacity.
- **Strengthening the capacity of Africa's large development finance network will improve the allocation of sustainable finance.** The 102 African development finance institutions (DFIs) can act as intermediaries between international finance and local projects, in line with national development agendas. The international community can channel more resources to well-managed DFIs and deliver on existing obligations, for instance, by increasing the allocation of climate adaptation finance. African governments and DFIs can also scale up the use of innovative de-risking and financing tools, including green, social, sustainability, and sustainability-linked bonds or local currency financing solutions emerging in many countries. Developing and interconnecting capital markets and stock exchanges will contribute to the growth of African firms.
- **Regional integration policies will improve and harmonise Africa's investment landscape.** Cross-border initiatives such as development corridors and digital infrastructures can reduce trade frictions and market fragmentation. At the same time, small and medium-sized enterprises need targeted support to seize investment opportunities along regional value chains. The African Continental Free Trade Area (AfCFTA) Investment Protocol aims to harmonise the African investment policy landscape but requires effective monitoring mechanisms and public-private alliances.

The five regional chapters of this report highlight how African regions can accelerate sustainable investments in strategic sectors. African regions can better leverage their unique assets to accelerate sustainable development and productive transformation. Regional case studies propose ways of operationalising the continental policy recommendations in specific sectors.

Policy recommendations to accelerate sustainable investments in African regions

Region	Case study	Policy recommendations
Southern Africa	Renewable energies	• Harmonise regulatory frameworks and accelerate regional initiatives on renewable energy infrastructures • Enhance public-private alliances and development finance based on national energy priorities • Adopt targeted policy solutions to scale up off-grid renewable energy projects in rural areas
Central Africa	Natural ecosystems	• Improve natural capital accounting to better inform investors and stakeholders • Establish institutional frameworks for the monetisation of natural ecosystems • Ensure local ownership when developing innovative financing mechanisms
East Africa	Renewable energies	• Enhance regulatory frameworks and energy utilities' capacity to improve investor confidence • Strengthen local financial institutions to catalyse resources for renewable energy projects • Support the growth of innovative enterprises through regional integration policies like the AfCFTA
North Africa	Climate finance	• Improve assessment of financing needs based on national and multi-sectorial priorities • Adopt and implement inclusive regulatory frameworks on sustainable finance • Encourage the development of sustainable finance markets (nationally and regionally)
West Africa	Agri-food value chains	• Increase smallholder farmers' access to financial products focused on productivity and sustainability • Strengthen regional agricultural policies and place-based programmes like agro-industrial parks • Support food security and agricultural practices through agro-poles, incubators and technical partnerships

Overview

The African continent offers large untapped potential for sustainable investments

Sustainable investments are essential for Africa's economic, social and environmental development. Investments are sustainable if their economic, social and environmental benefits outweigh their total cost. When mobilising and allocating investments, African countries need to manage tensions between economic, social and environmental goals such as productive transformation, social inclusion and resilience to climate change. This includes balancing energy production and carbon mitigation, developing agricultural land use and conserving ecosystems, or creating mass employment while promoting labour standards. The *Africa's Development Dynamics 2023* report provides an evidence-based analysis of Africa's investment landscape and identifies important investment-related policies that promote sustainable development on the continent as a whole and in each of its five regions.

Africa's sustainable financing gap can be bridged

At about 7% of the continent's gross domestic product (GDP), Africa's sustainable financing gap is small in comparison to its financial resources and to those available worldwide. This gap between the financing needed to achieve the Sustainable Development Goals and the availability of financial resources averaged USD 194 billion annually for 2015-21 (Figure 1). This sum equals 34% of Africa's investments in 2021 (gross fixed capital formation, defined as the acquisition of produced assets). The amount appears small relative to capital available: it is equivalent to less than 0.2% of the global and 10.5% of the African-held stock of assets under management – financial assets that wealth management firms handle on behalf of investors. A hypothetical annual reallocation of just 0.2% of global assets under management would bring their total allocation to Africa from currently under 1% to around 2.3% by 2030. This amount would still remain below the continent's share of global GDP (2.9% in 2020).

Figure 1. **Africa's sources of finance and sustainable financing gap, 2015-21 (USD billion)**

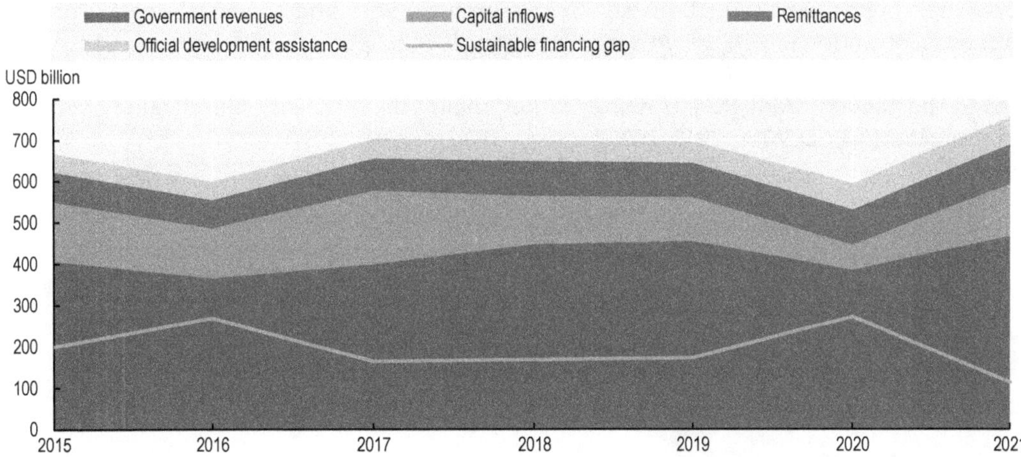

Source: Authors' calculations based on OECD (2022a), *Global Outlook on Financing for Sustainable Development 2023*, https://doi.org/10.1787/fcbe6ce9-en and other sources. See Annex 1.A for details on data sources and methodology.

StatLink https://stat.link/xcpd4f

Africa's financing shortfall has recently increased due to the COVID-19 pandemic, the global repercussions of conflicts and climate change. Government revenues decreased due to the COVID-19 pandemic: in 2020, Africa's average tax-to-GDP ratio declined by 0.3 percentage points to 16.0% (OECD/ATAF/AUC, 2022). International conflicts have led to disruptions in supply chains, affecting critical imports (food, energy and fertilisers). Climate financing needs have consistently not been met: between 2019 and 2020, USD 11.4 billion of Africa's total climate financing went to adaptation – almost five times less than the USD 53 billion per year set under the nationally determined contributions of the Paris Agreement (GCA, 2022).

Global uncertainty and inflation have escalated the costs of debt for most African countries. Debt levels have risen across Africa over the past decade, with the cost of debt service rising from 3% to over 5% of gross national income over the 2010-20 period. More recently, crisis-induced global uncertainty led to risk repricing. The average inflation rate for the continent is projected to reach 15.5% in 2023 – the highest level in 27 years – with peaks above 15% in 11 African countries. The increase in borrowing costs for African countries excluded countries with lower credit ratings from international capital markets and prevented debt refinancing (IMF, 2023a). For instance, Eurobond yields multiplied from 2021 to 2022 for many African countries, and the spread on an average African Eurobond (a measure for the potential cost of borrowing on capital markets) across 20 countries reached a 15-year high of about 10 percentage points in September 2022, eclipsing previous peaks of the COVID-19 crisis in 2020 and the global financial crisis in 2008 (Smith, 2022). Between April 2022 and April 2023, no African country has been able to issue new Eurobonds (IMF, 2023a). As of February 2023, the International Monetary Fund (IMF) considered 8 African countries in debt distress and 13 more at a high risk of debt distress (IMF, 2023b).

With unique assets, African countries represent the world's investment frontier

Africa has enjoyed high growth supported by investment, but the continent needs more transformative, sustainable growth. Since the turn of the 21st century, Africa has boasted the world's second-highest rate of economic growth after developing Asia. African growth is bouncing back since the global recession of 2020: real growth is projected at 3.7% in 2023 and 4.2% in 2024[1] – after developing Asia and before Latin America and the Caribbean, respectively at 5.0% and 1.6% in 2023 and 4.9% and 2.2% in 2024. High investment rates boosted Africa's growth, with the contribution of gross fixed capital formation to GDP growth reaching a peak of 1.2 percentage points in 2017-19, before declining during the COVID-19 pandemic in 2020-22 (Figure 2). Overall, growth has not led to the needed productive transformation, including job creation and value chain integration (AUC/OECD, 2018, 2019, 2022).

Figure 2. **Components of economic growth in Africa and other world regions, 2011-22**

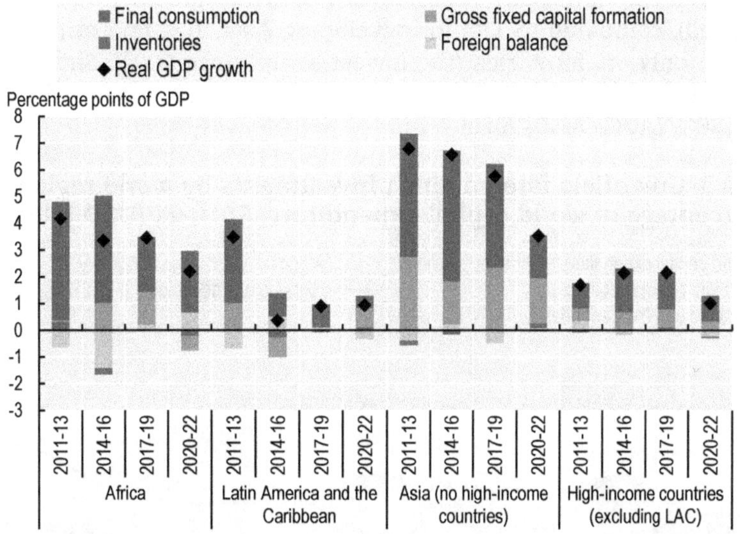

Note: See note under Figure 1.1 in Chapter 1.

Sources: Authors' calculations based on IMF (2022), *World Economic Outlook Database*, October 2022 Edition, www.imf.org/en/Publications/WEO/weo-database/2022/October.

StatLink https://stat.link/14zp78

The African continent holds unique human and natural capital for sustainable investment. Africa has the world's youngest population, with a median age of 19 years, compared to 30 for Latin America and the Caribbean, 31 for developing Asia and 42 for Europe. By 2050, Africa's population will almost double, from about 1.4 billion inhabitants to nearly 2.5 billion. More than half of the world's population growth will happen on the continent (AfDB/OECD/UNDP, 2015; UN DESA, 2022). The proportion of African youth completing an upper-secondary or tertiary education could reach 34% by 2040, up from 23% in 2020 and 18% in 2010 (AUC/OECD, 2021). From 2011 to 2020, African forests increased carbon stock by 11.6 million kilotons of CO_2-equivalent net emissions, while carbon stocks in forests outside Africa declined by 13 million kilotons. Of this increase, 59% was in Central African forests, now recognised as the world's largest carbon sink (FAO, 2022). The continent boasts 60% of the best solar resources globally (IEA, 2022). Natural capital accounts for 19% of Africa's total wealth, compared to 7% for Latin America and the Caribbean and 3% for developing Asia (World Bank, 2021).

Risk perceptions and information shortages have lowered investor confidence and increased the cost of capital in Africa more than in other world regions

Despite its potential, Africa attracts the lowest share of capital from institutional investors, compared to other world regions. In 2017-18, global pension funds and insurance companies allocated only 0.5% of their capital to African assets, compared to 1.2% for Latin America and the Caribbean and 4.2% for developing Asia. Africa's share of global investment capital has remained low (below 1%), even though global assets under management grew from USD 48 trillion in 2010 to over USD 112 trillion in 2021, despite economic downturns (BCG, 2022).

Africa's share of global foreign direct investment (FDI) and participation in global value chains have stagnated. In the last decade, global greenfield FDI – i.e. announced FDI projects that create new production facilities instead of acquiring existing ones – has decreased at an average rate of 3% per year. Moreover, since 2016, new investments have been shifting from developing countries to high-income countries (Figure 3). The COVID-19 pandemic accelerated this trend: in 2020-21, high-income countries outside of Latin America and the Caribbean attracted 61% of global greenfield FDI (the highest share ever recorded), compared to 17% for developing Asia, 10% for Latin America and the Caribbean and only 6% for Africa (the lowest share since 2004). Similarly, Africa's participation in global value chains has stagnated since the 2008 global financial crisis: it was only 1.7% in 2019 (AUC/OECD, 2022).

Figure 3. **Greenfield foreign direct investments by world region, as a percentage of world capital expenditure, 2010-21 (USD billion)**

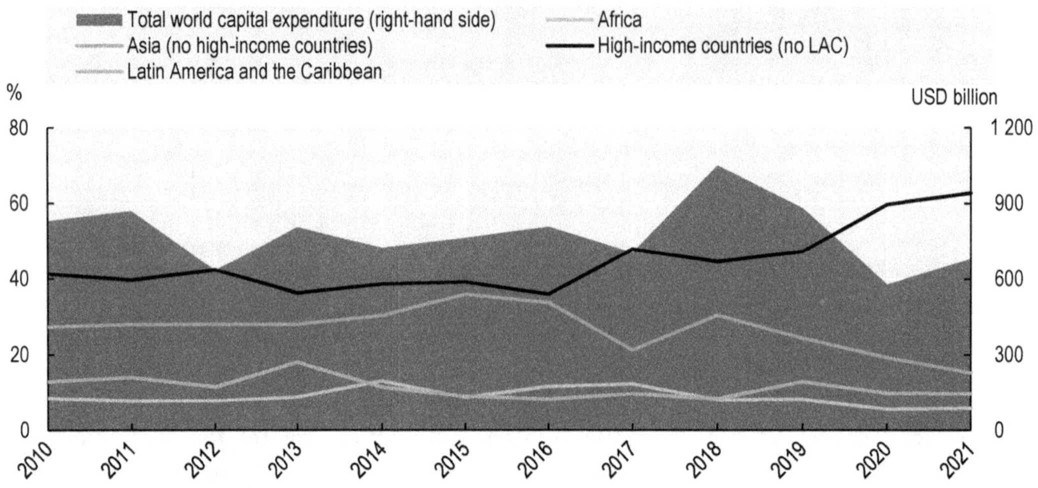

Note: LAC = Latin America and the Caribbean.

Source: Authors' calculations based on fDi Intelligence (2022), *fDi Markets* (database), www.fdiintelligence.com/fdi-markets.

StatLink https://stat.link/yr8mj9

Risks and information shortages persist as barriers to investment mobilisation in many African countries. Representatives of global multinational enterprises surveyed and interviewed for this report emphasised macroeconomic risks, policy instability and the lack of regulatory capacity as persisting barriers to their investments in African countries (Figure 4). Yet, some highlighted that investors with in-country experience can generate higher rates of return in Africa compared to other world regions. An overall lack of information inhibits assessments of investment opportunities in African markets: limited information and data may result in delays (investors "wait and see") and amplify "perception premiums".

Figure 4. **Responses to the AUC/OECD investor survey question "Which of the following risks have been most important for your investments in African countries?"**

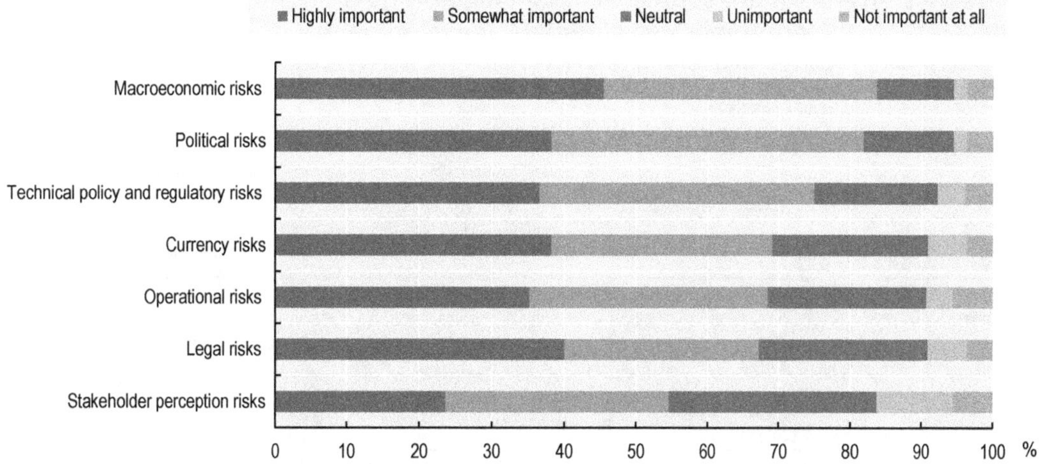

Note: n = 52 to 55. The AUC/OECD survey was administered in September 2022 to the networks of African business councils and the EU-Africa Business Forum. For further information, see Figure 1.6 in Chapter 1.

StatLink https://stat.link/vu9l0w

The poor credit ratings of many African countries may overestimate risks and result in excessive cost of capital. As of December 2022, leading global credit rating agencies gave investment-grade ratings only to Botswana and Mauritius, followed by Côte d'Ivoire, Morocco and South Africa in the non-investment grade speculative category (Trading Economics, 2022). Credit rating agencies may lack detailed data and insights on African countries. A recent UNDP (2023) study compared neutral model-based ratings with those issued by credit rating agencies, estimating that the latter led to higher interest rates and dampened investment mobilisation, creating a total opportunity cost of up to USD 74.5 billion for African countries. Country credit ratings also serve as a benchmark for private debt holders, thereby affecting the cost of private capital as well (e.g. interest rates and longevity of loans). The high cost of capital has been a barrier to investment mobilisation especially in sectors where large upfront capital expenditures are required. This is the case in the energy sector where, in 2021, the weighted average cost of capital in Africa was about seven times higher than in Europe and North America (IEA, 2022).

Better allocating existing sources of finance can support Africa's regional integration and sustainable development

Africa's external and domestic sources of finance show untapped potential to drive sustainable investments on the continent. Table 1 examines strengths and weaknesses of some of Africa's major potential sources of sustainable investments. The potential of FDI and remittances to contribute to sustainable growth remains underexploited due to limited integration with productive activities on the continent. Official development assistance (ODA) showed resilience during the COVID-19 pandemic but remains below pledged levels. Sustainability-oriented private investments such as impact investing and philanthropy still have limited scale and impact, while being prone to specific sectoral and country biases. Among domestic sources of investment, regional multinational enterprises and institutional investors offer untapped potential to support sustainable and resilient growth. Government revenues represent the largest source of finance in most countries, but their allocation towards sustainability objectives remains limited and insufficiently reported. Mobilising domestic resources is necessary to widen the fiscal space of national governments and reduce debt burdens, as well as attract sustainable investments from the private sector.

Table 1. **Africa's main sources of financing and their potential for promoting sustainable development**

	Sources	Amounts % of Africa's GDP	Strengths	Weaknesses
External	**Foreign direct investment**	USD 83 billion 2.6% GDP (2021)	Productivity spillovers for local suppliers; training for the local workforce	Limited alignment with sustainable development; spillovers reliant on effective linkages; vulnerable to shocks
	Remittances	USD 96 billion 3.8% GDP (2021)	Connections with local economies and the informal sector	Limited co-ordination of funds; limited focus on productive transformation
	Official development assistance	USD 65 billion 2.5% GDP (2021)	Resilience to global shocks; focus on social and ecological sustainability	Remaining below pledges; limited mobilisation of private investments in low-income countries
	Global impact investors	USD 24.3 billion 1.0% GDP (2019) (assets under management allocated to Africa)	Focus on transformative sectors (e.g. energy, finance, and small and medium-sized enterprises)	Focus on large and more advanced economies
	Private philanthropy	USD 2.1 billion 0.1% GDP (2018-19)	Focus on social sectors (e.g. health and education)	Relatively small amounts; not targeting the poorest countries
Domestic	**Government revenues**	USD 466 billion 16.7% GDP (2021)	Largest source of financing in most countries; resilient towards international monetary conditions	Country-specific challenges; decreases in revenue on a real per-capita basis; limited data on allocation towards sustainable development
	Multinational enterprises based in Africa	USD 2.7 billion 0.1% GDP (2021) (FDI outflows)	Regional footprint; resilience to global shocks	Limited amounts of financing; risk of reinforcing regional inequalities
	Domestic institutional investors	USD 1.8 trillion 73.3% GDP (2020) (assets under management held in Africa)	Vast financial resources; embedded in local financial markets	Risk aversion; limited investments in sustainable assets

Note: "Amounts" refers to financial flows during the reference period with the exception of "Global impact investors" and "Domestic institutional investors", which refer to end-of-period stocks (assets under management). Financial sources may overlap and cannot be aggregated. Global impact investors (GIIN, 2020) and private philanthropy (OECD, 2021a) are considered external sources of finance, as they mostly originate outside the African continent.
Source: Authors' compilation based on various sources. For further information, see Table 1.2 in Chapter 1.

External financial inflows represent important sources of finance for development on the African continent (Figure 1), but their sustainable development impacts remain limited.

- In 2021, FDI and remittances remained the largest external financial flows (6.4% of Africa's GDP); but their potential to promote sustainable development remains underexploited. For example, USD 1 million in FDI creates 14 jobs in textiles, 10 in electronic equipment and 9 in automotive, but these job-intensive sectors attracted only 4.5% of greenfield FDI to African countries over 2003-20.
- ODA increased in response to COVID-19 but remained at about 0.36% of donor countries' gross national income – well below the pledged level of 0.7% set by the 2030 Agenda for Sustainable Development. In 2022, bilateral ODA to Africa declined by 7.4% compared to the previous year, despite a general increase at the global level (OECD, 2023). Moreover, ODA shows specific sectoral and country biases: while private finance mobilised through ODA grew fivefold in Africa between 2012 and 2020 (from only USD 4 billion to USD 22 billion), less than 30% of the amounts mobilised targeted low-income countries (OECD, 2022b).
- Sustainability-oriented private investments (impact investing and philanthropy) are still small and unbalanced. For example, Southern Africa has a GDP (purchasing

power parity) per capita three times larger than Central Africa but, over 2016-19, received over four times more philanthropic inflows per capita.

FDI with linkages to local economies and suppliers can contribute to sustainable development. While effects can take time to materialise, FDI can enhance growth and innovation in the host country (Diallo, Jacolin and Rabaud, 2021; OECD, 2022c). Our analysis of firm-level data from the World Bank Enterprise Surveys shows that, on average, foreign firms operating in African countries rely less on inputs sourced from local suppliers than their peers in Asia, notably in agro-processing and manufacturing.

Mobilising diaspora investment can help develop local production. Between 20% and 30% of global remittances target economic activities (IFAD/World Bank, 2015). Diaspora investments are well-placed to support local production networks as most diaspora investors tend to establish more connections with local suppliers (Amendolagine et al., 2013). However, most of these investments are channelled towards informal activities (Asquith and Opoku-Owusu, 2020). Structured diaspora investment products could tap into the estimated USD 33.7 billion annual diaspora savings (Faal, 2019). Careful planning, regulatory approval in host countries and competitive pricing are key for successful African diaspora bond initiatives (AUC/OECD, 2021).

Intra-African greenfield FDI was more resilient to global shocks than FDI from outside Africa, and it has room to grow. From 2017 to 2021, intra-African FDI flows accounted for only 9% of total greenfield FDI to African countries. It showed resilience during the COVID-19 pandemic: in 2020-21, intra-African greenfield FDI decreased by 20% compared to 2018-19, while the drop in greenfield FDI from outside the continent was about 3 times more (-58%). Africa-based investors have increased new investment projects in ICT, renewable energies and metals (fDi Intelligence, 2022). Analysis of firm-level data from the *Orbis* database highlights that the vast majority (69%) of Africa-based listed companies is active in growing service-oriented sectors such as financial services (29%), retail (8%), real estate (6%), and information and communication technologies (6%).

Assets held by African institutional investors have grown rapidly, with much potential for investments in sustainable economic activities. According to estimates, in 2020, African institutional investors had assets under management of about USD 1.8 trillion, a 48% increase from 2017 (Juvonen et al., 2019). OECD data show that pension funds across 15 African countries accumulated USD 380 billion of assets by 2020, with South Africa accounting for almost 80% of the total (OECD, 2021b). This translates into an average GDP share of 25% for Africa (mostly driven by South Africa, Namibia and Botswana), compared to 22% in Latin America and the Caribbean and 3% in developing Asia. Yet, alternative assets – such as infrastructure, real estate, green and sustainable assets, private equity, and venture capital – accounted for less than 3% of portfolios in an assessment of five African pension markets, namely Ghana, Kenya, Namibia, Nigeria and South Africa (AfDB/IFC/MFW4A, 2022). Half of the major African pension funds state that sustainability is an important goal of their investments; however, they share limited information on their sustainability strategies (Stewart, 2022). This mirrors global trends among institutional investors (OECD, 2021c).

Better data, African-led partnerships and regional policies can accelerate sustainable investments across the continent

Which policies can help African countries mobilise greater investments and allocate them towards Agenda 2063 and priorities for sustainable development? Effectively allocating existing African financial and fiscal resources towards sustainability outcomes offers the largest potential. While the international community needs to meet its sustainable finance obligations towards developing countries, African governments, the private sector and civil society must work closer together to attract more sustainable investments into African economies. This report proposes three main policy priorities to accelerate sustainable investments on the continent (Table 2).

Table 2. **Investing in Africa's sustainable development: Three main policy agendas for the continent**

Challenge	Policy agenda	Policy action
Low investor confidence and high cost of capital	Informing risk assessments and sustainability measurements	Enhance national statistical capacity for country risk assessments Inform investor due diligence and project risk assessments with detailed data Support locally adapted sustainability frameworks and data collection
	African-led partnerships to deliver on frameworks and tools	Deepen regional capital markets to support African corporate growth and broaden the availability of financial products for investors Increase the capacity of local financial institutions to align sustainable finance with national priorities Adapt and expand innovative financing instruments fit for local contexts
Frameworks needed to explore African assets and steer investments towards sustainable development	Regional integration to widen impacts	Harmonise policies, improve digital infrastructures and development corridors Provide support for small and medium-sized enterprises to integrate into regional value chains Ensure effective implementation of the African Continental Free Trade Area Investment Protocol

African regions can better leverage their assets to accelerate productive transformation and sustainable development. The report's five regional chapters highlight how African regions can accelerate sustainable investments in strategic sectors (see Table 3 and Chapters 3-7). Case studies propose ways of operationalising the continental policy recommendations presented in Table 2 in specific sectors and regions while suggesting how productive transformation and sustainable development outcomes can be mutually reinforcing.

- Southern Africa accounts for about 60% of Africa's installed solar energy capacity, while the Rift Valley in East Africa holds the continent's richest geothermal potential. The renewable energy sector offers these regions opportunities to combine energy security and climate mitigation with job and enterprise creation.
- Central Africa's forests contain 62% of the continent's biomass carbon stock, or 11% of the global stock. Preserving the region's natural ecosystems promises both financial and ecological gains.
- Climate-related blended finance to North Africa increased by a factor of 4.9, from an average of USD 91 million over the period 2012-16 to USD 447 million in 2017-21, compared to a factor of 2.4 for developing Asia and 3.4 for Latin America and the Caribbean. Harmonised and deepened institutional frameworks on such financial instruments can help the region mobilise the funds needed for effective climate adaptation.
- Agriculture, forestry and fishing value added in West Africa was 24.4% of GDP in 2021, compared to 16.5% for Africa and 4.3% for the world. Upgrading the region's supply chains for processed food products would reduce imports and informality in the sector.

Table 3. **Investing in Africa's sustainable development: Policy recommendations by region**

Region	Case study	Policy recommendations
Southern Africa	Renewable energies	• Harmonise regulatory frameworks and accelerate regional initiatives on renewable energy infrastructures • Enhance public-private alliances and development finance based on national energy priorities • Adopt targeted policy solutions to scale up off-grid renewable energy projects in rural areas
Central Africa	Natural ecosystems	• Improve natural capital accounting to better inform investors and stakeholders • Establish institutional frameworks for the monetisation of natural ecosystems • Ensure local ownership when developing innovative financing mechanisms
East Africa	Renewable energies	• Enhance regulatory frameworks and energy utilities' capacity to improve investor confidence • Strengthen local financial institutions to catalyse resources for renewable energy projects • Support the growth of innovative enterprises through regional integration policies like the African Continental Free Trade Area and the East African Economic Community
North Africa	Climate finance	• Improve assessments of financing needs based on national and multi-sectorial priorities • Adopt and implement inclusive regulatory frameworks on sustainable finance • Encourage the development of sustainable finance markets (nationally and regionally)
West Africa	Agri-food value chains	• Increase smallholder farmers' access to financial products focused on productivity and sustainability • Strengthen regional agricultural policies and place-based programmes like agro-industrial parks • Support food security and agricultural practices through agro-poles, incubators and technical partnerships

Increased information and data availability leads to better resource allocation and investor confidence

Strengthening the national statistical capacities of African countries can make country risk assessments more accurate and reduce the cost of debt servicing. International organisations and partnerships could step up their support for national statistical capacities in ministries of finance and statistical offices. At the country level, most governments can increase public expenditure on statistical capacities to 0.15% of national budgets (up from an Africa-wide average of only 0.07% in 2021), as committed through the *Strategy for the Harmonization of Statistics in Africa 2017-2026* (AUC/AfDB/UNECA/ACBF, 2017; AUDA-NEPAD, 2022). A large number of African countries could improve their sovereign bond spreads by 14.5 basis points and decrease their external debt by about USD 400 million by putting their average levels of data transparency (i.e. adherence to international data standards and best practices) on par with that of better-performing countries (Kubota and Zeufack, 2020). Enhancing the statistical capacities of tax authorities would also help African countries recuperate a portion of the USD 50 billion in illicit financial flows that they lose each year, for instance, by allowing authorities to enforce country-by-country financial reporting for multinational enterprises or match tax records with business registration data (High Level Panel on Illicit Financial Flows from Africa, 2021).

Table 4. **Policy recommendations to enhance information and data availability**

Type of risk assessment	Specific policy actions	Illustration
Sovereign risk assessments	• Improve data collection and dissemination, in particular macroeconomic data • Adopt licensing and disclosure requirements for credit rating agencies	In 2021, less than 30% of African countries had a fully funded statistical plan, compared to 44% in Latin America and the Caribbean and 47% in developing Asia.
Project risk assessments	• Partner with third parties to share detailed market, technical and legal information for targeted sectors • Strengthen business-to-government dialogue, enabling feedback about policies and investment barriers	The African Automotive Data Network compiles detailed data on vehicle sales, demand, motorisation rates and assembly plants.
Sustainability assessments	• Harmonise and enforce methodologies on sustainability assessments and reporting • Provide small and mid-sized enterprises with the capacity to collect sustainable investment data	The AUC/OECD investor survey shows that supply chain partners' lacking capacity, unclear sustainability criteria and limited measurement capacity represent important barriers.

Note: See Table 2.2 in Chapter 2 for additional examples.

Public entities and international organisations, in partnership with private actors, can aggregate and share sectoral information and sustainability data. Results from the AUC/OECD investor survey show that investors demand more official and specialised information on incentives and statistical data (Figure 5). Investment promotion agencies, regulators and other public entities should provide such information at the national level, regularly updating data and presenting them in harmonised and user-friendly formats. Likewise, African governments can encourage the collection of sustainability data through national frameworks that can become the groundwork for a continental sustainable finance architecture (Were, 2022; Chapter 7).

In **Central Africa**, improving natural capital accounting could unlock additional finance for the region's sustainable development (Chapter 4). Despite representing the largest carbon sink in the world, valued at USD 55 billion per year, only 12% of international finance allocated to sustainable forest management went to Congo River Basin forests over the past decade, behind the Amazon River Basin (34%) and Southeast Asia's forests (55%). Adherence to international frameworks such as the United Nations System of Environmental Economic Accounting, as done by Burundi and Cameroon, can help governments provide reliable estimates of natural capital, assess opportunities and improve the allocation of sustainable finance.

Figure 5. **Responses to AUC/OECD investor survey question "Which sources of information should there be more of?"**

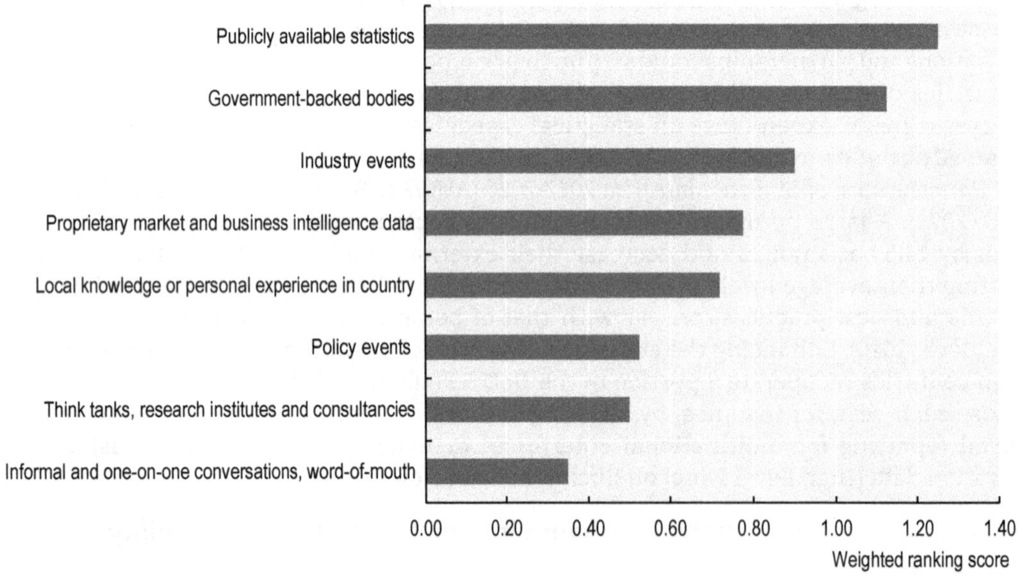

Note: n = 40. The AUC/OECD investor survey was administered in September 2022 to the networks of African business councils and the EU-Africa Business Forum. Results show a weighted ranking score. For further information, see Figure 2.1 in Chapter 2.

StatLink *https://stat.link/t9cobl*

Strong African-led institutions and partnerships can make sustainable finance more effective

Expanding and interconnecting local stock exchanges could mobilise additional finance to support the growth of African firms. The market capitalisation of the 28 national and 2 regional stock exchanges in Africa remains far below comparable developing economies: in 2021, the total value of African initial public offerings (IPO) represented less than USD 1 billion (compared to USD 14 billion in Brazil and 17 billion in India). Over the 2017-21 period, African IPOs accounted for less than 1% of the USD 1.5 trillion global value of IPOs (PwC, 2021). During the same period, 77% of all capital raised through Africa-based IPOs originated from only three markets (Egypt, Nigeria and South Africa). Interconnecting stock exchanges can reduce transaction costs, increase trading activity and allow for greater integration of capital markets. Improving the transparency of listing requirements on African stock exchanges could unlock finance for smaller firms. For instance, the African Exchanges Linkage Project, launched in 2022, enables seamless cross-border securities trading across seven African stock exchanges representing about USD 1.5 trillion in capitalisation.

Improving the capitalisation of African development finance institutions (DFIs) can allow them to support national development objectives. Africa is home to 102 DFIs, representing about 20% of their total number globally. Yet, African DFIs rarely manage assets worth more than 2-3% of their country's GDP. Given African governments' constrained fiscal positions, donors could increase African DFIs' capitalisation to strengthen their ability to channel investment. Initiatives such as the Global Climate Fund's (GCF) Readiness Programme can assist African DFIs in diversifying their funding. It provides grants of up to USD 1 million per year and technical assistance to local institutions across 35 African countries to receive accreditations and secure GCF funding (GCF, n.d.). The international community could also consider reallocating part of the IMF's Special Drawing Rights to well-managed African financial institutions to ensure alignment with regional priorities. The African Development Bank and the African Union chairperson called for the reallocation of USD 100 billion in Special Drawing Rights through the African Development Fund to provide concessional financing in low-income countries (AfDB, 2022).

Leveraging innovative financing instruments can unlock additional sustainable investments. African governments can tap innovative instruments such as "green, social, sustainability and sustainability-linked" bonds or carbon credits to scale up climate financing (Dembele, Schwarz and Horrocks, 2021; Chapters 4, 5 and 6). For instance, in 2021, Gabon became the first African country to receive funds (USD 17 million) as part of the USD 150 million results-based agreement with the Central African Forest Initiative, for the country's efforts in reducing deforestation over 2016-17 (CAFI, 2021). The issuance of green bonds across nine African countries mobilised USD 4.5 billion over 2014-21. It could be scaled up with supportive regulatory reforms, as implemented in Latin America and the Caribbean, which attracted 32.8 billion over the same period. Implementing carbon credit trading systems could mobilise up to USD 245 billion (Wambui, 2022; Yu et al., 2021). The Africa Carbon Markets Initiative launched at COP27 aims to mobilise USD 6 billion and create 30 million jobs by 2030. Finally, local currency financing solutions and other risk mitigation tools can make projects more viable and affordable for local investors. For example, InfraCredit Nigeria provides local currency guarantees and has mobilised close to USD 240 million from domestic pension funds to finance infrastructure assets since 2017.

> In **North and West Africa**, African-led partnerships advance the development of green financing tools (Chapters 6 and 7). Multi-stakeholder consultations and regulatory reforms enabled Egypt and Morocco to mobilise USD 1.1 billion through green bond issuance, or 25% of total green bond issuances in all of Africa over 2014-21. The West African Initiative for Climate Smart Agriculture, a blended finance fund, works through local financial institutions and third parties to offer technical assistance and loans at subsidised interest rates to farmers' organisations and agribusinesses that use climate-resilient agricultural practices.

Effective regional integration policies can help mobilise sustainable investments

Harmonising national investment policies and productive transformation strategies can increase sustainable investment opportunities. Small domestic markets, macroeconomic risks, unfit regulatory environments, and frail licensing and incorporation regimes increase risks and the cost of searching for investment opportunities. Investment policy frameworks and productive transformation strategies can work in tandem to address such issues. African governments can put sustainability at the centre of investment policies and regulatory effectiveness, particularly in strategic sectors such as renewable energy (see Chapters 3 and 5).

Development corridors and digital infrastructures can be expanded to reduce deficits, increase sustainability and facilitate trade. By 2030, USD 411 billion will be required for all transport equipment – trucks, railway vehicles, aircraft and ships – to accommodate the increase in trade brought about by the African Continental Free Trade Area (AfCFTA) (UNECA, 2022). In the context of the Programme for Infrastructure Development in Africa, the African Union has placed development corridors high on Africa's regional integration agenda (AU, 2017). A holistic and multi-dimensional approach to development corridors can help address infrastructure deficits on the continent and contribute to social and environmental sustainability (AU, 2020). Expanding digital infrastructures through the Pan-African Payment and Settlement System aims to facilitate trade, notably by reducing the cost of foreign exchange in the 42 African currencies (AUC/OECD, 2021, 2022).

Establishing linkages between multinational enterprises and local small and medium-sized enterprises takes time and requires policy support to generate sustainable outcomes. The impact of such linkages can take up to 15 years to materialise, as lead firms need time to invest financial, human and technological resources (Jenkins et al., 2007). Policy makers can deploy complementary support services – such as supplier development programmes, matchmaking services and data provision, targeted incentives, inclusive clustering policies, and support to meet international standards – to foster value chain linkages (AUC/OECD, 2022; OECD, 2021d). Support from third parties like training or certification agencies can enhance the benefits that lead firms transfer to SMEs through value chain linkages (see Chapter 7).

The AfCFTA Investment Protocol promises to harmonise the African investment policy landscape. Currently, 852 bilateral investment treaties exist between African countries and between African and non-African countries (UNECA/AU/AfDB/UNCTAD, 2019). Liberalising trade and harmonising investment, competition and intellectual property rights laws under the AfCFTA could boost Africa's FDI stock by 122% from outside the continent and by 68% from other African countries compared to 2017 levels (Echandi, Maliszewska and Steenbergen, 2022). Implementing the AfCFTA Investment Protocol, approved at the African Union Summit in February 2023, requires monitoring mechanisms; experiences from African regional economic communities – such as the ECOWAS Investment Climate Monitoring Scorecard and SADC Investment Policy Framework – and from other world regions provide examples of how to co-ordinate policies and monitor progress. Continuous exchange with private sector representatives, such as through the AfroChampions initiative, would help promote investment opportunities throughout the AfCFTA implementation process.

> In **East and Southern Africa**, cross-border projects can support the development of renewable energy and cross-border trade of renewable power (Chapters 3 and 5). The African Clean Energy Corridor, connecting the Eastern Africa Power Pool and the Southern African Power Pool, aims to increase electricity supply by 2.5 times, meeting 40-50% of power needs in both regions by 2030 while cutting annual CO_2 emission levels by 310 megatons.

Note

1. GDP growth per capita is projected to be lower, at 1.3% in 2023 and 1.8% in 2024, due to strong demographic growth.

References

AfDB (2022), "President Macky Sall and African Development Bank Group head Dr Akinwumi Adesina call for substantial support for Africa's low-income countries", 17 September, African Development Bank article, www.afdb.org/fr/news-and-events/president-macky-sall-and-african-development-bank-group-head-dr-akinwumi-adesina-call-substantial-support-africas-low-income-countries-54845.

AfDB/IFC/MFW4A (2022), *Gauging Appetite of African Institutional Investors for New Asset Classes*, African Development Bank, International Finance Corporation and Making Finance Work for Africa, www.mfw4a.org/sites/default/files/resources/gauging_appetite_of_african_institutional_investors_for_new_asset_classes_-_published.pdf.

AfDB/OECD/UNDP (2015), *African Economic Outlook 2015: Regional Development and Spatial Inclusion*, OECD Publishing, Paris, https://doi.org/10.1787/aeo-2015-en.

Amendolagine, V. et al. (2013), "FDI and local linkages in developing countries: Evidence from sub-Saharan Africa", *World Development*, Vol. 50, pp. 41-56, https://doi.org/10.1016/j.worlddev.2013.05.001.

Asquith, P. and S. Opoku-Owusu (2020), "Diaspora investment to help achieve the SDGs in Africa: Prospects and trends", in *Foreign Direct Investment Perspective through Foreign Direct Divestment*, IntechOpen, London, www.intechopen.com/chapters/72728.

AU (2020), *The Integrated Corridor Approach - "A Holistic Infrastructure Planning Framework to Establish PIDA-PAP 2"*, Strategic Note, African Union, https://pp2.au-pida.org/wp-content/uploads/2020/04/English-Strategic-Note_Integrated-Corridor-Approach-and-Selection-Criteria-AUC.pdf.

AU (2017), "Infrastructure corridors are key to Africa's intra-regional trade, job creation: Stakeholders agree at PIDA Session", Press Release, African Union, https://au.int/en/pressreleases/20171127/infrastructure-corridors-are-key-africa%E2%80%99s-intra-regional-trade-job-creation.

AUC/AfDB/UNECA/ACBF (2017), *Strategy for the Harmonization of Statistics in Africa 2017-2026 (SHaSA 2)*, https://au.int/sites/default/files/documents/34580-doc-34577-doc-shasa_ii_strategy_eng_full_web.pdf.

AUC/OECD (2022), *Africa's Development Dynamics 2022: Regional Value Chains for a Sustainable Recovery*, AUC, Addis Ababa/OECD Publishing, Paris, https://doi.org/10.1787/2e3b97fd-en.

AUC/OECD (2021), *Africa's Development Dynamics 2021: Digital Transformation for Quality Jobs*, AUC, Addis Ababa/OECD Publishing, Paris, https://doi.org/10.1787/0a5c9314-en.

AUC/OECD (2019), *Africa's Development Dynamics 2019: Achieving Productive Transformation*, OECD Publishing, Paris/AUC, Addis Ababa, https://doi.org/10.1787/c1cd7de0-en.

AUC/OECD (2018), *Africa's Development Dynamics 2018: Growth, Jobs and Inequalities*, OECD Publishing, Paris/AUC, Addis Ababa, https://doi.org/10.1787/9789264302501-en.

AUDA-NEPAD (2022), *Second Continental Report on the Implementation of Agenda 2063*, African Union Development Agency, South Africa, www.nepad.org/microsite/2nd-continental-report-implementation-of-agenda-2063.

BCG (2022), *Global Asset Management 2022: From Tailwinds to Turbulence*, Boston Consulting Group, https://web-assets.bcg.com/c8/5a/2f2f5d784302b945ba1f3276abbc/global-asset-management-2022-from-tailwinds-to-turbulence-may-2022.pdf.

CAFI (2021), "Gabon: First in Africa to receive payments for preserved rainforests", Central African Forest Initiative, www.cafi.org/countries/gabon/gabon-first-africa-receive-payments-preserved-rainforests.

Dembele, F., R. Schwarz and P. Horrocks (2021), *Scaling Up Green, Social, Sustainability and Sustainability-linked Bond Issuances in Developing Countries*, OECD Publishing, Paris, www.oecd.org/dac/financing-sustainable-development/blended-finance-principles/documents/scaling-up-green-social-sustainability-sustainability-linked-bond-issuances-developing-countries.pdf.

Diallo, A., L. Jacolin and I. Rabaud (2021), "Foreign direct investment and domestic private investment in sub-Saharan African countries: Crowding-in or out", *Ferdi Working Papers*, No. 292, https://ferdi.fr/dl/df-MtwJiRQa4ZgpWvN5BBwKh5X3/ferdi-p292-foreign-direct-investment-and-domestic-private-investment-in.pdf.

Echandi, R., M. Maliszewska and V. Steenbergen (2022), *Making the Most of the African Continental Free Trade Area: Leveraging Trade and Foreign Direct Investment to Boost Growth and Reduce Poverty*, International Bank for Reconstruction and Development/World Bank, Washington, DC, https://documents1.worldbank.org/curated/en/099305006222230294/pdf/P1722320bf22cd02c09f2b0b3b320afc4a7.pdf.

Faal, G. (2019), *Strategic, Business and Operational Framework for an African Diaspora Finance Corporation: African Union Legacy Project on Diaspora Investment, Innovative Finance and Social Enterprise in Africa*, African Union Commission, Addis Ababa, https://au.int/sites/default/files/documents/40847-doc-EN_-_ADFC_Business_and_Operational_Framework_-_May_2019.pdf.

FAO (2022), *FAOSTAT* (database), Food and Agriculture Organization of the United Nations, www.fao.org/faostat/en/#home, (accessed October 2022).

fDi Intelligence (2022), *fDi Markets* (database), www.fdiintelligence.com/fdi-markets (accessed 19 September 2022).

GCA (2022), *State and Trends in Adaptation in Africa 2022*, Global Center on Adaptation, Rotterdam, https://gca.org/reports/sta22/.

GCF (n.d.), "Overview", Green Climate Fund webpage, www.greenclimate.fund/readiness (accessed 2 February 2023).

GIIN (2020), *Annual Impact Investor Survey*, Global Impact Investing Network, https://thegiin.org/assets/GIIN%20Annual%20Impact%20Investor%20Survey%202020.pdf.

High Level Panel on Illicit Financial Flows from Africa (2021), *Track it! Stop it! Get it! Report of the High Level Panel on Illicit Financial Flows from Africa*, AU/UNECA Conference of Ministers of Finance, Planning and Economic Development, https://au.int/sites/default/files/documents/40545-doc-IFFs_REPORT.pdf.

IEA (2022), *Africa Energy Outlook 2022*, International Energy Agency, Paris, www.iea.org/reports/africa-energy-outlook-2022.

IFAD/World Bank (2015), *The Use of Remittances and Financial Inclusion*, International Fund for Agricultural Development, Rome, www.ifad.org/documents/38714170/40187309/gpfi.pdf/58ce7a06-7ec0-42e8-82dc-c069227edb79.

IMF (2023a), *Regional Economic Outlook Africa, April 2023*, IMF Publication Services, International Monetary Fund, Washington, DC, www.imf.org/en/Publications/REO/SSA/Issues/2023/04/14/regional-economic-outlook-for-sub-saharan-africa-april-2023.

IMF (2023b), "List of LIC DSAs for PRGT-eligible countries", International Monetary Fund, Washington, DC, www.imf.org/external/Pubs/ft/dsa/DSAlist.pdf.

IMF (2022), *World Economic Outlook Database*, October 2022 Edition, International Monetary Fund, www.imf.org/en/Publications/WEO/weo-database/2022/October (accessed October 2022).

Jenkins, B. et al. (2007), *Business Linkages: Lessons, Opportunities, and Challenges*, International Finance Corporation, International Business Leaders Forum and the Kennedy School of Government, Harvard, www.hks.harvard.edu/sites/default/files/centers/mrcbg/programs/cri/files/report_16_BUSINESS%2BLINKAGESFINAL.pdf.

Juvonen, K. et al. (2019), "Unleashing the potential of institutional investors in Africa", *AfDB Working Papers*, No. 325, African Development Bank, Abidjan, www.afdb.org/sites/default/files/documents/publications/wps_no_325_unleashing_the_potential_of_institutional_investors_in_africa_c_rv1.pdf.

Kubota, M. and A. Zeufack (2020), "Assessing the returns on investment in data openness and transparency", *World Bank Policy Research Working Paper*, No. 9139, World Bank, Washington, DC, https://openknowledge.worldbank.org/entities/publication/5dad280a-b4a8-538b-a34b-407980c8a848.

OECD (2023), "ODA Levels in 2022 – preliminary data: Detailed summary note", OECD, Paris, www.oecd.org/dac/financing-sustainable-development/ODA-2022-summary.pdf.

OECD (2022a), *Global Outlook on Financing for Sustainable Development 2023*, OECD Publishing, Paris, https://doi.org/10.1787/fcbe6ce9-en.

OECD (2022b), "Mobilisation", *Flows Based on Individual Projects (CRS)* (dataset), OECD Publishing, Paris, https://stats-1.oecd.org/Index.aspx?DataSetCode=DV_DCD_MOBILISATION (accessed December 2022).

OECD (2022c), *FDI Qualities Policy Toolkit*, OECD Publishing, Paris, www.oecd-ilibrary.org/finance-and-investment/fdi-qualities-policy-toolkit_7ba74100-en.

OECD (2021a), *Private Philanthropy for Development: Data for Action Dashboard* (database), OECD Publishing, Paris, https://oecd-main.shinyapps.io/philanthropy4development/ (accessed November 2022).

OECD (2021b), *OECD Global Pension Statistics* (database), https://doi.org/10.1787/pension-data-en (accessed October 2022).

OECD (2021c), *Mobilising Institutional Investors for Financing Sustainable Development in Developing Countries: Emerging Evidence of Opportunities and Challenges*, OECD Publishing, Paris, www.oecd.org/dac/financing-sustainable-development/Mobilising-institutional-investors-for-financing-sustainable-development-final.pdf.

OECD (2021d), "Enabling SME linkages with foreign firms in global value chains", in *Middle East and North Africa Investment Policy Perspectives*, OECD Publishing, Paris, https://doi.org/10.1787/824a45f1-en.

OECD/ATAF/AUC (2022), *Revenue Statistics in Africa 2022*, OECD Publishing, Paris, https://doi.org/10.1787/ea66fbde-en-fr.

PwC (2021), *Africa Capital Markets Watch 2021*, PricewaterhouseCoopers, www.pwc.co.za/en/assets/pdf/africa-capital-markets-watch-2021.pdf.

Smith, G. (3 October 2022), "African Eurobonds in Q3 2022", LinkedIn, www.linkedin.com/pulse/african-eurobonds-q3-2022-gregory-smith/.

Stewart, F. (18 January 2022), "The elephant in the room: Bringing sustainable investment to Africa", World Bank Private Sector Development Blog, https://blogs.worldbank.org/psd/elephant-room-bringing-sustainable-investment-africa.

Trading Economics (2022), "Indicators: Credit Rating | Africa", *Trading Economics* (database), https://tradingeconomics.com/country-list/rating?continent=africa (accessed January 2023).

UN DESA (2022), "World Population Prospects: The 2022 Revision", *United Nations* (database), United Nations Department of Economic and Social Affairs, New York, https://population.un.org/dataportal/data/indicators/67/locations/903/start/2000/end/2030/table/pivotbylocation (accessed October 2022).

UNDP (2023), *Lowering the Cost of Borrowing in Africa: The Role of Sovereign Credit Ratings*, United Nations Development Program, New York, www.undp.org/africa/publications/lowering-cost-borrowing-africa-role-sovereign-credit-ratings.

UNECA (2022), *The African Continental Free Trade Area and Demand for Transport Infrastructure and Services*, United Nations Economic Commission for Africa, Addis Ababa, https://hdl.handle.net/10855/47596.

UNECA/AU/AfDB/UNCTAD (2019), *Assessing Regional Integration in Africa (ARIA IX): Next Steps for the African Continental Free Trade Area*, United Nations Economic Commission for Africa, African Union, African Development Bank and United Nations Conference on Trade and Development, Addis Ababa, https://archive.uneca.org/sites/default/files/PublicationFiles/aria9_report_en_4sept_fin.pdf.

Wambui, R. (2022), "Scaling up sustainable finance and investment in the Global South: A case study of sub-Saharan Africa", in *Scaling Up Sustainable Finance and Investment in the Global South*, CEPR Press, London, https://cepr.org/system/files/publication-files/175477-scaling_up_sustainable_finance_and_investment_in_the_global_south.pdf.

Were, A. (2022), "The impacts of climate change continue to compromise the livelihoods of hundreds of millions of Africans", FSD Kenya Blog, 21 October, www.fsdkenya.org/blogs-publications/blog/how-to-develop-a-green-project-pipeline-in-africa/.

World Bank (2021), *The Changing Wealth of Nations 2021: Managing Assets for the Future*, World Bank, Washington, DC, http://hdl.handle.net/10986/36400.

Yu, S. et al. (2021), "The potential role of Article 6 compatible carbon markets in reaching net-zero", *School of Public Policy and IETA Working Paper*, International Emissions Trading Association and University of Maryland, www.ieta.org/resources/Resources/Net-Zero/Final_Net-zero_A6_working_paper.pdf.

Chapter 1

Africa's sustainable investments in times of global crises

This chapter makes the case that African countries need more sustainable investments to create jobs and promote inclusive growth. It outlines the extent to which sustainable investments and financing have not met the many opportunities that the continent offers and analyses the potential for improvement. The chapter first assesses the sustainable investment landscape that is emerging from the concurrent crises of the COVID-19 pandemic, the global repercussions of conflicts and climate change and provides an estimate for the continent's sustainable financing gap. Second, it examines low investor confidence and the high cost of capital as specific investment barriers that these crises have amplified. Third, the chapter identifies investment linkages with small and medium-sized enterprises, intra-African investments and institutional investors as three domains offering untapped potential to support Africa's regional integration and sustainable growth.

IN BRIEF

As a result of three global crises (the COVID-19 pandemic, the global repercussions of conflicts and the climate crisis), Africa's sustainable financing needs are growing. At the onset of the COVID-19 pandemic, in 2020, Africa's sustainable financing gap reached USD 272 billion, the highest level since projections began in 2015. Yet, this gap appears small compared to capital available worldwide and on the continent: the USD 194 billion average sustainable financing gap for 2015-21 calculated in this report is equivalent to less than 0.2% of the global and 10.5% of the African-held stock of assets under management – financial assets that wealth management firms handle on behalf of investors.

The recent global shocks have amplified investment barriers by lowering investor confidence and exacerbating information shortages while increasing the cost of capital in Africa more than in other world regions. Risks related to global shocks and information shortages remain the primary reasons for Africa's limited investment attractiveness. Due to unfavourable country credit ratings and heightened risk aversion among international investors, the costs of public and private capital are far above global averages in many African countries, especially in the renewable energy sector. The limited availability of data is a pervasive issue, hindering risk assessments and mitigation strategies and increasing the cost of searching for investment opportunities. A lack of data also makes it difficult to measure the allocation of funds towards sustainable development and impacts.

Current sources of investment can better support regional integration, job creation and inclusive growth. Better integrating foreign direct investment into local economies can create jobs and improve Africa's participation in global and regional value chains. African regional lead firms and institutional investors hold great potential to boost sectors that can better balance economic, social and environmental sustainability, such as information and communications technology, finance, and renewable energy.

Africa's sustainable investments in times of global crises

Africa's USD 194 billion annual sustainable financing gap can be bridged

with Africa's unique assets...

Median age

19 Africa

42 Europe

African forests increased carbon stock by almost 12 million kilotons of CO_2-equivalent net emissions

2011

2020

... and available resources

The annual gap is equivalent to:

% of the global stock of financial assets: 0.2

% of African-held stock of financial assets: 10.5

Investor confidence is much lower in Africa than in other world regions

Cost of capital for energy projects:

Europe and North America

Africa: x7

Africa received a tiny fraction of capital from global pension funds and insurance companies

Africa: 0.5%

Latin America and the Caribbean: 1.2%

Developing Asia: 4.2%

Attracting sustainable investment: Where to look

External financial inflows

USD 1 million greenfield FDI creates:

14 jobs in textiles

9 in automotive

10 in electronic equipment

and yet...

these sectors combined attracted only 4.5% of greenfield FDI to African countries over 2003-20

Regional lead firms

Intra-African FDI was about 3 times more resilient during the pandemic than non-African FDI

and yet...

it accounts for only 9% of greenfield FDI to Africa

Africa's institutional investors

Assets held by Africa-based institutional investors amount to USD **1.8 trillion,** or 73% of GDP

and yet...

alternative and green assets represent less than 3% of portfolios in Africa's major pension fund markets

Africa continental profile

Figure 1.1. Components of economic growth and sources of financing in Africa

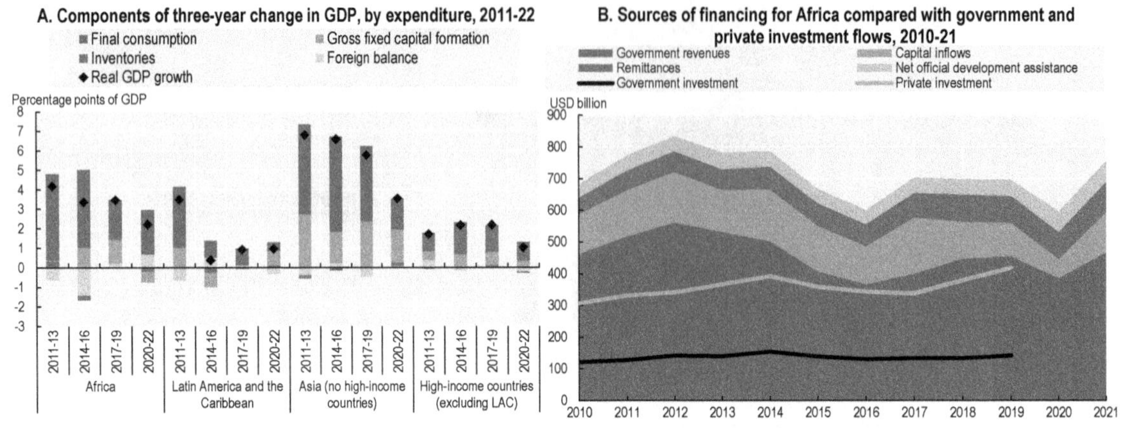

Note: The components of GDP growth are calculated on an annual basis by using real annual GDP growth to estimate the increase in real US dollars. Aggregate figures are calculated by taking the average of the national figures weighted by GDP in purchasing-power-parity dollars. The components of GDP growth over three-year periods were calculated by taking the difference between the geometric average of the annual real GDP growth over the period and the real GDP growth when setting each component to zero for individual years. Foreign balance is the difference between imports and exports. Imports contribute negatively to GDP. "High-income countries" refers to countries classified as "high-income" according to the World Bank Country and Lending Groups outside of Latin America and the Caribbean. Government revenues include all tax and non-tax government revenues minus debt service and grants received. Capital inflows include foreign direct investment (FDI), portfolio investment and other investment inflows reported by the International Monetary Fund under asset/liability accounting. Figures for capital inflows should be interpreted with some caution as some figures for 2021 and for portfolio inflows are missing.

Sources: Authors' calculations based on IMF (2022a), *World Economic Outlook Database*, www.imf.org/en/Publications/WEO/weo-database/2022/October; OECD (2022a), *OECD Development Assistance Committee* (database), https://stats-1.oecd.org/Index.aspx?DataSetCode=TABLE2A; World Bank (2022a), *World Development Indicators* (database), https://datatopics.worldbank.org/world-development-indicators/; IMF (2022b), *Balance of Payments and International Investment Position Statistics (BOP/IIP)* (database), https://data.imf.org/?sk=7A51304B-6426-40C0-83DD-CA473CA1FD52; IMF (2022c), *Investment and Capital Stock Dataset (ICSD)* (database), https://data.imf.org/?sk=1CE8A55F-CFA7-4BC0-BCE2-256EE65AC0E4; and World Bank-KNOMAD (2022), *Remittances* (database), www.knomad.org/data/remittances.

StatLink https://stat.link/06793s

Figure 1.2. Greenfield foreign direct investment flows to Africa, by activity, source and destination, 2017-22

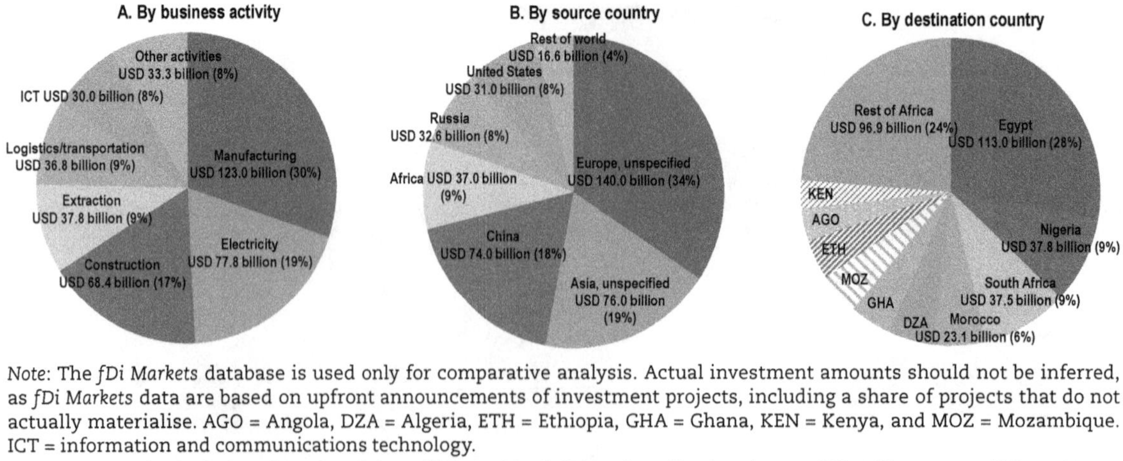

Note: The *fDi Markets* database is used only for comparative analysis. Actual investment amounts should not be inferred, as *fDi Markets* data are based on upfront announcements of investment projects, including a share of projects that do not actually materialise. AGO = Angola, DZA = Algeria, ETH = Ethiopia, GHA = Ghana, KEN = Kenya, and MOZ = Mozambique. ICT = information and communications technology.

Source: Authors' calculations based on fDi Intelligence (2022), *fDi Markets* (database), www.fdiintelligence.com/fdi-markets.

StatLink https://stat.link/xftpb6

Sustainable investments have not yet met the opportunities African economies offer

African countries represent the world's investment frontier, holding important assets. Africa has by far the youngest population of all continents, with a median age of 19 years, compared to 30 for Latin America and the Caribbean, 31 for developing Asia as the next youngest regions and 42 for Europe as the oldest (UN DESA, 2022). By 2050, Africa's population will almost double, from about 1.4 billion inhabitants to nearly 2.5 billion. More than half of the world's population growth will happen on the continent, including in rural areas (UN DESA, 2022; AfDB/OECD/UNDP, 2015). In 2022, Africa was the only world region with positive year-on-year growth in start-up funding (5%) (Cuvellier, 2023). Estimates suggest that agricultural yields for cereals and grains in large parts of Africa could double or triple, adding 20% to global output (McKinsey, 2019). The Democratic Republic of the Congo's cobalt production makes up 70% of the global total – providing a key input for battery production (ANRC, 2021). From 2011 to 2020, African forests increased carbon stock by 11.6 million kilotons of CO_2-equivalent net emissions, while carbon stocks in forests outside Africa declined by 13 million kilotons. Of this increase, 59% was in Central African forests, now recognised as the world's largest carbon sink. The continent boasts 60% of the best solar resources globally (IEA, 2022a).

Africa has enjoyed high growth, supported by investment, but this has not sufficiently driven productive transformation. Since the turn of the 21st century, Africa has boasted the world's second-highest rate of economic growth after developing Asia. African growth is bouncing back since the global recession of 2020: growth estimates are at 3.7% in 2023 and projected in 2024 at 4.2% – after developing Asia and before Latin America and the Caribbean, respectively at 5% and 1.6% for 2023 and 4.9% and 2.2% for 2024. High investment rates boosted Africa's growth, with the contribution of gross fixed capital formation to gross domestic product (GDP) growth reaching a peak of 1.2 percentage points in 2017-19, before declining during the COVID-19 pandemic in 2020-22 (Figure 1.1). Overall, high growth has not sufficiently catalysed productive transformation, including job creation and value chain integration (AUC/OECD, 2018, 2019, 2022).

Sustainable investments are essential to steer the productive transformation towards inclusion and resilience. When mobilising and allocating investments, African countries need to manage tensions between economic goals of productive transformation and social and environmental goals such as inclusion and resilience to climate change (Box 1.1). This is the case, for example, when balancing energy production and carbon mitigation, agricultural land use and conservation, or mass employment creation and labour standards. To face the emerging global challenges of the 21st century, African countries can use sustainable investments to make the most of the continent's unique assets while reducing their vulnerability to crises and shocks.

Box 1.1. Agenda 2063 and sustainable investments: This report's approach

The African Union's Agenda 2063 provides a blueprint for a transformation that combines productivity and sustainability. Agenda 2063 codifies the goal of a "prosperous Africa, based on inclusive growth and sustainable development" (AU, 2015). While creating quality jobs and developing highly productive sectors remain essential (AUC/OECD, 2018), the African continent now faces a growing opportunity to steer its economic transformation towards responses to climate change and the preservation of natural environments. Agenda 2063 explicitly considers environmental sustainability, stating that "Africa's unique natural endowments, its environment and ecosystems [should be] healthy, valued and protected, with climate resilient economies and communities" (AU, 2015).

Box 1.1. **Agenda 2063 and sustainable investments: This report's approach** ***(continued)***

Investments are sustainable if their total economic, social and environmental benefits can be predicted to outweigh their total cost. Economic sustainability refers to the long-term viability of a market-based activity for all actors involved. Social sustainability consists of effects on human development, individual well-being and collective outcomes such as peace and social cohesion (UN Global Compact, 2022). Environmental sustainability is achieved if the investment's activity does not surpass the boundaries of ecological systems that support life on Earth (considering issues such as climate change, chemical pollution and freshwater use) (NBS, 2022). Global frameworks to track sustainability outcomes include the United Nations' Sustainable Development Goals (SDGs) and various environmental, social and governance standards (OECD, 2022b).

The *Africa's Development Dynamics 2023* report investigates which investments offer the best balance and minimise trade-offs between economic, social and environmental sustainability, with each dimension hinging on Africa-specific challenges:

- **Economic: Regional integration.** Recent crises have demonstrated the need for Africa to reduce its vulnerability to global shocks through better market integration and stronger regional supply chains (AUC/OECD, 2022).
- **Social: Employment creation and inclusive growth.** Given Africa's population growth and rural-urban inequalities, the creation of large numbers of high-quality jobs and opportunities for Africa's poor populations are foundational for social sustainability (AUC/OECD, 2018, 2019, 2021).
- **Environmental: Climate resilience and a just energy transition.** In view of Africa's small contribution to climate change and its vulnerability to extreme weather events, climate adaptation and a nationally specific mix of energy investments are priorities.

To capture the complexity of sustainable investments, the *Africa's Development Dynamics 2023* report analyses public and private sources of sustainable finance, comparing them across regions, countries and sectors. It covers a range of databases, including on foreign direct investment (FDI) and multinational enterprises, government revenues, pension funds, official development assistance (ODA), impact investing and philanthropy, complemented by primary data from a survey and interviews with multinational investors. The report compares sustainability outcomes across sectors based on current literature and available indicators such as greenhouse gas emissions and job creation. It features additional analyses on specific sectors with high sustainability potential, such as renewable energies and infrastructure.

Despite the impact of global crises, Africa's sustainable financing gap can be bridged

The COVID-19 pandemic, the global repercussions of conflicts and climate change are widening Africa's sustainable financing needs.

- In 2020, the annual sustainable financing gap (i.e. the gap between the financing needed to achieve the SDGs and the availability of financial resources) reached USD 272 billion, the highest level since projections began in 2015 (Figure 1.3), largely as a result of the COVID-19 pandemic. While available financing rebounded in 2021, worsening macroeconomic conditions in 2022 are likely to widen the gap yet again.
- The repercussions of conflicts are creating additional investment needs and strains on Africa's finances. Recent conflicts have led to disruptions in supply chains

and increases in the prices of critical imports (food, energy and fertilisers) while fuelling inflation and triggering a global tightening in monetary policies. This could add an estimated financing need of USD 6 to 10 billion per annum for African commodity-importing countries (IMF, 2022d).

- To keep global warming below 1.5°C by 2030, African countries need an estimated USD 277 billion per year to implement their nationally determined contributions as per the Paris Agreement – almost ten times more than the USD 29.5 billion mobilised so far (CPI, 2022).

Figure 1.3. **Available financing and sustainable financing gap, 2015-21**

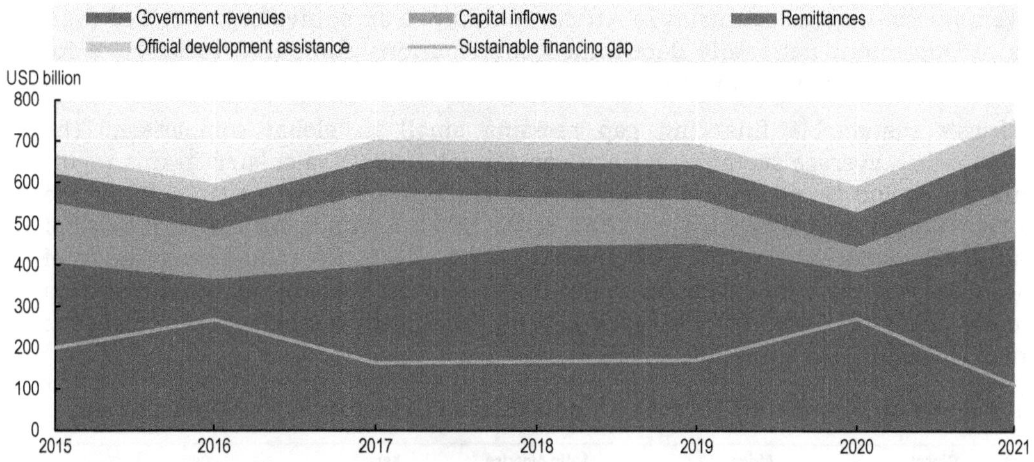

Note: See Annex 1.A for details.

Source: Authors' calculations based on OECD (2022b), *Global Outlook on Financing for Sustainable Development 2023: No Sustainability Without Equity*, https://doi.org/10.1787/fcbe6ce9-en; IMF (2022a), *World Economic Outlook Database*, www.imf.org/en/Publications/WEO/weo-database/2022/October; OECD (2022a), *OECD Development Assistance Committee* (database), https://stats-1.oecd.org/Index.aspx?DataSetCode=TABLE2A; World Bank (2022a), *International Debt Statistics* (database), https://databank.worldbank.org/source/international-debt-statistics; IMF (2022b), *Balance of Payments and International Investment Position Statistics (BOP/IIP)* (database), https://data.imf.org/?sk=7A51304B-6426-40C0-83DD-CA473CA1FD52; and World Bank-KNOMAD (2022), *Remittances* (database), www.knomad.org/data/remittances; UNCTAD (2020b), "Economic Development in Africa Report 2020: Press Conference", Press Release, https://unctad.org/osgstatement/economic-development-africa-report-2020-press-conference.

StatLink https://stat.link/uvlh0r

Decreasing tax revenues and rising debts and interest rates are putting many African countries in debt distress. While government revenues continue to represent by far the largest individual source of finance, they decreased sharply in reaction to the COVID-19 pandemic (Figure 1.3) while per-capita GDP dropped by 4.1% in 2020. African governments collected on average 6.2% less revenues in 2020 than in 2015, on a real per-capita basis (taking into account population growth and inflation). Rising debt levels, increasingly owed to private creditors, contributed to raising the cost of debt service from only 3% to over 5% of gross national income over the 2010-20 period. The rise in global interest rates since March 2022 has added constraints for African governments by impacting global liquidity and exchange rates and triggering portfolio investment outflows. By February 2023, the International Monetary Fund (IMF) considered 8 African countries in debt distress,[1] plus 13 countries[2] at a high risk of debt distress (IMF, 2023). For instance, between 2021 and 2022, Eurobond yields more than tripled for Ghana and roughly doubled for Egypt, Gabon, Kenya, Nigeria and Tunisia, pricing these countries out of the market (Smith, 2022). Debt relief mechanisms can address part of the debt burden; these include the G20 Debt Service Suspension Initiative (DSSI) or the G20 / Paris Club Common Framework for Debt Treatments beyond the DSSI (Ekeruche, 2022; IMF, 2021a).

ODA to Africa must continue to increase, especially for adapting to climate change. ODA increased in response to COVID-19, with African countries receiving around USD 65 billion in 2020 and 2021, compared to less than 51 billion in 2019. However, in 2020, this increase did not compensate for shortfalls in spending by African governments and in financial inflows (Figure 1.3). ODA has also not yet met the levels pledged by the international community. In 2020, high-income countries provided and mobilised USD 83.3 billion for climate action in developing countries, missing the USD 100 billion target set at the United Nations Climate Summit in Copenhagen in 2009 (OECD, 2022c). From 2019 to 2020, international public climate finance for African countries grew only marginally from USD 22.3 to USD 24.3 billion (CPI, 2022). The most fiscally constrained countries are also the most vulnerable to climate change: on average, low-income countries in Africa would need an equivalent of 21% of their GDPs to implement nationally determined contributions compared to only 9% for middle-income countries (CPI, 2022).

Africa's sustainable financing gap remains small in global comparison. The USD 194 billion average sustainable financing gap for 2015-21 calculated in this report (Figure 1.3) would be equivalent to an annual reallocation of less than 0.2% of the USD 112 trillion total global stock, or 10.5% of the USD 1.8 trillion African-held stock of assets under management (BCG, 2022; Juvonen et al., 2019). An annual reallocation of 0.2% would bring the total allocation of global assets under management to Africa from currently under 1% (Table 1.1) to around 2.3% by 2030, still well below the continent's share of global GDP (2.9% in 2020).

Table 1.1. **Allocation of selected sources of institutional investment to world regions**

Type of investment	Global	Africa	Latin America and the Caribbean	Asia	Year
Venture capital	USD 600 billion	USD 5 billion (0.8%)	n.a.	n.a.	2021
Equity financing	USD 250.1 billion	USD 1.7 billion (0.7%)	USD 5.3 billion (2%)	USD 63.3 billion (25%)	2022 Q1&Q2
Pension funds	USD 3.3 trillion	USD 24.5 billion (~0.7%)	USD 57.9 billion (1.76%)	USD 180 billion (5.46%)	2017-18
Insurance companies	USD 1.8 trillion	USD 0.36 billion (~0.02%)	USD 2.88 billion (0.16%)	USD 32.76 billion (1.8%)	2017-18

Note: Venture capital and equity financing figures are based on comprehensive data sources. Pension fund and insurance companies data are derived from the 2019 edition of the OECD *Annual Survey of Large Pension Funds and Public Pension Reserve Funds* (OECD, 2019). Thirty-six pension funds and 30 insurance companies provided data. Figures for pension funds and insurance companies have been extrapolated from their declarations of total investments in developing countries.

Source: Authors' compilation based on AVCA (2022), *Venture Capital in Africa Report*, www.avca-africa.org/media/2967/62644-avca-avca-venture-capital-in-africa-report-v13.pdf, CB insights (2022), *State of Venture*, www.cbinsights.com/reports/CB-Insights_Venture-Report-Q2-2022.pdf; and OECD (2021a), *Mobilising Institutional Investors for Financing Sustainable Development in Developing Countries: Emerging Evidence of Opportunities and Challenges*, www.oecd.org/dac/financing-sustainable-development/Mobilising-institutional-investors-for-financing-sustainable-development-final.pdf.

The African continent's share of global investment has stagnated

Due to global crises, uncertainty, risk and sovereign debt have become more prevalent as investment barriers for African countries. The "Lucas paradox", after Robert Lucas' seminal article (Lucas, 1990), captures the phenomenon that global capital does not flow from rich to poor countries despite higher marginal returns in poorer economies. Empirical studies have suggested that domestic institutional factors such as government stability and bureaucratic quality have been the dominant explanations of this puzzle (Alfaro et al., 2008). Yet, the recent global crises have had little effect on institutional factors, while exacerbating alternative explanatory factors: capital market imperfections, specifically uncertainty, risk, sovereign debt and home biases (Leimbach and Bauer, 2022; Ndikumana and Boyce, 2003).

Recent global events have accelerated an increasing preference for new greenfield FDI in high-income over developing countries, have reduced Africa's participation in global value chains and may be increasing poverty. In the last decade, global greenfield FDI – new FDI projects reflecting future investment trends – has decreased at an average annual rate of 3%. Since 2016, new investments have been shifting from developing countries to high-income countries (Figure 1.4). The COVID-19 pandemic accelerated this trend: in 2020-21, high-income countries outside of Latin America and the Caribbean attracted 61% of global greenfield FDI (the highest share ever recorded), compared to 17% for developing Asia, 10% for Latin America and the Caribbean and only 6% for Africa (the lowest share since 2004). Similarly, Africa's participation in global value chains has stagnated since the 2008 global financial crisis and was only 1.7% in 2019 (AUC/OECD, 2022). The pandemic exacerbated this trend, in part due to multinational enterprises in high-income countries reshoring or near-shoring their production to reduce their exposure to supply chain shocks or postponing investment decisions in the face of global instability. The World Bank (Brenton, Ferrantino and Maliszewska, 2022) estimates that a shift towards global reshoring to high-income countries and the People's Republic of China (hereafter "China") could drive an additional 52 million people into extreme poverty, more than 80% of them in Africa.

Figure 1.4. **Greenfield foreign direct investments by world region, as a percentage of world capital expenditure, 2010-21**

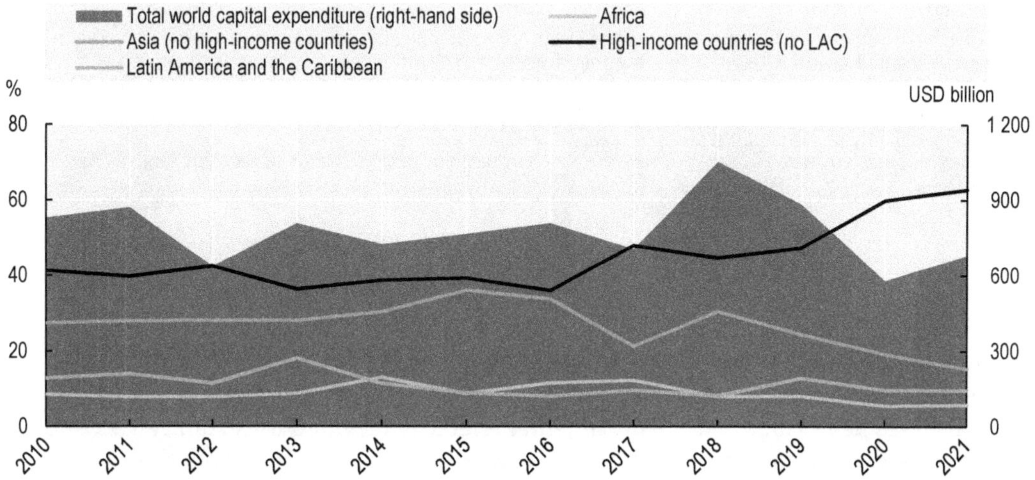

Note: LAC = Latin America and the Caribbean.
Source: Authors' calculations based on fDi Intelligence (2022), *fDi Markets* (database), www.fdiintelligence.com/fdi-markets.

StatLink https://stat.link/yr8mj9

Returns to FDI in Africa have narrowed compared to FDI in high-income countries. Narrowing FDI return differentials between developing and advanced economies have contributed to declining shares of FDI inflows to developing countries (Evenett and Fritz, 2021). In Africa, the decline in FDI returns has been mostly driven by resource-rich economies due to a downward trend in oil prices from 2011 until prices rebounded in 2021 (Figure 1.5). In contrast, FDI inflows to non-resource exporters (such as Ethiopia, Kenya, Madagascar and Mauritius) have been relatively more resilient (Ideue, 2019).

Africa attracts the lowest share of capital from institutional investors compared to other world regions. In the last decade, global assets under management grew from

USD 48 trillion in 2010 to over USD 112 trillion in 2021, despite economic downturns. Even during the first year of the COVID-19 pandemic, global assets under management further grew at a record 12% (BCG, 2022). Africa receives the lowest share of global capital across different types of investors, ranging from 0.8% for venture capital to as low as 0.02% for insurance companies (Table 1.1).

Figure 1.5. **Rates of return on foreign direct investment inflows by world region, 2011-20**

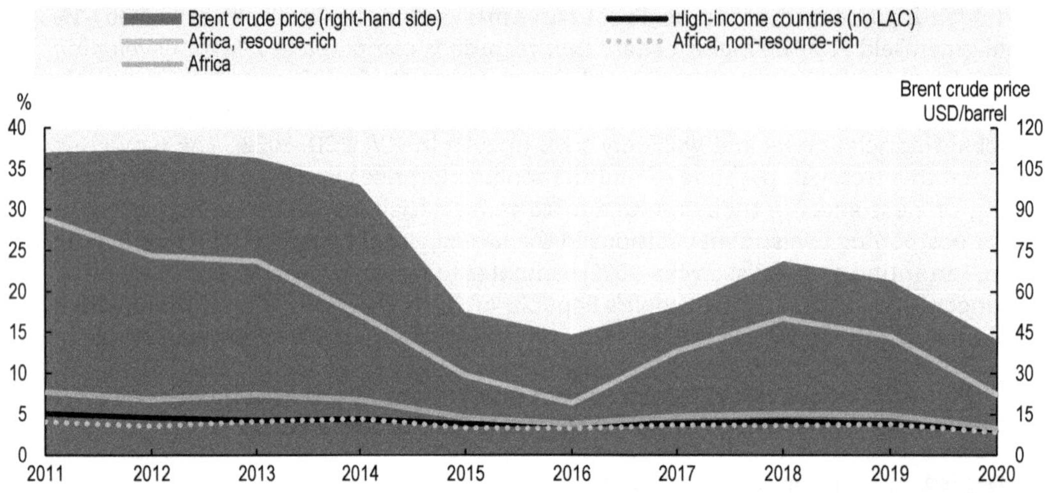

Note: FDI rates of return are calculated as the ratio of FDI income debit at year t over the average of FDI positions' liabilities at year t and t-1 (UNCTAD, 2019). Data for Africa cover 28 countries. Of the 9 resource-rich African countries, a complete time series is only available for Angola and Nigeria. LAC = Latin America and the Caribbean.

Source: Authors' calculations based on IMF (2022b), *Balance of Payments and International Investment Position Statistics (BOP/IIP)* (database), https://data.imf.org/?sk=7A51304B-6426-40C0-83DD-CA473CA1FD52.

StatLink https://stat.link/cfjan3

Lower investor confidence and the higher cost of capital help explain why investment remains weaker in many African countries compared to other world regions

Among the many factors that can attract a greater share of global investments, African countries can focus on improving investor confidence and reducing the cost of capital. The global crises have amplified the detrimental effects of elevated uncertainty, risk and information asymmetries that characterise investments in many – though not all – African countries. Addressing the specific barriers to investor confidence and decision making is essential to reverse current trends and sustain high levels of investment, even during future shocks.

Risks and information shortages persist as barriers to investment in many African countries

Foreign investors continue to point to economic and political risks as barriers to investment. Current survey data suggest that factors that have weighed on investor confidence for several decades – such as macroeconomic conditions, political risk, weak regulatory systems, rising debt and currency volatility (Collier and Pattillo, 2000) – continue to be of concern (Figure 1.6). Representatives of global multinational enterprises (interviewed for this report) emphasised policy instability and the lack of regulatory capacity as barriers, mentioning abrupt shifts in these leading them to withdraw investments. Interviewees expressed their wish, in particular, for better transparency in the negotiation process of the African Continental Free Trade Area (AfCFTA), pointing to limited public information and insufficient opportunities to provide technical inputs.

Figure 1.6. **Responses to the AUC/OECD investor survey question "Which of the following risks have been most important for your investments in African countries?"**

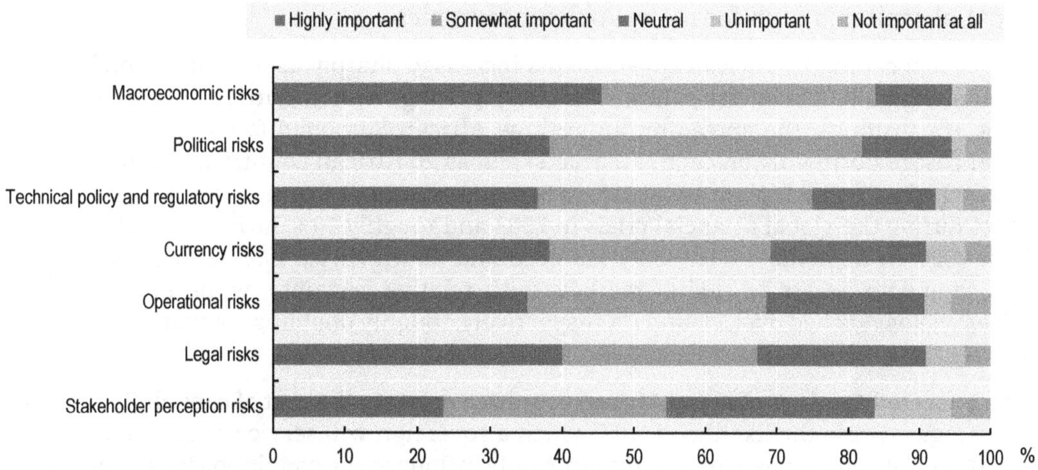

Note: n = 52 to 55. The survey was administered in September 2022 to the networks of African business councils and the EU-Africa Business Forum. Risk dimensions are ranked by weighted average. The following examples were provided to illustrate risk categories: macroeconomic risks – economic volatility, government default; currency risks – devaluation, fluctuation; operational risks – fragile supply chains, resource availability; legal risks – enforceability of contracts; political risk – protectionism, favouritism, retroactive policy changes; technical policy and regulatory risks – licensing, taxation, regulations, procurement processes; stakeholder perception risk – management or shareholders opposed to invest in Africa.

StatLink https://stat.link/vu9l0w

Investors take into account risks related to political and policy factors, including governance. While investors have traditionally looked to Africa for market access, growth and natural resources (Onyeiwu and Shrestha, 2016; Cheung et al., 2012), recent evidence suggests that preconditions of political and policy factors can be as important (Andoh and Cantah, 2020; Calderon et al., 2019; Osabutey and Okoro, 2015). Good governance is especially conducive to investment once countries reach a minimum threshold of government stability, democratic accountability, law and order, and bureaucratic quality (Yeboua, 2020).

Non-equity modes of entry into foreign markets, which can limit exposure to risks, have become more prevalent. Modes of entry into foreign markets that do not require investors to acquire an ownership stake (i.e. licensing, franchising and management contracts) have increased rapidly over the past two decades, outpacing the growth of FDI (Qiang, Liu and Steenbergen, 2021). Since these agreements lie between arm's-length trade and FDI, they can enable technology-driven multinational enterprises to access overseas markets through contracts and digital channels without a significant physical presence (UNCTAD, 2020b).

Information shortages and limited data availability, amplified by fragmented African markets, hinder investments. In-depth interviews, literature review and the AUC/OECD investor survey conducted for this report confirm that an overall lack of information and data inhibits assessments of investment opportunities in African markets (see also Pineau, 2014). Limited data may result in delays (investors "wait and see") and thwarted investment activity (where information is insufficient for an informed decision). Despite ongoing progress on the implementation of the AfCFTA, African markets remain heterogenous and fragmented, with varying statistical capacities, which increase search costs and prevent economies of scale for market-seeking foreign investment.

Information shortages can fuel "perception premiums". A lack of information such as statistical data creates uncertainty, thereby amplifying the detrimental effects of real risks on investment mobilisation. As risks become more difficult to assess, subjective perceptions gain importance, potentially affecting investment decisions directly (Jaspersen et al., 2000) or indirectly via the increasing cost of capital (Fofack, 2021).

The cost of capital is high for many African countries

The cost of capital for African governments increased sharply as a result of conflicts and tightening global financial policy, effectively pricing most countries out of capital markets. For instance, the spread on an average African Eurobond (a measure for the potential cost of borrowing on capital markets) across 20 African countries issuing such bonds reached a 15-year high of about 12% in September 2022, eclipsing previous peaks of about 9% during the global financial crisis in 2008 and roughly 10% during the COVID-19 crisis in 2020. In September 2022, only Morocco and South Africa had bond yields low enough to ensure access to capital markets with relative certainty, while even these countries' yields reached over 7% and 8% respectively, roughly doubling compared to 2021 (Smith, 2022).

The poor credit ratings of many African countries drive up the cost of capital. Country credit ratings express the likelihood with which a sovereign will service or default on its foreign financial obligations. Credit ratings not only influence the conditions for sovereign debt but also serve as a benchmark for private debt holders (UN, 2022). They influence the cost of both public and private capital (e.g. interest rates and longevity of loans). Private investors mostly rely on ratings published by credit rating agencies (Box 1.2), while export credit agencies (e.g. Coface, SACE) and international organisations (e.g. IMF, OECD) develop ratings to determine the financial conditions that sources of public finance can offer. The high cost of capital acts as an investment barrier, especially in sectors where high upfront capital expenditures are required (Box 1.3).

Box 1.2. The influence of credit rating agencies on the cost of capital in Africa

Country risk ratings published by global credit rating agencies (CRAs), such as Moody's, Standard & Poor's, and Fitch, are foundational for investment risk assessments. In addition to quantifiable factors (such as public revenues or debt levels), CRAs use qualitative, expertise-based subjective judgments and predictions by analysts, notably to determine political risk (Bouchet et al., 2003). As of December 2022, leading CRAs gave Botswana and Mauritius investment-grade ratings based on high political stability and commitment to debt repayments, followed by Côte d'Ivoire, Morocco and South Africa in the non-investment grade speculative category (Trading Economics, 2022).

Critiques contend that CRAs lack accountability and overestimate risks for African countries. Critiques of how CRAs rate African countries intensified after 17 African countries were downgraded in 2020 at the onset of the COVID-19 pandemic – the highest number for developing regions (OECD, 2022d). Such downgrades are often pro-cyclical, increasing the cost of capital for African countries at a time when spending should be expanded (Fofack, 2021). Critics contend that CRAs tend to overestimate African country risk due to information shortages. African countries may lack the detailed and historic data that CRA methodologies depend on while leading CRAs have a narrow capacity for direct and in-depth risk assessments of African governments and firms. This may result in "herding", with CRAs following each other's rating trends, rather than relying on independent assessments (Mutize, 2022; Pandey, 2020). For most African

Box 1.2. **The influence of credit rating agencies on the cost of capital in Africa *(continued)***

countries, credit ratings are unsolicited (Ahouassou, 2011), which may incentivise agencies to lower the rating score (Fulghieri et al., 2014). While African governments have initiated several rejections and appeals, so far such efforts have not resulted in any rating revisions, in part because appeals are administered directly by CRAs (Mutize, 2022). CRAs also disincentivise African governments from restructuring their debt, as they consider restructuring a sovereign default, affecting the rating negatively (AU/UNECA, 2021).

Policy makers can engage CRAs to adopt fairer market behaviour, make their methodologies more transparent and share more data. Ambitious proposals include the establishment of new, impartial rating agencies, either at the global level or through the African Union (Fofack, 2021; Sovereign Group, 2022). South Africa pursued the more immediate approach of requiring CRAs to be licensed locally, enabling regulatory review of alleged anti-competitive practices of CRAs and the imposition of fines (Mutize, 2022). The transparency and accountability of CRAs could be improved by mandating them to specify the extent to which ratings are based on models or on subjective judgments, to discern short-term and long-term ratings that take into account climate transition pathways and to co-ordinate and share data with an international organisation such as the IMF (Fofack, 2021; UN 2022; see also Chapter 2).

Box 1.3. **Africa's renewable energy sector and the high cost of capital**

Renewable energy production is an unequivocal sustainable investment opportunity for Africa. Investments in renewable energy production can support several of Africa's development priorities, such as access to electricity, the mitigation of carbon emissions, reduced dependence on natural resource extraction and fuel imports, and employment creation (IEA, 2022a; OECD/World Bank/UNEP, 2021; RES4Africa, 2022; UNECA 2016).

New investments in Africa's energy sector have increasingly gone towards renewables rather than fossil fuels, but following the global energy crisis in 2022, investment in some African oil and gas markets is resurgent. The share of renewable energy in total energy greenfield FDI increased from 5% in 2010 to 61% in 2021 (Figure 1.7). Despite a general downward trend across all sectors during the COVID-19 pandemic, the value of international project finance deals in Africa's renewable energy sector increased by 19% in 2020 and 117% in 2021 (UNCTAD, 2022b). Solar has become a major contributor to African renewable energy production over the last decade. It is projected to become by far the cheapest source of energy in Africa by 2030 (USD 18-49 per MWh compared to USD 33-86 for onshore wind and USD 30-110 for gas) (IEA, 2022a). Driven by companies such as ZOLA Electric (Off Grid Electric), EcoZoom, M-Kopa and Mobisol (Engie Energy Access), Africa has become the leading destination for investments in off-grid solutions, attracting 70% (USD 1.7 billion) of the global total between 2010 and 2020 (IRENA and AfDB, 2022, based on data from Wood Mackenzie, 2021). Nonetheless, in 2022 Europe's attempts to diversify away from Russian natural gas fuelled investment in some African oil and gas markets which are secured against international off-take. In July 2022, the governments of Algeria, Niger and Nigeria signed a memorandum of understanding to build a trans-Saharan gas pipeline, a project estimated at USD 13 billion that could send up to 30 billion cubic meters of gas a year to Europe (Chikhi, 2022).

Box 1.3. **Africa's renewable energy sector and the high cost of capital** ***(continued)***

Figure 1.7. **Greenfield foreign direct investment to Africa's energy sectors, capital expenditures, 2003-21**

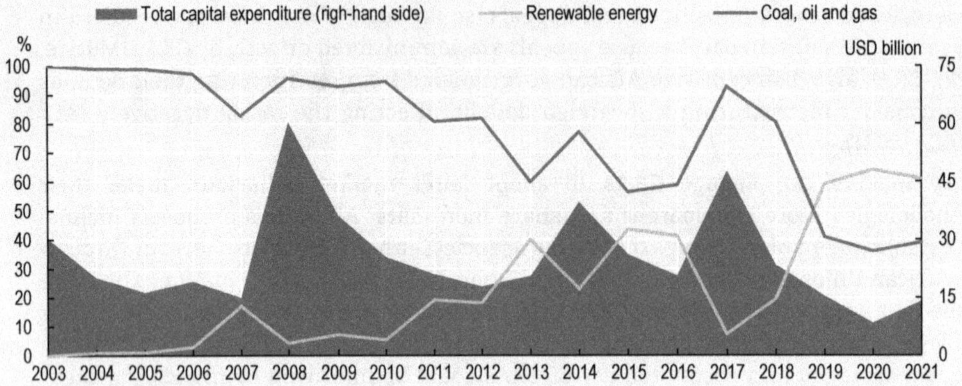

Source: Authors' calculations based on the fDi Intelligence (2022), *fDi Markets* (database), www.fdiintelligence.com/fdi-markets.

StatLink https://stat.link/npmug9

The high cost of capital is particularly detrimental to investments in the renewable energy sector. For instance, after Ghana's central bank raised its benchmark rate to 17% (the comparable United States [US] prime rate is 3.5%), the cost per kilowatt-hour for solar energy systems increased eight times more than that for a gas plant (Kincer and Moss, 2022). The COVID-19 pandemic reversed a slow downward trend in the weighted average cost of capital for energy projects in Africa, which in 2021 was about seven times higher than in Europe and North America (IEA, 2022a). The weighted average cost of capital for renewable energy projects varies widely across Africa (between 8% and 32%). The highest risk premiums often materialise in the countries with the greatest need for investments (Ameli et al., 2021).

Investments remain far below the levels necessary for Africa to achieve its clean energy production targets. The continent is home to 60% of the best solar resources globally, yet only 1% of global installed solar PV capacity (IEA, 2022a). Achieving full access to clean modern energy in Africa by 2030 would require investments totalling USD 25 billion per year until 2030, which is slightly above 1% of total energy investments globally. Current annual investments fall far short of these targets and would need to increase by almost eight times for Africa to achieve universal energy access by 2030 (IEA, 2022a). Investments will need to shift from fuel supply towards power supply and end uses such as energy-efficient buildings. Achieving Africa's sustainable energy transition would require private capital to cover 60% of the cumulative energy investment between now and 2030 (IEA, 2022a).

Africa's better investment performance compared to other world regions does not necessarily result in increased investment amounts. Historically, superior returns on investments in African countries have not translated into rising investment amounts, as investors expect higher returns to compensate for higher risk (Asiedu, 2002). For instance, over the past decade, risk-adjusted rates of return have been depressed as a result of policy uncertainty (e.g. around protectionist measures) (Evenett and Fritz, 2021). Market-seeking FDI in sectors such as retail, information and communications technology (ICT), financial services, and other consumer services in Africa has increased less than in other parts of the world, despite higher returns. For instance, US-based companies active in wholesale trade, finance and insurance earn significant premium returns on their activities on the continent compared to those in other world regions, though less than 1% of their foreign investments takes place in Africa (mostly in Egypt, Nigeria and South Africa) (Figure 1.8).

Figure 1.8. **Within-sector shares and rates of return of outward foreign direct investment from the United States, by investment destination and sector, 2017-21**

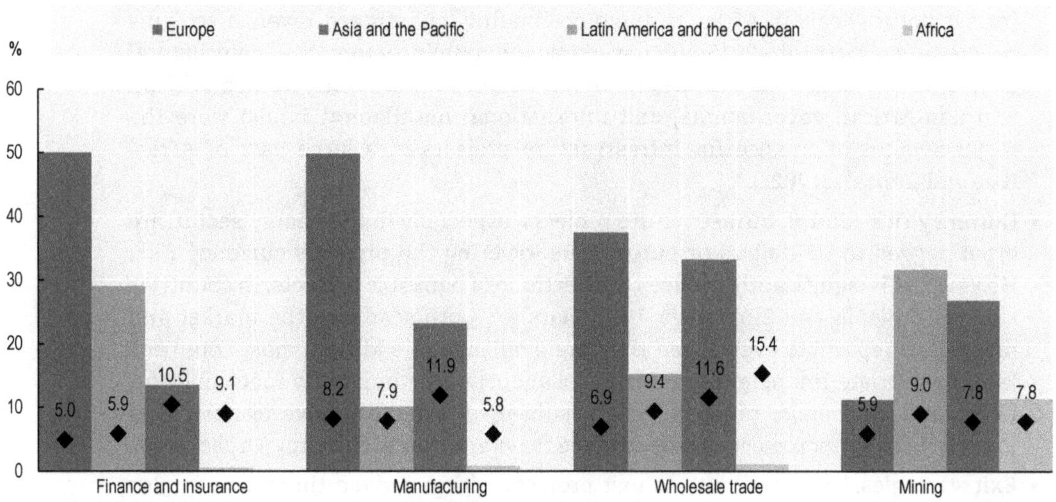

Note: Bars show within-sector shares of outward US FDI stocks by investment destination. Diamonds show US FDI rates of return by sector and investment destination, calculated as the ratio of US FDI income abroad at year t over the average of US FDI end-year stocks abroad at year t and t-1 (UNCTAD, 2019). The figure shows averages over the 2017-21 period and covers selected sectors and destinations. Sectors are sorted in descending order by total FDI stock.

Source: Authors' calculations based on the U.S. Bureau of Economic Analysis (2022), *U.S. BEA* (database), https://apps.bea.gov/iTable/iTable.cfm?ReqID=2&step=1.

StatLink https://stat.link/u85jez

The majority of infrastructure projects in African countries lack the investment necessary to succeed, but some countries' specificities benefit experienced investors. In infrastructure, 80% of projects fail at the feasibility and business-plan stage, as only a few projects meet investors' risk-return expectations (OECD/ACET, 2020; McKinsey, 2020). At the same time, Africa shows the lowest default rates on infrastructure project finance debt at 5.3%, compared to 6.1% in Asia and 10.1% in Latin America (Kelhoffer, 2021). Multinational enterprises interviewed for this report emphasised that Africa-specific experience allows them to generate higher rates of return in Africa compared to other world regions. Once the upfront costs for risk mitigation are borne (see Box 1.4), virtuous cycles between recognition by other market actors, operational expertise, government relations, economies of scale and innovation can unfold. New investors frequently rely on experienced intermediaries to compensate for information shortages, creating competitive disadvantages for smaller investors that are unable to afford such services.

Box 1.4. **Risk mitigation strategies used by infrastructure investors**

Extensive due diligence and risk mitigation measures help explain lower selection and default rates for infrastructure projects in African countries. Several asset managers with experience on the continent identified the following approaches to deal with typical challenges for infrastructure projects:

- **Due diligence.** Asset managers operating in African countries often need to build local knowledge over time through desk research, lengthy local due diligence processes and organisational efforts (Deloitte, 2016). While these long-term

Box 1.4. **Risk mitigation strategies used by infrastructure investors *(continued)***

efforts improve comfort with investing in the region and increase the overall quality of infrastructure projects, the significant upfront effort often discourages inexperienced or smaller asset owners.

- **De-risking.** Governments and development finance institutions often back infrastructure deals in Africa through co-funding, guaranteed revenue streams or credit support. In 2015-20, non-domestic public actors (i.e. multilateral development banks, bilateral development finance institutions, foreign African and non-African governments, and international multilateral funds) were the major sources of finance for infrastructure projects in a large part of Africa (Lee and Gonzalez, 2022).
- **Currency risk control.** Infrastructure projects, especially in the energy sector, are often pegged to US dollars or euros, thus lowering the project's currency risk. However, this significantly reduces the portfolio of bankable projects. In countries such as Ethiopia and Zimbabwe, US dollars are both scarce in the market and difficult to repatriate even when they are available. In addition, most countries lack appropriate financial products in local currency markets to meet investor needs and fund major projects. As a result, investors often have to borrow in foreign currency for projects where revenue flows are in local currency (Orbitt, 2020).
- **Exit strategies.** The possibility to exit projects within a given timeframe is also a concern for most investors with a medium-term investment horizon (Deloitte, 2016). According to a study by African Infrastructure Investment Managers, the exit environment for African infrastructure investments has improved in recent years. It is providing better refinancing opportunities once projects are operational and earning revenues. Nonetheless, narrow and underdeveloped financial markets, capital controls and weak legal frameworks can often slow down or increase the cost of exiting.

Source: Authors' elaboration based on Mercer (2018), *Investment in African Infrastructure: Challenges and Opportunities*, and Eyraud, Pattillo and Selassie (14 June 2021), "How to attract private finance to Africa's development", www.imf.org/en/Blogs/Articles/2021/06/14/blog-how-to-attract-private-finance-to-africa-s-development.

Existing channels for investment show untapped potential to support Africa's regional integration and sustainable development

External financial inflows and domestic sources of investment can be better exploited for sustainable growth

External financial inflows represent important sources of finance for development on the African continent (Table 1.2). In 2021, as in previous years, FDI and remittances made up the largest external financial flows (6.4% of Africa's GDP); yet their potential to promote sustainable growth remains underexploited due to limited integration with productive activities on the continent. ODA and sustainability-oriented private investments (impact investing and philanthropy) are still small and show specific sectoral and country biases (Box 1.5).

Similarly, among domestic sources of investment in African countries, regional multinational enterprises and institutional investors offer untapped potential to support sustainable and resilient growth (Table 1.2). Mobilising domestic resources is necessary to widen the fiscal space of national governments and reduce debt burdens, as well as attract sustainable investments from the private sector.

Table 1.2. **Africa's external and domestic potential sources of sustainable finance**

External/domestic	Sources	Amounts	% of Africa's GDP
External	Foreign direct investment	USD 83 billion (2021)	2.6% (2021)
	Portfolio investment	USD -9.7 billion (2021)	-0.1% (2021)
	Remittances	USD 96 billion (2021)	3.8% (2021)
	Official development assistance	USD 65 billion (2021)	2.5% (2021)
	Global impact investors	USD 24.3 billion (2019) (assets under management invested in Africa)	1.0% (2019)
	Private philanthropy	USD 2.1 billion (2018-19)	0.1% (2019)
Domestic	Government revenues	USD 466 billion (2021)	16.7% (2021)
	Multinational enterprises based in Africa	USD 2.7 billion (2021) (FDI outflows)	0.1% (2021)
	Domestic institutional investors	USD 1.8 trillion (2020) (assets under management based in Africa)	73.3% (2020)

Note: "Amounts" refers to financial flows during the reference period with the exception of "Global impact investors" and "Domestic institutional investors", which refer to end-of-period stocks (assets under management). Financial sources may overlap and cannot be aggregated. Government revenues exclude grants and expenditures on debt services. Global impact investors (GIIN, 2020) and private philanthropy (OECD, 2021b) are considered external sources of finance as they mostly originate outside the African continent.

Source: Authors' compilation based on UNCTAD (2022c), *UNCTADstat* (database), https://unctadstat.unctad.org/EN/; IMF (2022b), *Balance of Payments and International Investment Position Statistics (BOP/IIP)* (database), https://data.imf.org/?sk=7A51304B-6426-40C0-83DD-CA473CA1FD52; IMF (2022c), *Investment and Capital Stock Dataset (ICSD)* (database), https://data.imf.org/?sk=1CE8A55F-CFA7-4BC0-BCE2-256EE65AC0E4; World Bank-KNOMAD (2022), *Remittances* (database), www.knomad.org/data/remittances; OECD (2022a), *OECD Development Assistance Committee* (database), https://stats-1.oecd.org/Index.aspx?DataSetCode=TABLE2A; GIIN (2020), *Annual Impact Investor Survey*, https://thegiin.org/assets/GIIN%20Annual%20Impact%20Investor%20Survey%202020.pdf; OECD (2021b), *OECD Private Philanthropy for Development: Data for Action* (database), https://oecd-main.shinyapps.io/philanthropy4development/; IMF (2022a), *World Economic Outlook* (database), www.imf.org/en/Publications/WEO/weo-database/2022/October; Juvonen et al. (2019), "Unleashing the potential of institutional investors in Africa", *AfDB Working Papers*, No. 325, www.afdb.org/sites/default/files/documents/publications/wps_no_325_unleashing_the_potential_of_institutional_investors_in_africa_c_rv1.pdf.

Box 1.5. **Africa's external sources of sustainable finance**

Official development assistance rose during the COVID-19 pandemic, prioritising social sectors especially in Africa's low-income countries. In 2020, 18 African countries received a larger increase in ODA than in any other year since 2015, partly offsetting the contraction in public finance. On average, net ODA accounted for 9% of GDP for low-income African countries in 2020, compared to only 1.4% and 0.5% for lower- and upper-middle-income counties. Consistent with bilateral ODA allocation recorded in the past decade, over half went to support social sectors in 2020, such as health (28%) and education (9%) or to address humanitarian emergency situations (20%).

Private funding mobilised through ODA has increased, though low-income countries have not been the main recipients. Private finance mobilised through ODA intervention grew fivefold in Africa between 2012 and 2020, from only USD 4 billion to USD 22 billion. About three-quarters of the amounts targeted three sectors: banking and financial services (31%), industry, mining and construction (27%), and energy (20%). However, less than 30% of the amounts mobilised targeted low-income countries (OECD, 2022e).

Despite risk perceptions, appetite for impact investing is expected to grow among global institutional investors, but current assets are held largely in two African countries. Impact investing refers to "investments made with the intention to generate positive, measurable social and environmental impact alongside a financial return".[3] According to the 2020 Annual Impact Investor Survey (GIIN, 2020), African countries are attracting more than 21% of assets worldwide (USD 24.3 billion), and 52% of global impact investors plan to expand their investments in Africa by 2025. Until 2015, about 50% of impact investments went to Kenya and South Africa (GIIN, 2015, 2016). Policy uncertainty may

Box 1.5. Africa's external sources of sustainable finance *(continued)*

prevent Africa from fully realising its potential for impact investment, with 35% of investors citing currency and country risks as severe.

Though Africa receives a larger share of private philanthropic giving than other parts of the world, its poorest regions are not the main beneficiaries, and several obstacles exist. Between 2016-19, Africa attracted 39% of philanthropic flows of global cross-border philanthropy, while Latin America and the Caribbean and developing Asia received 33% and 23% respectively. East Africa received most of Africa's philanthropic inflows with USD 2.4 billion, followed by West Africa with USD 1.7 billion (see Figure 1.9). Cross-border philanthropic giving does not focus on Africa's poorest regions: for example, Southern Africa has a GDP (purchasing power parity) per capita three times larger than Central Africa but received over four times more philanthropic inflows per capita. The major obstacles to philanthropic flows to African countries include political uncertainty, strict regulations, currency volatility and perceptions of corruption (Indiana University Lilly Family School of Philanthropy, 2022; Murisa, 2022).

Figure 1.9. Cross-border philanthropy inflows by African region and sector, USD million, 2016-19

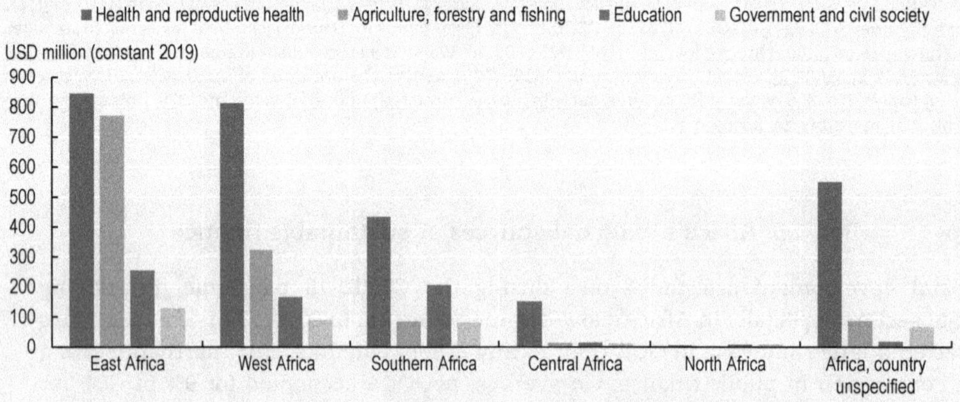

Source: Authors' calculations based on OECD (2021b), *OECD Private Philanthropy for Development: Data for Action* (database), https://oecd-main.shinyapps.io/philanthropy4development/.

StatLink https://stat.link/i7knqp

Better foreign direct investment integration with local economies can create jobs and spillovers that benefit African firms

Foreign direct investment can contribute to sustainable development beyond the capital invested and can have long-term crowding-in effects. Through spillovers to local suppliers and domestically owned firms and through training the workforce, FDI can enhance growth and innovation in the host country and contribute to its sustainable development (Box 1.6). A recent study finds that FDI in Africa has little effect on domestic private investment in the short run but creates significant crowding-in effects in the long run: a one percentage point increase of the share of FDI in GDP led to a 0.3% rise in private domestic investment in a large sample of African countries, with weaker effects in non-diversified commodity-exporting countries (Diallo, Jacolin and Rabaud, 2021).

Box 1.6. OECD FDI Qualities Indicators in Africa

The OECD FDI Qualities Indicators seek to shed light on how FDI contributes to sustainable development, focusing on productivity and innovation, job quality and skills, gender equality, and the low-carbon transition (OECD, 2022f). The OECD FDI Qualities Policy Toolkit further supports governments in identifying policies and institutional arrangements to improve FDI impacts on sustainable development (OECD, 2022g).

Economies in developing and emerging regions, whose domestic technology is often further away from the technological frontier, can particularly benefit from FDI through the transfer of more advanced foreign technologies. Across Africa, the share of foreign firms using technology from abroad is 32%, compared to 13% for domestic firms. This difference is lower than in Latin America and the Caribbean but higher than in developing Asia and OECD countries (Figure 1.10, Panel A). By providing more training opportunities for their employees, foreign firms in African regions contribute significantly to on-the-job skill development (Figure 1.10, Panel B). In most African regions, female employment rates are similar to those for foreign and domestic firms, whereas the share of female top managers is higher in domestic than in foreign companies. This pattern suggests that FDI can create employment opportunities for women, while foreign companies do not necessarily offer better career advancement opportunities for their female workforce in general (Figure 1.10, Panels C and D).

Figure 1.10. OECD FDI Qualities Indicators for Africa and other world regions

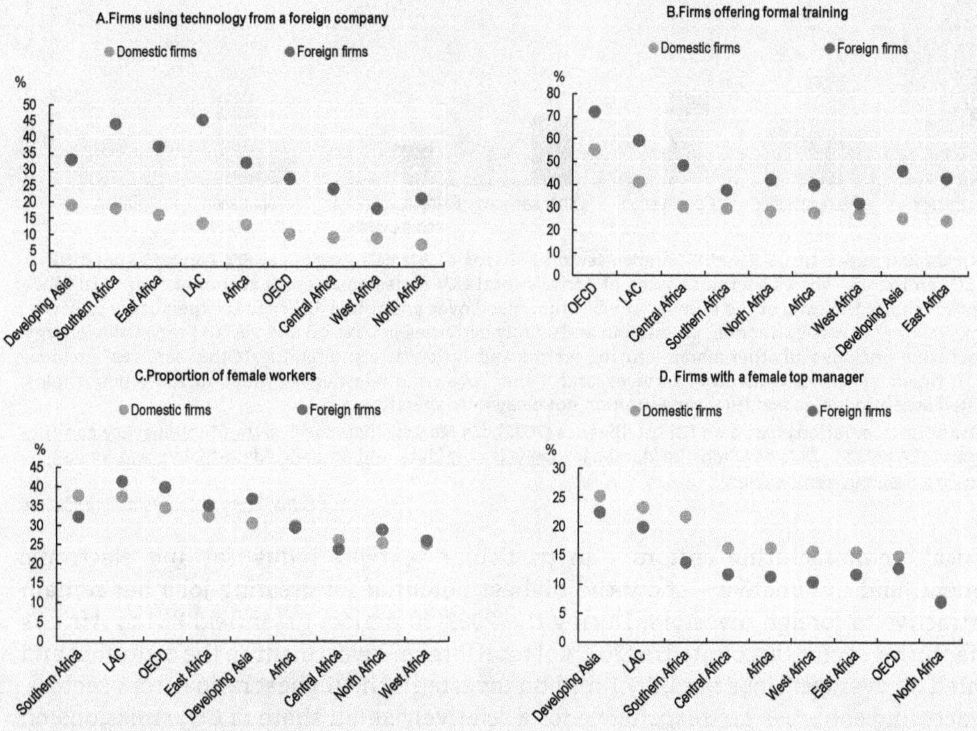

Note: The FDI Qualities Indicators cover 153 countries globally, of which 38 are in Africa. Depending on data availability, some regions do not fully cover all countries. Southern Africa excludes South Africa. LAC = Latin America and the Caribbean.

Source: OECD (2022g), *FDI Qualities Policy Toolkit*, https://doi.org/10.1787/7ba74100-en.

StatLink https://stat.link/h92cj4

In the last two decades, Africa's coal, oil and gas industry attracted the largest share of greenfield FDI, but recent trends show increasing market-seeking investments in Africa's services sectors, such as retail and ICT. In 2003-20, the largest share of greenfield FDI in the continent went to the energy sector (36%), mostly targeting activities in the coal, oil and gas industry (30%), with renewable energy investments representing only 6% of the total. About 60% of the greenfield FDI that went into coal, oil and gas came from Europe and North America. These investments generated on average only 0.25 jobs per USD 1 million of capital expenditure while feeding Africa's most polluting industry, responsible for almost 50% of continental CO_2 emissions since the beginning of the century (Figure 1.11). While this industry has represented the largest source of government revenues and accounted for half of the exports outside the continent for many resource-rich African countries (IEA, 2022a), it has not led to productive transformation and regional integration. In recent years, the emergence of new technologies and booming domestic consumption markets meant that new FDI has focused less on Africa's extractive sectors and more on retail, ICT, financial services and other consumer services (AUC/OECD 2021).

Figure 1.11. **Greenfield foreign direct investment to Africa by sector and selected sustainability indicators, 2003-20**

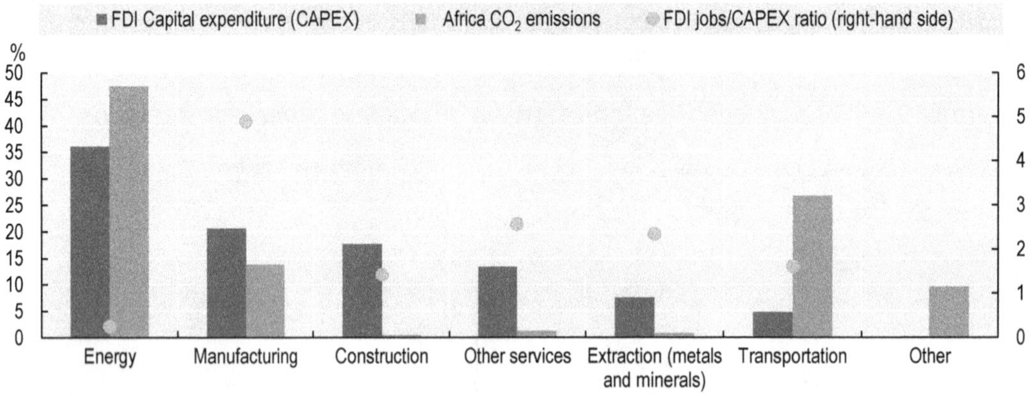

Note: "FDI Capital expenditure (CAPEX)" shows sectoral shares of Africa's greenfield FDI capital expenditures. "Africa CO_2 emissions" shows sectoral shares of Africa's total CO_2 emissions from fuel combustion. "FDI jobs / CAPEX ratio" shows the ratio of the number of jobs announced over greenfield FDI capital expenditure to Africa, by sector. "Energy" covers extraction, production and supply activities in coal, oil and gas and renewable energy, "Manufacturing" includes all other manufacturing sectors and agriculture and fishing, "Other services" includes retail, ICT, financial services and other services, and "Other" is a residual category which includes households, unallocated auto-producers and final consumption not elsewhere specified.

Source: Authors' calculations based on fDi Intelligence (2022), *fDi Markets* (database), www.fdiintelligence.com/fdi-markets and IEA (2022b), *Data and Statistics* (database), www.iea.org/data-and-statistics/data-tools/greenhouse-gas-emissions-from-energy-data-explorer.

StatLink https://stat.link/cie2mg

Africa's manufacturing sectors – in particular textiles, industrial and electronic equipment, and automotive – show the highest potential for creating jobs but remain less attractive to foreign investors. During the 2003-20 period, greenfield FDI to Africa's manufacturing sectors accounted for 20.6% of total foreign investment on the continent and generated on average 5 jobs per USD 1 million invested – the highest ratio across sectors. Manufacturing activities are responsible for a relatively small share of CO_2 emissions on the continent (Figure 1.11). The specific sub-sectors of textiles, industrial and electronic equipment, and automotive have the best records in terms of job creation (14, 10 and 9 jobs per USD 1 million invested respectively), but they attracted only 4.5% of total greenfield FDI capital expenditures in Africa over 2003-20.[4]

Linkages between local affiliates of multinational enterprises and domestic suppliers are important channels for productivity spillovers from FDI. Such linkages can help domestic firms and small and medium-sized enterprises upgrade (Amendolagine et al., 2019; Javorcik and Spatareanu, 2008) through several spillover channels (Table 1.3).

Table 1.3. **Examples of spillovers from foreign to domestic firms**

Spillover channel	Short description	Example
Demand creation	Foreign firms open up market opportunities for local suppliers	A World Bank firm-level study of multinational enterprise suppliers in Rwanda (Qiang, Liu and Steenbergen, 2021) shows that supply linkages with multinational enterprises increase by 2% the probability for a domestic firm to become an exporter. The effect is greater in more complex value chains that require higher product standards and deeper interactions, such as textiles, chemicals and professional services.
Knowledge and technology transfer	Foreign firms provide training and technical assistance to local suppliers	In 2022, Renault Trucks, Toyota Tsusho Corporation and Carrier Global Corporation partnered with the World Food Programme and the Government of Ghana to build a Transport Training Centre in Accra. The centre aims at enhancing transport and logistics capacities across West Africa through free online and hands-on training for up to 400 people per year (WFP, 2022).
Certification	Foreign firms facilitate input quality certification processes within local suppliers	In 2015, the Zurich-based manufacturer Barry Callebaut launched a certification programme to promote sustainable farming within its cocoa supply chain. By February 2022, the programme registered about 121 000 farmers in Ghana, 101 000 in Côte d'Ivoire, 19 000 in Cameroon and 1 700 in Nigeria (Cocoa Horizons, 2022).

Source: Authors' compilation based on literature review.

Foreign firms are less likely to source supplies locally in Africa than in Asia, and the extent of local sourcing varies among African countries. Analysis of firm-level data from the World Bank Enterprise Surveys shows that, on average, foreign firms operating in African countries rely less on inputs sourced from local suppliers compared to their peers in Asia (Figure 1.12). Sector-specific factors, value chain structures and policy considerations can explain variations across African countries: for example, in Ethiopia and Morocco, advanced local supplier capabilities exist in key sectors such as textiles and automotive, allowing foreign manufacturers to source locally. Differences in shares of local sourcing by foreign investors can result from legal and regulatory requirements, as in Egypt (OECD, 2020a) and Tunisia (OECD, 2021c).

Figure 1.12. **Local sourcing of inputs by foreign manufacturing firms in selected countries in Africa and Asia, % of total sourcing**

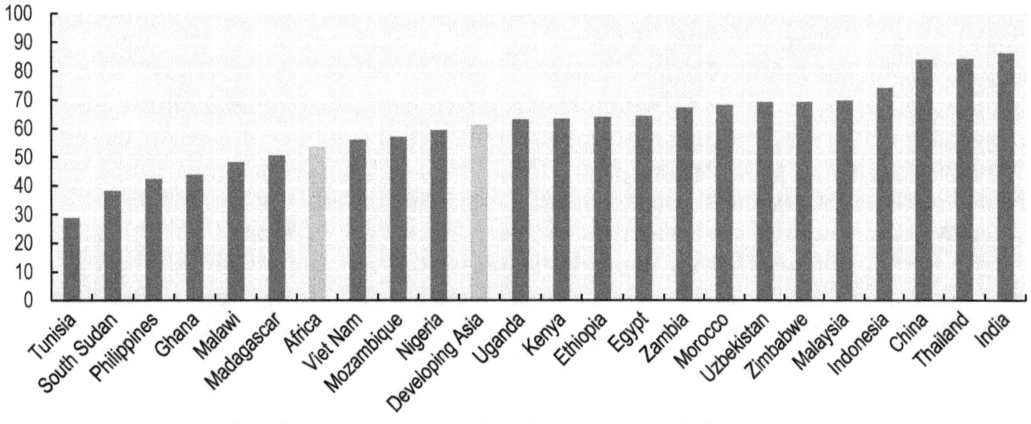

Note: Countries covering less than 50 survey respondents have been excluded.
Source: Authors' calculations based on World Bank (2022b), *Enterprise Surveys* (database), www.enterprisesurveys.org.
StatLink https://stat.link/v5yfiq

The transfer of knowledge and technology from multinational enterprises depends on the absorptive capacity of Africa's small and medium-sized enterprises, which often suffer from a high level of informality and information asymmetries. Absorptive capacity – defined as the production and technology gap between domestic and foreign firms – shapes the ability of local firms and small and medium-sized enterprises to benefit from technological spillovers from multinational enterprises (Lugemwa, 2014; Vu, 2018). A recent study on 100 manufacturing firms in Kenya shows that absorptive capacity plays a statistically significant role in FDI's boosting firm performance, implying that firms need some level of knowledge and technology capacity to fully tap the benefits of FDI (Wanjere et al., 2021). However, investments targeted at African small and medium-sized enterprises are often hampered by informality and information asymmetries (Box 1.7).

Box 1.7. **Sustainable investments in African small and medium-sized enterprises: Coupling financing with impact assessments**

The numerous financial challenges that many African small and medium-sized enterprises (SMEs) face make it difficult for them to attract traditional investors, especially for sustainable investments. The capital requirements of Africa's SMEs typically range between USD 2 000 and USD 100 000, depending on a country's income levels. This "mesofinance" segment of companies is not a well-established target group for typical financing channels: SMEs are often too large for microfinance but too small and unstructured to attract traditional banks and investors. Most entrepreneurs are not trained in business planning, lack documented financial data and – apparently the most significant barrier to accessing credit – are unable to provide collateral in obtaining credit (e.g. land, buildings or equipment) (EIB, 2022). Some entrepreneurs are also unwilling to open their books to equity investors, as they are loath to have their decisions challenged or are unfamiliar with this type of finance. Due to lacking liquidity in financial markets, investors cannot easily sell their shares in SMEs and achieve profitable exits, especially in Francophone Africa and its least developed countries. These challenges are even more pronounced for attracting sustainable investments that seek to expand SMEs while also improving their social and environmental practices.

While SMEs remain unattractive to traditional financiers, specialised investors that couple funding with business advisory can provide sustainable investments. For example, Investisseurs & Partenaires (I&P), a social investor focusing on Africa's least developed countries, provides dedicated solutions for start-ups and high-potential SMEs (I&P, n.d. a; Severino, 2018). I&P developed an impact scorecard to determine a project's alignment with I&P's impact pillars (e.g. the provision of essential goods and services, gender promotion, and environmental impact). It carries out an environmental and social audit to assess a company's current practices and define an action plan to mitigate identified risks. So far, I&P has carried out over 150 investments, with 87% located in the least developed countries and around 75% contributing directly to the SDGs. With an average post-investment employment growth of around 50%, these micro enterprises and SMEs have maintained or created nearly 9 000 direct jobs (with 96% of employees benefiting from health coverage) and have indirectly impacted nearly 50 000 family members (I&P, n.d. b; Coulibaly, 2022). The investor's experience suggests that SMEs may continue to yield lower financial returns for impact investors but offer the greatest additionality for social and environmental impacts.

Mobilising remittances as part of diaspora investment can help develop local production networks. According to International Fund for Agricultural Development (IFAD/World Bank, 2015), up to 30% of remittances target economic activities. However, most of these remittances are channelled towards informal activities and micro, small and medium-sized enterprises through extended family ties and social networks, rather than towards structured diaspora investment products. This is due to limitations including a lack of knowledge about investment opportunities along with low confidence in regulatory and political systems (Asquith and Opoku-Owusu, 2020). Diaspora investments can support the development of local production networks as most diaspora investors tend to establish more connections with local suppliers than non-diaspora foreign investors (Amendolagine et al., 2013). Structured diaspora investment products could tap into the estimated USD 33.7 billion annual diaspora savings, channelling some of these funds more directly towards productive investments on the continent (Faal, 2019).

The growth of intra-African investment can support job creation and regional integration

African multinational enterprises account for a minor share of greenfield FDI to the continent but have increased their investment in specific sectors. From 2017 to 2021, intra-African FDI flows accounted for only 9% of total greenfield FDI to the continent.[4] However, in 2020-21, despite a sharp reduction in total greenfield FDI to Africa during the COVID-19 pandemic, Africa-based investors increased their engagement in new investment projects in ICT, renewable energies and metals (Figure 1.13). For example, in 2020, MTN Nigeria (a subsidiary of the South Africa-based MTN Group) announced plans to invest over USD 1.6 billion in 4G network infrastructure across the country until 2023 (NIPC, 2020).

Figure 1.13. **Greenfield foreign direct investment to Africa by source region and sector, % change in capital expenditures between 2018-19 and 2020-21**

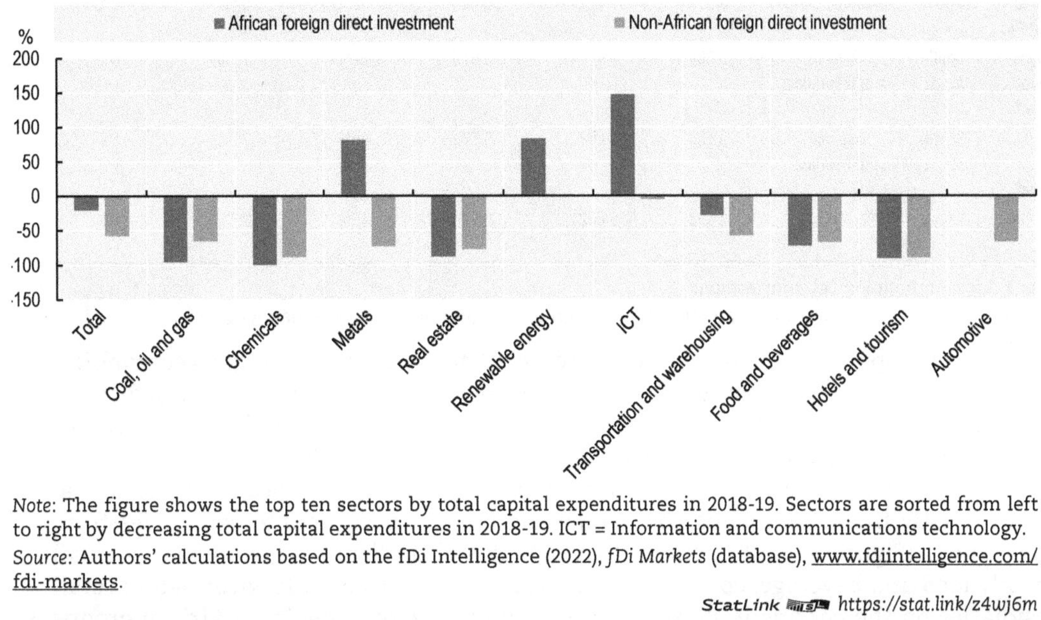

Note: The figure shows the top ten sectors by total capital expenditures in 2018-19. Sectors are sorted from left to right by decreasing total capital expenditures in 2018-19. ICT = Information and communications technology.
Source: Authors' calculations based on the fDi Intelligence (2022), *fDi Markets* (database), www.fdiintelligence.com/fdi-markets.

StatLink https://stat.link/z4wj6m

Original analysis for this report shows that the growth of African multinational enterprises in services – such as finance and retail – has increased the potential for job creation, but they are highly dominated by South African groups. Overall, Africa's services sectors combine comparatively low environmental impact with a relatively positive job creation potential (Figure 1.11). For example, greenfield FDI in retail generates on average 5.6 jobs per USD 1 million of capital expenditures.[4] In South Africa, Africa's top FDI source and destination in 2021, the retail sector accounts for 21.5% of total employment (Statistics South Africa, 2022), mostly due to the dominance of large domestic retail companies. Analysis of firm-level data from the *Orbis* database across 521 African private companies listed on a stock market with subsidiaries in Africa highlights the dominance of South African firms as intra-African investors (Table 1.4). They represented 34% of firms included in the sample and three-quarters of turnover and market capitalisation. While 23% of Africa-based listed firms in the sample operate in manufacturing, the vast majority (69%) is active in service-oriented sectors such as financial services (29%), retail (8%), real estate (6%), and information and communication technologies (6%).

Table 1.4. **The top ten Africa-based listed companies by market capitalisation**

Rank	Company name	Country	Sector	Turnover (USD million)	Employees	Market capitalisation (USD million)	% of domestic subsidiaries	% of continental subsidiaries	% of subsidiaries outside Africa
1	Naspers Limited	South Africa	ICT	5 934	28 445	89 883	30%	2%	68%
2	Firstrand Limited	South Africa	Finance and insurance	7 710	-	28 560	81%	12%	7%
3	Standard Bank Group Limited	South Africa	Finance and insurance	8 426	49 224	21 180	54%	32%	14%
4	Sasol Limited	South Africa	Manufacturing	14 275	28 949	19 108	56%	4%	41%
5	Sanlam Limited	South Africa	Finance and insurance	6 892	-	12 726	56%	32%	12%
6	MTN Group Limited	South Africa	ICT	11 455	16 390	12 294	17%	56%	27%
7	Dangote Cement Plc	Nigeria	Manufacturing	3 378	17 747	10 040	8%	89%	4%
8	Nedbank Group Limited	South Africa	Finance and insurance	3 667	-	9 915	62%	22%	16%
9	Absa Group Limited	South Africa	Finance and insurance	5 404	35 267	9 782	66%	28%	6%
10	Safaricom PLC	Kenya	ICT	2 593	5 852	9 646	70%	20%	10%

Note: See Annex 1.B for methodological information.
Source: Bureau van Dijk (2022), *Orbis* (database), www.bvdinfo.com/en-gb/our-products/data/international/orbis.

African groups in financial services and retail tend to have a larger geographical footprint. Based on the analysis of the *Orbis* database, on average Africa-based listed companies have established 17 subsidiaries on the continent, compared to 8 for Western European companies, 4 for North American companies and only 3 for Asian companies. African groups hold three-quarters of subsidiaries operating in Africa in the financial sector – mostly financial holding companies and banks – compared to companies from other regions (Figure 1.14). While less than 10% of African listed firms operate in retail – mostly food and beverage, construction materials – they account for over half of retail subsidiaries on the continent, illustrating the dominance of a few large African groups (e.g. Shoprite, Pick n Pay).

Figure 1.14. **Subsidiaries of listed companies active in Africa, by sector and home region of company group**

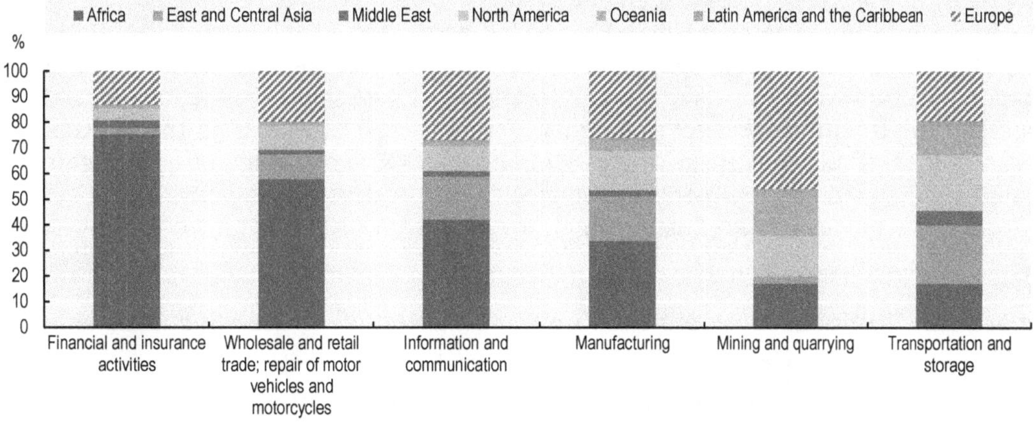

Note: The figure shows the top six sectors by number of African subsidiaries. The sample includes 521 Africa-based listed private companies and 2 355 non-Africa-based listed private companies with subsidiaries in Africa. See Annex 1.B for further methodological information.

Source: Authors' calculations based on Bureau van Dijk (2022), *Orbis* (database), www.bvdinfo.com/en-gb/our-products/data/international/orbis.

StatLink https://stat.link/5bzk8m

Manufacturing and retail are the most job-intensive sectors, but sectors with high market value – financial and ICT – can indirectly create jobs. Manufacturing and retail account for over 50% of direct employment among Africa-based listed firms. In contrast, the financial and ICT sectors represent over 60% of market capitalisation, but they create less than one-fourth of total direct employment: about 500 000 employees (Figure 1.15). However, the financial and ICT sectors offer the potential for indirect job creation through increasing financial inclusion and digital upgrading in the rest of the economy (AUC/OECD, 2021).

Figure 1.15. **Shares of market capitalisation and employment among Africa-based listed companies**

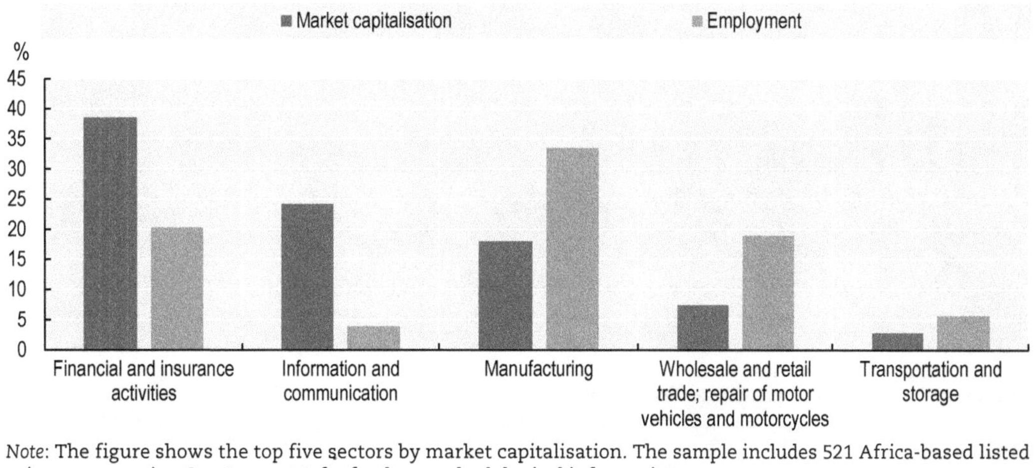

Note: The figure shows the top five sectors by market capitalisation. The sample includes 521 Africa-based listed private companies. See Annex 1.B for further methodological information.

Source: Bureau van Dijk (2022), *Orbis* (database), www.bvdinfo.com/en-gb/our-products/data/international/orbis.

StatLink https://stat.link/g3iyza

African firms expanding within the continent often have better knowledge of the new business environments than non-African firms. Formal and informal knowledge of the business environment often helps regional pioneers enter neighbouring markets by facilitating investment decisions and reducing costs (Kathuria, Yatawara and Zhu, 2021). Using such knowledge, Dangote Cement, for instance, has successfully competed against non-African incumbent companies and expanded across ten African countries (World Bank, 2016). Firms can acquire capabilities in their domestic market that can allow them to expand to countries that have similar institutional settings; this appears crucial to succeed in difficult market environments (Verhoef, 2011). Research on the location strategies of three South African firms – SABMiller, MTN and Massmart – highlights the ability to implement non-market strategies as well as leverage important political connections to navigate weak institutional environments (White, Kitimbo and Rees, 2019).

Domestic institutional investors hold untapped potential to unlock sustainable finance

African institutional investors have grown, while their investments in alternative assets remain negligible. According to the latest estimates, in 2020, African institutional investors had assets under management of about USD 1.8 trillion, registering a 48% increase from 2017 (Juvonen et al., 2019). OECD data show that pension funds across 15 African countries accumulated USD 380 billion of assets by 2020, with South Africa accounting for almost 80% of the total (OECD, 2021d). This translates into an average GDP share of 25% for Africa (mostly driven by South Africa, Namibia and Botswana), compared to 22% in Latin America and the Caribbean and 3% in developing Asia (Figure 1.16). Yet, alternative assets – such as infrastructure, real estate, green and sustainable assets, private equity, and venture capital – accounted for less than 3% of portfolios in an assessment of five African pension markets, namely Ghana, Kenya, Namibia, Nigeria and South Africa (AfDB/IFC/MFW4A, 2022).

Figure 1.16. **Assets under management of pension funds, 2015-20, % of GDP**

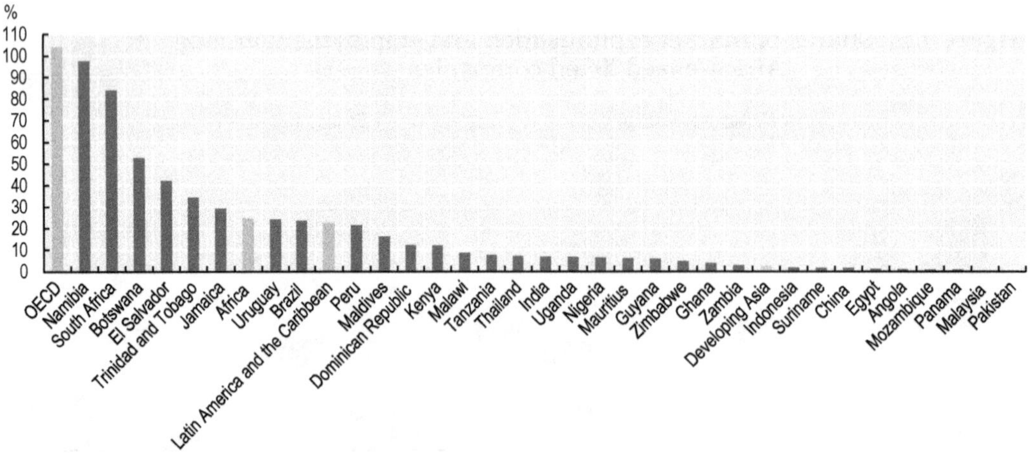

Note: OECD includes 38 countries, Africa includes 15 countries, Latin America and the Caribbean includes 10 countries and Developing Asia includes 7 countries.

Source: Authors' calculations based on OECD (2021d), *OECD Global Pension Statistics* (database), https://doi.org/10.1787/pension-data-en.

StatLink https://stat.link/9tdoye

The absence of environmental, social and governance (ESG) frameworks, capacity constraints and a lack of information for investors limit sustainable investment in African countries. Specific sustainable investment frameworks are still missing across the African continent, with South Africa's implementation of an ESG taxonomy in April 2022 as one exception. Data and management capacity constraints make accurate ESG criteria assessments more difficult, which can lower ESG scores and increase the risk of exclusion from international sustainable investment (OECD, 2022b). In a survey of 70 African banks, 70% saw green lending as an opportunity, but 60% cited technical capacity as a barrier to implementation (EIB, 2022). Mirroring global trends among institutional investors (OECD, 2021a), half of the major African pension funds provide information on the importance of sustainability to their investments. And these share only limited information on their specific strategies and implementations (Stewart, 2022).

Better institutional governance and co-operation across countries can help Africa's sovereign wealth funds (SWFs) attract private capital for sustainable investments. Total assets under management of Africa's SWFs amount to USD 100 billion across 30 funds (Global SWF, 2022). Several SWFs have established private equity funds for sectors such as healthcare and renewable energy to attract foreign investors to sustainable investment opportunities (Table 1.5). In a recent survey of senior executives of African SWFs, all respondents underlined the importance of independent and effective institutional governance as the first priority to generate the trust of international and domestic partners. Eighty-three per cent of respondents said that the current collaboration between the continent's SWFs was insufficient and that much more needs to be done also in the context of the AfCFTA (IFSWF and Templeton, 2021). In June 2022, African SWFs, with collective assets under management of USD 12.6 billion, formed the African Sovereign Investors Forum, a new shared platform to accelerate co-ordination to mobilise capital for sustainable investments (AfDB, 2022).

Table 1.5. **Examples of sustainable investment projects by African sovereign wealth funds**

Sovereign wealth fund	Country	Assets under management (2020)	Sustainable investment projects
Fonds Souverain d'Investissements Stratégiques (Fonsis)	Senegal	USD 846 million	Since 2017, Fonsis has set up four solar farms which today represent more than 50% of the solar capacity of Senegal, energy supply for nearly a million households and the potential to save 160 tons of carbon dioxide annually.
Ghana Infrastructure Investment Fund (GIIF)	Ghana	USD 330 million	In 2017, GIIF committed USD 51 million to a public-private partnership with a local ICT company to establish 880 km of in-land fibre optic cables for an extensive high-quality broadband network in the west of Ghana. The project connected major towns and created approximately 12 000 direct and indirect jobs during the construction phase.
The Sovereign Fund of Egypt (TSFE)	Egypt	USD 12.7 billion	TSFE has signed memorandums of understanding representing USD 40 billion of investment in green hydrogen with power and transport companies (Furness, 2022).
Nigeria Sovereign Investment Authority (NSIA)	Nigeria	USD 1.8 billion	NSIA completed a USD 12.5 million investment project to upgrade, equip, maintain and operate an outpatient cancer treatment facility, the first of its kind in Nigeria. The upgraded centre provides advanced external radiotherapy, brachytherapy and chemotherapy and is equipped with a world-class training facility for oncology professionals. It has treated over 4 000 patients since being established in May 2019.

Source: Authors' compilation based on IFSWF and Templeton (2021), *Investing for Growth and Prosperity: In Africa Sovereign Wealth Funds Focus on G, S and E*, www.ifswf.org/sites/default/files/IFSWF_Africa_Paper_v2.pdf and desk research.

Pension and sovereign wealth funds may be willing to invest in African infrastructure projects, provided quality criteria are met. In a 2018 study on institutional investment and commercial project development in Africa, all surveyed pension and sovereign wealth funds stated they were willing to consider investing in African infrastructure projects that are already generating revenues. While only 11% of pension funds reported interest in infrastructure projects under development (greenfield projects), most indicated a willingness to invest indirectly in the early stage of project preparation through investment vehicles and entities that strictly meet their investment criteria, such as high-quality bonds, funds, banks and corporations. Most investors surveyed ranked public-sector commitment and experienced project management among their top investment requirements (Danso and Samuels, 2018).

Annex 1.A. The estimation of Africa's sustainable financing gap

The estimation of Africa's sustainable financing gap in this report draws on the methodology outlined in the OECD's *Global Outlook on Financing for Sustainable Development 2023* (OECD, 2022b). While other estimation methodologies exist (e.g. UNCTAD, 2022a), the OECD methodology can be replicated with data that is available for almost all African countries over time. Based on original projections of the annual financing needs of African countries to achieve the SDGs and the financial resources available to meet those needs conducted in 2015 (UNCTAD, 2014, 2016), this report assumes a baseline USD 200 billion sustainable financing gap per annum for the African continent until 2030 in a scenario where financing conditions remain constant (UNCTAD, 2020b). As per the OECD (2022b) approach, the baseline is adjusted according to changes in Africa's main (foreign and domestic) sources of finance compared to 2015 as the year in which the baseline was projected (Annex Table 1.A.1).

In contrast to the OECD (2022b) approach, this report presents the available financing and the sustainable financing gap from 2015-21 (Figure 1.3). For this purpose, the methodology deviates from OECD (2022b) in that 2015 instead of 2019 is used as a baseline while one-off COVID-19-related fiscal measures were omitted. To calculate official development finance, only net ODA data were used instead of data from the *Total Official Support for Sustainable Development* (TOSSD, 2022) database, which are not available for all African countries for the time period 2015-21.

Annex Table 1.A.1. **Calculation of Africa's sustainable financing gap in 2020**

Financial flows		Value	Description	Source
Baseline estimate of annual sustainable financing gap		USD 200.0 billion	Africa's average annual sustainable financing gap projected in 2015	UNCTAD, 2020b
+	Decrease in available government revenues (excluding grants and external debt service)	USD 21.6 billion	Change in government revenues between 2015 and 2020	Calculations based on IMF, 2022a, and World Bank, 2022a
+	Decrease in capital inflows	USD 82.7 billion	Change in FDI, portfolio investment and other investment inflows between 2015 and 2020	IMF, 2022b
-	Increase in remittances	USD 12.6 billion	Change in remittance flows between 2015 and 2020	World Bank-KNOMAD, 2022
-	Increase in official development assistance	USD 19.8 billion	Change in official development assistance between 2015 and 2020	OECD, 2022a
Sustainable financing gap in 2020		USD 271.9 billion		

Note: Capital inflows include foreign direct investment (FDI), portfolio investment, and other investment inflows reported by the International Monetary Fund under asset/liability accounting. Figures for capital inflows should be interpreted with some caution as some portfolio inflows figures are missing.

Sources: Authors' calculations and elaboration based on OECD (2022b), *Global Outlook on Financing for Sustainable Development 2023: No Sustainability Without Equity*, https://doi.org/10.1787/fcbe6ce9-en; IMF (2022a), *World Economic Outlook Database*, www.imf.org/en/Publications/WEO/weo-database/2022/October; OECD (2022a), *OECD Development Assistance Committee* (database), https://stats-1.oecd.org/Index.aspx?DataSetCode=TABLE2A; World Bank (2022a), *International Debt Statistics* (database), https://databank.worldbank.org/source/international-debt-statistics; IMF (2022b), *Balance of Payments and International Investment Position Statistics (BOP/IIP)* (database), https://data.imf.org/?sk=7A51304B-6426-40C0-83DD-CA473CA1FD52; UNCTAD (2020b), "Economic Development in Africa Report 2020: Press Conference", Press Release, https://unctad.org/osgstatement/economic-development-africa-report-2020-press-conference and World Bank-KNOMAD (2022), *Remittances* (database), www.knomad.org/data/remittances.

Annex 1.B. Analysis of African lead firms

The *Orbis* database[5]

The Orbis database from Bureau van Dijk (BvD) – a Moody's Analytics company – provides harmonised financial and ownership information at the firm level, across more than 100 countries and over 400 million private and public listed firms. Data are collected from over 160 different government and commercial information providers (national business registers). While BvD harmonises the data in a standard "global" format, the data are not nationally representative (see Kalemly-Ozcan et al., 2022, for more information).

Sample selection criteria[6]

In order to extract a sample of companies active in Africa from the *Orbis* database, the following data selection criteria were applied:

- active privately owned companies with subsidiaries (minimum 10% of direct ownership)[7] located in African countries
- companies with "latest year of accounts" not older than five years (2017-2021)
- publicly listed companies registered as Global Ultimate Owners (GUO).[8]

For each company, consolidated accounts are reported. When these are not available, unconsolidated accounts are reported.

Due to data quality considerations (see also OECD, 2020b), the analysis is focused on listed firms for which data are of higher coverage and quality to allow cross-sector and country analysis.

Notes

1. Republic of Congo, Malawi, Mozambique, São Tomé and Príncipe, Somalia, Sudan, Zambia and Zimbabwe.
2. Burundi, Cameroon, Central African Republic, Chad, Comoros, Djibouti, Ethiopia, Gambia, Ghana, Guinea-Bissau, Kenya, Sierra Leone and South Sudan.
3. https://thegiin.org/impact-investing/
4. Authors' calculations based on fDi Intelligence (2022).
5. https://www.nber.org/papers/w21558
6. The data were downloaded on 15 September 2022.
7. The 10% threshold is defined in accordance with the OECD definition of FDI relationship: https://www.oecd.org/daf/inv/investment-policy/2487495.pdf.
8. In the *Orbis* database, a Global Ultimate Owner (GUO) is the individual or entity at the top of the corporate ownership structure. The GUO filtering condition is applied to identify the company group and avoid the selection of multiple entities belonging to the same group.

References

AfDB (2022), "African Development Bank, Africa50 and the newly launched African Sovereign Investors Forum signal strong desire to jointly mobilize capital for infrastructure projects", Press Release, www.afdb.org/en/news-and-events/press-releases/african-development-bank-africa50-and-newly-launched-african-sovereign-investors-forum-signal-strong-desire-jointly-mobilize-capital-infrastructure-projects-52677.

AfDB/IFC/MFW4A (2022), *Gauging Appetite of African Institutional Investors for New Asset Classes*, African Development Bank, International Finance Corporation and Making Finance Work for Africa, www.mfw4a.org/sites/default/files/resources/gauging_appetite_of_african_institutional_investors_for_new_asset_classes_-_published.pdf.

AfDB/OECD/UNDP (2015), *African Economic Outlook 2015: Regional Development and Spatial Inclusion*, OECD Publishing, Paris, https://doi.org/10.1787/aeo-2015-en.

Ahouassou, A. (24 May 2011), "African countries credit ratings: Key for effective resource mobilization on international capital markets", African Development Bank, www.afdb.org/fr/news-and-events/african-countries-credit-ratings-key-for-effective-resource-mobilization-on-international-capital-markets-8023.

Alfaro, L. et al. (2008), "Why doesn't capital flow from rich to poor countries? An empirical investigation", *Review of Economics and Statistics*, Vol. 90/2, pp. 347–368, https://doi.org/10.1162/rest.90.2.347.

Ameli, N. et al. (2021), "Higher cost of finance exacerbates a climate investment trap in developing economies", *Nature Communications*, Vol. 12, https://doi.org/10.1038/s41467-021-24305-3.

Amendolagine, V. et al. (2019), "Local sourcing in developing countries: The role of foreign direct investments and global value chains", *World Development*, Vol. 113, pp. 73-88, https://doi.org/10.1016/j.worlddev.2018.08.010.

Amendolagine, V. et al. (2013), "FDI and local linkages in developing countries: Evidence from sub-Saharan Africa", *World Development*, Vol. 50, pp. 41-56, https://doi.org/10.1016/j.worlddev.2013.05.001.

Andoh, F. K. and W. G. Cantah (2020), "Foreign Direct Investment in Sub-Saharan Africa: Is Tax Obligation Still an Issue?", *Global Business Review*, Vol. 23/5, pp. 1236-1251, https://doi.org/10.1177/0972150919890241.

ANRC (2021), *Lithium-Cobalt Value Chain Analysis for Mineral Based Industrialization in Africa*, African Natural Resources Centre, Abidjan, www.afdb.org/pt/documents/lithium-cobalt-value-chain-analysis-mineral-based-industrialization-africa.

Asiedu, E. (2002), "On the determinants of foreign direct investment to developing countries: Is Africa different?", *World Development*, Vol. 30/1, pp. 107-119, http://dx.doi.org/10.2139/ssrn.280062.

Asquith, P. and S. Opoku-Owusu (2020), "Diaspora investment to help achieve the SDGs in Africa: Prospects and trends", in *Foreign Direct Investment Perspective through Foreign Direct Divestment*, IntechOpen, London, www.intechopen.com/chapters/72728.

AUC (2015), *Agenda 2063: The Africa We Want*, African Union Commission, Addis Ababa, https://au.int/sites/default/files/documents/36204-doc-agenda2063_popular_version_en.pdf.

AUC/UNECA (2021), *Africa sovereign Credit Rating Review: 2021 End of Year Outlook*, United Nations Economic Commission for Africa and African Union Commission, Addis Ababa, https://hdl.handle.net/10855/47399.

AUC/OECD (2022), *Africa's Development Dynamics 2022: Regional Value Chains for a Sustainable Recovery*, AUC, Addis Ababa/OECD Publishing, Paris, https://doi.org/10.1787/2e3b97fd-en.

AUC/OECD (2021), *Africa's Development Dynamics 2021: Digital Transformation for Quality Jobs*, AUC, Addis Ababa/OECD Publishing, Paris, https://doi.org/10.1787/0a5c9314-en.

AUC/OECD (2019), *Africa's Development Dynamics 2019: Achieving Productive Transformation*, AUC, Addis Ababa/OECD Publishing, Paris, https://doi.org/10.1787/c1cd7de0-en.

AUC/OECD (2018), *Africa's Development Dynamics 2018: Growth, Jobs and Inequalities*, AUC, Addis Ababa/OECD Publishing, Paris, https://doi.org/10.1787/9789264302501-en.

AVCA (2022), *Venture Capital in Africa Report*, African Private Equity and Venture Capital Association, www.avca-africa.org/media/2967/62644-avca-avca-venture-capital-in-africa-report-v13.pdf.

BCG (2022), *Global Asset Management 2022: From Tailwinds to Turbulence*, Boston Consulting Group, https://web-assets.bcg.com/c8/5a/2f2f5d784302b945ba1f3276abbc/global-asset-management-2022-from-tailwinds-to-turbulence-may-2022.pdf.

Bouchet, M. et al. (2003), *Country Risk Assessment: A Guide to Global Investment Strategy*, Wiley Finance, West Sussex, https://developingfinance.org/download/Wiley-Finance-Country-Risk-Assessment-A-Guide-to-Global-Investment-Strategy.pdf.

Brenton, P., M. J. Ferrantino and M. Maliszewska (2022), *Reshaping Global Value Chains in Light of COVID-19: Implications for Trade and Poverty Reduction in Developing Countries*, World Bank, Washington, DC, https://doi.org/10.1596/978-1-4648-1821-9.

Bureau van Dijk (2022), *Orbis* (database), www.bvdinfo.com/en-gb/our-products/data/international/orbis (accessed October 2022).

Calderon, C. et al. (2019), "Drivers of gross capital inflows: Which factors are more important for sub-Saharan Africa?", *Policy Research Working Paper*, No. 8777, World Bank, Washington, DC, https://openknowledge.worldbank.org/handle/10986/31403.

CB Insights (2022), *State of Venture*, www.cbinsights.com/reports/CB-Insights_Venture-Report-Q2-2022.pdf.

Cheung, Y. W. et al. (2012), "China's outward direct investment in Africa", *Review of International Economics*, Vol. 20/2, John Wiley & Sons, Hoboken, https://doi.org/10.1111/j.1467-9396.2012.01017.x.

Chikhi, L. (9 July 2022), "Algeria, Niger and Nigeria sign MoU for Saharan gas pipeline", Reuters, www.reuters.com/business/energy/algeria-niger-nigeria-sign-mou-saharan-gas-pipeline-2022-07-28/.

Cocoa Horizons (2022), *The Cocoa Snapshot: 21/22 Mid-Year Review*, www.cocoahorizons.org/sites/www.cocoahorizons.org/files/Cocoa%20Snapshot%2021-22%20Half%20Year%20EN.pdf.

Collier, P. and C. Pattillo (2000), "Investment and Risk in Africa", in *Studies on the African Economies Series*, Palgrave Macmillan, London, https://doi.org/10.1007/978-1-349-15068-7_1.

Coulibaly, N. (23 July 2022), "Entrepreneuriat durable : I&P veut faire émerger 500 champions africains d'ici à 2030", JeuneAfrique, www.jeuneafrique.com/1362840/economie/entrepreneuriat-durable-ip-veut-faire-emerger-500-champions-africains-dici-a-2030/.

CPI (2022), *Landscape of Climate Finance in Africa*, Climate Policy Initiative, San Francisco, www.climatepolicyinitiative.org/wp-content/uploads/2022/09/Landscape-of-Climate-Finance-in-Africa.pdf.

Cuvellier, M. (24 January 2022), "Africa vs. The Rest of The World", Africa: The Big Deal, https://thebigdeal.substack.com/p/africa-vs-the-rest-of-the-world.

Danso H. and B. Samuels (2018), "Benchmark for Investing in African Infrastructure Project Development ("I4PD Benchmark")" in *Special Report Institutional Investment and Commercial Project Development in Africa*, www.africainvestor.com/wp-content/uploads/2022/02/I4PD-Benchmark-Report-2018-Update-D15-2.pdf.

Deloitte (2016), *Your Essential Guide to De-risking Africa: Unlocking the Value in Africa*, Deloitte www2.deloitte.com/content/dam/Deloitte/za/Documents/risk/ZA_De-risking%20Africa%20Brochure_FINAL_digi_spreads.pdf.

Diallo, A., L. Jacolin and I. Rabaud (2021), "Foreign direct investment and domestic private investment in sub-Saharan African countries: Crowding-in or out", *Ferdi Working Papers*, No. 292, https://ferdi.fr/dl/df-MtwJiRQa4ZgpWvN5BBwKh5X3/ferdi-p292-foreign-direct-investment-and-domestic-private-investment-in.pdf.

EIB (2022), *Finance in Africa: Navigating the Financial Landscape in Turbulent Times*, European Investment Bank, www.eib.org/attachments/lucalli/finance_in_africa_2022_en.pdf.

Ekeruche, M. A. (2022), *Africa's Rising Debt and the Emergence of New Creditors*, *African Debt Series*, Vol. 2, FES AU/AU, Addis Ababa, https://library.fes.de/pdf-files/bueros/fes-ua/19365.pdf.

Evenett, S. J. and J. Fritz (2021), *Advancing Sustainable Development with FDI: Why Policy Must Be Reset*, CEPR Press, London, www.globaltradealert.org/reports/75.

Eyraud, L., C. Pattillo and A. A. Selassie (14 June 2021), "How to attract private finance to Africa's development", IMF blogs, www.imf.org/en/Blogs/Articles/2021/06/14/blog-how-to-attract-private-finance-to-africa-s-development.

Faal, G. (2019), *Strategic, Business and Operational Framework for an African Diaspora Finance Corporation: African Union Legacy Project on Diaspora Investment, Innovative Finance and Social Enterprise in Africa*, African Union Commission, Addis Ababa, https://au.int/sites/default/files/documents/40847-doc-EN - ADFC Business and Operational Framework - May 2019.pdf.

fDi Intelligence (2022), *fDi Markets* (database), www.fdiintelligence.com/fdi-markets (accessed 19 September 2022).

Fofack, H. (2021), *The Ruinous Price for Africa of Pernicious' Perception Premiums*, Africa Growth Initiative at Brookings, www.brookings.edu/wp-content/uploads/2021/10/21.10.07_Perception-premiums.pdf.

Fulghieri, P. et al. (2014), "The Economics of Solicited and Unsolicited Credit Ratings", *The Review of Financial Studies*, Vol. 27/2, pp. 484-518, https://doi.org/10.1093/rfs/hht072.

Furness, V. (2 August 2022), "How Egypt's sovereign fund plans to green the country's strategic infrastructure", Capital Monitor, https://capitalmonitor.ai/regions/middle-east-and-africa/egypts-green-plans-sovereign-wealth-fund/.

GIIN (2020), *Annual Impact Investor Survey*, Global Impact Investing Network, https://thegiin.org/assets/GIIN%20Annual%20Impact%20Investor%20Survey%202020.pdf.

GIIN (2016), *The Landscape for Impact Investing in Southern Africa*, Global Impact Investing Network, https://thegiin.org/assets/documents/pub/Southern%20Africa/GIIN_SouthernAfrica.pdf.

GIIN (2015), *The Landscape for Impact Investing in East Africa*, Global Impact Investing Network, https://thegiin.org/research/publication/the-landscape-for-impact-investing-in-east-africa/.

Global SWF (23 August 2022), "African SWFs: The art of patience", https://globalswf.com/news/african-swfs-the-art-of-patience#:~:text=The%20biggest%20African%20SWF%20is,of%20around%20US%24100%20billion.

Indiana University Lilly Family School of Philanthropy (2022), *2022 Global Philanthropy Environment Index*, Indiana University Lilly Family School of Philanthropy, Indianapolis, www.developmentaid.org/api/frontend/cms/file/2022/04/IU2022GPEIGlobalReport-1.pdf.

I&P (n.d. a), "Notre approche", Investisseurs & Partenaires webpage, www.ietp.com/fr/node/1963/#approche-section (accessed 6 January 2023).

I&P (n.d. b), "Impact", Investisseurs & Partenaires webpage, www.ietp.com/fr/content/impact (accessed 6 January 2023).

Ideue, K. (2019), "Recent trends in foreign direct investment in sub-Saharan Africa", in *Connecting Asia and Africa: Challenges and Prospects*, Institute of Developing Economies, Chiba, www.ide.go.jp/library/Japanese/Publish/Reports/Seisaku/pdf/2018_1_10_001_ch03.pdf.

IEA (2022a), *Africa Energy Outlook 2022*, International Energy Agency, Paris, www.iea.org/reports/africa-energy-outlook-2022.

IEA (2022b), "Greenhouse gas emissions from Energy Data Explorer", *Data and Statistics* (database), www.iea.org/data-and-statistics/data-tools/greenhouse-gas-emissions-from-energy-data-explorer (accessed October 2022).

IFAD/World Bank (2015), *The Use of Remittances and Financial Inclusion*, International Fund for Agricultural Development, Rome, www.ifad.org/documents/38714170/40187309/gpfi.pdf/58ce7a06-7ec0-42e8-82dc-c069227edb79.

IFSWF and F. Templeton (2021), *Investing for Growth and Prosperity: In Africa Sovereign Wealth Funds Focus on G, S and E*, International Forum of Sovereign Wealth Funds, www.ifswf.org/sites/default/files/IFSWF_Africa_Paper_v2.pdf.

IMF (2023), "List of LIC DSAs for PRGT-eligible countries", International Monetary Fund, https://www.imf.org/external/pubs/ft/dsa/dsalist.pdf.

IMF (2022a), *World Economic Outlook Database*, October 2022 Edition, International Monetary Fund, www.imf.org/en/Publications/WEO/weo-database/2022/October (accessed October 2022).

IMF (2022b), *Balance of Payments and International Investment Position Statistics (BOP/IIP)* (database), International Monetary Fund, https://data.imf.org/?sk=7A51304B-6426-40C0-83DD-CA473CA1FD52 (accessed 22 November 2022).

IMF (2022c), *Investment and Capital Stock Dataset (ICSD)* (database), https://data.imf.org/?sk=1CE8A55F-CFA7-4BC0-BCE2-256EE65AC0E4 (accessed October 2022).

IMF (2022d), *Regional Economic Outlook Africa April 2022*, IMF Publication Services, International Monetary Fund, Washington, DC, www.imf.org/en/Publications/REO/SSA/Issues/2022/04/28/regional-economic-outlook-for-sub-saharan-africa-april-2022.

IMF (2021a), "Questions and Answers on Sovereign Debt Issues", International Monetary Fund webpage, www.imf.org/en/About/FAQ/sovereign-debt (accessed 12 January 2023).

IMF (2021b), *Database of Fiscal Policy Responses to COVID-19*, International Monetary Fund, www.imf.org/en/Topics/imf-and-covid19/Fiscal-Policies-Database-in-Response-to-COVID-19 (accessed October 2022).

IRENA and AfDB (2022), *Renewable Energy Market Analysis: Africa and Its Regions*, International Renewable Energy Agency and African Development Bank, Abu Dhabi and Abidjan, www.irena.org/publications/2022/Jan/Renewable-Energy-Market-Analysis-Africa.

Jaspersen, F. et al. (2000), "Risk and private investment: Africa compared with other developing areas", in *Studies on the African Economies Series*, Palgrave Macmillan, London, https://doi.org/10.1007/978-1-349-15068-7_3.

Javorcik, B. S. and M. Spatareanu (2008), "To share or not to share: Does local participation matter for spillovers from foreign direct investment?", *Journal of Development Economics*, Vol. 85/(1-2), pp. 194-217, https://doi.org/10.1016/j.jdeveco.2006.08.005.

Juvonen, K. et al. (2019), "Unleashing the potential of institutional investors in Africa", *AfDB Working Papers*, No. 325, African Development Bank, Abidjan, www.afdb.org/sites/default/files/documents/publications/wps_no_325_unleashing_the_potential_of_institutional_investors_in_africa_c_rv1.pdf.

Kalemli-Ozcan, S. et al. (2022), "How to construct nationally representative firm level data from the Orbis Global Database: New facts and aggregate implications", *NBER Working Papers*, No. 21558, https://doi.org/10.3386/w21558.

Kathuria, S., R. A. Yatawara and X. Zhu (2021), *Regional Investment Pioneers in South Asia: The Payoff of Knowing Your Neighbors*, World Bank, Washington, DC, https://doi.org/10.1596/978-1-4648-1534-8.

Kelhoffer, K. (September 2021), "Examining infrastructure as an asset class", Moody's Analytics, www.moodysanalytics.com/articles/2020/examining-infrastructure-as-an-asset-class.

Kincer, J. and T. Moss (22 April 2022), "Gas prices high, but renewables also at risk from rising interest rates", Energy for Growth blog, www.energyforgrowth.org/blog/gas-prices-high-but-renewables-also-at-risk-from-rising-interest-rates/.

Lee, N. and M. C. Gonzalez (2022), "Stuck near ten billion: Public-private infrastructure finance in sub-Saharan Africa", *CGD Policy Paper 251 February 2022*, www.cgdev.org/sites/default/files/stuck-near-ten-billion-public-private-infrastructure-finance-sub-saharan-africa.pdf.

Leimbach, M. and N. Bauer (2022), "Capital markets and the costs of climate policies", *Environmental Economics and Policy Studies*, Vol. 24/3, pp. 397-420, https://doi.org/10.1007/s10018-021-00327-5.

Lucas, R. E. (1990), "Why doesn't capital flow from rich to poor countries?", *The American Economic Review*, Vol. 80/2, pp. 92-96, www.jstor.org/stable/2006549.

Lugemwa, P. (2014), "Foreign direct investment and SME growth: Highlighting the need for absorptive capacity to support linkages between transnational corporations and SMEs in developing countries", *International Journal of Economics, Finance and Management Sciences*, Vol. 2, No. 4, pp. 245-256, http://dx.doi.org/10.11648/j.ijefm.20140204.13.

McKinsey (6 March 2020), "Solving Africa's infrastructure paradox", McKinsey & Company, www.mckinsey.com/capabilities/operations/our-insights/solving-africas-infrastructure-paradox.

McKinsey (15 February 2019), "Winning in Africa's agricultural market", McKinsey & Company, www.mckinsey.com/industries/agriculture/our-insights/winning-in-africas-agricultural-market.

Mercer (2018), *Investment in African Infrastructure: Challenges and Opportunities*, www.marshmclennan.com/content/dam/mmc-web/insights/publications/2018/dec/innovations-in-infrastructure/Investment-in-African-Infrastructure/gl-2018-wealth-investment-opportunities-in-african-infrastructure-full-report-mercer.pdf.

Murisa, T. (2022), "Region Report: Sub-Saharan Africa", 2022 Global Philanthropy Environment Index, SIVIO Institute, https://scholarworks.iupui.edu/bitstream/handle/1805/27917/2022GPEISub-SaharanAfrica.pdf.

Mutize (13 February 2022), "Moody's has bought a leading African rating agency: Why it's bad news", The Conversation, https://theconversation.com/moodys-has-bought-a-leading-african-rating-agency-why-its-bad-news-176827.

NBS (2022), "Environmental sustainability: Meaning, examples and importance", Network for Business Sustainability, https://nbs.net/environmental-sustainability-meaning-examples-importance/.

Ndikumana, L. and J. K. Boyce (2003), "Public debts and private assets: Explaining capital flight from sub-Saharan African countries", *World Development*, Vol. 31/1, pp. 107-130, https://doi.org/10.1016/S0305-750X(02)00181-X.

NIPC (2020), "MTN Nigeria to Invest 600bn in Network Expansion", Nigeria Investment Promotion Commission, www.nipc.gov.ng/2020/03/03/mtn-nigeria-to-invest-600bn-in-network-expansion/.

OECD (2022a), "Aid (ODA) disbursements to countries and regions", *OECD Development Assistance Committee* (database), https://stats-1.oecd.org/Index.aspx?DataSetCode=TABLE2A (accessed 15 December 2022).

OECD (2022b), *Global Outlook on Financing for Sustainable Development 2023: No Sustainability Without Equity*, OECD Publishing, Paris, https://doi.org/10.1787/fcbe6ce9-en.

OECD (2022c), *Climate Finance Provided and Mobilised by Developed Countries in 2016-2020: Insights from Disaggregated Analysis*, Climate Finance and the USD 100 Billion Goal, OECD Publishing, Paris, https://doi.org/10.1787/286dae5d-en.

OECD (2022d), *OECD Sovereign Borrowing Outlook 2022*, OECD Publishing, Paris, https://doi.org/10.1787/b2d85ea7-en.

OECD (2022e), "Mobilisation", *Flows Based on Individual Projects (CRS)* (dataset), OECD Publishing, Paris, https://stats-1.oecd.org/Index.aspx?DataSetCode=DV_DCD_MOBILISATION (accessed December 2022).

OECD (2022f), *FDI Qualities Indicators 2022*, www.oecd.org/fr/investissement/fdi-qualities-indicators.htm.

OECD (2022g), *FDI Qualities Policy Toolkit*, OECD Publishing, Paris, https://doi.org/10.1787/7ba74100-en.

OECD (2021a), *Mobilising Institutional Investors for Financing Sustainable Development in Developing Countries: Emerging Evidence of Opportunities and Challenges*, OECD Publishing, Paris, www.oecd.org/dac/financing-sustainable-development/Mobilising-institutional-investors-for-financing-sustainable-development-final.pdf.

OECD (2021b), *Private Philanthropy for Development: Data for Action Dashboard*, OECD Publishing, Paris, https://oecd-main.shinyapps.io/philanthropy4development/ (accessed November 2022).

OECD (2021c), "Enabling SME linkages with foreign firms in global value chains", in *Middle East and North Africa Investment Policy Perspectives*, OECD Publishing, Paris, https://doi.org/10.1787/824a45f1-en.

OECD (2021d), *OECD Global Pension Statistics* (database), https://doi.org/10.1787/pension-data-en (accessed October 2022).

OECD (2020a), *OECD Investment Policy Reviews: Egypt 2020*, OECD Publishing, Paris, https://doi.org/10.1787/9f9c589a-en.

OECD (2020b), "Coverage and representativeness of Orbis data", *OECD Science, Technology and Industry Working Papers*, No. 2020/06, OECD Publishing, Paris, https://doi.org/10.1787/c7bdaa03-en.

OECD (2019), *Annual Survey of Large Pension Funds and Public Pension Reserve Funds*, www.oecd.org/finance/survey-large-pension-funds.htm (accessed 17 February 2021).

OECD/ACET (2020), *Quality Infrastructure in 21st Century Africa: Prioritising, Accelerating and Scaling up in the Context of PIDA (2021-30)*, www.oecd.org/dev/Africa-Quality-infrastructure-21st-century.pdf.

OECD/World Bank/UNEP (2018), *Financing Climate Futures: Rethinking Infrastructure*, OECD Publishing, Paris, https://doi.org/10.1787/9789264308114-en.

Onyeiwu, S. and H. Shrestha (2016), "Determinants of foreign direct investment in Africa", *Journal of Developing Societies*, Vol. 20/1-2, pp. 89-106, https://doi.org/10.1177/0169796X04048305.

Orbitt (3 June 2020), "Managing currency risk in Africa: A playbook for decision-making", https://orbitt.capital/managing-currency-risk-in-africa-a-playbook-for-decision-making/.

Osabutey, E. L. C. and C. Okoro (2015), "Political risk and foreign direct investment in Africa: The case of the Nigerian telecommunications industry", *Thunderbird International Business Review*, Vol. 57/6, pp. 417-429, https://doi.org/10.1002/tie.21672.

Pandey, A. (14 September 2020), "Is Africa a victim of bias by international investors?", Deutsche Welle, www.dw.com/en/africa-imf-bias-discrimination-debt-international-investors/a-54564359.

Pineau, C. (2 September 2014), "The African data gap: What it means for business", Devex, www.devex.com/news/the-african-data-gap-what-it-means-for-business-84246.

Qiang, C. Z., Y. Liu and V. Steenbergen (2021), *An Investment Perspective on Global Value Chains*, World Bank, Washington, DC, https://openknowledge.worldbank.org/handle/10986/35526.

RES4Africa (2022), *Sustainable Electricity for a Prosperous Africa, Renewable Energy Solutions for Africa*, https://static1.squarespace.com/static/609a53264723031eccc12e99/t/628cea0bc18a56354ede110e/1653402171127/RES4Africa+5th+Flagship+Publication+2022+-+Sustainable+electricity+for+a+Prosperous+Africa_double+paged.pdf.

Severino, J. M. (20 March 2018), "Three things we have learned about investing in African small businesses and in fragile countries", OECD Development Matters blog, https://oecd-development-matters.org/2018/03/20/three-things-we-have-learned-about-investing-in-african-small-businesses-and-in-fragile-countries/.

Smith, G. (3 October 2022), "African Eurobonds in Q3 2022", LinkedIn, https://www.linkedin.com/pulse/african-eurobonds-q3-2022-gregory-smith/.

Sovereign Group (2022), "Africa Union moves to set up Africa-owned credit rating agency", webpage, www.sovereigngroup.com/news/news-and-views/africa-union-moves-to-set-up-africa-owned-credit-rating-agency/ (accessed October 2022).

Statistics South Africa (2022), "Quarterly employment statistics (QES)", Statistical Release P0277, Pretoria, www.statssa.gov.za/publications/P0277/P0277June2022.pdf.

Stewart, F. (18 January 2022), "The elephant in the room: Bringing sustainable investment to Africa", World Bank Private Sector Development Blog, https://blogs.worldbank.org/psd/elephant-room-bringing-sustainable-investment-africa.

TOSSD (2022), "TOSSD", *Total Official Support for Sustainable Development* (database), https://tossd.online/ (accessed October 2022).

Trading Economics (2022), "Indicators: Credit Rating | Africa", *Trading Economics* (database), https://tradingeconomics.com/country-list/rating?continent=africa (accessed January 2023).

UN (2022), *Financing for Sustainable Development Report 2022*, United Nations, New York, https://development finance.un.org/fsdr2022.

UN DESA (2022), "World Population Prospects: The 2022 Revision", *United Nations* (database), United Nations Department of Economic and Social Affairs, New York, https://population.un.org/dataportal/data/indicators/67/locations/903/start/2000/end/2030/table/pivotbylocation (accessed October 2022).

UN Global Compact (2022), "Social sustainability", webpage, www.unglobalcompact.org/what-is-gc/our-work/social (accessed October 2022).

UNCTAD (2022a), "Financing for development: Mobilizing sustainable development finance beyond COVID-19", Note by the UNCTAD secretariat, United Nations Conference on Trade and Development, https://unctad.org/system/files/official-document/tdb_efd5d2_en.pdf/.

UNCTAD (2022b), "Regional trends: Africa", Highlights of *World Investment Report 2022*, United Nations Conference on Trade and Development, United Nations Publishing, New York, https://unctad.org/system/files/non-official-document/WIR2022-Regional_trends_Africa_en.pdf.

UNCTAD (2022c), "Foreign direct investment: Inward and outward flows and stock, annual", *UNCTADstat* (database), United Nations Conference on Trade and Development, https://unctadstat.unctad.org/EN/ (accessed October 2022).

UNCTAD (2020a), *World Investment Report 2020*, United Nations Conference on Trade and Development, United Nations Publishing, New York, https://unctad.org/system/files/official-document/wir2020_en.pdf.

UNCTAD (2020b), "Economic Development in Africa Report 2020: Press Conference", Press Release, United Nations Conference on Trade and Development, https://unctad.org/osgstatement/economic-development-africa-report-2020-press-conference.

UNCTAD (2019), "Global investment trends and prospects", in *World Investment Report 2019: Special Economic Zones*, United Nations Publications, New York, https://unctad.org/system/files/official-document/WIR2019_CH1.pdf.

UNCTAD (2016), *Economic Development in Africa Report 2016: Debt Dynamics and Development Finance in Africa*, United Nations Conference on Trade and Development, United Nations Publishing, New York, https://unctad.org/system/files/official-document/aldcafrica2016_en.pdf.

UNCTAD (2014), *World Investment Report 2014: Investing in the SDGs*, United Nations Publishing, New York, https://unctad.org/system/files/official-document/wir2020_en.pdf.

UNECA (2016), "The policy framework for greening industrialization in Africa" in *Economic Report on Africa 2016*, Economic Commission for Africa, Addis Ababa, www.uneca.org/sites/default/files/chapterimages/era2016_chap4_en-rev6may.pdf.

U.S. Bureau of Economic Analysis (2022), "International data: Direct investment and MNE", *U.S. BEA* (database), https://apps.bea.gov/iTable/?ReqID=2&step=1 (accessed October 2022).

Verhoef, G. (2011), "The globalisation of South African conglomerates, 1990-2009", *Economic History of Developing Regions*, Vol. 26/2, pp. 83-106, https://doi.org/10.1080/20780389.2011.625242.

Vu, H. D. (2018), "Firm's absorptive capacity: The case of Vietnamese manufacturing firms", *Review of Economic Perspectives*, Vol. 18/3, pp. 301-325, https://doi.org/10.2478/revecp-2018-0015.

Wanjere, M. et al. (2021), "Mediating role of absorptive capacity on the relationship between foreign direct investment and local firm's performance", *European Journal of Business and Management Research*, Vol. 6/5, pp.256-263, https://doi.org/10.24018/ejbmr.2021.6.5.1134.

WFP (21 July 2022), "WFP and partners bring first-of-its-kind transport training centre to West Africa", World Food Programme, https://www.wfp.org/news/wfp-and-partners-bring-first-its-kind-transport-training-centre-west-africa.

White, L., A. Kitimbo and L. Rees (2019), "Institutions and the location strategies of South African firms in Africa", *Thunderbird International Business Review*, Vol. 61/1, pp. 61-73, https://doi.org/10.1002/tie.21965.

Wood Mackenzie (2021), "Off-Grid Renewable Investment", *Wood Mackenzie* (database), https://datahub.woodmac.com/app/main#/dashboards/5d3a1511d249d18c0f001758 (accessed October 2022).

World Bank (2022a), *World Development Indicators* (database), World Bank, Washington, DC, https://datatopics.worldbank.org/world-development-indicators/ (accessed 12 January 2023).

World Bank (2022b), *Enterprise Surveys* (database), www.enterprisesurveys.org (accessed October 2022).

World Bank (2021), "Migration and remittances data", *Annual Remittances Data May 2021* (database), www.worldbank.org/en/topic/migrationremittancesdiasporaissues/brief/migration-remittances-data (accessed October 2022).

World Bank (2016), *Breaking Down Barriers: Unlocking Africa's Potential through Vigorous Competition Policy*, World Bank, Nairobi, http://hdl.handle.net/10986/24688.

World Bank-KNOMAD (2022), *Remittances* (database), The Global Knowledge Partnership on Migration and Development (KNOMAD), World Bank, www.knomad.org/data/remittances (accessed 19 December 2022).

Yeboua, K. (2020), "Foreign direct investment and economic growth in Africa: New empirical approach on the role of institutional development", *Journal of African Business*, Vol. 22/3, pp. 361-378, https://doi.org/10.1080/15228916.2020.1770040.

Chapter 2

Policies to accelerate sustainable investments for Africa

This chapter identifies policy priorities for African policy makers to mobilise more sustainable investments and better allocate existing resources towards sustainable development. First, it outlines ways in which African institutions can enhance the availability of the information and data necessary for risk and sustainability assessments. Second, the chapter discusses how African-led partnerships and institutions can unlock sustainable finance in line with development priorities. Third, it outlines how effective regional integration policies can scale up sustainable investments.

IN BRIEF

The African continent faces the twin goals of mobilising greater resources and aligning them with its sustainable development priorities. To achieve both, African governments and all groups of stakeholders must collaborate, focusing on three policy priorities to accelerate sustainable investments in Africa:

- Enhancing data availability and comparability will increase investor confidence, transparency and accountability. Improving macroeconomic data may enable many countries to align credit ratings with real risks. Public-private alliances can permit government agencies to share official and market data that inform investors' risk assessment strategies and reduce the cost of gathering information. Global sustainability disclosure and data frameworks need to be adapted to African contexts, and complemented by direct support for investors and supply chain partners.
- Strengthening African-led partnerships and financial institutions will allow for a more effective allocation of sustainable finance. The international community must deliver on existing obligations and channel resources to well-managed African financial institutions, for instance, by making climate adaptation finance available or reallocating Special Drawing Rights. Local financial institutions can orchestrate project development and risk mitigation instruments while aligning efforts with national development agendas. Innovative sustainable financing tools, such as green, social, sustainability and sustainability-linked bonds, are emerging in many countries and could be scaled up. Developing and interconnecting capital markets and stock exchanges will spur Africa's corporate growth.
- Connecting and harmonising regional markets through effective national, regional and continental policies will catalyse sustainable investments at scale. National investment policy frameworks remain essential to attract sustainable investments, while cross-border investment projects reduce trade frictions and market fragmentation. Small and medium-sized enterprises, with their specific needs, require policy support to tap into sustainable investment opportunities and integrate into regional value chains led by larger firms. The successful operationalisation of the African Continental Free Trade Area Investment Protocol requires effective monitoring and private-sector partnerships at the regional and continental scales.

Policies to accelerate sustainable investments for Africa

Information and data improve resource allocation and investor confidence

Enhance national statistical capacity to improve debt transparency

Better data transparency could reduce African sovereign bond spreads by **14.5 basis points** and decrease external debt by at least **USD 400 million**

Improve the collection of sustainability data

Top **3** barriers for tracking the sustainability of investments:

1) lack of supply chain reporting
2) unclear sustainability standards
3) difficult measurements

African-led partnerships can make sustainable finance more effective

Between 2019 and 2020 an estimated USD **11.4 billion** went to climate change adaptation in Africa - significantly less than the USD 53 billion needed annually

African-based initial public offerings (IPO) represented less than **1%** of the USD 1.5 trillion global IPOs over 2017-21

Africa is home to **102** Development finance institutions (DFIs)

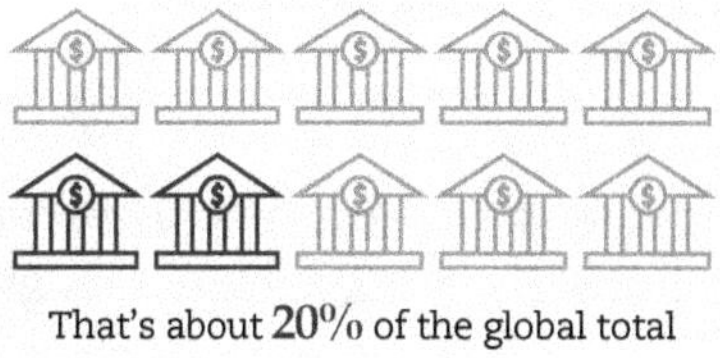

That's about **20%** of the global total

Yet, African DFIs rarely manage assets worth more than 2-3% of their country's GDP

Effective regional integration policies can scale up sustainable investments

By 2030, increased trade due to the AfCFTA will require **USD 411 billion** worth of investment in transport equipment

Investment in Africa's development corridors projects mostly comes from:

- Regional development banks: 31%
- National governments: 30%
- International development finance providers: 17%

African governments and all groups of stakeholders must collaborate to reduce the continent's sustainable financing gap. First, effectively allocating existing African resources towards sustainability outcomes offers the largest potential: domestic government revenues amounted to USD 466 billion in 2021, equivalent to 17% of gross domestic product (GDP), and assets held by African institutional investors amounted to USD 1.8 trillion in 2020, equivalent to 73% of GDP. Second, the international community needs to shoulder its responsibilities and meet its sustainable finance obligations. Third, African governments, the private sector and civil society must work ever closer together to attract more sustainable investments into African economies.

African countries are faced with the twin challenge of mobilising greater resources and allocating them towards their sustainable development priorities. This chapter proposes three main policy approaches that would allow policy makers to work towards these goals by directly addressing the two overarching challenges presented in the previous chapter (Table 2.1). Chapter 1 identified low investor confidence and the excessive cost of capital as investment barriers that global crises have exacerbated. It also showed that more and stronger frameworks and tools are needed for African countries to make the most of their unique assets and for the significant existing financial flows – including Africa's own resources – to be allocated more directly towards sustainable development, all across the continent.

Table 2.1. **Policy actions for mobilising and allocating sustainable investments, mapped against challenges**

Challenge	Policy agenda	Policy action
Low investor confidence and high cost of capital	Informing risk assessments and sustainability measurements	Enhance national statistical capacity for country risk assessments
		Inform investor due diligence and project risk assessments with detailed data
		Support locally adapted sustainability frameworks and data collection
	African-led partnerships to deliver on frameworks and tools	Deepen regional capital markets and stock exchanges to support African corporate growth
Frameworks needed to explore African assets and steer investments towards sustainable development		Increase the capacity of local financial institutions to align sustainable finance with national priorities
		Adapt and expand innovative financing instruments fit for local contexts
	Regional integration to widen impacts	Harmonise policies, improve digital infrastructures and development corridors
		Provide support for small and medium-sized enterprises to integrate into regional value chains
		Ensure effective implementation of the African Continental Free Trade Area Investment Protocol

Source: Authors' compilation.

The policy recommendations in this chapter represent a menu of options, aiming to stimulate participatory policy dialogue that involves African civil society. The chapter seeks to encourage evidence-based policy dialogue by presenting policy recommendations that tackle important barriers to sustainable investments identified in the previous chapter. It seeks to inform dialogue in forums by and for African policy makers, the private sector and civil society. African actors are invited to take ownership of the recommendations by further refining and adapting them for their purposes and contexts.

Holistic national strategies can combine individual policy recommendations in line with local priorities. Chapter 1 showed the magnitude of Africa's sustainable financing gap and highlighted that filling it requires tackling complex challenges and co-ordinating different sources of finance across national, regional, continental and global scales, often through multi-stakeholder partnerships. This chapter does not attempt to provide a definitive and all-encompassing solution. Instead, it offers a blueprint for key policy actions, illustrating them with policy examples from across the continent. Ultimately, the specific policy mix that works will differ for each African country, and the effective implementation of policies will require further tailoring them to country contexts.

Increased information and data availability leads to better resource allocation and investor confidence

Better information can improve risk assessments, align risk perceptions with real risks, decrease transaction costs and support the assessment of sustainability outcomes (Table 2.2). Investors lack awareness of investment opportunities in some African countries: they require more comprehensive, granular and reliable information to assess and navigate real risks (Chapter 1). Public and private institutions can improve the reporting on their expenditures and investments to increase the allocation of existing African resources to sustainable activities. Accurate data on country risks could improve credit ratings and lower the cost of capital, especially in the sectors with high potential for sustainability. Investment project data can facilitate opportunity search and due diligence, lowering barriers to entry for new investors. Data on sustainability investments' outcomes must be collected according to frameworks harmonised at regional and continental levels.

Enhanced national statistical capacity can improve country risk and sustainability assessments and debt transparency

Strengthened statistical capacities of African countries can make country risk assessments more accurate. Macroeconomic indicators, domestic revenue mobilisation and debt data are critical inputs for sovereign risk assessments; however, they are often not available in sufficient depth and detail in African countries (Chapter 1). In 2021, less than a third of African countries (30%) had a fully funded statistical plan compared to almost half the countries in LAC (44%) and in Developing Asia (47%) (PARIS21, 2023). With additional funding, international organisations and partnerships such as the Partnership in Statistics for Development in the 21st Century (PARIS21) could increase their efforts to support the statistical capacities in ministries of finance and statistical offices through secondments, communities of practice and grants (other examples appear in Table 2.2). At the same time, they could consider focusing more directly on the timely provision of data that is relevant for country risk (especially on private debt). Additional follow-through on the decision of African heads of state to allocate 0.15% of national budgets to statistical capacities is required (AUC/AfDB/UNECA/ACBF, 2017).

Regulations and data-sharing agreements can improve the transparency and consistency of country credit ratings. In parallel to efforts to establish an African credit rating agency (AU, 2022a), regulating credit rating agencies can guarantee the integrity, responsibility, good governance and independence of credit rating activities, with a view to ensuring quality ratings and high levels of investor protection. African regulators could follow the example of the Credit Services Act in South Africa, which requires local licensing for agencies and imposes disclosure requirements for ownership structures and methodologies (Pillay and Sikochi, 2022). Credit rating agencies and international financial institutions can publish long-term credit ratings that take into account climate transition pathways, while making model-based versus discretionary components of ratings transparent (UN, 2022). Data could be consolidated across different country risk ratings, such as from credit rating agencies, export credit agencies and development banks (e.g. the African Development Bank's [AfDB] Country Portfolio Performance Reviews [AfDB, n.d.] or the World Bank's IDA Country Performance Ratings [IDA, 2022]).

Table 2.2. **Policy actions and examples for enhancing information and data availability**

Policy action	Policy measure	Policy example	Impact	Level
Enhance national statistical capacity for country risk assessments	Increasing national statistical capacity on macroeconomic, domestic revenue and sovereign risk	*Revenue Statistics in Africa* by the OECD Development Centre, OECD Centre for Tax Policy and Administration, African Tax Administration Forum and African Union Commission	The annual publication *Revenue Statistics in Africa* presents internationally comparable indicators on domestic resources mobilisation for 31 African countries to inform tax policy analysis and reforms (OECD/ATAF/AUC, 2022).	N
	Sharing sovereign risk data	African Regional Technical Assistance Centers (AFRITACs) of the International Monetary Fund	Five AFRITACs strengthen the macroeconomic statistical capacities of African ministries and statistical offices. For example, AFRITAC East has supported the harmonisation of fiscal data and GDP statistics across East Africa (IMF, n.d.).	R/C/G
	Imposing licensing and disclosure requirements for credit rating agencies	South African Credit Rating Services Act	The European Securities and Markets Authority deemed the South African Credit Rating Services Act as stringent as European Union (EU) rules, allowing EU agencies to endorse ratings issued by the six agencies registered in South Africa (FSCA, 2023; Pillay and Sikochi, 2022).	N
Inform investor due diligence and project risk assessments with detailed data	Aggregating detailed information about investment projects	*Global Emerging Markets Risk Database*	The database aggregates data from multilateral banks and financial institutions on credit defaults in emerging markets. While the database is expanding its coverage, so far, only public sector-linked entities input data, recovery rates are not provided and default data cannot be disaggregated by country, sector or type of credit instrument (Lee, Forster and Paxton, 2021).	G
	Partnering with third parties to make disaggregated, sectoral data available	African Automotive Data Network (AADN)	Through the AADN, the African Association of Automotive Manufacturers compiles detailed data on vehicle sales, demand, motorisation rates and assembly plants (AADN, n.d.).	C
	Publishing up-to-date and forward-looking technical and legal information	The African Development Bank's Electricity Regulation Index (ERI)	Regulations vary widely across African energy sectors, with only 27 out of 43 countries surveyed having conducted cost-of-service studies and implementing quality-of-service and transmission grid regulations in 2022. Nine countries do not publish any tariff methodologies (AfDB, 2021).	C
	Strengthening business-to-government dialogue, allowing for feedback about policies and investment barriers	African Union - European Union (AU-EU) Digital for Development (D4D) Hub	The AU-EU D4D Hub launched an online platform, D4D Access, aimed at facilitating experience sharing between African and European actors on inclusive and sustainable digital transformation. The D4D Hub facilitated the France-Rwanda 2023 investment deal to modernise and harmonise the network infrastructure of central and local administrations (D4D Hub, 2023).	G
Support locally adapted sustainability frameworks and data collection	Harmonising and enforcing methodologies on sustainability assessments and reporting	Egypt's reforms on environmental, social and governance (ESG) disclosure	As of 2022, the Financial Regulation Authority of Egypt requires quarterly ESG compliance reports from all companies listed on the Egyptian Stock Exchange with issued capital above EGP 100 million (over 230 companies) (Atef, 2022).	N
	Providing firms with the capacity to collect sustainable investment data	Investisseurs & Partenaires (I&P)	I&P is a social investor focusing on micro, small and medium-sized enterprises, assessing their practices through social and environmental audits and measuring sustainability impacts against a scorecard. It has carried out over 150 investments which have maintained or created nearly 9 000 direct jobs, with around 75% contributing directly to the Sustainable Development Goals (I&P, n.d.).	R

Note: N = national, R = regional, C = continental, G = global.
Source: Authors' compilation.

African governments, statistical offices and financial institutions can do more to track the allocation and impacts of sustainable finance. Chapter 1 showed that Africa's sustainable financing gap is unlikely to be filled uniquely by mobilising more investments. African stakeholders can also fill the gap by increasing the allocation of existing resources towards sustainable development; however, this requires a more granular understanding of financial flows. Sustainability assessment frameworks should be implemented for all major financial flows (government revenues, capital flows, remittances and official development assistance), drawing on benchmarks from sustainable finance (OECD/UNDP, 2021) and complementing overarching sustainable development outcome assessments (UNECA/AfDB/AU/UNDP, 2022).

African governments can share data with international institutions to enable harmonised country risk and sustainability assessments and improve debt transparency. The ongoing process of operationalising the African Union's 2nd Strategy for the Harmonisation of Statistics in Africa (AUC/AfDB/UNECA/ACBF, 2017) could focus more directly on macroeconomic and sustainability data; STATAFRIC, the pan-African statistics institute recently founded under the strategy, is well-positioned to lead such an effort over time. Organisations like the International Monetary Fund (IMF) could facilitate data collection and aggregation (Mutize, 2022). International organisations and credit rating agencies could co-ordinate their data collection exercises to regularise the flow of data and avoid duplication of the work of strained national statistical offices. Regional entities, such as the IMF's African Regional Technical Assistance Centers (IMF, n.d.), could act as focal points for macroeconomic data while African think tanks, such as Afrobarometer, could support sustainability assessments. Comprehensive data on publicly and privately held sovereign debt can also feed into better co-ordination of debt relief among traditional and emerging creditors (Box 2.1; Ekeruche, 2022). Investing in data transparency can significantly reduce the costs of debt service. Research at the World Bank shows that a large number of African countries could have improved their sovereign bond spreads by 14.5 basis points if their average level of data transparency was on par with that of better-performing countries (Kubota and Zeufack, 2020).

Box 2.1. **Debt transparency in Africa**

Improved debt transparency can improve African governments' borrowing capacity. Debt transparency contributes to higher credit ratings, lower borrowing costs and improved investment inflows. In Burkina Faso, improved capacity in the national debt management office triggered a decrease in borrowing costs across all debt instruments and extended the maturity of bonds from five to ten years (World Bank, 2022a). However, as of 2021, 40% of low-income countries had never published any debt data or had not updated their data in the previous two years (Rivetti, 2021). The latest revision of the World Bank's International Debt Statistics added almost USD 200 billion in previously unreported loan commitments, the largest increase in 50 years. In 11 African countries, the revision surpassed the initially reported debt stock by over 10% (Horn, Mihalyi and Nickol, 2022).

International partners can support African governments' debt reporting and management. Empowering African countries to report data on debt could help public and private lenders overcome their unwillingness to disclose information and facilitate risk assessments. Multilateral initiatives on debt management can assist governments in creating costed development plans and in improving project appraisals and public investment management (AfDB, 2022a; World Bank/IMF, 2017). In 2021, the OECD also launched the OECD Debt Transparency Initiative to support the voluntary disclosure of granular data on commercial loans extended to low-income countries (OECD, 2023).

Enhancing transparency in debt issuance could facilitate debt restructuring. Debt restructuring processes have been slow in the cases of Chad, Ethiopia and Zambia. Umbrella rescue packages like the Brady Plan or the Heavily Indebted Poor Countries Initiative have had limited applicability in the more fragmented contemporary debt landscape. For instance, the Debt Service Suspension

Box 2.1. **Debt transparency in Africa *(continued)***

Initiative has seen limited participation by private creditors despite their growing relevance (Ekeruche, 2022). However, responses such as including enhanced collective action clauses in sovereign bond issuances can encourage private creditor participation in debt restructuring processes (AUC/OECD, 2021). Also, an African regulator to improve tax transparency, fiscal management, and the fight against illicit financial flows could improve debt transparency and management (AU, 2022a).

Investors require detailed data to inform due diligence and risk assessments

Public entities like investment promotion agencies (IPAs), in partnership with private actors, can aggregate and publicly share information and data. Successful investments hinge on comprehensive risk assessment and mitigation strategies, before and after a decision to invest (see Box 1.4 in Chapter 1). Results from the AUC/OECD investor survey show that, in addition to first-hand experience, investors request more official and specialised information on incentives and statistical data (Figure 2.1). IPAs and other public entities should provide such information, regularly updating data and presenting them in user-friendly formats (e.g. using live dashboards). IPAs can aggregate investor surveys conducted by chambers of commerce and collaborate with business intelligence providers such as Asoko Insights. They should focus particularly on project-level data within priority sectors, anonymised and investment performance data and loan defaults, or the co-ordination of technical assistance from international organisations.

Figure 2.1. **Responses to AUC/OECD investor survey question: "Which sources of information should there be more of?"**

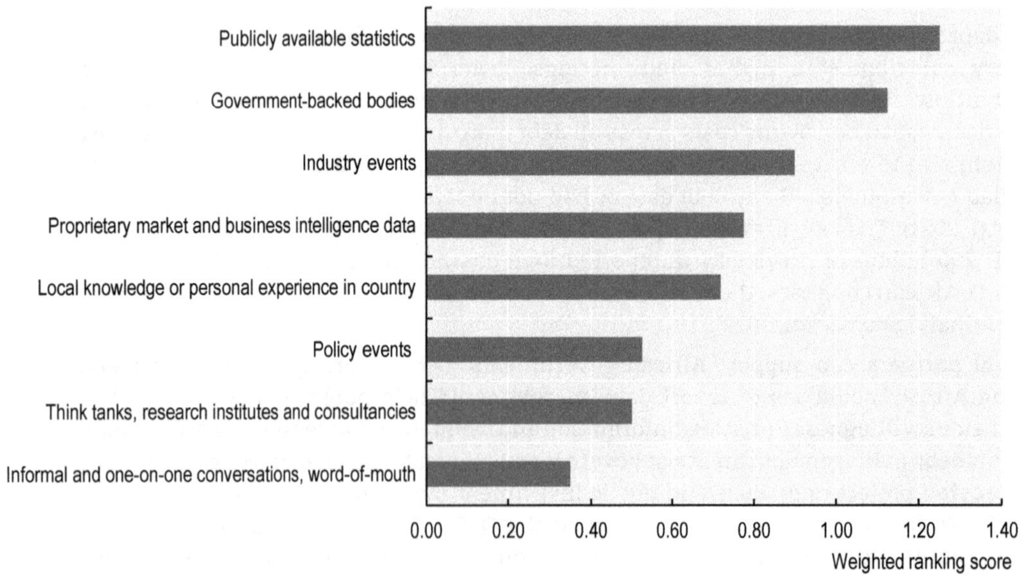

Note: n = 40. The survey was administered in September 2022 to the networks of African business councils and the EU-Africa Business Forum. Results show a weighted ranking score, where the top-three-ranked answers were attributed scores from three to one (i.e. higher score for highest ranked as "should there be more of"). "Government-backed bodies" were explained to participants as "investment promotion agencies, export credit and investment insurance agencies".

Source: Authors' compilation.

StatLink *https://stat.link/t9cobl*

With public and donor support, academic institutions and business associations can offer detailed sectoral and value chain data. For example, the African Market Observatory monitors prices and market dynamics in agri-food supply chains in East and Southern Africa (CCRED, n.d.), while the African Automotive Data Network compiles detailed data on the continent's automotive industry (Table 2.2).

Investors benefit from information on national policies, risks and development plans, and regulators can often provide this information. Investors evaluate not only policies and regulations currently in force but also specific technical and legal risk factors, such as their eligibility for tax incentives or the prior dependability of policy plans and regulatory decisions. Detailed infrastructure development plans and precedents of legal disputes between investors and regulators can be an important source of information in densely regulated sectors with a high potential for sustainability, like energy (RES4Africa/PwC Italy, 2021). Regulators can increase the publication of such details at the national level, while also contributing to pan-African information-gathering efforts including the African Investment Observatory, a forthcoming collaboration between the African Union Commission and the OECD.

Public bodies can deepen dialogue with the private sector and institutional investors. International investors would benefit from additional channels for business-government dialogue to share their feedback about policies and investment barriers, such as accessible policy focal points, formal consultation processes and interactive events (Table 2.2). In Uganda for instance, the Presidential Investors' Round Table serves to convene foreign and Ugandan investors and facilitate business-to-government dialogue, emphasising sectors that are key within the national investment strategy.

Locally adapted frameworks and direct support for investors and supply chain partners can strengthen the collection and assessment of sustainability data

Global climate finance is mismatched with needs, risks and firm informality in African markets. International climate finance standards for compliance and reporting are fragmented and have mostly been developed outside the African continent (OECD, 2022a). While the continent is vulnerable to the impacts of climate change across sectors such as agriculture, water, tourism, fisheries and forestry, global climate finance tends to focus on mitigation (reducing greenhouse emissions) rather than adaptation (reducing the impacts of climate change) (Were, 2022a). Between 2019 and 2020, USD 11.4 billion of climate financing to Africa went to adaptation – significantly less than the USD 52.7 billion needed annually by 2030 (GCA, 2022). Climate finance providers often have limited experience in deploying solutions in African countries, leading to high risk perceptions, high cost of capital and financial products that do not account for locally specific climate risks or the large share of informal firms (Ameli et al., 2021; Mullan and Ranger, 2022; see also Chapters 1 and 6).

African governments can encourage the collection of sustainability data through national frameworks that can become the groundwork for a continental sustainability finance architecture. Results of the AUC/OECD investor survey suggest that measurement standards and partners' lacking capacity represent major barriers to the systematic collection and assessment of sustainability data (Figure 2.2). African policy makers can facilitate sustainability assessments through disclosure requirements for insurers and multinational enterprises (in particular, for climate risks and impacts which are relatively easy to measure) while providing small and informal firms with the capacity to collect sustainable investment data through training, incentives and accessible databases (Table 2.2). Governments could also subsidise risk data collection for the most vulnerable communities, as they are the least likely to be the focus of private risk management products (Mullan and Ranger, 2022). Over time, nationally collected data can feed into shared sustainable finance architectures, especially for climate finance, where growing international commitments require co-ordination and targeted allocation at the national and regional levels (Were, 2022b; Chapter 7).

Figure 2.2. **Responses to AUC/OECD investor survey question: "What major barriers did you face in ensuring the sustainability of your investments in African countries?"**

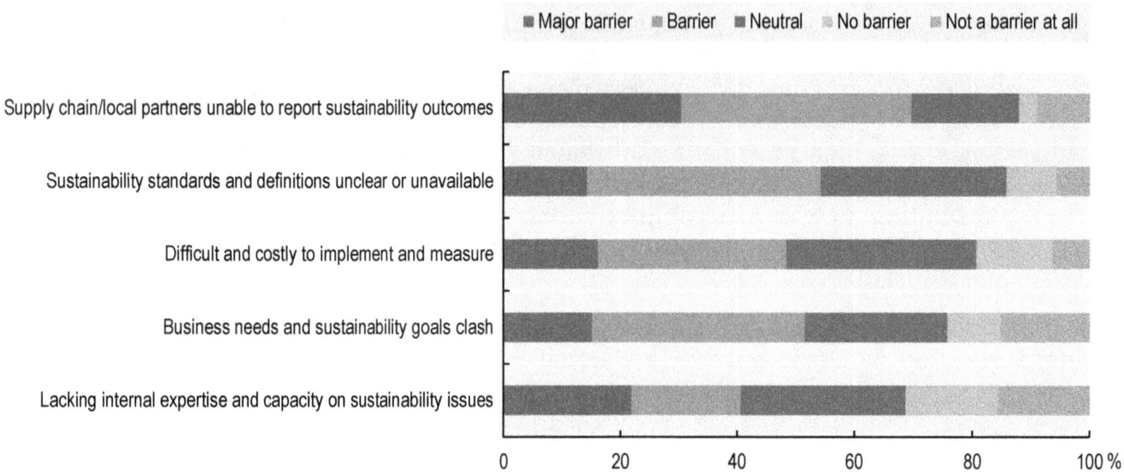

Note: n = 31 to 35. The survey was administered in September 2022 to the networks of African business councils and the EU-Africa Business Forum. Risk dimensions are ranked by weighted average.
Source: Authors' compilation.

StatLink https://stat.link/ptz1ga

IPAs can play a larger role in measuring the contribution of investment to sustainable development. IPAs are beginning to establish relevant metrics and key performance indicators (KPIs) that capture sustainability aspects while supporting investors and their supply chain partners to collect and assess data. This is an emerging area for IPAs around the world, not only in Africa. In a recent survey of IPAs in OECD countries, on average, only 16% said they track their contributions to the Sustainable Development Goals through specific indicators. According to the survey, the most often used KPIs on sustainability and inclusiveness to orient investment projects are those relating to productivity and innovation, followed by those on jobs. About half of the surveyed IPAs use KPIs related to low carbon transitions, while other KPIs are rare (OECD, 2021a).

Strengthened African-led partnerships can make sustainable finance more effective

African-led financial institutions and partnerships offer viable ways to better pool sustainable finance and allocate it in line with development priorities (Table 2.3). Assets held by African institutional investors can be channelled into sustainable investment finance while capital markets in many African countries inhibit cross-border investments (Chapter 1). The linkages between and capacity of existing African financial institutions can be strengthened to strategically channel finance in alignment with policy agendas. Innovative financing instruments can help monetise untapped assets and improve domestic resource mobilisation. The further development of African capital markets can unlock finance to support Africa's corporate growth and broaden the availability of financial products for local and foreign investors.

Table 2.3. **Policy actions and examples for strengthening African-led institutions and partnerships for sustainable finance**

Policy action	Policy measure	Policy example	Impact	Level
Deepen regional capital markets and stock exchanges to support African corporate growth	Interconnecting stock markets to reduce transaction costs and increase trading activity and liquidity of domestic markets	African Exchanges Linkage Project (AELP)	The AELP Trading Link, launched in 2022, enables seamless cross-border securities trading across seven African stock exchanges representing about USD 1.5 trillion in capitalisation (AfDB, 2022b).	R
	Facilitating listings to unlock finance for local firms	ELITE programme of the Casablanca stock exchange	In Morocco, the ELITE programme certified 20 local companies, enabling them to raise capital on domestic stock exchanges by the end of 2018 (UNECA, 2020).	N
Increase the capacity of local financial institutions to align sustainable finance with national priorities	Enhancing governance and capitalisation of domestic financial institutions	Seychelles' blue bond allocation	The Development Bank of Seychelles, together with a conservation trust and technical support from the World Bank, co-managed the allocation of a USD 15 million blue bond to support marine conservation and fishery projects (World Bank, 2019).	N
	Providing early-stage project development, technical assistance and risk mitigation instruments aligned with national development priorities	Africa50 project preparation facility (PPF)	Africa50's PPF managed to bring a 400-megawatt solar plant in Egypt to financial close twice as fast as is typical for such projects (Nassiry et al., 2018).	C
Adapt and expand innovative financing instruments fit for local contexts	Pooling of assets from large and small investors to de-risk investment projects	Kenya Pension Funds Investment Consortium (KPFIC)	The KPFIC aims to pool at least USD 250 million from the 1 300 pension funds operating in the country. In 2022, it had already mobilised KES 16 billion (Kenyan shilling) (USD 124 million) to finance road infrastructure (Taarifa News, 2022).	N
	Promoting local currency financing solutions to reduce foreign exchange risk and attract local investors	InfraCredit Nigeria	InfraCredit provides local currency guarantees to finance infrastructure assets in Nigeria. Since 2017, it has mobilised close to NGN 110 billion (Nigerian naira) (USD 240 million) from domestic pension funds, brought 9 infrastructure projects to financial close and created an estimated 2 300 jobs (InfraCredit, 2023).	N
	Valuing Africa's natural resources to mobilise climate financing	Central African Forest Initiative (CAFI)	In 2021, Gabon became the first African country to receive funds (USD 17 million) from CAFI for its efforts in reducing deforestation over 2016-17 (CAFI, 2021).	R
	Devising tailored regulatory frameworks to support the uptake of innovative tools	Namibia's Regulation 29	Namibia's Regulation 29 facilitates investments from domestic pension funds into unlisted companies via regulated special-purpose investment vehicles. Following its introduction in 2018, investments in private equity increased by nearly 50% over 2017-18 (World Bank, 2020).	N

Notes: N = national, R = regional, C = continental, G = global.
Source: Authors' compilation.

Deeper capital markets will support African corporate growth and broaden the availability of financial products for investors

Deepening local capital markets could improve the availability of formal investable products. Currently, most institutional investors target relatively risk-free and liquid assets such as fixed-income securities, equities or government bonds, largely due to the dearth of alternative investment instruments. For example, Kenya's pension industry holds about 75% of its assets in fixed-income securities. In contrast, countries with more developed capital markets, such as Mauritius and Nigeria, allocate less than a third to government securities (IFC, 2021). Regional initiatives implemented together with African industry stakeholders, including the Africa Private Equity and Debt Programme, can support the development of local capital markets and help diversify domestic investors' portfolios (FSD Africa, 2022).

If activity on African stock exchanges was comparable to other developing countries, additional finance for African firms would become available. So far, the market capitalisation of the 28 national and 2 regional stock exchanges in Africa remains far below comparable developing economies. Over the 2017-21 period, African initial public offerings (IPO) represented less than 1% of the USD 1.5 trillion global value of IPOs. During the same period, 77% of all capital raised through Africa-based IPOs originated from only three markets (Egypt, Nigeria and South Africa), raising a combined USD 6 billion, mostly in the services and information and communications technology sectors. Across all capital raising activities recorded on stock exchanges in Africa, 80% were African firm listings on national exchanges, 15% were non-African firm listings on African exchanges, and the rest consisted of intra-African and extra-continental listings (5% and 3% respectively) (Figure 2.3).

Figure 2.3. **Activity on African stock exchanges, 2017-21**

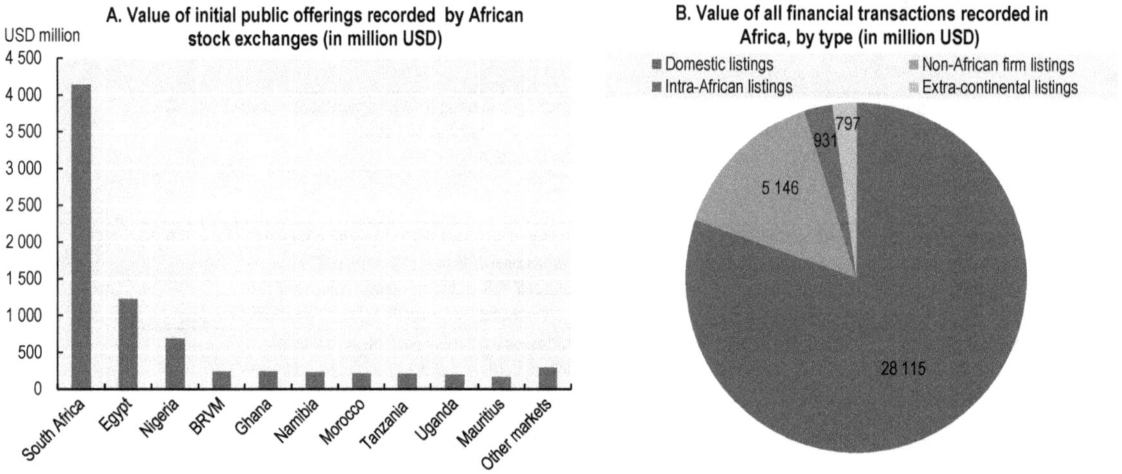

Note: BRVM (Bourse Régionale des Valeurs Mobilières) is a stock exchange serving these West African countries: Burkina Faso, Côte d'Ivoire, Mali, Niger, Senegal and Togo. "Other markets" include ten African capital markets registering a total IPO value of less than USD 100 million over the 2017-21 period – namely Botswana, Malawi, Tunisia, Mozambique, Zambia, Rwanda, Algeria, BVMAC (Central African Stock Exchange), Kenya and Zimbabwe (ranked from highest to lowest value). "Financial transactions" refer to both initial public offerings and further offers (i.e. issuance of additional shares to existing shareholders or new investors) recorded on stock exchanges. Four types of financial transactions are recorded: i) "domestic listings": African companies listing on a domestic exchange; ii) "intra-African listings": African companies listing on any African exchange other than their local exchange; iii) "extra-continental listings": African companies listing on an exchange outside of Africa; and iv) "non-African firm listings": non-African companies listing on an African exchange.

Source: PwC (2021), *African Capital Markets Watch 2021*, www.pwc.co.za/en/assets/pdf/africa-capital-markets-watch-2021.pdf.

StatLink https://stat.link/bcj6lx

Interconnecting stock exchanges can reduce transaction costs, increase trading activity and allow for greater integration of capital markets. Linking domestic stock exchanges could create opportunities for diversification and greater efficiency while reducing costs for cross-border investments (Soumaré et al., 2021). The national stock exchange in Mauritius has introduced automated trading systems allowing for assets trading via web browsers and a mobile application called mySEM (AfDB, 2022c). At the regional level, the East African Community (EAC) connected four domestic stock exchanges (Tanzania, Rwanda, Burundi and Uganda) through the EAC Capital Markets Infrastructure platform, reducing the time needed to trade cross-listed shares from over one month to three days. These efforts for interconnection can also lay the groundwork for further integration of capital markets, for instance, through the co-listing of African enterprises on different stock exchanges or the designation of some exchanges as regional hubs (Cercle des Économistes, 2022).

Improving the transparency of listing requirements on African stock exchanges could unlock finance for smaller firms. Lengthy administrative procedures for listing, lack of training and knowledge about capital markets, as well as the broader lack of transparency limit domestic firms' ability to access African capital markets. Stock markets could establish targeted programmes to facilitate the listing of small and medium-sized enterprises (SMEs) or sector-specific firms. Since the early 2000s, 15 African countries created alternative markets to help SMEs access long-term capital (Johnson and Kotey, 2018). In 2018, the London Stock Exchange partnered with Morocco and the West African Monetary and Economic Union's stock exchanges to implement the ELITE programme offering mentoring and advice and enabling local SMEs to enter capital markets (UNECA, 2020).

With the right governance and partnerships, African institutions can effectively channel sustainable finance towards national priorities

Improving the capitalisation of African development finance institutions (DFIs) can allow them to support national development objectives, including via the reallocation of Special Drawing Rights (SDRs). African DFIs rarely manage assets worth more than 2-3% of GDP (Figure 2.4). Given African governments' constrained fiscal positions, diversifying African DFIs' capitalisation would strengthen their ability to channel investment. The international community could consider reallocating part of the IMF's SDRs to well-managed African financial institutions to ensure alignment with regional priorities (AfDB, 2022d). In 2021, African countries received only 5% (USD 33 billion) of the one-time USD 650 billion global allocation of SDRs for COVID-19 recovery. While G20 economies pledged to re-channel USD 100 billion in SDRs to developing economies, most of the funds would flow through the IMF's Poverty Reduction and Growth Trust or the Resiliency and Sustainability Trust in the form of concessional loans with restrictive eligibility criteria (CEPR, 2022).

African DFIs are well positioned to act as intermediaries between international finance and local projects, in line with national sustainability priorities. Currently, Africa is home to 102 DFIs, representing about 20% of the global total (Figure 2.4). Given their knowledge of local markets, African regional and national DFIs are well placed to strategically channel international finance towards viable projects responding to national development priorities (see the example in Box 2.2 and Chapter 7). Since 2011, the AfDB and other multilateral lenders issued USD 1.1 billion of guarantees through the African Guarantee Fund to 161 local DFIs across 40 African countries; they supported lending to SMEs, women and youth and to projects related to climate adaptation and mitigation of value chains (AGF, 2022). While most African DFIs are multi-sectoral (41%), some hold mandates to target specific sectors or groups such as micro enterprises and SMEs (26%), rural development (10%), housing (8%) or infrastructure (6%) (Xu et al., 2021). For example, the efforts of the Development Bank of Nigeria to alleviate financing constraints faced by micro enterprises and SMEs led to the Impact Credit Guarantee, a mechanism for domestic commercial banks to provide guarantees for loans to SMEs (Fitch, 2021). During the COVID-19 pandemic, African public development banks demonstrated a high level of adaptability, implementing counter-cyclical responses to help sustain investments and shifting focus to new sectors (e.g. health and the green transition) (Attridge, Chen and Getzel, 2022). Major new sustainable investment initiatives, such as the European Union's EUR 150 billion Global Gateway Investment Package,[1] will benefit from steering and co-ordination through national DFIs.

Figure 2.4. **Number and capitalisation of operational development finance institutions in developing regions**

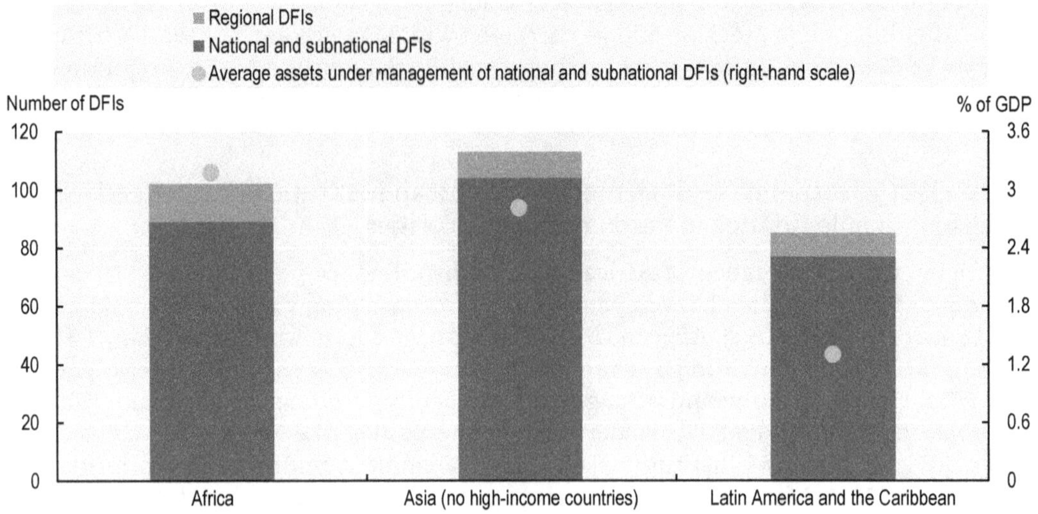

Source: Xu et al. (2021), "What are public development banks and development financing institutions? – Qualification criteria, stylized facts and development trends", *China Economic Quarterly International*, Vol. 1/4, https://doi.org/10.1016/j.ceqi.2021.10.001.

StatLink https://stat.link/2jghrl

Box 2.2. **Creating investment opportunities in Portuguese-speaking African countries**

Portuguese-speaking African (PALOP) countries – Angola, Cabo Verde, Guinea-Bissau, Mozambique, and São Tomé and Príncipe – are looking to attract more sustainable investments. Private investments remain highly volatile in PALOP countries, with foreign direct investment (FDI) inflows ranging from 10.7% of GDP in 2015 to 0.8% in 2021. Over 2015-21, more than 90% of greenfield FDI targeted only two countries, Angola and Mozambique, mostly in manufacturing and extractive industries. More than three-quarters of FDI originated from the People's Republic of China (hereafter "China"), European countries and the United States. PALOP countries are seeking to develop new sustainable investment opportunities, notably in green sectors. For instance, the paper producer Portucel invested over USD 2.3 billion in sustainable forestry activities in Mozambique, planting over 20 million trees – a carbon stock of 1.7 million tonnes. The investment also aims to support food security and income generation across 7 000 rural households through its USD 40 million Community Development Program.

Co-operation between African DFIs and international partners offers opportunities to overcome obstacles and diversify project portfolios in PALOP countries. The Lusophone Development Compact, an investment platform created with the support of the AfDB and the Portuguese government, aims to drive private sector growth in PALOP countries. It does so through three core mechanisms: lowered financing cost, risk mitigation instruments and capacity building to improve project bankability (AfDB, 2019). Compact members have developed country-specific agreements in line with PALOP countries' development priorities. For instance, in São Tomé and Príncipe, the Zuntámon Compact Initiative aims to stimulate the agriculture and tourism industries, particularly for women and youth-led businesses. It is expected to improve market access for 60 SMEs through technical and business development training and finance, yielding an average of 10% growth in business sales by 2025 (AfDB, 2023). On September 2022, the Portuguese government and the AfDB signed an agreement under which Portugal will provide guarantees of up to EUR 400 million exclusively to bank-financed projects approved under the Lusophone Compact.

African project preparation facilities (PPFs) can create pipelines of financially viable projects through early-stage project development and continued assistance. Scaling up African PPFs with successful track records can facilitate the pathway from project feasibility studies to financial closing. For instance, Africa50's PPF managed to bring a 400 MW solar plant in Egypt to financial close twice as fast as is typical for such projects (Nassiry et al., 2018). National PPFs could also streamline project preparation, handing projects over to global facilities that often support projects only from the pre-feasibility stage (CEPA, 2015). In South Africa, the National Treasury together with South Africa's Development Bank provided early-stage project preparatory financing to kick-start the Renewable Energy IPP Procurement (REIPPP) Programme, which later mobilised USD 14 billion of private sector investment (GIH, 2019).

Improvements in corporate governance, transparency and risk management enhance local DFI performance. Governance reforms can help African DFIs implement results-oriented models and shelter them from political interference (UNECA, 2022a). The Ugandan Development Bank's corporate governance reforms helped better integrate development priorities and reduced non-performing loan ratios from 60% to less than 10% over 2014-19 (Griffith-Jones, Attridge and Gouett, 2020). The Prudential Standards, Guidelines and Rating System, developed by the Association of African Development Finance Institutions with inputs from central, commercial and multilateral banks, can assist African DFIs in monitoring performances. Reviews over the 2011-18 period across more than 30 African DFIs highlighted significant improvements in management independence, transparency and liquidity (AADFI, 2017).

Co-operation between African DFIs and international stakeholders can increase information sharing, transparency and capacity building. The Infrastructure Consortium for Africa's PPF Network gathers 15 global and regional PPFs to enhance information and data sharing on projects, governance practices and cross-funding opportunities (ICA, 2017). Multilateral co-operation can help ensure that international finance providers and African DFIs operate under transparent rules to improve the allocation of sustainable finance (Box 2.3). Initiatives include the Global Climate Fund's (GFC) Readiness Programme; it provides grants of up to USD 1 million per year and technical assistance to local institutions across 35 African countries to receive the accreditations necessary to secure GCF funding (GCF, n.d.). Another such initiative is Africa's first co-guarantee platform (CGP), which aims at scaling up risk mitigation capacity by improving co-operation across African DFIs including export credit agencies. The current CGP project pipeline, co-developed with the African Union Development Agency-New Partnership for Africa's Development, includes 20 projects, worth more than USD 12 billion, in sectors such as energy, infrastructure, agribusiness and regional trade (AfDB, 2022e).

Box 2.3. Strengthening information sharing and financial allocation between export credit agencies

Export credit agencies (ECAs) benefit African countries by providing finance and mitigating risks. ECAs represent a significant source of finance for African countries' development. ECAs are financial institutions with a public mandate, providing financial instruments such as interest rate support, guarantees, insurance or refinancing. These instruments mitigate risks for exporters from ECAs' home countries that seek to finance projects in foreign markets.

ECAs from OECD member countries differ from others:

- ECAs from OECD member countries – except for Chile, Costa Rica and Iceland – adhere to the 1978 Arrangement on Officially Supported Export Credit. This framework sets common financing terms and considerations around anti-corruption, debt sustainability, and environmental and social due diligence. According to the OECD Export Credits Group,

Box 2.3. **Strengthening information sharing and financial allocation between export credit agencies *(continued)***

Africa indirectly received an annual average of USD 5.9 billion[2] in export credit finance over the 2012-21 period, mostly in the energy, transport and storage, mineral resources and mining, and the industry sectors.

- In recent years, ECAs falling outside of the OECD agreement gained in importance. By 2018, arrangement-regulated activities accounted for only 36% of global trade-related support, while the role of ECAs from China and India has been growing (EBF/BIAC/ICC, 2019). In Africa, ten countries[3] have operational ECAs providing trade finance to local exporters along with two regional ECAs (the African Export-Import Bank and the African Trade Insurance Agency) promoting regional trade and investment.

Multilateral co-operation can increase information sharing and financial allocation between ECAs, including for considerations related to climate change and sustainability. International platforms such as the OECD Export Credits Group or the Berne Union offer opportunities to increase collaboration, information gathering and knowledge sharing between African and non-African ECAs operating on the continent. Multilateral co-operation can also encourage better allocation of ECA finance. A recent survey across 32 international ECAs highlighted that climate- and sustainability-related considerations are still limited but growing in importance (OECD, 2021b). Commitments include both the creation of the "Export Finance for Future" coalition from seven European countries in 2021, seeking to align export finance with the Paris Climate Agreement, and China's pledge to stop financing coal projects, leading to the cancellation of coal power plants in South Africa, Tanzania and Zimbabwe (CREA, 2022).

African governments' voices in international negotiations are necessary to ensure that climate and energy finance commitments are met. The African Group of Negotiators on Climate Change played a key role in COP27 negotiations; it led to the adoption of the Global Shield, a loss and damage insurance system that is set to receive an initial USD 200 million of financial aid to the countries that are most vulnerable to climate change (Werners and Okunola, 2023). Strengthening co-ordination with international partners will be crucial to ensure that high-income countries deliver on and scale up climate adaptation finance beyond the USD 25 billion committed by 2025 (Kabukura, 2022). International climate finance should also align with African priorities to balance support for the just energy transition and universal energy access while delivering on job creation and industrialisation goals (AU, 2022b).

Innovative financing instruments need to adapt to local contexts to expand sustainable financing

Pooling financial assets from large and small investors provides opportunities for risk mitigation. At the national level, the Kenya Pension Fund Investment Consortium pools finance from the 1 300 domestic pension funds. It has potentially unlocked over USD 1 billion of investment following a revision of pension investment rules enabling the funds to invest up to 10% of their assets in infrastructure. The initiative has received support from multilateral partners, attracting investments from international pension funds alongside domestic ones (Davis et al., 2022). Regional initiatives such as Africa50 Infrastructure Fund and AfDB's Pan African Infrastructure Development Fund also provide one-stop shops, including for risk mitigation mechanisms, to facilitate joint investments in the infrastructure sector. Pooled financial products can also reach smaller investor bases such as diaspora investors. For example, Ethiopia's Diaspora Trust Fund raised over USD 5 million from 25 000 people across 93 countries over the 2018-20 period (EDTF, 2022).

Local currency financing can be used to mobilise finance from domestic investors. Local currency financing solutions offset the risk of asset-liability mismatches at terms and can make projects more viable and affordable for local investors. For instance, the Nigerian Sovereign Investment Authority partnered with GuarantCo to establish the Nigerian Infrastructure Credit Enhancement Facility (InfraCredit), providing local currency guarantees to finance infrastructure assets (Halland et al., 2021). Since 2017, InfraCredit has mobilised NGN 110 billion from domestic pension funds, bringing 9 infrastructure projects to financial close and creating an estimated 2 300 jobs in the country. Similarly, a partnership between the West African Development Bank and BPI France (the French export credit agency) facilitated access to both international and local currencies to cover costs of La Mé River's water purification plant, which is expected to deliver about a third of the drinking water for Abidjan by 2025.

Leveraging Africa's natural capital could help scale up climate financing. In most African countries, natural capital (e.g. land, forest, solar energy capacity and water) accounts for 30% to 50% of total national wealth (UNEP, 2016). To protect and generate economic value from this wealth, African governments are increasingly leveraging innovative instruments such as green, social, sustainability and sustainability-linked bonds or carbon credits (Dembele, Schwarz and Horrocks, 2021; Chapters 4, 5 and 6). For instance, Gabon became the first African country to receive funds (USD 17 million) for its efforts in reducing deforestation over 2016-17 (CAFI, 2021). The issuance of green bonds across nine African countries mobilised USD 4.5 billion over 2014-21, while implementing carbon credit trading systems could mobilise up to USD 245 billion (Wambui, 2022; Yu et al., 2021). The Africa Carbon Markets Initiative launched at COP27 and regional initiatives such as the West African and Eastern African Alliances on Carbon Markets and Climate Finance are examples of institutional frameworks that can help scale up sustainable finance (BAFU, 2022).

Co-operation between regulators and investors can support the emergence of innovative financial assets. Regulatory bodies can engage with institutional investors via public-private platforms and forums to improve the clarity of regulations and raise awareness of new financial instruments (AfDB/IFC/MFW4A, 2022). For instance, regulators and close to 50 institutional investors engaged in consultations in the design phase of a new inclusive bond product (Box 2.4). In Namibia, context-specific regulations in the form of a revised governance framework, Regulation 29, have helped overcome underdeveloped capital markets and governance issues. It facilitates local direct investment from domestic pension funds via regulated special-purpose investment vehicles and more than doubled equity investments in unlisted firms just one year after implementation (Gratcheva and Stewart, 2020).

Box 2.4. **Designing innovative investment products: Insights from inclusive bonds**

UNECA and its partners' inclusive bond programme aims to provide affordable and sustainable finance to SMEs and to informal and micro businesses. The bond will tap a large range of investment sources including domestic and international institutional investors as well as national and diaspora savings. The state, DFIs and beneficiaries will provide guarantees to reassure investors and reduce interest rates while local microfinance institutions will manage loans to selected businesses with limited default risks, engaging in consultations with business groups and co-operatives.

Box 2.4. **Designing innovative investment products: Insights from inclusive bonds** ***(continued)***

Multi-stakeholder consultations are conducted to ensure the adequacy of the programme in local contexts:

- **Setting development priorities with governments:** The first issuances of the bond target two pilot countries in Central and West Africa. Relevant sectors have been identified with governments to identify relevant sectors based on national development priorities in the context of the African Continental Free Trade Area (AfCFTA), including agriculture, transport and cross-border trade.
- **Ensuring feasibility and risk mitigation with regulators.** Given the lack of a track record in dealing with such a bond, feasibility studies will be conducted with local regulators to ensure local authorities and investors of the project's viability.
- **Raising awareness among beneficiaries and investors.** Technical workshops will be delivered to set up monitoring practices (including due diligence and impact reporting) and educate entrepreneurs and investors on the benefits of the bond.

Source: Authors' compilation based on an interview with UNECA.

Effective regional integration policies can catalyse sustainable investments at scale

Regional integration projects and harmonised investment policies at the national, regional and continental levels can accelerate sustainable investment and improve its allocation (Table 2.4). FDI should be better integrated into local economies, and sustainable investments from Africa's lead firms and institutional investors should be increased, given their unique potential, as suggested in Chapter 1. To achieve these goals, harmonised national investment policy frameworks must be complemented with effective regional projects that reduce non-tariff barriers and enhance market integration. SMEs are key economic actors within Africa's regional value chains but need policy support to tap into sustainable investment opportunities. The AfCFTA Investment Protocol has the potential to catalyse sustainable investments at continental scale but requires effective monitoring mechanisms and partnerships with the private sector.

Table 2.4. **Policy actions and examples for regional integration and harmonisation**

Policy action	Policy measure	Policy example	Impact	Level
Harmonise policies, improve digital infrastructures and development corridors	Adopting policy frameworks for sustainable investments	Rwanda's 2021 Law on investment promotion and facilitation	In January 2021, Rwanda enacted an Investment Promotion and Facilitation Law, which introduces new priority sectors and tax incentives aimed at improving the competitiveness and productivity of the economy and making Kigali a hub for innovative investors and startups (ALN, 2021).	N
	Reducing barriers to regional investment projects	Pan-African Payment and Settlement System (PAPSS)	PAPSS seeks to simplify cross-border transactions and ease instant payments across Africa's 42 local currencies. As of June 2022, the PAPSS network consists of 8 central banks, 28 commercial banks and 6 payment services providers (Annex 2.C).	C
	Improving cross-border development corridors and special economic zones	Northern Economic Corridor	Between 2014 and 2015, following the operationalisation of several One-Stop Border Posts, the turnaround time for trucks driving along the Northern Economic Corridor between Mombasa and Kampala was reduced from 18 to 4 days (Nugent and Soi, 2020).	R
Provide support for small and medium-sized enterprises to integrate into regional value chains	Increasing linkages between multinational enterprises and local SMEs	Ghana Supply Chain Development Program	The USAID-funded Ghana Supply Chain Development Program trained 650 employees from 254 SMEs in 96 training workshops. The Program led to 78 contracts, worth USD 18.5 million, being awarded (PYXERA Global, 2018).	N
	Supporting local SMEs to meet international standards and certifications	Alliance for Product Quality in Africa	In Ghana, the project supported fairafric, an organic chocolate producer, to obtain two quality certifications by providing training and financial support. The certifications boosted the company's sales by about 20%, including through exports to France, Japan and the United States, allowing for the creation of 20 direct and 5 indirect jobs (Alliance for Product Quality in Africa, 2022).	N
Ensure effective implementation of the AfCFTA Investment Protocol	Monitoring progress at the national level through regional co-operation	ECOWAS (Economic Community of West African States) Investment Climate Monitoring Scorecard	The ECOWAS Investment Climate Monitoring Scorecard was developed within the Improved Business and Investment Climate in West Africa Project as a tool for benchmarking member states' investment-related reforms (ECOWAS, 2020).	R
	Engaging regional private sector networks to catalyse investments at the continental scale	Trillion Dollar Investment Framework for Africa	Through the AfroChampions initiative, the African Union aims to promote the AfCFTA via a private-sector blended finance vehicle that will fund investments in strategic projects (Sasi, 2022).	C

Notes: N = national, R = regional, C = continental, G = global.
Source: Authors' compilation.

Harmonised policies, better digital infrastructures and development corridors can increase cross-border sustainable investments

Harmonising national investment policies and productive transformation strategies can help African countries increase sustainable development opportunities. Small domestic markets, high macroeconomic risks, weak regulatory environments, and frail licensing and incorporation regimes increase risks and the cost of searching for investment opportunities to prohibitive levels in many African countries (Chapter 1). Investment policy frameworks (Annex 2.A) and productive transformation strategies can work in tandem to address such issues. In addition to identifying investment priorities and clarifying how they contribute to advancing sustainable development objectives, productive transformation strategies cover a range of enabling policies – from regulatory frameworks to logistics and trade costs, from digital payments to tariffs and from human resource development to sectoral industrialisation strategies (AUC, 2019; AUC/OECD, 2019; OECD et al., 2021). African governments can increase the sustainability aspects of investment policy frameworks and productive transformation strategies by focusing, for instance, on FDI or the regulation of sectors such as energy (Annex 2.A and Annex 2.B).

Tax incentives to attract sustainable investments need careful design and systematic evaluation. Tax incentives have the potential to increase output, employment, productivity and other sustainability objectives. Yet, poorly designed incentives may reduce revenue-raising capacity, create economic distortions, erode equity, increase administrative and compliance costs, and potentially trigger harmful tax competition. Redundancy rates – the percentage of investors who claim that they would have invested even without tax incentives – exceeded 70% in 10 out of the 14 surveys on developing and emerging economies in a 2015 study (IMF/OECD/UN/World Bank, 2015). Research across seven African countries found that tax incentives reduce effective corporate tax rates by 30% on average, while detailed contextualised mappings of existing incentives can support the design of a coherent incentive framework (Celani, Dressler and Wermelinger, 2022).

Digital infrastructure represents an important path towards increasing market integration. Expanding digital infrastructures such as the Pan-African Payment and Settlement System (Annex 2.C) could further enhance regional integration (AUC/OECD, 2021, 2022). The upcoming AfCFTA protocol on e-commerce could take inspiration from existing agreements like the Singapore-New Zealand-Chile Digital Economy Partnership Agreement by including provisions on digital payments and adopting international standards on anti-money laundering and combating the financing of terrorism (AML/CFT) and on electronic data exchange (Elms, 2021).

Upgrading transport infrastructure and logistics remains key for cross-border investments. Limited transport infrastructure, fragmented regulations and delays at border posts continue to weigh on investment projects that rely on imports and exports. Programmes such as the Programme for Infrastructure Development in Africa (PIDA) can mobilise investments and contribute to the upgrading of current infrastructure networks. A recent UNECA study shows that, by 2030, USD 411 billion will be required for all transport equipment – trucks, railway vehicles, aircraft and ships – to accommodate increased trade due to the AfCFTA. Of the 69 projects to be implemented under the second PIDA Priority Action Plan, one-third targets transport infrastructures across 44 countries (11 projects in road, 6 in rail, 5 in maritime transports/ports and 1 in a border post) (UNECA, 2022b).

Regional development corridors and cross-border special economic zones (SEZs) can offer "quick wins" to attract regional sustainable investments. Development corridors represent important ways of addressing the infrastructure deficits on the continent, but they should undergo detailed multi-dimensional assessments to provide fully sustainable outcomes (Box 2.5). Similarly, cross-border SEZs are emerging as means to catalyse private investment. For instance, the Musina-Makhado SEZ is located near the Beitbridge Border Post between South Africa and Zimbabwe, a gateway to Southern African Development Community (SADC) countries and a critical location on the region's North-South trade corridor. The SEZ is intended to boost regional trade in energy and manufacturing, especially in the metal industry, while creating at least 50 000 job opportunities over the next ten years (UNCTAD, 2021).

Box 2.5. **Africa's regional development corridors**

Within Africa's development agenda, cross-border development corridors represent established solutions to accelerate regional integration. Development corridors comprise large hard and soft infrastructure projects in extensive, often transnational geographical areas that seek sustainable investments (Juffe-Bignoli et al., 2021). As part of PIDA, the African Union has placed development corridors high on Africa's regional integration agenda (AU, 2017, 2020). According to the African Development Corridor Database, which collects information on 79 corridors on the continent, the predominant form of infrastructure in Africa's development corridors is roads (35%), followed by wet ports (21%), passenger and freight railways (18%), and airports (8%). Most projects are based in Kenya (19%), followed by Tanzania (10%), South Africa and the Democratic Republic of the Congo (9% each). The average cost of a corridor ranges between USD 3.5 billion and USD 4 billion. Regional development banks and national governments respectively invested in 31% and 30% of all development corridors' projects, followed by multilateral banks (11%), the

Box 2.5. **Africa's regional development corridors *(continued)***

international development community (6%) and regional economic communities (5%). Private companies and national banks invest in a small percentage of development corridors' projects (4% and 3%, respectively) (Thorn et al., 2022).

Development corridors can facilitate cross-border trade, but comprehensive assessments of environmental pressures must guide current and future projects. For example, between 2014 and 2015, following the operationalisation of several One-Stop Border Posts, the turnaround time for trucks driving along the Northern Economic Corridor between Mombasa and Kampala was reduced from 18 to 4 days (Nugent and Soi, 2020). Yet, corridors also open extensive areas of land to new environmental pressures. A 2015 study on 33 planned and existing corridors in Africa showed that, collectively, the corridors would bisect over 400 existing protected areas and could degrade a further 1 800 by advancing habitat disruption near or inside the reserves (Laurance et al., 2015).

Small and medium-sized enterprises require policy support to access sustainable investments along regional value chains

Establishing linkages between multinational enterprises and local SMEs takes time and requires policy support but can have sustainable outcomes. The impact of linkages with SMEs can take up to 15 years to materialise, as lead firms need time to invest financial, staff and technological resources in business partnerships (Jenkins et al., 2007). Since direct linkages to multinational enterprises require high standards that can be challenging to attain for SMEs, large national local firms can play an intermediary role. Policy makers can deploy complementary support services to foster the creation of value chain linkages (AUC/OECD, 2022; OECD, 2021c), depending on objectives and implementation settings (Table 2.5). Once linkages are established, support services can leverage the position of lead firms in value chains to channel investments towards SMEs and guide them towards sustainable outcomes (see Chapter 7 for examples from West Africa's agri-food industry).

Table 2.5. **Examples of policy tools to promote linkages between multinational enterprises and local SMEs**

Policy tool	Description	Implementation challenges	Example
Supplier development programmes	Improve the quality of the supplier base in strategic sectors to meet foreign investors' demands	• Is complex and costly to manage and implement	USAID-funded Ghana Supply Chain Development Programme trained 650 individuals from 254 SMEs in 96 training workshops. The programme led to 78 contracts, worth USD 18.5 million, being awarded (PYXERA Global, 2018).
Matchmaking and data provision	Reduce information asymmetries between foreign and domestic firms	• Requires a suitable supplier base • Is costly to implement and update	In Tunisia, government agencies provide matchmaking services and a local supplier database including information on businesses with quality certifications (OECD, 2021c).
Targeted tax incentives	Locally integrate groups of companies	• Requires a suitable supplier base • Has fiscal and administrative costs • Can distort competition	South Africa's Strategic Investment Programme offers an initial capital allowance of 50% or 100% for foreign companies that extend linkages to domestic firms (Sabha, Liu and Willem, 2020).
Targeted non-tax incentives	Reduce regulatory and administrative barriers to facilitate linkages	• Requires a suitable supplier base • Requires institutional capacity and effective co-operation mechanisms	Egypt eased the regulatory and administrative procedures on local firms that supply businesses in zones which have duty-free regimes (OECD, 2020).
Inclusive special economic zones and industrial clusters	Favour linkages through multi-purpose industrial geographical agglomerations open to local firms	• Requires a suitable supplier base • Is complex and costly to manage and implement • Requires institutional capacity	In Kenya, the Export Business Accelerator was launched in 2013 to provide business support to SMEs that intended to establish their activities in the Athi River Export Processing Zone. The number of local firms in the zone rose from 25% in 2012 to 38% in 2018 (UNCTAD, 2021).

Source: Authors' compilation based on literature review.

Business development and supply chain partnerships by private stakeholders can help upgrade the production capacity of SMEs and facilitate linkages. For example:

- ACET Business Transform is a business accelerator and incubator programme by the African Center for Economic Transformation that aims to make selected SMEs in Ghana investment-ready for integration into global value chains. The programme includes mentorship services by executives in lead firms, providing local SMEs with access to knowledge and business networks.[4]
- In August 2021, Ethiopian Airlines and DHL signed a memorandum of understanding with the African Electronic Trade Group for establishing the East African Smart Logistics and Fulfilment Hub at Addis Ababa Bole International Airport. The partnership aims to integrate all trade and logistics activities (online e-commerce, warehouse, transportation and door-to-door delivery) within a multi-purpose platform to promote affordable services to SMEs and foster regional trade (AU, 2021).[5]

Harmonised quality standards and certifications can enable local firms to tap into regional investment opportunities. International partners can provide technical assistance to governments and directly assist local producers to meet international standards and obtain certifications (Box 2.6).

Box 2.6. **Alliance for Product Quality in Africa**

The Alliance for Product Quality in Africa seeks to assist local firms and institutions operating in export-relevant sectors from selected countries in complying with international standards or obtaining certifications. The German Agency for International Cooperation GmbH (GIZ) and the German National Metrology Institute (PTB) launched the project in 2019 as part of the Special Initiative on Training and Job Creation of the German Federal Ministry for Economic Cooperation and Development (BMZ). The programme focuses on Côte d'Ivoire, Egypt, Ethiopia, Ghana, Morocco, Rwanda, Senegal and Tunisia, offering the following:

- Facilitating local companies' adoption of international standards and certifications to establish long-term supplier relationships with European companies while creating local jobs (see example of fairafric in Table 2.4).
- Supporting governmental institutions in partner countries to strengthen national quality infrastructure. The project provides technical capacity building, peer learning and public-private dialogue, for example, to improve pesticide residue testing by the Rwanda Standards Board for agricultural produce. By adhering to international standards, Rwanda's agricultural producers are expected to improve their competitiveness.

Source: BMZ and GIZ contributions.

The effective implementation of the AfCFTA Investment Protocol is key to harmonising Africa's sustainable investment landscape

The AfCFTA Investment Protocol aims to harmonise the African investment policy landscape. Currently, 852 bilateral investment treaties exist between African countries and between African and non-African countries (UNECA/AU/AfDB/UNCTAD, 2019). Building on the Pan-African Investment Code, a non-binding instrument introduced in 2017 to guide intra-continental investments, the AfCFTA Investment Protocol aims to i) facilitate and protect sustainable investments, ii) manage investment dispute resolution and iii) enable co-operation regarding investment promotion and facilitation. The protocol also seeks to establish a Pan-African Investment Agency to provide financial resource mobilisation, business development and technical support to states, national investment promotion agencies and the private sector (Tralac, 2021). The protocol's draft was concluded in October 2022 and adopted by the AfCFTA Council of Ministers. Next, the text will be submitted to the Assembly of Heads of States for review and adoption (IISD, 2022).

Implementation of the AfCFTA could stimulate global and intra-African investments in strategic sectors and increase wages for women. Successful trade liberalisation and harmonisation of investment, competition and intellectual property rights laws under the AfCFTA could increase FDI stocks to Africa from outside the continent by 122% and from inside the continent (intra-Africa FDI) by 68%, compared to 2017 levels (Echandi, Maliszewska and Steenbergen, 2022). The realisation of these gains, however, is not automatic and depends in part on the availability of local productive capabilities. Removing barriers could also stimulate investments in value chains with high potential, such as automotives, services and pharmaceuticals. For instance, the AfCFTA Secretariat, Afreximbank and the African Association of Automotive Manufacturers have joined efforts to develop the Pan-African Auto Pact (PAAP). The ongoing PAAP strategy seeks to connect trading automotive manufacturers, ultimately increasing vehicle sales from 1 to 5 million units by 2035 (AAAM/Deloitte, 2020; AUC/OECD, 2022: Chapter 3). In addition, since in large parts of Africa more than 50% of women work in agriculture, increased agricultural investments through regional integration could raise women's wages by at least 10% compared to current levels (UNDP/AfCFTA Secretariat, 2021; World Bank, 2022b).

Experiences from African regional economic communities and other world regions show how to co-ordinate policies and monitor progress. Regional monitoring mechanisms can help effectively implement the AfCFTA Investment Protocol at the national level. Previous regional policy initiatives offer valuable insights (Table 2.6).

Table 2.6. **Examples of monitoring mechanisms of regional trade and investment policies**

Regional policy initiative	Description
Association of Southeast Asian Nations (ASEAN) free trade units	The monitoring mechanism under the ASEAN Free Trade Area (AFTA) led to the establishment of AFTA National Units in the capital cities of most ASEAN member countries. The units are responsible for ensuring that necessary enactments of tariff reductions are legislated and implemented at the national level (ASEAN, 2012).
EU foreign investment screening mechanism	In 2020, the European Union introduced a foreign investment screening mechanism, establishing formal contact points and secure channels in each member state and within the European Commission, enabling information sharing, analysis and co-ordinated actions (EC, 2020).
ECOWAS Investment Climate Monitoring Scorecard	The ECOWAS Investment Climate Scorecard was developed within the Improved Business and Investment Climate in West Africa Project as a tool for benchmarking member states' investment-related reforms. Through this tool, the project helped deepen regional integration, especially in the area of regional investment in the ECOWAS common market (ECOWAS, 2020).
SADC Investment Policy Framework	The SADC Secretariat, in collaboration with the OECD, developed a set of indicators to benchmark and monitor member states' progress in implementing the SADC Investment Policy Framework. The SADC Secretariat assumes the central monitoring responsibility while devolving specific reporting functions to dedicated national contact points in each member state (OECD/SADC, 2017).

Source: Authors' compilation.

Further exchange with private sector representatives, such as the AfroChampions initiative, would help promote investment opportunities. Through the AfroChampions initiative, the African Union aims to mobilise private sector-driven investments in key business areas. This investment and financing framework is dubbed the Trillion Dollar Investment Framework for Africa. Its goal is to establish a blended finance vehicle that will fund investments in strategic projects through collaborative efforts with project developers, investors, financiers, multinational enterprises, SMEs, business associations, governments, regional bodies and development finance institutions (Sasi, 2022).

Annex 2.A. The OECD Policy Framework for Investment and FDI Qualities Policy Toolkit in African countries

The OECD has been working with many countries worldwide to promote investment climate reforms on the basis of its Policy Framework for Investment (PFI) (OECD, 2015). This comprehensive multilaterally backed instrument was developed in 2006 and updated in 2015. The PFI emphasises policy coherence, a whole-of-government approach, and the fundamental principles of rule of law, transparency, non-discrimination and the protection of property rights. Based on the PFI, almost 40 Investment Policy Reviews have been conducted, with 10 in Africa: Morocco is currently in its second Investment Policy Review, Mauritius and Zambia have requested a second review, and Rwanda has submitted a first request.

Building on the FDI Qualities Indicators (Box 1.6 in Chapter 1), the FDI Qualities Policy Toolkit (OECD, 2022b) complements the PFI by addressing the impact of foreign direct investment on jobs and skills, SMEs, innovation, and gender equality. The development of the Toolkit involved a detailed mapping of policies and institutional arrangements governing the sustainable development impacts of investment across ten countries, including Morocco, Rwanda, Senegal and Tunisia (Annex Figure 2.A.1). Within Africa, FDI Qualities Reviews are planned for Egypt and Tunisia in 2023.

An added value of Investment Policy Reviews and FDI Qualities Reviews is the engagement with an inter-ministerial taskforce and consultation with the private sector and other stakeholders. This approach ensures that recipient governments and stakeholders take ownership of reform suggestions. In addition, the FDI Qualities Guide for Development Co-operation (OECD, 2022c), launched in October 2022, seeks to strengthen the role of development co-operation for mobilising foreign direct investment and enhancing its impact.

Annex Figure 2.A.1. Targeted policy measures to promote sustainable foreign direct investment in selected countries

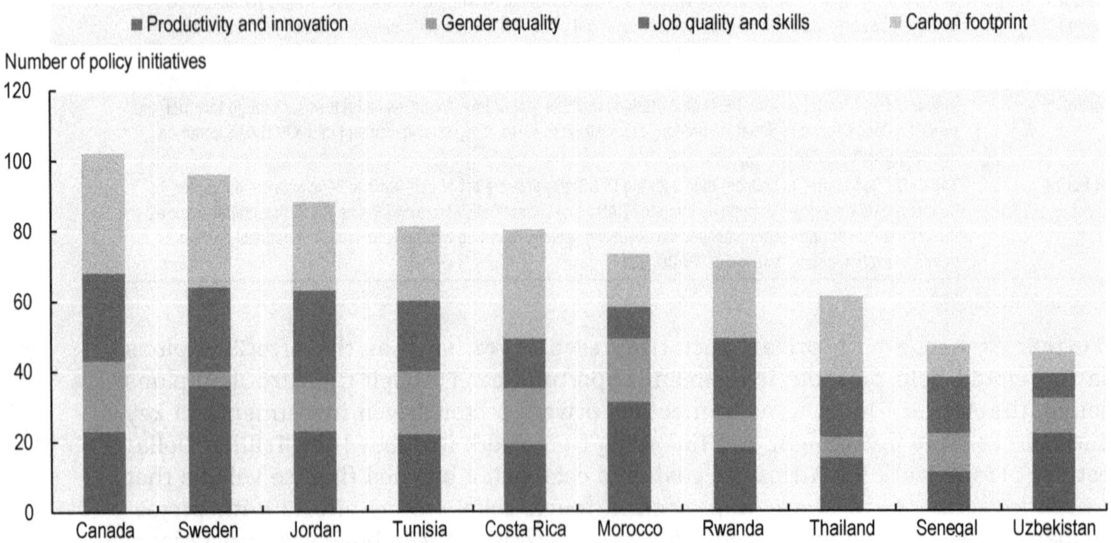

Source: FDI Qualities Mapping of Policies and Institutions from OECD (2022b), *FDI Qualities Policy Toolkit*, https://doi.org/10.1787/7ba74100-en.

StatLink https://stat.link/7itywf

Annex 2.B. Regulatory effectiveness in Africa's energy sector

Energy utilities' worsening financial situation has negatively impacted regulatory effectiveness (AfDB, 2021). Given limited budgets, African public agencies and regulators often struggle to overcome institutional legacies that privilege fossil fuel production and find it hard to implement technically complex, long-term-oriented regulations (Pueyo, 2018; RES4Africa, 2022; UNECA, 2016). In the eyes of private investors, energy regulators in many countries are not fulfilling essential functions such as licensing, wholesale pricing and grid management; private investors also believe countries lack independence, capacity and accountability mechanisms such as dispute resolution (AfDB, 2021; RES4Africa/PwC Italy, 2021). Accordingly, private investors in renewable energy assess regulatory risks as higher than public investors do (RES4Africa/PwC Italy, 2021).

Regulatory effectiveness in the form of detailed energy plans and other best practices is a key determinant for attracting investments in African energy systems (Falchetta et al., 2021). An immediate priority for any African energy regulators is the establishment of detailed national energy plans that set specific targets for developing renewable energy sources and new infrastructures (such as grid interconnections) and for co-ordinating power supply with bordering countries (IEA, 2022; RES4Africa, 2022; Chapters 3 and 5). Fundamental regulatory and utility best practices to attract investments include tariff restructuring, reverse auctions and standardised power purchasing agreements, while carbon markets and taxes can be explored by more advanced regulators, following the lead of Côte d'Ivoire, Senegal and South Africa (IEA, 2022; OECD/World Bank/UNEP, 2018; Chapter 3). The Moroccan Agency for Sustainable Development is a promising example of an agency that administers tenders while also functioning as a central power off-taker and hub for investor requests and queries (IEA, 2022).

Each country has its specific energy concerns and level of readiness to set targets, and policy makers need to consider these (see Chapters 3 and 5 on the renewable energy industry in Southern and Eastern Africa). Pueyo (2018) found that, in Ghana, an unreliable off-taker and macroeconomic and regulatory volatility inhibited investments in renewable energy; while in Kenya, limited demand, incomplete grids, utility governance and land rights were major barriers. Fossil fuel-producing countries should pursue the decarbonisation of extractive industries and exit strategies in parallel while leveraging traditional energy producers' commitments to renewables and carbon reductions (OECD, 2022d). Policy makers need to be flexible and prioritise carefully according to their country's and region's specific issues. They should also acknowledge different levels of country readiness. The few African countries that have already set renewable energy targets and established initial local value chains (including Egypt, Kenya, Morocco and South Africa) can now focus on different policy reforms compared to countries where such fundamentals have yet to be implemented (RES4Africa, 2022).

Annex 2.C. The Pan-African Payment and Settlement System

Africa's lack of an integrated continental payment infrastructure for cross-border transactions results in high costs. Only 20% of intra-African cross-border payments are cleared within the continent. The rest are routed through overseas banks, where African currencies are exchanged for dollars, pounds or euros before being converted back into a different African currency. When standard transfer and bank fees are included, the total costs across Africa of this process amount to USD 5 billion per year (PAPSS, 2022).

The Pan-African Payment and Settlement System (PAPSS) seeks to simplify cross-border payments between Africa's 42 local currencies. Jointly developed by the AfCFTA Secretariat and the African Export-Import Bank (Afreximbank), PAPSS aims to streamline and secure money flows across African borders. The PAPSS platform centralises validation checks, reducing the need for costly overseas intermediaries. The system aims to complete transactions in less than two minutes for a low fee.

The continental roll-out of PAPSS is underway. In 2022, the pilot phase was completed in the six countries that are part of the West Africa Monetary Zone: The Gambia, Ghana, Guinea, Liberia, Nigeria and Sierra Leone. As of June 2022, the PAPSS network consists of 8 central banks, 28 commercial banks and 6 payment service providers (Leadership, 2022).

Notes

1. https://commission.europa.eu/strategy-and-policy/priorities-2019-2024/stronger-europe-world/global-gateway/eu-africa-global-gateway-investment-package_en.
2. This average excludes ECA-backed aircraft deals that fall under specific rules and account for an average of USD 577 million annually.
3. Algeria, Egypt, Ghana, Morocco, Nigeria, Senegal, South Africa, Sudan, Tunisia and Zimbabwe.
4. According to an interview with ACET representatives.
5. Confirmed in an interview with African Electronic Group representatives.

References

AADFI (2017), *Report on the 7th Peer Review with the AADFI Prudential Standards, Guidelines and Rating System (PSGRS) in 2017*, Association of African Development Finance Institutions, Abuja, https://adfi-ci.org/wp-content/uploads/2022/05/aadfi_doc_en_20171114082330.pdf.

AAAM/Deloitte (2020), *Africa Automotive Forum, Summary Report*, African Association of Automotive Manufacturers/Deloitte, www2.deloitte.com/content/dam/Deloitte/za/Documents/za_AAAM-Africa-Automotive-Forum-2020-Summary.pdf.

AADN (n.d.), "About", Africa Automotive Data Network webpage, www.africaautomotivedatanetwork.co.za (accessed 2 February 2023).

AfDB (n.d.), "Country Portfolio Performance Review", African Development Bank webpage, www.afdb.org/en/documents/project-operations/country-portfolio-performance-review (accessed 2 February 2023).

AfDB (2023), "Sao Tome and Principe - Zuntamon Lusophone Compact Initiative - Phase I", African Development Bank, https://projectsportal.afdb.org/dataportal/VProject/show/P-ST-H00-003 (accessed 2 February 2023).

AfDB (2022a), "African Development Bank to launch public financial management academy to build capacity in African countries", African Development Bank article, 9 June, www.afdb.org/en/news-and-events/press-releases/african-development-bank-launch-public-financial-management-academy-build-capacity-african-countries-52335.

AfDB (2022b), "African Development Bank, African Securities Exchange Association launch AELP E-Platform linking seven African capital markets with $1.5 trillion market capitalization", African Development Bank article, 8 December, www.afdb.org/en/news-and-events/press-releases/african-development-bank-african-securities-exchange-association-launch-aelp-e-platform-linking-seven-african-capital-markets-15-trillion-market-capitalization-57245.

AfDB (2022c), "Mauritius: National bourse launches new automated trading platform", African Development Bank article, 20 May, www.afdb.org/en/news-and-events/press-releases/mauritius-national-bourse-launches-new-automated-trading-platform-51728.

AfDB (2022d), "President Macky Sall and African Development Bank Group head Dr Akinwumi Adesina call for substantial support for Africa's low-income countries", African Development Bank article, 17 September, www.afdb.org/fr/news-and-events/president-macky-sall-and-african-development-bank-group-head-dr-akinwumi-adesina-call-substantial-support-africas-low-income-countries-54845.

AfDB (2022e), "Africa Investment Forum: Harnessing guarantees and insurance to close the continental financing gap – The Africa Co-Guarantee Platform leads the way", African Development Bank article, 27 October, www.afdb.org/en/news-and-events/africa-investment-forum-harnessing-guarantees-and-insurance-close-continental-financing-gap-africa-co-guarantee-platform-leads-way-55839.

AfDB (2021), *Electricity Regulatory Index for Africa 2021*, African Development Bank Group, Abidjan, https://africa-energy-portal.org/sites/default/files/2021-12/08122021%20ERI%20report%202021.pdf.

AfDB (2019), *The Lusophone Development Compact: Accelerating Sustainable, Inclusive and Private Sector Growth*, African Development Bank, www.afdb.org/sites/default/files/news_documents/lusophone_compact_brochure_en.pdf.

AfDB/IFC/MFW4A (2022), *Gauging Appetite of African Institutional Investors for New Asset Classes*, African Development Bank/International Finance Corporation/Making Finance Work for Africa, www.mfw4a.org/sites/default/files/resources/gauging_appetite_of_african_institutional_investors_for_new_asset_classes_-_published.pdf.

Alliance for Product Quality in Africa (2022), "Audrey: More jobs in chocolate production through certifications", www.allianceforproductquality.de/en/projekte/schokoladenproduktion-zertifizierungen/.

ALN (2021), "Impact of Rwanda's new investment facilitation and promotion law on doing business", Legal Alert, African Legal Network, www.rfl.rw/docs/LEGAL_ALERT_ALN.pdf.

Ameli, N. et al. (2021), "Higher cost of finance exacerbates a climate investment trap in developing economies", *Nature Communications*, Vol. 12, https://doi.org/10.1038/s41467-021-24305-3.

ASEAN (2012), "AFTA and National AFTA Units", webpage, Association of Southeast Asian Nations, https://asean.org/afta-and-national-afta-units/.

Atef, N. A. (2022), "Scaling up sustainable finance and investment in the Middle East and North Africa", in *Scaling Up Sustainable Finance and Investment in the Global South*, Centre for Economic Policy Research (CEPR) Press, London, https://cepr.org/system/files/publication-files/175477-scaling_up_sustainable_finance_and_investment_in_the_global_south.pdf.

Attridge, S., Y. Chen and B. Getzel (2022), "Weathering the storm: African public development banks' response to Covid-19 and their recovery role", *ODI Working Paper*, Overseas Development Institute, London, https://cdn.odi.org/media/documents/ODI_Working_paper_Weathering_the_storm_African_public_development_banks_response.pdf.

AU (2022a), "Ministers of Finance conclude discussions on access to finances; debt restructuring and Africa's credit rating", Press Release, African Union, https://au.int/en/pressreleases/20220726/ministers-finance-conclude-discussions-access-finances-debt-restructuring-and.

AU (2022b), "Africa speaks with unified voice as AU Executive Council adopts African Common Position on Energy Access and Just Energy Transition", Press Release, African Union, https://au.int/en/pressreleases/20220722/africa-speaks-unified-voice-au-executive-council-adopts-african-common.

AU (2021), "Ethiopian Airlines A-e Trade Group, sign MoU to establish East African smart logistics and fulfilment hub at ADD to support AfCFTA", Press Release, African Union, https://au.int/en/pressreleases/20210803/ethiopian-airlines-e-trade-group-sign-mou-establish-east-african-smart.

AU (2020), *The Integrated Corridor Approach - "A Holistic Infrastructure Planning Framework to establish PIDA-PAP 2"*, Strategic Note, African Union, https://pp2.au-pida.org/wp-content/uploads/2020/04/English-Strategic-Note_Integrated-Corridor-Approach-and-Selection-Criteria-AUC.pdf.

AU (2017), "Infrastructure corridors are key to Africa's intra-regional trade, job creation: Stakeholders agree at PIDA Session", Press Release, African Union, https://au.int/en/pressreleases/20171127/infrastructure-corridors-are-key-africa%E2%80%99s-intra-regional-trade-job-creation.

AUC (2019), *What Public Policies are Good for Productive Transformation in Africa?*, African Union Commission Department of Economic Affairs, Addis Ababa, https://au.int/sites/default/files/newsevents/workingdocuments/35970-wd-1.1._new_paper_stc_transformation_productive_eng.pdf.

AUC/AfDB/UNECA/ACBF (2017), *Strategy for the Harmonization of Statistics in Africa 2017-2026 (SHaSA 2)*, https://au.int/sites/default/files/documents/34580-doc-34577-doc-shasa_ii_strategy_eng_full_web.pdf.

AUC/OECD (2022), *Africa's Development Dynamics 2022: Regional Value Chains for a Sustainable Recovery*, OECD Publishing, Paris, https://doi.org/10.1787/2e3b97fd-en.

AUC/OECD (2021), *Africa's Development Dynamics 2021: Digital Transformation for Quality Jobs*, AUC, Addis Ababa/OECD Publishing, Paris, https://doi.org/10.1787/0a5c9314-en.

AUC/OECD (2019), *Africa's Development Dynamics 2019: Achieving Productive Transformation*, AUC, Addis Ababa/OECD Publishing, Paris, https://doi.org/10.1787/c1cd7de0-en.

BAFU (2022), "Bilateral climate agreements", webpage, Federal Office for the Environment (FOEN), www.bafu.admin.ch/bafu/en/home/themen/thema-klima/klimawandel-stoppen-und-folgen-meistern/klima--internationales/staatsvertraege-umsetzung-klimauebereinkommen-von-paris-artikel6.html (accessed 2 February 2022).

CAFI (2021), "Gabon: First in Africa to receive payments for preserved rainforests", Central African Forest Initiative, www.cafi.org/countries/gabon/gabon-first-africa-receive-payments-preserved-rainforests.

CCRED (n.d.), "African Market Observatory (AMO): What do we do", Centre for Competition, Regulation and Economic Development webpage, www.competition.org.za/africanmarketobservatory (accessed 2 February 2023).

Celani, A., L. Dressler and M. Wermelinger (2022), "Building an Investment Tax Incentives database: Methodology and initial findings for 36 developing countries", *OECD Working Papers on International Investment*, No. 2022/01, OECD Publishing, Paris, https://doi.org/10.1787/62e075a9-en.

CEPA (2015), *Mobilising Finance for Infrastructure: A study for the Department for International Development*, Cambridge Economic Policy Associates Ltd, https://assets.publishing.service.gov.uk/media/57a0897fe5274a31e00000e8/61319-DfID_1_Synthesis_Report_Final.pdf.

CEPR (2022), *The Case for More Special Drawing Rights: Rechanneling Is No Substitute for a New Allocation*, Center for Economic Policy and Research, https://cepr.net/report/the-case-for-more-special-drawing-rights/.

Cercle des Économistes (2022), *Relançons le Débat Économique 2022*, https://lecercledeseconomistes.fr/wp-content/uploads/2022/05/rlde_16_cercle_unionafricaine.pdf.

CREA (2022), "Briefing: 12.8 GW of Chinese overseas coal projects cancelled, but 19 GW could still go ahead", Centre for Research on Energy and Clean Air, https://energyandcleanair.org/wp/wp-content/uploads/2022/04/Final_Chinese-overseas-briefing_April2022.pdf.

Davis, R. M. et al. (2022), "Mobilising long-term finance in the Global South: Lessons from the 'South' and 'North'", in *Scaling Up Sustainable Finance and Investment in the Global South*, CEPR Press, London, https://cepr.org/system/files/publication-files/175477-scaling_up_sustainable_finance_and_investment_in_the_global_south.pdf.

Dembele, F., R. Schwarz and P. Horrocks (2021), *Scaling up Green, Social, Sustainability and Sustainability-linked Bond Issuances in Developing Countries*, OECD Publishing, Paris, https://www.oecd.org/dac/financing-sustainable-development/blended-finance-principles/documents/scaling-up-green-social-sustainability-sustainability-linked-bond-issuances-developing-countries.pdf.

D4D Hub (2023), "Rwanda and France sign new deal to improve digital public services and support innovations with high development potential", https://d4dhub.eu/fr/news/rwanda-and-france-sign-new-deal-to-improve-digital-public-services-and-support-innovations-with-high-development-potential.

EBF/BIAC/ICC (2019), *Joint Business Position on the Modernisation of the OECD Arrangement: Ensuring a Global Level Playing Field*, European Banking Federation/Business at OECD/International Chamber of Commerce, www.ebf.eu/wp-content/uploads/2019/11/Final-version-Joint-business-position-on-Future-of-OECD-Arrangement.pdf.

EC (2020), "EU foreign investment screening mechanism becomes fully operational", Press Release, European Commission, https://ec.europa.eu/commission/presscorner/detail/en/ip_20_1867.

Echandi, R., M. Maliszewska and V. Steenbergen (2022), *Making the Most of the African Continental Free Trade Area: Leveraging Trade and Foreign Direct Investment to Boost Growth and Reduce Poverty*, International Bank for Reconstruction and Development/World Bank, Washington, DC, https://documents1.worldbank.org/curated/en/099305006222230294/pdf/P1722320bf22cd02c09f2b0b3b320afc4a7.pdf.

ECOWAS (2020), "ECOWAS launches 'Improved Business & Investment Climate in West Africa Project' website", Press Release, Economic Community of West African States, https://ecowas.int/ecowas-launches-improved-business-investment-climate-in-west-africa-project-website/.

EDTF (2022), "Building a better Ethiopia together", Ethiopian Diaspora Trust Fund, www.ethiopiatrustfund.org/ (accessed 26 October 2022).

Ekeruche, M. A. (2022), *Africa's Rising Debt and the Emergence of New Creditors: A Review of the Trends, Challenges and Prospects (2000 - 2021)*, African Debt Series, Vol. 2, https://library.fes.de/pdf-files/bueros/fes-ua/19365.pdf.

Elms, D. (2021), *Increasing Access and Interoperability of Cross-border E-payments in Asia*, Hinrich Foundation, https://static1.squarespace.com/static/5393d501e4b0643446abd228/t/606ea7b0363d76436e5ce51a/1617864635266/E-payments+in+Asia_Hinrich+Foundation.pdf.

Falchetta, G. et al. (2021), "The role of regulatory, market and governance risk for electricity access investment in sub-Saharan Africa", *Energy for Sustainable Development*, Vol. 62, https://doi.org/10.1016/j.esd.2021.04.002.

Fitch (2021), *The Revival of African National Development Banks*, Fitch Rating Special Report, www.fitchratings.com/research/banks/the-revival-of-african-national-development-banks-19-04-2021.

FSCA (2023), "Registered Credit Rating Agencies", webpage, Financial Sector Conduct Authority, www.fsca.co.za/Regulated%20Entities/Pages/Credit-Rating-Agencies.aspx (accessed 2 February 2023).

FSD Africa (2022), "Africa Private Equity and Debt Programme", webpage, https://fsdafrica.org/projects/africa-private-equity-and-debt-programme/.

GCA (2022), *State and Trends in Adaptation in Africa 2022*, Global Center on Adaptation, Rotterdam, Netherlands, https://gca.org/reports/sta22/.

GCF (n.d.), "Overview", Green Climate Fund webpage, www.greenclimate.fund/readiness (accessed 2 February 2023).

GIH (2019), *Leading Practices in Governmental Processes Facilitating Infrastructure Project Preparation*, Global Infrastructure Hub, https://cdn.gihub.org/umbraco/media/2344/gih_project-preparation_full-document_final_art_web.pdf.

Gratcheva, E. M. and F. E. Stewart (2020), *Leveraging Pension Fund Investment for Domestic Development: Namibia's Regulation 29 Approach*, World Bank Group, Washington, DC, http://documents.worldbank.org/curated/en/125241594367606090/Leveraging-Pension-Fund-Investment-for-Domestic-Development-Namibia-s-Regulation-29-Approach.

Griffith-Jones, S., S. Attridge and M. Gouett (2020), *Securing Climate Finance through National Development Banks*, Oversees Development Institute, https://cdn.odi.org/media/documents/200124_ndbs_web.pdf.

Halland, H. et al. (2021), "Mobilising institutional investor capital for climate-aligned development", *OECD Development Policy Papers*, No. 35, OECD Publishing, Paris, https://doi.org/10.1787/e72d7e89-en.

Horn, S., D. Milhalyi and P. Nickol (3 March 2022), "Systematic underreporting of public debt statistics: 50 years of evidence and recent progress", World Bank Blogs, https://blogs.worldbank.org/developmenttalk/systematic-underreporting-public-debt-statistics-50-years-evidence-and-recent.

I&P (n.d.), "Impact", Investisseurs & Partenaires webpage, www.ietp.com/fr/content/impact (accessed 6 January 2023).

ICA (2017), "Project Preparation Facilities Network (PPFN)", Infrastructure Consortium for Africa, www.icafrica.org/en/project-preparation/project-preparation-facilities-network-ppfn/ (accessed 3 February 2023).

IDA (2022), "IDA Country Performance Ratings (CPR)", International Development Association webpage, https://ida.worldbank.org/en/financing/resource-management/ida-country-performance-ratings (accessed 2 February 2023).

IEA (2022), *Africa Energy Outlook 2022*, International Energy Agency, www.iea.org/reports/africa-energy-outlook-2022.

IFC (2021), *How the COVID-19 Crisis is Impacting African Pension Fund Approaches to Portfolio Management*, International Finance Corporation, www.ifc.org/wps/wcm/connect/61e14b0d-b283-4f8f-8d17-4bce3f54d4a1/African+pension+funds_FINAL-10-9-20.pdf?MOD=AJPERES&CVID=nkeOGIJ.

IISD (26 December 2022), "AfCFTA Protocol on Investment was concluded", Investment Treaty News, www.iisd.org/itn/en/2022/12/26/afcfta-protocol-on-investment-was-concluded/.

IMF (n.d.), "Regional Technical Assistance Centers", International Monetary Fund webpage, www.imf.org/external/np/exr/key/rtacs.htm (accessed 2 February 2023).

IMF/OECD/UN/World Bank (2015), *Options for Low Income Countries' Effective and Efficient Use of Tax Incentives for Investment: A Report to the G-20 Development Working Group by the IMF, OECD, UN and World Bank*, International Monetary Fund, OECD, United Nations and the World Bank, www.oecd.org/tax/options-for-low-income-countries-effective-and-efficient-use-of-tax-incentives-for-investment.pdf.

InfraCredit (2023), Infrastructure finance website, https://infracredit.ng/ (accessed 28 February 2023).

Jenkins, B. et al. (2007), *Business Linkages: Lessons, Opportunities, and Challenges*, International Finance Corporation, International Business Leaders Forum and the Kennedy School of Government, Harvard, www.hks.harvard.edu/sites/default/files/centers/mrcbg/programs/cri/files/report_16_BUSINESS%2BLINKAGESFINAL.pdf.

Johnson, B. and R. A. Kotey (2018), “The influence of small and medium enterprises (SMEs) listing on the Ghana Alternative Market (GAX): Prevailing factors”, *Academic Journal of Economic Studies*, Vol. 4/4, pp. 142-156, http://hdl.handle.net/10419/215860.

Juffe-Bignoli, D. et al. (2021), “Mitigating the impacts of development corridors on biodiversity: A global review”, *Frontiers in Ecology and Evolution*, Vol. 9, https://doi.org/10.3389/fevo.2021.683949.

Kabukura, W. (2022), “As Africa’s climate warms, rich countries pledge more funds”, Public Broadcasting Service, 5 September, www.pbs.org/newshour/world/as-africas-climate-warms-rich-countries-pledge-more-funds.

Kubota, M. and A. Zeufack (2020), “Assessing the returns on investment in data openness and transparency”, *World Bank Policy Research Working Paper*, No. 9139, World Bank, Washington, DC, http://hdl.handle.net/10986/33295.

Laurance, W. F. et al. (2015), “Estimating the environmental costs of Africa’s massive ‘development corridors’”, *Current Biology*, Vol. 25/24, pp. 3202-3208, www.sciencedirect.com/science/article/pii/S0960982215013093?via%3Dihub.

Leadership (2022), “PAPSS goes live as FBN, Ghana Bank consummate 1st transaction”, article, 6 October, https://leadership.ng/papss-goes-live-as-fbn-ghana-bank-consummate-1st-transaction/ (accessed 26 October 2022).

Lee, N., G. Forster and S. Paxton (2021), “MDBs could do more to build markets just by releasing more data”, Center for Global Development blog post, 29 June, www.cgdev.org/blog/mdbs-could-do-more-build-markets-just-releasing-more-data.

Mullan, M. and N. Ranger (2022), “Climate-resilient finance and investment: Framing paper”, *OECD Environment Working Papers*, No. 196, OECD Publishing, Paris, https://doi.org/10.1787/223ad3b9-en.

Mutize, M. (2022), “Moody’s has bought a leading African rating agency: Why it’s bad news”, The Conversation, 13 February, https://theconversation.com/moodys-has-bought-a-leading-african-rating-agency-why-its-bad-news-176827.

Nassiry, D. et al. (2018), *Clean Energy Project Preparation Facilities: Mapping the Global Landscape*, Oversees Development Institute, https://cdn.odi.org/media/documents/12504.pdf.

Nugent P. and I. Soi (2020), “One-stop border posts in East Africa: State encounters of the fourth kind”, *Journal of Eastern African Studies*, Vol. 14/3, pp. 433-454, www.tandfonline.com/doi/full/10.1080/17531055.2020.1768468.

OECD (2023), “OECD Debt Transparency Initiative”, OECD webpage, www.oecd.org/finance/debt-transparency/ (accessed 2 February 2023).

OECD (2022a), *Global Outlook on Financing for Sustainable Development 2023: No Sustainability Without Equity*, OECD Publishing, Paris, https://doi.org/10.1787/fcbe6ce9-en.

OECD (2022b), *FDI Qualities Policy Toolkit*, OECD Publishing, Paris, https://doi.org/10.1787/7ba74100-en.

OECD (2022c), *FDI Qualities Guide for Development Co-operation: Strengthening the Role of Development Co-operation for Sustainable Investment*, OECD Development Policy Tools, OECD Publishing, Paris, https://doi.org/10.1787/7f251bac-en.

OECD (2022d), *Equitable Framework and Finance for Extractive-based Countries in Transition (EFFECT)*, OECD Development Policy Tools, OECD Publishing, Paris, https://doi.org/10.1787/7871c0ad-en.

OECD (2021a), *Together or Apart: Investment Promotion Agencies’ Prioritisation and Monitoring and Evaluation for Sustainable Investment Promotion*, OECD Investment Insights, www.oecd.org/daf/inv/investment-policy/Investment-Insights-Investment-Promotion-Prioritisation-OECD.pdf.

OECD (2021b), *Responses to the Survey of Climate-related and Sustainability-related Policies and Practices*, OECD Working Party on Export Credits and Credit Guarantees, www.oecd.org/officialdocuments/publicdisplaydocumentpdf/?cote=TAD/ECG(2021)10&docLanguage=En.

OECD (2021c), “Enabling SME linkages with foreign firms in global value chains”, in *Middle East and North Africa Investment Policy Perspectives*, OECD Publishing, Paris, https://doi.org/10.1787/824a45f1-en.

OECD (2020), *OECD Investment Policy Reviews: Egypt 2020*, OECD Investment Policy Reviews, OECD Publishing, Paris, https://doi.org/10.1787/9f9c589a-en.

OECD (2015), “The Policy Framework for Investment (PFI)”, webpage, www.oecd.org/investment/pfi.htm (accessed 1 February 2022).

OECD et al. (2021), *Production Transformation Policy Review of Egypt: Embracing Change, Achieving Prosperity*, OECD Development Pathways, OECD Publishing, Paris, https://doi.org/10.1787/302fec4b-en.

OECD/ATAF/AUC (2022), *Revenue Statistics in Africa 2022*, OECD Publishing, Paris, https://doi.org/10.1787/ea66fbde-en-fr.

OECD/SADC (2017), *Role of Monitoring for Implementation: Advancing Investment Policy Reforms in the Southern African Development Community*, OECD, Paris/Southern African Development Community, Gaborone.

OECD/UNDP (2021), *OECD-UNDP Impact Standards for Financing Sustainable Development*, OECD Publishing, Paris, https://doi.org/10.1787/744f982e-en.

OECD/World Bank/UNEP (2018), *Financing Climate Futures: Rethinking Infrastructure*, OECD Publishing, Paris, https://doi.org/10.1787/9789264308114-en.

PAPSS (2022), "Connecting payments: Accelerating Africa's trade", Pan-African Payment and Settlement System presentation to the African Union Commission and the OECD, virtual event, Enhancing Cross-border Digital Payment Systems for Africa's Regional Trade and Integration, 28 June 2022.

PARIS21 (2023), *Statistical Capacity Monitor* (database), Paris, https://statisticalcapacitymonitor.org/ (accessed 28 February 2023).

Pillay, S. and A. Sikochi (2022), "The credit rating agency market in Africa", *Harvard Business School Working Paper*, No. 22-074, www.hbs.edu/faculty/Pages/item.aspx?num=62480.

Pueyo, A. (2018), "What constrains renewable energy investment in Sub-Saharan Africa? A comparison of Kenya and Ghana", *World Development*, Vol. 109, pp. 85-100, https://doi.org/10.1016/j.worlddev.2018.04.008.

PwC (2021), *Africa Capital Markets Watch 2021*, PricewaterhouseCoopers, www.pwc.co.za/en/assets/pdf/africa-capital-markets-watch-2021.pdf.

PYXERA Global (2018), *Ghana Supply Chain Development Program – PYXERA*, https://vdocuments.mx/ghana-supply-chain-development-program-pyxera-supply-chain-development-program.html?page=1.

RES4Africa (2022), *Sustainable Electricity for a Prosperous* Africa, Renewable Energy Solutions for Africa, https://static1.squarespace.com/static/609a53264723031eccc12e99/t/628cea0bc18a56354ede110e/1653402171127/RES4Africa+5th+Flagship+Publication+2022+-+Sustainable+electricity+for+a+Prosperous+Africa_double+paged.pdf.

RES4Africa/PwC Italy (2021), *Investor Survey on Sub Saharan Africa*, RES4Africa and PricewaterhouseCoopers Italy, https://static1.squarespace.com/static/609a53264723031eccc12e99/t/6180ffb91e351d4c7fcdd981/1635844031170/Investor+survey+on+Sub+Saharan+Africa_RES4Africa+PwC+%281%29.pdf.

Rivetti, D. (2021), *Debt Transparency in Developing Economies*, World Bank, Washington, DC, http://documents.worldbank.org/curated/en/743881635526394087/Debt-Transparency-in-Developing-Economies.

Sabha, Y., Y. Liu and D. Willem (2020), *Investment Linkages and Incentives: Promoting Technology Transfer and Productivity Spillovers from Foreign Direct Investment (FDI)*, FCI in Focus, World Bank, Washington, DC, http://documents.worldbank.org/curated/en/354781589316916550/Investment-Linkages-and-Incentives-Promoting-Technology-Transfer-and-Productivity-Spillovers-from-Foreign-Direct-Investment-FDI.

Sasi, I. (20 April 2022), "AfCFTA operationalization: The USD 1 trillion investment framework", Fie-Consult article, https://fieconsult.com/afcfta-operationalization-the-usd-1-trillion-investment-framework/.

Soumaré, I. et al. (2021), "Capital market development in sub-Saharan Africa: Progress, challenges and innovations", *ODI Working Paper* 2, a joint FSD Africa–ODI research programme for financial sector development in Africa, Overseas Development Institute, London, https://cdn.odi.org/media/documents/ODI_Working_Paper_2_Capital_markets_development_in_SSA_FINAL_clean.pdf.

Taarifa News (2022), "KEPFIC to inject Kshs16B into infrastructure projects this year", https://taarifanews.co.ke/kepfic-to-inject-kshs16b-inti-infrastructure-projects-this-ye/.

Thorn, J. P. R. et al. (2022), "The African Development Corridors Database: A new tool to assess the impacts of infrastructure investments", *Scientific Data*, Vol. 9/679, https://doi.org/10.1038/s41597-022-01771-y.

Tralac (2021), *Protocol on Investment to the Agreement Establishing the African Continental Free Trade Area*, Trade Law Centre NPC, www.tralac.org/documents/resources/cfta/4613-protocol-on-investment-to-the-agreement-establishing-the-afcfta-zero-draft-november-2021/file.html.

UN (2022), *Financing for Sustainable Development Report 2022*, United Nations, New York, https://developmentfinance.un.org/fsdr2022.

UNCTAD (2021), *Handbook on Special Economic Zones in Africa: Towards Economic Diversification across the Continent*, United Nations Conference on Trade and Development, https://unctad.org/system/files/official-document/diaeia2021d3_en.pdf.

UNDP/AfCFTA Secretariat (2021), *Futures Report 2021*, United Nations Development Programme and the African Continental Free Trade Area Secretariat, www.undp.org/africa/publications/futures-report-2021.

UNECA (2022a), *Assessing the Effectiveness of National Development Banks in Africa*, United Nations Economic Commission for Africa, Addis Ababa, https://repository.uneca.org/bitstream/handle/10855/49159/b12021684.pdf?sequence=1&isAllowed=y.

UNECA (2022b), *The African Continental Free Trade Area and Demand for Transport Infrastructure and Services*, United Nations Economic Commission for Africa, Addis Ababa, https://hdl.handle.net/10855/47596.

UNECA (2020), "Tapping into the potential of African markets", in *Economic Report on Africa 2020: Innovative Finance for Private Sector Development in Africa*, United Nations Economic Commission for Africa, Addis Ababa, https://uneca.org/sites/default/files/chapterimages/CHAPTER%204_TAPPING%20INTO%20THE%20POTENTIAL%20OF%20AFRICAN%20MARKETS_ERA2020.pdf.

UNECA (2016), "The policy framework for greening industrialization in Africa", in *Economic Report on Africa 2016*, Economic Commission for Africa, Addis Ababa, www.uneca.org/sites/default/files/chapterimages/era2016_chap4_en-rev6may.pdf.

UNECA/AfDB/AU/UNDP (2022), *2020 Africa Sustainable Development Report*, African Union, United Nations Economic Commission for Africa, African Development Bank, and United Nations Development Programme, New York, www.afdb.org/en/documents/2020-africa-sustainable-development-report.

UNECA/AU/AfDB/UNCTAD (2019), *Assessing Regional Integration in Africa (ARIA IX): Next Steps for the African Continental Free Trade Area*, United Nations Economic Commission for Africa, African Union, African Development Bank and United Nations Conference on Trade and Development, Addis Ababa, https://archive.uneca.org/sites/default/files/PublicationFiles/aria9_report_en_4sept_fin.pdf.

UNEP (2016), "Is Africa's natural capital the gateway to finance its development?", United Nations Environment Programme article, 21 September, www.unep.org/news-and-stories/story/africas-natural-capital-gateway-finance-its-development.

Wambui, R. (2022), "Scaling up sustainable finance and investment in the Global South: A case study of sub-Saharan Africa", in *Scaling Up Sustainable Finance and Investment in the Global South*, CEPR Press, London, https://cepr.org/system/files/publication-files/175477-scaling_up_sustainable_finance_and_investment_in_the_global_south.pdf.

Were, A. (2022a), "How can Africa benefit from the private sector's growing interest in climate finance?", OECD Development Matters article, 17 March, https://oecd-development-matters.org/2022/03/17/how-can-africa-benefit-from-the-private-sectors-growing-interest-in-climate-finance/.

Were, A. (2022b), "The impacts of climate change continue to compromise the livelihoods of hundreds of millions of Africans", FSD Kenya Blog, 21 October, www.fsdkenya.org/blogs-publications/blog/how-to-develop-a-green-project-pipeline-in-africa/.

Werners, S. and O. H. Okunola (2023), "COP27 in review: Climate talks delivered big gains for Africa, but also several challenges", The Conversation, 4 January, https://theconversation.com/cop27-in-review-climate-talks-delivered-big-gains-for-africa-but-also-several-challenges-196582.

World Bank (2022a), "Why one African country opted for full disclosure on debt", World Bank Feature Story, 10 July, www.worldbank.org/en/news/feature/2022/07/10/why-one-african-country-opted-for-full-disclosure-on-debt.

World Bank (2022b), "Free trade deal boosts Africa's economic development", World Bank article, 30 June, www.worldbank.org/en/topic/trade/publication/free-trade-deal-boosts-africa-economic-development.

World Bank (2020), *Leveraging Pension Fund Investment for Domestic Development: Namibia's Regulation 29 Approach*, Finance, Competitiveness and Innovation Insight, World Bank, Washington, DC, https://openknowledge.worldbank.org/handle/10986/34332.

World Bank (2019), "Case study - Seychelles: Introducing the world's first sovereign blue bond", IBRD Financial Products webpage, World Bank Treasury, https://thedocs.worldbank.org/en/doc/242151559930961454-0340022019/original/CasestudyBlueBondSeychellesfinal6.7.2019.pdf.

World Bank/IMF (2017), *The Medium-Term Debt Management Strategy: An Assessment of Recent Capacity Building*, World Bank/International Monetary Fund, https://documents1.worldbank.org/curated/en/300771500775277965/pdf/Board-Paper-2017-MTDS-Assessment-of-Recent-Capacity-Building-Final-Clean-06272017.pdf.

Xu, J. et al. (2021), "What are public development banks and development financing institutions?—Qualification criteria, stylized facts and development trends", *China Economic Quarterly International*, Vol. 1/4, https://doi.org/10.1016/j.ceqi.2021.10.001.

Yu, S. et al. (2021), "The potential role of Article 6 compatible carbon markets in reaching net-zero", *IETA Working Paper*, University of Maryland and International Emissions Trading Association, www.ieta.org/resources/Resources/Net-Zero/Final_Net-zero_A6_working_paper.pdf.

Chapter 3

Investing in renewable energies for Southern Africa's sustainable development

This chapter examines the development of sustainable investments with a focus on the renewable energy sector in Southern Africa (Angola, Botswana, Eswatini, Lesotho, Malawi, Mozambique, Namibia, South Africa, Zambia and Zimbabwe). The first section shows that multiple global crises have exacerbated sustainable investment needs, while the region's sources of finance offer untapped potential to spur sustainable growth. The second section explores how investments in the region's renewable energy sector can generate social, economic and environmental development gains. It identifies major constraints hampering the investments that are needed to achieve energy security and a just energy transition. The third section proposes policy priorities to catalyse investments in Southern Africa's renewable energy sector.

IN BRIEF

The slow pace of public and private investments has contributed to sluggish gross domestic product (GDP) growth in Southern Africa, while global crises have exacerbated the region's investment needs. Southern Africa's domestic sources of finance hold untapped potential to catalyse sustainable investment. The regional pension fund market is the largest on the continent, and South African multinationals represent 75% of turnover and market capitalisation of Africa's listed companies. Despite available resources, investment is taking place, neither at the required scale, nor in sectors critical for sustainable development.

Energy is a case in point. Investments in renewable energy can help improve energy security, overcome energy poverty and generate sustainable development gains in Southern Africa. Renewable energies can significantly lower carbon dioxide (CO_2) emissions and generate positive social and economic returns on investments. For example, solar energy creates twice as many jobs in operations and maintenance as fossil fuels. Despite recent global shocks, the renewable energy sector has grown, but the investments needed to achieve universal clean energy access remain large. South Africa's energy transition alone will demand about USD 250 billion in the next three decades. In 2016-20, 79% of the Southern African population in urban areas had access to electricity compared to only 26% in rural areas. Improving access to affordable energy and accelerating the region's just energy transition will require mobilising public and private finance for renewable energy projects.

This chapter identifies three priorities for policy makers in Southern Africa to catalyse investments in renewable energies: strengthening regional co-operation to harmonise regulatory frameworks and scale up investments in renewable energy infrastructures; de-risking private sector investments in renewable energy projects, including through public-private partnerships and development finance; and adopting dedicated policies and financing solutions to increase clean energy access in rural areas.

Southern Africa

Decreasing investment → low growth

Annual GDP growth percentage points

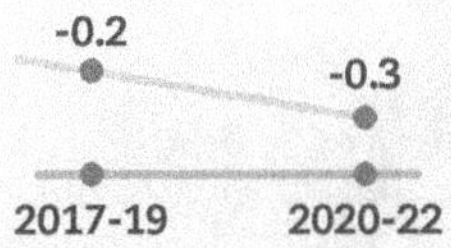

Domestic sources of finance → untapped potential

Total turnover and market capitalisation of Africa's listed companies

Pension funds as % of GDP

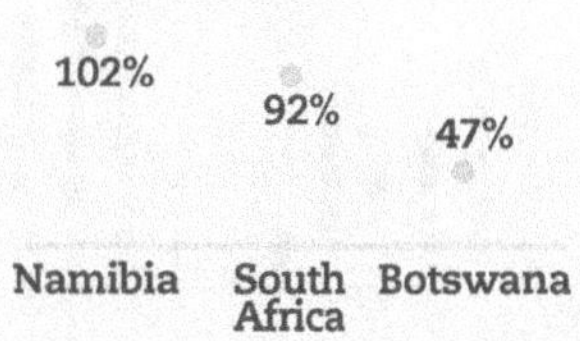

Renewable energy has potential for sustainable development

Southern Africa's share of the continent's installed electricity capacity:

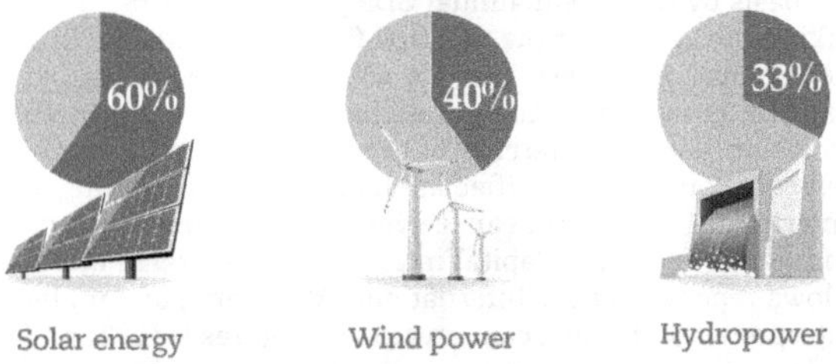

Solar energy creates twice as many jobs in operations and maintenance as fossil fuels

More investments can achieve energy security and universal clean energy access

Access to electricity (% of population), 2016-20

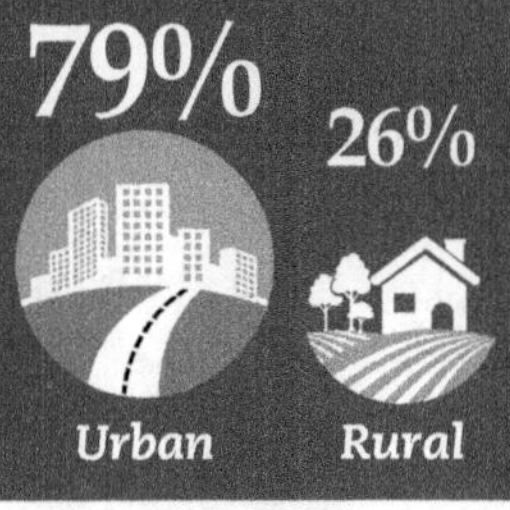

Electricity **blackouts** in South Africa's coal-based energy system are estimated to drag growth by **2 percentage points** in 2023

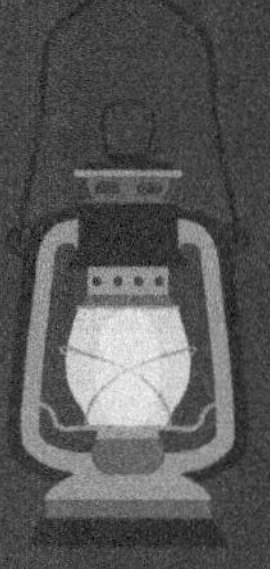

What's next?

- **Harmonise regulatory frameworks and accelerate regional initiatives** on renewable energy infrastructures
- **Enhance public-private alliances and development finance** based on national energy priorities
- **Adopt targeted policy solutions** to scale up off-grid renewable energy projects **in rural areas**

Southern Africa regional profile

Figure 3.1. Components of economic growth and sources of financing in Southern Africa

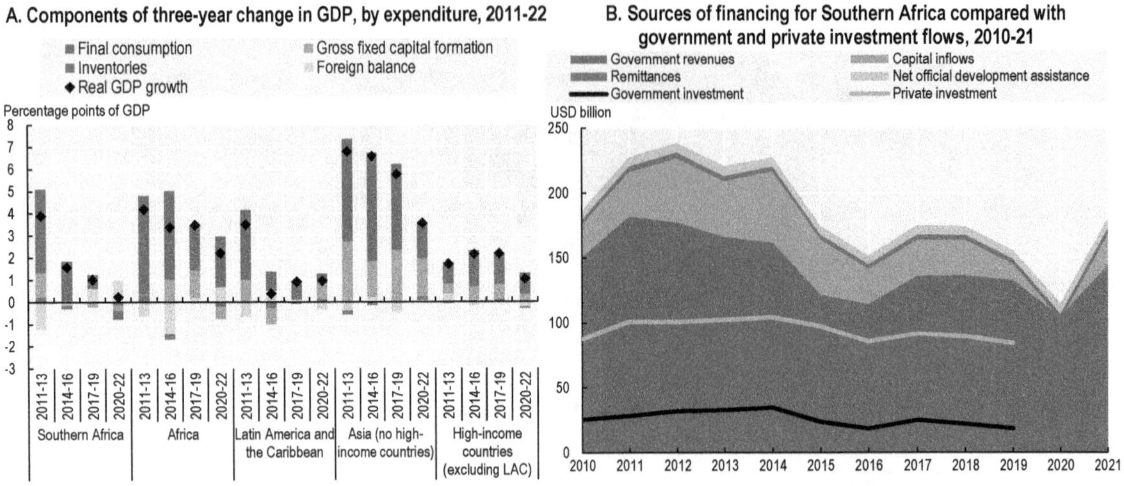

Note: The components of GDP growth are calculated on an annual basis by using real annual GDP growth to estimate the increase in real US dollars. Aggregate figures are calculated by taking the average of the national figures weighted by GDP in purchasing-power-parity dollars. The components of GDP growth over three-year periods were calculated by taking the difference between the geometric average of the annual real GDP growth over the period and the real GDP growth when setting each component to zero for individual years. Foreign balance is the difference between imports and exports. Imports contribute negatively to GDP. "High-income countries" refers to countries classified as "high-income" according to the World Bank Country and Lending Groups outside of Latin America and the Caribbean. Government revenues include all tax and non-tax government revenues minus debt service and grants received. Capital inflows include foreign direct investment (FDI), portfolio investment and other investment inflows reported by the International Monetary Fund under asset/liability accounting. Figures for capital inflows should be interpreted with some caution as some figures for 2021 and for portfolio inflows are missing.

Sources: Authors' calculations based on IMF (2022a), *World Economic Outlook Database*, www.imf.org/en/Publications/WEO/weo-database/2022/October; OECD (2022a), *OECD Development Assistance Committee* (database), https://stats-1.oecd.org/Index.aspx?DataSetCode=TABLE2A; World Bank (2022a), *World Development Indicators* (database), https://data.worldbank.org/products/wdi; IMF (2022b), *Balance of Payments and International Investment Position Statistics (BOP/IIP)* (database), https://data.imf.org/?sk=7A51304B-6426-40C0-83DD-CA473CA1FD52; IMF (2022c), *Investment and Capital Stock Dataset (ICSD)* (database), https://data.imf.org/?sk=1CE8A55F-CFA7-4BC0-BCE2-256EE65AC0E4; and World Bank-KNOMAD (2022), *Remittances* (database), www.knomad.org/data/remittances.

StatLink https://stat.link/0fkbli

Figure 3.2. Greenfield foreign direct investment flows into Southern Africa, by activity, source and destination, 2017-22

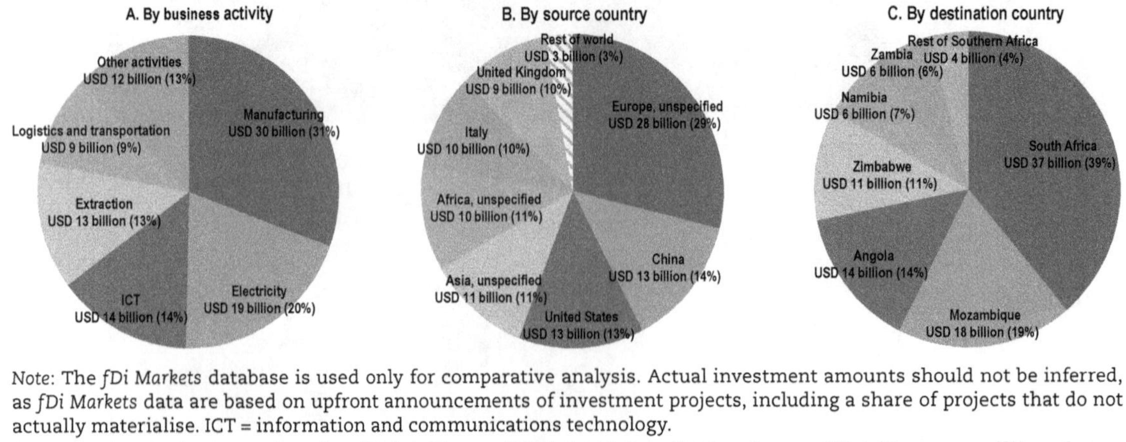

Note: The *fDi Markets* database is used only for comparative analysis. Actual investment amounts should not be inferred, as *fDi Markets* data are based on upfront announcements of investment projects, including a share of projects that do not actually materialise. ICT = information and communications technology.

Source: Authors' calculations based on fDi Intelligence (2022), *fDi Markets* (database), www.fdiintelligence.com/fdi-markets.

StatLink https://stat.link/029wqf

Southern Africa needs to mobilise more and better investments for sustainable development

Current global crises are exacerbating Southern Africa's investment needs

In recent years, decreasing investments have contributed to sluggish GDP growth in Southern Africa. The average GDP growth[1] for Southern Africa over the 2020-22 period was the lowest in Africa (0.3%, compared to 2.3% for Africa as a whole). Mostly driven by South Africa, which made up 68% of the region's GDP in 2021, the regional annual GDP growth stagnated around 1% over 2017-19 and plummeted to -5.7% in 2020 during the COVID-19 pandemic. Decreasing investment reduced Southern Africa's annual GDP growth by 0.2 percentage points over the 2017-19 period, and 0.3 percentage points over the 2020-22 period (Figure 3.1, Panel A). During the pandemic – between 2019 and 2020 – gross fixed capital formation in the region dropped by 23%, reaching its lowest level since 2006, mostly due to lower investments in South Africa (64%), Zambia (14%) and Angola (13%). The projected real GDP growth for Southern Africa is 1.4% for 2023 and 2.4% for 2024 (IMF, 2023a).

The COVID-19 pandemic further lowered investment flows and heightened sovereign debt risk. Public and private investments were already on a downward trend before the COVID-19 pandemic (Figure 3.1, Panel B). In 2020-21, South Africa, the region's largest recipient of foreign direct investment (FDI) (receiving 48% of total FDI to the region in 2015-19),[2] witnessed large capital outflows. Due to rising global risk aversion (see Chapter 1), net sales of local currency-denominated sovereign bonds by non-residents drove down portfolio investment flows; FDI decreased by 39% in 2020, but rose to a record high in 2021, mirroring developments in domestic growth (Goel and Miyajima, 2021; UNCTAD 2022a, 2021). Further, the region attracted higher official development assistance (ODA) and remittance flows during the pandemic: in 2020, ODA increased by 27% on an annual basis, mostly due to higher flows to Malawi, Mozambique and South Africa, while higher remittances mostly benefited Zimbabwe. Government revenues rebounded in 2021 and averaged 25% of GDP in 2020-21, in line with the pre-pandemic period. However, rising government expenditures to address the effects of the pandemic contributed to an increase of 13 percentage points in the average debt-to-GDP ratio of the region between 2019 and 2020. According to the International Monetary Fund, as of February 2023, four of the eight African countries in debt distress are in Southern Africa (i.e. Malawi, Mozambique, Zambia and Zimbabwe) (IMF, 2023b).

The ramifications of international conflicts exacerbate the vulnerability of some countries to external shocks. International conflicts have contributed to rising global food and energy prices, which has in turn created deep economic uncertainty across the region: net imports of food and fuel account for over 5% of GDP in Botswana, Lesotho and Zimbabwe (IEA, 2022a) while Malawi, Mozambique, Namibia and South Africa import more than 30% of their wheat directly from Russia and Ukraine (UNCTAD, 2022b). Even in Angola, the region's largest oil exporter, increased public revenues due to rising global oil prices have been partly offset by the country's dependency on imported refined petroleum and high costs of fuel subsidies (Kozul-Wright, 2023; Ver Angola, 2023).

Investments in climate change adaptation and mitigation and in clean energy access are needed to improve resilience. Malawi, Mozambique and Zimbabwe ranked among the five countries in the world most affected by extreme weather events in 2019 (Eckstein, Künzel and Schäfer, 2021). South Africa's coal-based economy is the leading CO_2 emitter on the continent: in 2020 the country accounted for 4.8% of the African population, 11% of African GDP and 32.7% of continental CO_2 emissions (IEA, 2022a). Estimates show that the economic costs associated with frequent electricity outages have reduced South Africa's GDP by 1% to 1.3% annually since 2007 (Gbadamosi, 2023).

Foreign and domestic sources of finance can be better allocated to support sustainable development

South Africa's information and communications technology (ICT) sector is highly attractive to foreign investors, but more productive investments across the region are needed to drive sustainable growth. In 2017-22, Angola, Mozambique and South Africa attracted more than 70% of the region's greenfield FDI capital expenditures (Figure 3.2, Panel C). ICT received the largest share of FDI to South Africa, while most of the FDI flows in Angola and Mozambique went to manufacturing, energy and extraction. On average, foreign investment into manufacturing showed the highest job creation potential in the region, with more than two jobs created for every USD 1 million invested (Figure 3.3). However, this ratio is about three times lower than in East Africa and two times lower than in North Africa. The automotive sector in South Africa shows high potential for creating jobs, thanks to its important linkages with neighbouring countries (AUC/OECD, 2022, Chapter 3). Investments in other countries (such as Angola, Mozambique and Zimbabwe) mostly target the processing of coal, oil and gas, and chemicals, resulting in lower job creation and a higher environmental footprint (see also Chapter 1).

Figure 3.3. **Greenfield foreign direct investment to Southern Africa, capital expenditures and job creation, by business activity, 2017-21**

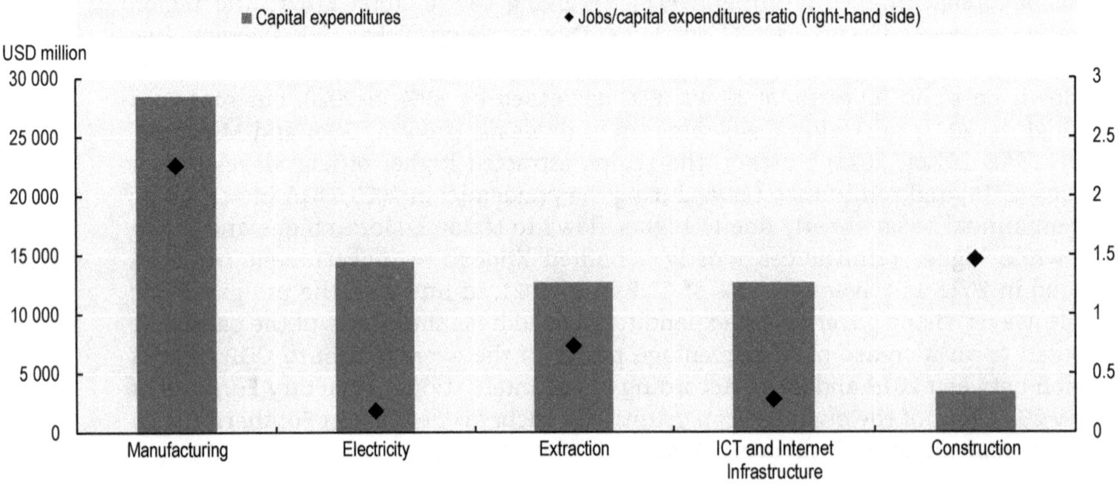

Note: ICT = information and communications technology. The figure shows the top five business activities by capital expenditure in 2017-21.

Source: Authors' calculations based on fDi Intelligence (2022), *fDi Markets* (database), www.fdiintelligence.com/fdi-markets.

StatLink https://stat.link/zneswf

ODA can support social sustainability, but its capacity to mobilise private finance in the most vulnerable countries remains limited. In 2020, during the COVID-19 pandemic, 75% of ODA flows to the region targeted social infrastructure and services (such as health and education), and ODA registered a 58% increase compared to 2019.[3] However, between 2012 and 2020, ODA mobilised the largest share of private finance in Southern Africa's infrastructure and productive sectors (Figure 3.4). In 2018-20, Mozambique was the only Least Developed Country among the top 20 recipients of mobilised private finance; in 2020, the largest volumes of the country's private finance mobilised through ODA were concentrated in a few large-scale liquefied natural gas projects (Bartz-Zuccala et al., 2022). Today, only around 30% of ODA reaches the 20 countries with the highest electricity access deficit; thus, aligning ODA with climate action would require increased efforts towards clean energy projects in low-income countries (Moreira Da Silva, 2021; OECD, 2019).

Figure 3.4. **Private finance mobilised through official development assistance in Southern Africa, 2012-20, USD million**

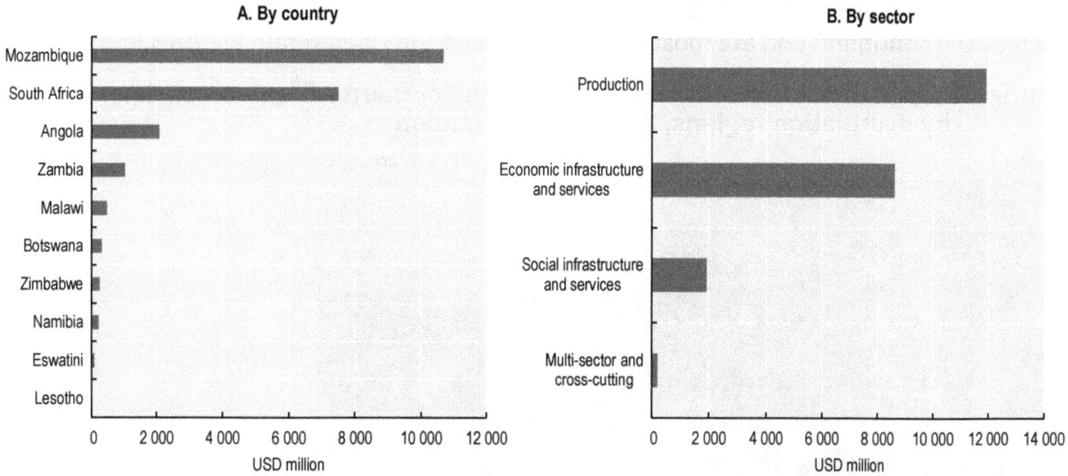

Source: Authors' calculations based on OECD (2022b), "Mobilisation", *OECD.Stat* (dataset), https://stats.oecd.org/Index.aspx?DataSetCode=DV_DCD_MOBILISATION.

StatLink https://stat.link/oink6m

Impact investing[4] is highly concentrated in South Africa, and the country has introduced enabling environmental, social and governance (ESG) policies. According to the latest available data (GIIN, 2016), nearly three-quarters of all impact capital invested in the region has been disbursed to South Africa (mostly in energy and finance), amounting to USD 29.1 billion (of which more than USD 24.2 billion originated from development finance institutions). This is close to 15 times the amount deployed in Zambia, which ranks second in the region in terms of impact capital disbursed. South Africa has implemented substantial enabling policies over the past decade to encourage institutional investors to incorporate ESG factors into their investment strategies (GIIN, 2020).

Large domestic institutional investors such as pension funds offer untapped potential for impact investing in the region. The regional pension fund market is the largest on the continent, with total assets in retirement savings plans accounting for 102% of GDP in Namibia (2020), 92% in South Africa (2018) and 47% in Botswana (2019).[5] However, regulatory and market barriers hold back institutional investors, including in the most developed markets. A recent survey of 139 pension funds in South Africa, representing 74% of assets under management in the country, shows that most pension funds identify a lack of both impact investing products and an impact investment pipeline as a top constraint in directing investments to green and climate-focused assets, followed by difficulty in monitoring and reporting on impacts of investments (IFC, 2020a).

Intra-regional investment is limited, but South African multinationals can catalyse investments at scale

Most FDI in the region comes from high-income countries, while intra-regional FDI flows are limited. In 2017-21, high-income countries represent the largest share of greenfield FDI inflows to the region, mostly targeting South Africa, Angola and Mozambique (in that order). In line with continental figures, only 11% of greenfield FDI capital expenditures to Southern Africa comes from other African countries, which includes 5% from countries in the region.[6]

South Africa-based company groups active in finance, ICT and retail have the potential to drive sustainable investments at regional and continental scale. In terms of greenfield FDI outflows, South Africa is the largest African investor both on the continent (USD 9 billion and 31% of intra-African FDI in 2017-21) and outside the continent (USD 7 billion and 58% of African FDI outside the continent in 2017-21) thanks to the internationalisation activities of its large company groups. In many cases, their FDI capital expenditures expand across other African countries, mostly in Southern and West Africa (Figure 3.5). South Africa-based companies represent 75% of the turnover and market capitalisation of listed companies on the continent[7] and are mostly active in finance, ICT and retail (Figure 3.6).

Figure 3.5. **Greenfield foreign direct investment outflows from Southern African countries, by destination regions, 2017-21, USD million**

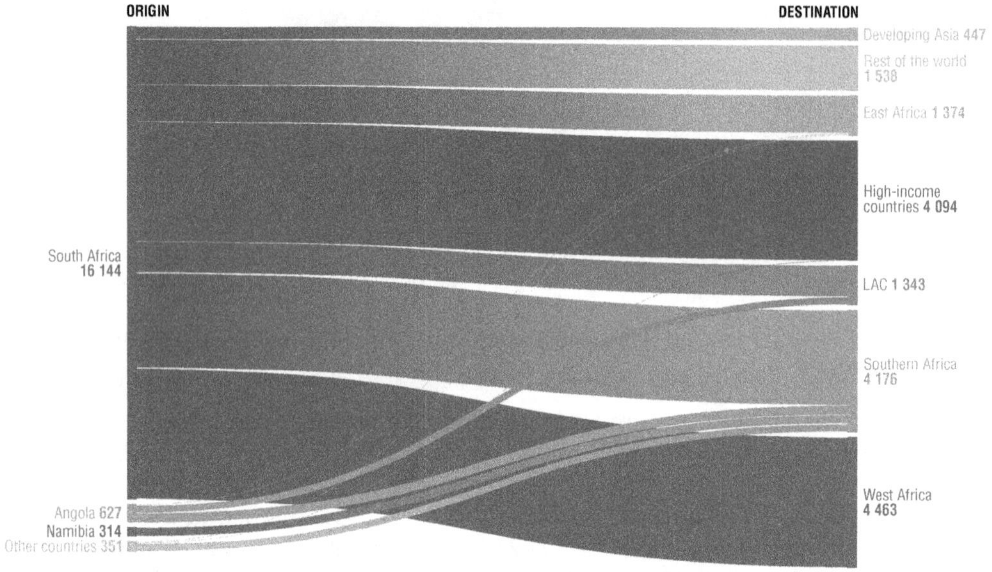

Note: "Other countries" includes Botswana (USD 282 million), Zimbabwe (USD 66 million) and Zambia (USD 3.5 million) while "Rest of the world" includes countries in Central Africa (USD 94 million), North Africa (USD 82 million) and other regions not specified in the chart (USD 1 362 million).
Source: Authors' calculations based on fDi Intelligence (2022), *fDi Markets* (database), www.fdiintelligence.com/fdi-markets.
StatLink https://stat.link/xo32zs

Figure 3.6. **The ten Southern African companies with the highest market capitalisation**

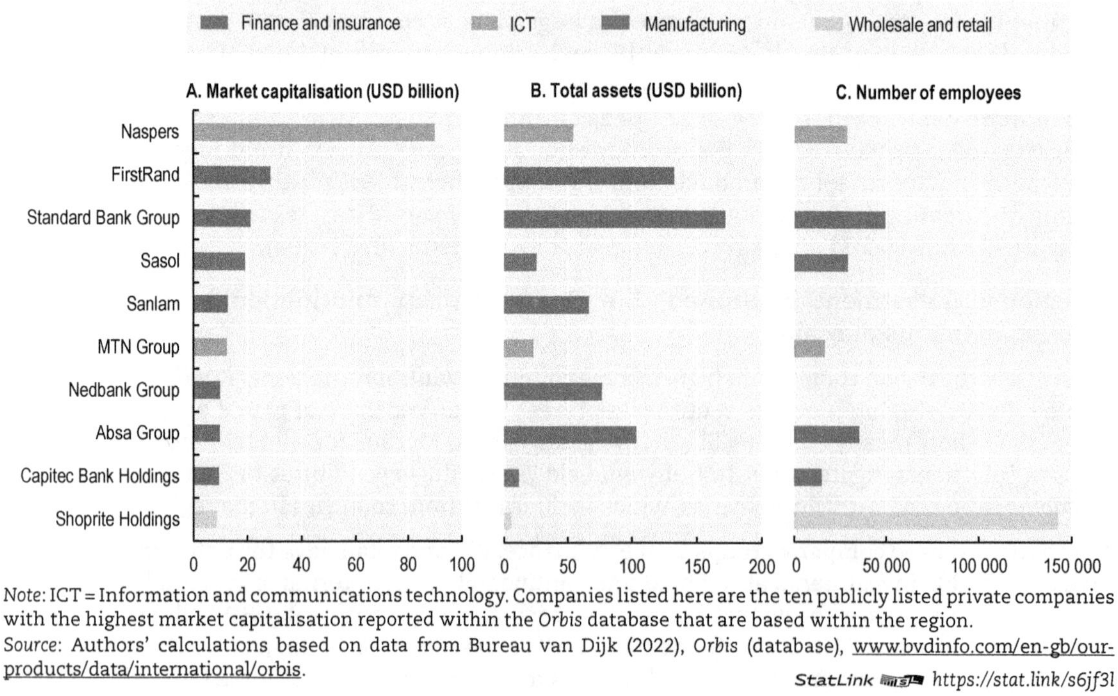

Note: ICT = Information and communications technology. Companies listed here are the ten publicly listed private companies with the highest market capitalisation reported within the *Orbis* database that are based within the region.
Source: Authors' calculations based on data from Bureau van Dijk (2022), *Orbis* (database), www.bvdinfo.com/en-gb/our-products/data/international/orbis.
StatLink https://stat.link/s6jf3l

Investments in Southern Africa's renewable energy potential can generate inclusive and sustainable development

Investments in renewable energy can generate economic, social and environmental development gains in Southern Africa

Southern Africa's renewable energy market is growing fast and holds high potential. Southern Africa accounts for about 60% of Africa's installed solar energy capacity, 40% of the continent's installed wind power and 33% of its renewable hydropower capacity. In 2021, the total renewable electricity installed capacity in the region reached 21.4 gigawatts (GW), representing a 37% increase since 2017.[8] South Africa is leading the region's energy transition with large investments in solar, wind and green hydrogen, which will help reduce the country's high reliance on coal. Mozambique and Zambia are boosting their hydropower capacity. Namibia is investing in the solar, wind and green hydrogen industries. Botswana and Angola are starting solar deployments. The International Renewable Energy Agency estimates technical installable capacities in the region of 908 GW for solar and 53 GW for wind, assuming a 1% land-utilisation factor (IRENA/AfDB, 2022).

The renewable energy sector can become an important source of job creation. In 2021, the renewable energy sector in Southern Africa accounted for about 19% of total renewable energy jobs in Africa.[9] In South Africa, renewable energy technologies provide more jobs in operations and maintenance than fossil fuels (Figure 3.7). Following the country's Renewable Energy Independent Power Producer Procurement Programme, renewable energy jobs doubled from 31 207 in 2016-17 to 63 291 in 2021. However, 75% of these jobs were in the construction sector, which typically provides short-term employment, while only 25% were in more permanent operations and maintenance occupations (IRENA/ILO, 2022; AUC/OECD, 2022). Due to its linkages to other productive sectors, renewable energy investment can create jobs across several industrial sectors (such as the steel, fibreglass and electrical equipment industries) and support services (such as legal, financial and engineering design). According to a recent study, an injection of USD 4 billion into renewable energy production in South Africa can create more than 30 000 jobs by 2030 across the energy value chain (GreenCape, 2021).

Figure 3.7. **Operations and maintenance jobs created per gigawatt hour by energy source in South Africa**

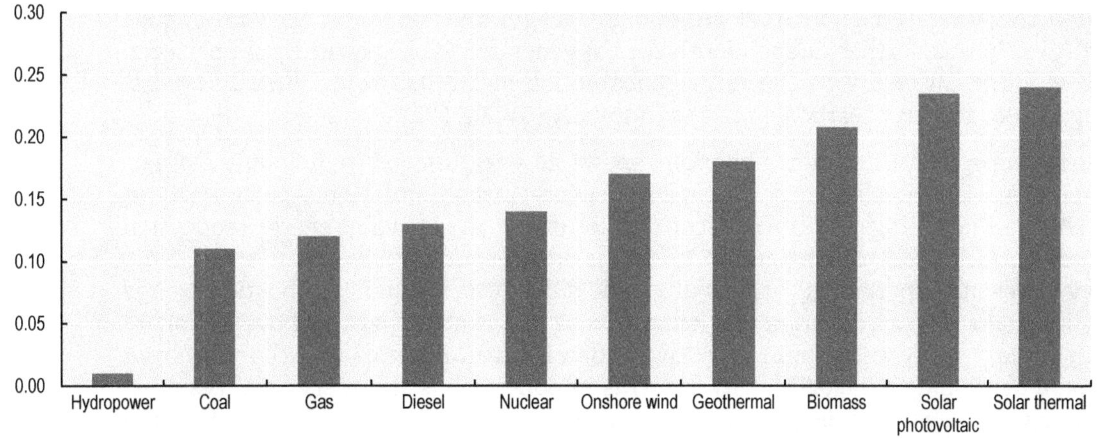

Source: COBENEFITS (2019), *Future Skills and Job Creation through Renewable Energy in South Africa: Assessing the Co-benefits of Decarbonising the Power Sector*, https://www.cobenefits.info/wp-content/uploads/2019/03/COBENEFITS-Study-South-Africa-Employment.pdf.

StatLink https://stat.link/qa7fkn

Southern Africa's energy sector is a major contributor to continental carbon emissions. Greenhouse gas emissions per capita in Southern Africa (2.5 tonnes of CO_2-equivalent per capita) are higher than in Africa as a whole (0.9) and Latin America and the Caribbean (2.1) but lower than in developing Asia (3.6) and high-income countries (9.2) (Figure 3.8). Relative to other African regions, Southern Africa has the largest share of CO_2-equivalent emissions in the energy sector (58.3%) and in electricity and heating (51.3%). Other energy-reliant sectors – such as commercial and public services (49.0%), manufacturing and construction (37.9%), and agriculture and forestry (37.8%) – are also major emitters at the continental level.[10]

Figure 3.8. **Southern Africa's greenhouse gas emissions, tonnes of CO_2-equivalent per capita, 2020**

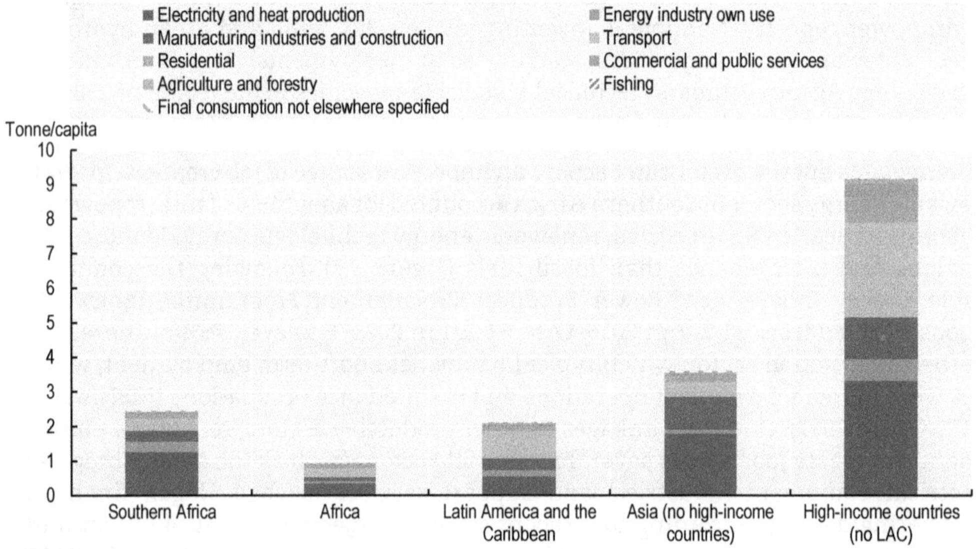

Note: LAC = Latin America and the Caribbean.

Source: OECD (2022c), "GHG Emissions from fuel combustion (summary)", *IEA CO_2 Emissions from Fuel Combustion Statistics: Greenhouse Gas Emissions from Energy* (database), https://doi.org/10.1787/445ec5dd-en.

StatLink https://stat.link/1pcdkw

Renewable energy use in the region is associated with lower CO_2 emissions. Researchers estimate that, in South Africa, a 1% increase in hydroelectricity consumption brings about a 0.52% reduction in CO_2 emissions (Udeagha and Ngepah, 2021). The Kangnas Wind Farm in the Northern Cape (South Africa) generates 513 gigawatt hours per year, which is sufficient to meet the energy consumption of 155 000 South African homes, saving 550 000 tonnes of carbon emissions annually (GWEC, 2022).

The development of non-combustion renewable energies and sustainable biofuels technologies must accelerate to significantly reduce carbon emissions, particularly in South Africa. The average share of non-combustion energy in renewable energy production in Southern Africa (21%) for the period 2010-20 is only second to that of East Africa (35%). However, despite experiencing an upward trend since 2010, the non-combustion energy share in total energy production was only 2% in 2020. That is slightly above the share for Africa as a whole (1.9%) but much lower than in Latin America and the Caribbean (10%) and developing Asia (6.3%).[11] Investments in non-combustion energy sources must be accompanied by the development of sustainable biofuels technologies to significantly reduce carbon emissions (Stafford et al., 2019).

Renewable energy can underpin economic growth through positive returns on investments and resilience to economic shocks. Espoir, Sunge and Bannor (2023) find that a 1% increase in renewable energy consumption in the Southern Africa Development Community (SADC) leads to a bigger impact (0.55%) on economic growth than a 1% increase in non-renewable energy consumption (0.47%). According to Wang et al. (2018), renewable energy's effect on economic growth is positive in countries with lower overall risks and more stable economic environments. Relatedly, a recent report shows higher long-term portfolio returns for renewable energy compared with non-renewable energy in emerging and developing economies, but large return differentials exist vis-à-vis advanced economies (IEA/CCFI, 2021). Investments in renewable energy were also far less impacted by the economic shocks due to COVID-19. For example, while total greenfield FDI capital expenditures to South Africa decreased by 19% between 2018-19 and 2020-21, they increased by 72% in the renewable energy sector.[12]

Unlocking public and private finance in renewable energy can improve energy security

South Africa is driving renewable energy investments in the region, but the country's inefficient coal-based energy system continues to cause socio-economic harm for the most vulnerable. Between 2012 and 2021, the renewable energy share in Southern Africa's total electricity capacity increased from 14.7% to 28.6%, above Africa's average (23%) (Figure 3.9). Southern Africa was the main recipient of renewable energy investment in Africa, having attracted over 40% (USD 22.4 billion) of total flows over the 2010-20 decade. Solar energy projects accounted for 60% of that investment (USD 13.5 billion) followed by wind at 35% (USD 7.8 billion). South Africa, through its Renewable Energy Independent Power Producer Procurement Programme, attracted 85% of the region's renewable energy investment between 2010 and 2020. In 2020, with 5.9 GW, the country represented 57% of Africa's installed solar generation capacity (IRENA/AfDB, 2022). Nonetheless, the country's outdated and mismanaged coal-based energy system continues to generate prolonged electricity blackouts, which are estimated to reduce South Africa's growth by 2 percentage points in 2023, with severe socio-economic consequences for the most vulnerable (Bhargav, Gumbi and Winning, 2023; De Jonghe, 2022).

Figure 3.9. **Installed electricity capacity in Southern Africa, by energy source, 2000-21**

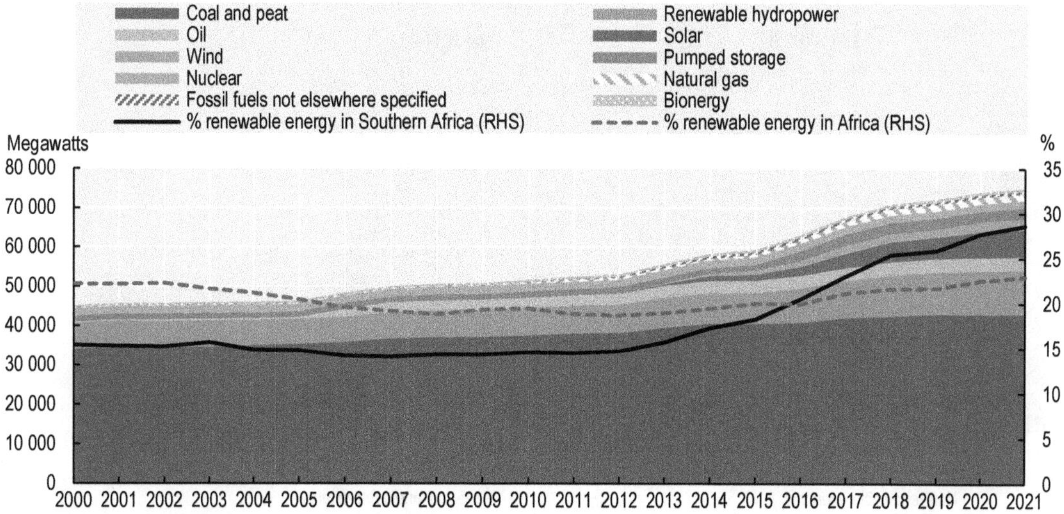

Note: RHS = right-hand side.

Source: Authors' calculations based on IRENA (2022a), IRENASTAT (database), https://pxweb.irena.org/pxweb/en/IRENASTAT/IRENASTAT__Power%20Capacity%20and%20Generation/RECAP_2022_cycle2.px/.

StatLink https://stat.link/loub3s

Public funds could be better allocated to accelerate Southern Africa's clean energy development. In the last decade, non-renewable energy has received more public funds than renewable energy, despite rising investments in solar energy production. Cumulative public investment flows into total energy production amounted to USD 23.9 billion, of which 44% went to the oil sector (in Angola) and only 28% to renewable energy across the region (mostly in hydropower and solar) (Figure 3.10). If Angola invested in its high potential in hydropower, solar and wind energy production, it would achieve its 60% electrification target by 2025 (Ayukegba, 2022). Sonangol – the former Angolan fuel concessionaire – seeks to diversify its energy sources as part of its new Energy Transition strategy, making the transition from an oil and gas company to an energy company (ITA, 2022).

The decreasing costs of renewable energy technologies represent an opportunity to reduce the region's reliance on hydropower and increase resilience to external shocks. The low diversification of public investments into renewables has contributed to a narrow energy technology mix in the region (Figure 3.10). Hydropower has been used in Africa for many decades owing to the presence of the continent's large rivers; the Zambezi River, for example, provides hydropower to Mozambique, South Africa, Zambia and Zimbabwe. In 2021, hydropower represented 15% of Southern Africa's total electricity capacity and 52% of its renewable electricity capacity. In Malawi, Mozambique and Zambia, hydropower's share in electricity generation exceeds 80% (IRENA/AfDB, 2022). Hydropower is increasingly vulnerable to climate shocks, which calls for comprehensive cost-benefit analyses of new and existing facilities (IEA, 2020). At the same time, the falling installation costs of alternative energy technologies such as wind and solar can be an opportunity to invest in diversifying the current renewable energy mix (Figure 3.11). For example, according to the International Energy Agency, "[w]ith further cost declines, Africa has the potential to produce 5 000 megatonnes of hydrogen per year at less than USD 2 per kilogramme – equivalent to global total energy supply today" (IEA, 2022a). Namibia's government recently launched a new strategy aimed at delivering up to 12 tonnes of green hydrogen annually by 2050 and making the country the first green hydrogen provider on the continent. The initiative will require up to USD 190 billion in investments and is expected to create 600 000 jobs by 2040 (Rust and Ossenbrink, 2022).

Figure 3.10. **Cumulative public investment flows into renewable and non-renewable energy in Southern Africa, 2001-20, USD million**

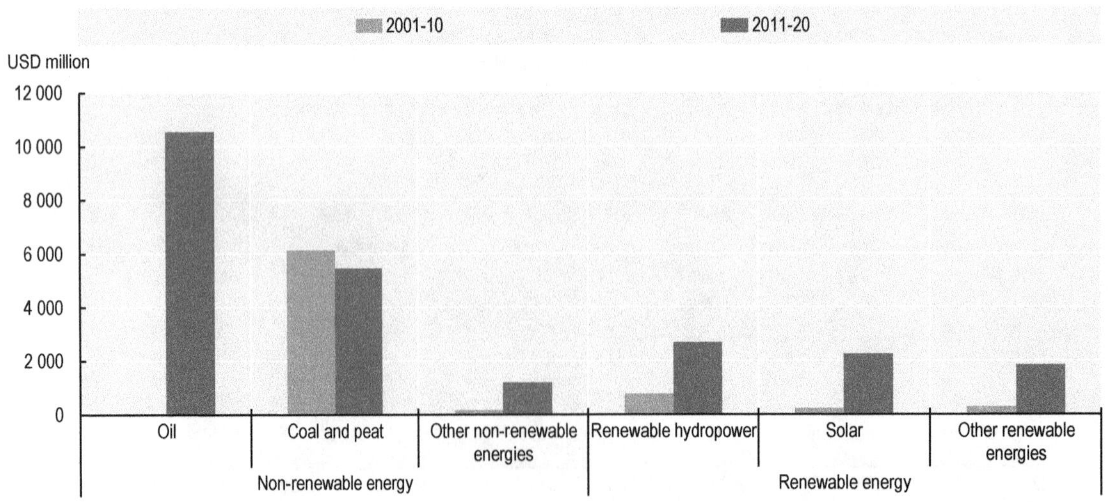

Source: Authors' calculations based on IRENA (2022a), *IRENASTAT* (database), https://pxweb.irena.org/pxweb/en/IRENASTAT/IRENASTAT__Power%20Capacity%20and%20Generation/RECAP_2022_cycle2.px/.

StatLink https://stat.link/3b8ric

Figure 3.11. **Global weighted average total installed costs by energy source, 2010-20**

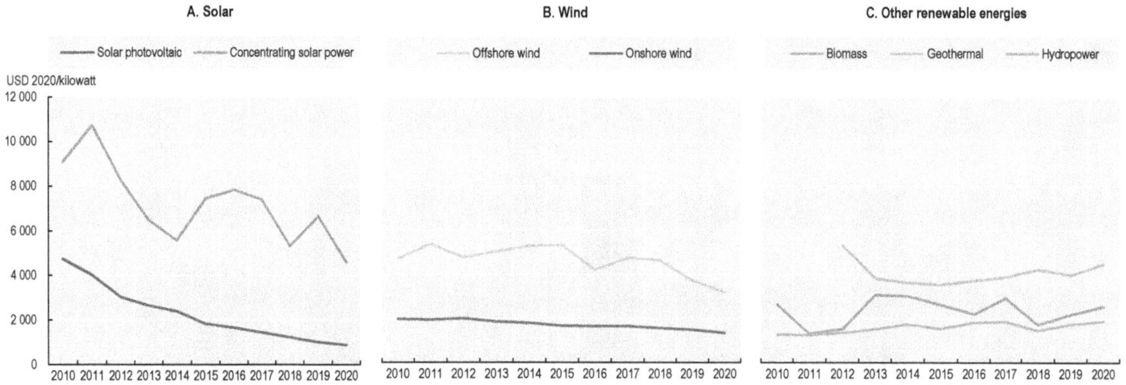

Source: IRENA (2021), *Renewable Power Generation Costs in 2020*, www.irena.org/-/media/Files/IRENA/Agency/Publication/2021/Jun/IRENA_Power_Generation_Costs_2020.pdf?rev=c9e8dfcd1b2048e2b4d30fef671a5b84.

StatLink https://stat.link/kfc7jy

High risks and inefficient public utilities discourage private investment in many countries in the region. Public investment through state-owned enterprises plays a larger role in energy sector investment in Africa than in other world regions, as most of its projects are not able to attract private capital owing to political, legal and economic risks (IEA, 2022a; IRENA/AfDB, 2022; see also Chapters 1 and 5). Estimated operating losses among all African utilities exceeded USD 150 billion in 2020. Attracting private investment requires strengthening the capacity of local energy authorities through better governance, transparent regulations and effective incentives (IEA, 2022a).

A lack of capital market instruments and rigid regulations inhibit investments from large institutional investors based in the region. A recent survey shows that Africa-based institutional investors represent 3.6% of global institutional investors with direct investments in renewable energy projects compared to close to 0% of those with indirect investments in renewable energy funds. Capital market instruments needed for indirect portfolio investments (such as renewable energy funds or green bonds) are less available in African markets (IRENA, 2020). Moreover, rigid regulatory regimes are often identified as major obstacles to pension funds' investment in infrastructure. Botswana, Namibia and South Africa are Africa's largest pension fund markets as a share of GDP (see above and Chapter 1). South Africa's pension system is more advanced in terms of infrastructure finance, while Botswana and Namibia invest less in infrastructure, in part because of more constraining regulations (Sy, 2017).

Scaling up investments in off-grid renewable energy solutions can help reduce the rural-urban divide in energy access

Off-grid renewable energy solutions can increase electricity access in rural areas and create opportunities for small-scale entrepreneurship. On average, 53% of Southern Africa's population had access to electricity over the period 2016-20 compared to 41% in 2001-05, but large differences persist between urban (79%) and rural areas (26%) (Figure 3.12). Significant investments in small-scale and portable off-grid renewable energy solutions can help increase clean energy access in rural areas while creating opportunities for small-scale investors and entrepreneurs. For example, off-grid solutions can enable a shift away from wood and charcoal to cleaner energy sources for cooking (CCA, 2021), with large benefits in terms of reduced air pollution, fewer premature deaths and opportunities for small entrepreneurs (Box 3.1).

Figure 3.12. **Access to electricity in Southern Africa, five-year average share of population by location**

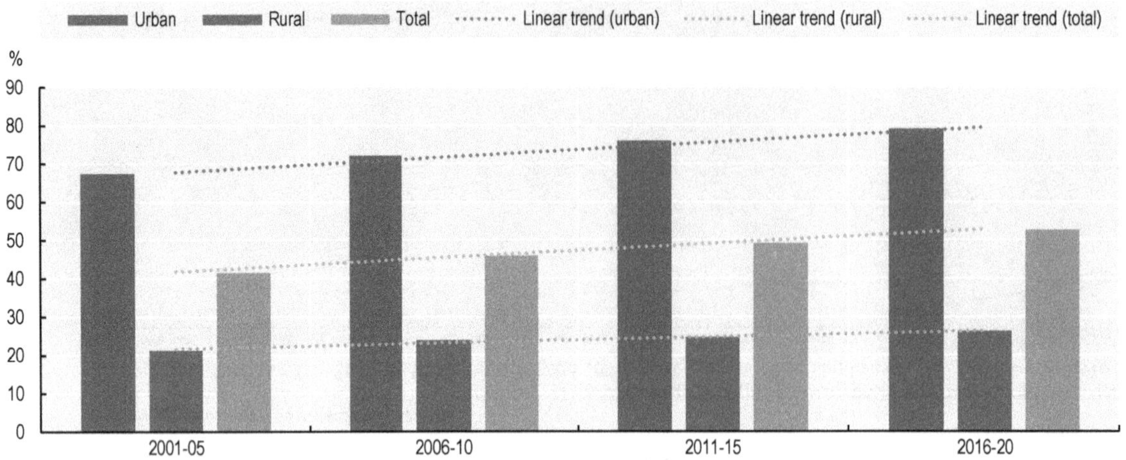

Source: Authors' compilation from World Bank (2022a), *World Development Indicators* (database), https://data.worldbank.org/products/wdi.

StatLink *https://stat.link/62tusv*

Box 3.1. **Access to clean cooking in Southern Africa**

Clean cooking – the use of modern stoves and clean fuels for cooking – is a cross-cutting solution to advance various sustainability objectives such as health and climate protection, affordable energy, and women's empowerment (CCA, n.d.). In Southern African countries excluding South Africa, the estimated welfare cost per capita of premature deaths from household air pollution in 2019 was approximately 2.5 times higher than in South Africa and 1.5 times higher than Africa's average.[13] Eighty-seven per cent of the South African population had access to clean cooking in 2020, compared to an average of 37% in other Southern African countries and 30% in Africa as a whole. Since 2000, the share increased by 31 percentage points in South Africa, compared to an average increase of only 7 percentage points in other Southern African countries over the same period (Figure 3.13).

Box 3.1. **Access to clean cooking in Southern Africa *(continued)***

Figure 3.13. **Share of the population with access to clean cooking in Southern Africa, 2000 and 2020**

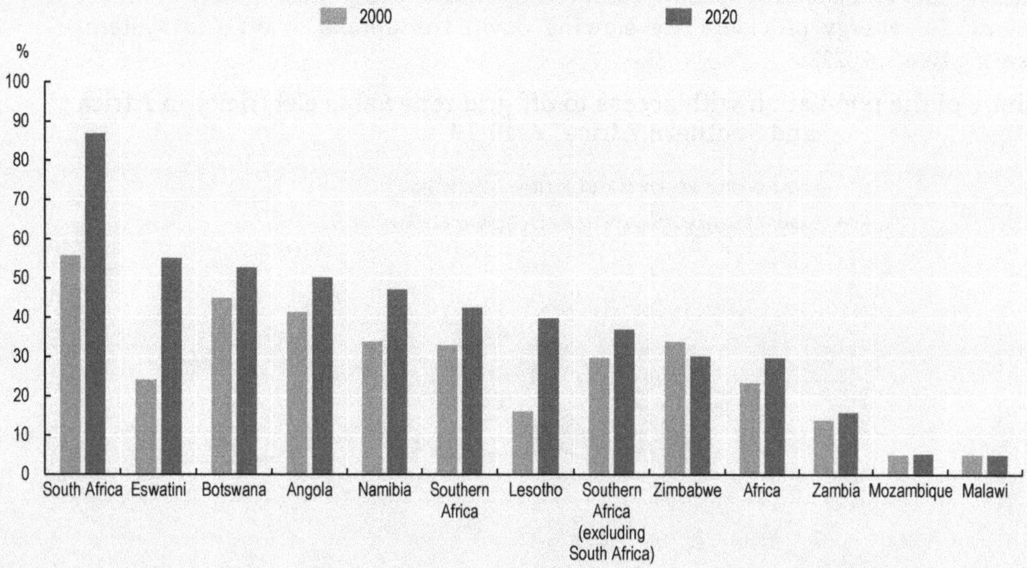

Note: In Malawi and Mozambique, the reported share is less than 5%.

Source: IEA (2021a), *World Energy Outlook-2021*, www.iea.org/reports/world-energy-outlook-2021 based on WHO (2021), *Household Energy Database*, www.who.int/data/gho/data/themes/air-pollution/who-household-energy-db and IEA (2021b), *World Energy Balances 2021* (database), www.iea.org/data-and-statistics/data-product/world-energy-balances.

StatLink https://stat.link/bck2ra

Investing in clean cooking solutions can contribute to social and environmental sustainability while creating opportunities for small entrepreneurs. Mozambique and Zambia provide examples:

- **Mozambique.** In 2012, CleanStar Mozambique (CSM), a small to medium-sized enterprise, designed a profitable ethanol-fuelled cooking stove to reduce indoor air pollution and deforestation from the use of wood and charcoal for cooking. The CSM project involves a value chain starting with a contract farming scheme that generates cash for smallholder farmers who supply raw materials to the CSM plant. Ethanol-based fuel and cook stoves are then produced and distributed. The CSM target of supplying 25 000 stoves annually is expected to prevent the deforestation of 14 000 hectares of forest and save 169 000 tonnes of carbon (CCA, 2022).
- **Zambia.** In 2019, Emerging Cooking Solutions Zambia, a social enterprise, received EUR 1 million in funding from Energy and Environment Partnership Africa to scale up the use of its pay-as-you-go clean cooking stove in Zambia. Each stove saves 4 tonnes of CO_2 and EUR 50 per year while improving family health. The project aims at substituting charcoal with sustainably produced biomass pellets for 20 000 households and is expected to create 100 direct jobs (EEP Africa, 2021).

Due to lower investments into off-grid renewable electricity capacity, access to off-grid electricity in Southern Africa has grown sluggishly compared to the rest of Africa (Figure 3.14). In 2010-20, Southern Africa attracted only 3% (USD 52 million) of total investment in off-grid renewables in Africa. Mozambique and Zambia received 65% of all commitments to the region (IRENA/AfDB, 2022). In South Africa, prohibitive energy and installation costs and a lack of specific contracting solutions (e.g. green power purchase agreements) for energy providers are slowing down the uptake of off-grid systems (Engineering News, 2022).

Figure 3.14. **Share of the population with access to off-grid renewable electricity in Africa and Southern Africa, 2010-19**

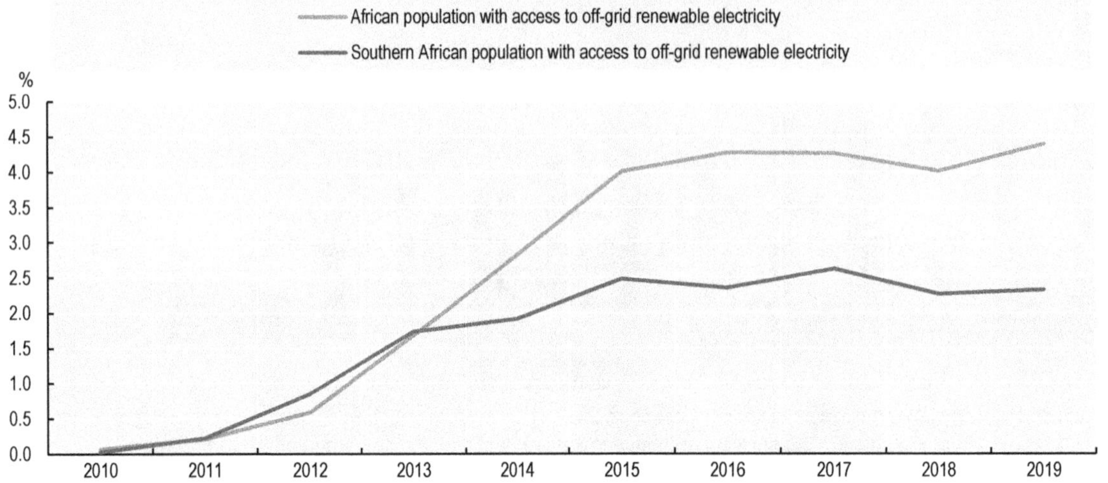

Note: Off-grid renewable electricity includes electricity through mini-grids, solar home systems, solar lights, hydropower, and biogas (IRENA, 2022a).

Source: Authors' calculations based on IRENA (2022a), *IRENASTAT* (database), https://pxweb.irena.org/pxweb/en/IRENASTAT/IRENASTAT__Power%20Capacity%20and%20Generation/RECAP_2022_cycle2.px/ and UN DESA (2022), "World Population Prospects: The 2022 Revision", *United Nations* (database), https://population.un.org/dataportal/data/indicators/67/locations/903/start/2000/end/2030/table/pivotbylocation.

StatLink https://stat.link/71cxl6

Public policies can catalyse investments in Southern Africa's renewable energy sector

Advancing energy security and a just energy transition in Southern Africa requires co-ordinated policies based on national and local contexts. As shown in the previous sections, investments in renewable energies have the potential to enhance energy security and reduce carbon emissions in Southern Africa. They can increase access to clean energy for the most vulnerable, hence generating social and economic returns. However, each country in the region is unique in terms of energy access and production capacity (Figure 3.15). Different policy solutions are needed to address challenges and opportunities at the national level. Taking that into account, this section discusses three priority areas for policy makers to catalyse renewable energy investments in the region:

- **Strengthening regional co-operation to harmonise regulatory frameworks and scale up investments in renewable energy infrastructures.** Closer co-operation among all countries in Southern Africa is key to setting realistic energy transition objectives, assessing investment needs, harmonising regulatory procedures and ensuring effective policy implementation and monitoring. Regional initiatives on cross-border infrastructures can accelerate renewable energy uptake.

- **De-risking private sector investments in renewable energy projects, including through public-private partnerships and development finance.** For example, countries relying on large fossil fuel production capacity and more advanced regulatory frameworks (e.g. Angola and South Africa) can make the best use of public-private partnerships to accelerate the transition towards clean energy production. Through development finance institutions, international co-operation can play a major role in mobilising private capital in more vulnerable countries with significant renewable energy potential, low access to electricity and lower regulatory capacity (e.g. Malawi, Mozambique, Zambia and Zimbabwe).
- **Dedicating specific policies and financing solutions to increase access to clean energy in rural areas.** Less than 15% of the rural population has access to electricity in Angola, Malawi, Mozambique and Zambia (World Bank, 2022a). Dedicated policies and financing instruments can help scale up off-grid renewable energy solutions (e.g. mini-grids or stand-alone systems) and accelerate access to clean energy while creating opportunities for small entrepreneurs in rural areas.

Figure 3.15. **Installed electricity capacity and access to electricity in Southern African countries, 2020-21**

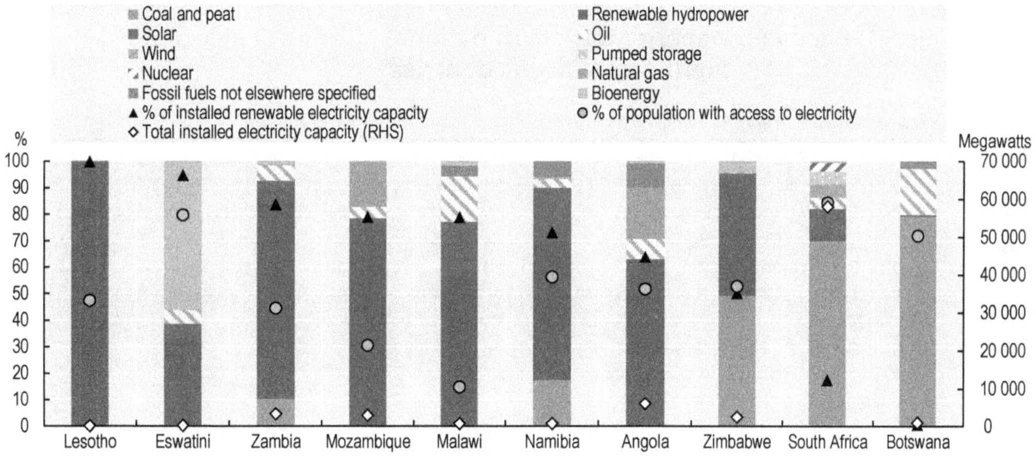

Note: RHS = right-hand side. Data on installed electricity capacity refer to 2021, while data on access to electricity refer to 2020.

Source: Authors' calculations based on IRENA (2022a), *IRENASTAT* (database), https://pxweb.irena.org/pxweb/en/IRENASTAT/IRENASTAT__Power%20Capacity%20and%20Generation/RECAP_2022_cycle2.px/ and World Bank (2022a), *World Development Indicators* (database), https://data.worldbank.org/products/wdi.

StatLink https://stat.link/ojbxf7

Regional co-operation is key to harmonise regulatory frameworks and scale up investments in renewable energy infrastructures

Harmonising regulatory frameworks and implementing action plans at the regional level can help reduce constraints on investment, such as high cost of capital, across countries. As seen in Chapter 1, the weighted average cost of capital for energy projects can be up to seven times higher in Africa than in Europe and North America (IEA, 2022a). Almost all renewable energy policies of countries in Southern Africa (Table 3.1) highlight the high initial cost of capital as the major constraint to renewable energy investment. Other key constraints are inadequate regulatory frameworks on renewable energy procurement, limited funding options and the lack of skilled personnel to design, install and maintain renewable energy systems. Hence, there is a large scope for regional co-ordination on these matters. The 2016-2030 Renewable Energy and

Energy Efficiency Strategy and Action Plan (REEESAP) was adopted in July 2017 in Eswatini by the SADC ministers responsible for energy. The plan provides a framework for SADC member states to develop their own strategies and action plans for renewable energy and energy efficiency, through common strategic guidelines on regulatory and institutional frameworks, financing mechanisms and capacity building, among others. The SADC Centre for Renewable Energy and Energy Efficiency was formed as part of the implementation of the REEESAP to lead the development and implementation of a holistic regional renewable energy and energy efficiency programme (SACREEE, 2019). Ensuring a coordinated and effective implementation of the REEESAP at national level will be crucial to improve the renewable energy investment landscape across the region.

Most Southern African countries have set renewable energy targets within their national policies. Most countries in Southern Africa included renewable energy targets within their national policies, but their timeframes and specifications vary (Table 3.1). All 16 countries in the SADC submitted nationally determined contributions (NDCs) in the context of the Paris Agreement. Of the 16 NDCs, all but Botswana's include renewable energy objectives, but only 11 are quantifiable. The SADC-aggregated quantifiable NDC renewable energy targets amount to 29.6 GW of renewable energy installed capacity by 2030 (Muñoz Cabré et al., 2020).

Table 3.1. **Renewable energy targets in national policies of selected Southern African countries**

Country	Energy transition targets	National policy
Angola	By 2025: 5 000 megawatts (MW) of large hydropower, 500 MW of biomass, 100 MW of solar, 100 MW of wind and 100 MW of small hydropower.	2014 Angola Renewable Energy Strategy
Botswana	By 2025: 100 MW of solar photovoltaics (PV). By 2030: 25% renewable energy.	2007 and 2016 National Development Plans (NDP 10 and 11)
Eswatini	By 2030: 50% renewable energy penetration in the electricity mix.	Energy Masterplan 2034
Mozambique	By 2043: 4 900 ca. MW hydropower, 530-980 MW solar and 150-270 MW wind.	2018 Integrated Master Plan of Energy Infrastructures
Namibia	By 2030: 49% to 70% renewable electricity. Under the 70% scenario: 530 MW of solar PV, 349 MW of wind, 347 MW of hydropower, 150 MW of concentrated solar power and 40 MW of biomass.	2016 National Renewable Energy Policy
South Africa	By 2030: 39.7% of renewable generation capacity, 17 742 MW of wind, 8 288 MW of solar PV, 4 600 MW of hydropower and 600 MW of concentrated solar power.	2019 Integrated Resource Plan for Electricity
Zambia	By 2030: 2 015 MW of grid-connected renewable energy and 1 886 gigawatt hours of off-grid renewable energy provided by PV mini-grids and solar home systems.	Renewable Energy Strategy and Action Plan 2022
Zimbabwe	By 2030: 26.5% renewable electricity, 1 575 MW of solar PV, 275 MW of bioenergy, 150 MW of small hydropower, 100 MW of wind, 250 000 solar water heaters, 8 000 domestic bio-digesters and 288 institutional bio-digesters.	2019 National Renewable Energy Policy

Source: Authors' compilation based on Muñoz Cabré et al. (2020), *Expanding Renewable Energy for Access and Development: The Role of Development Finance Institutions in Southern Africa*, and desk research.

Policy makers can increase cooperation at the regional level to accelerate the transition towards renewable energy. The Southern Africa Power Pool Plan 2017 includes a "high renewables" scenario with 53% renewables in the energy mix by 2040, which has been set as a feasible high-level policy target for the SADC region (Muñoz Cabré et al., 2020). Under this scenario, the SADC region would need an estimated annual investment of USD 2.4 billion to add 2.8 GW per year until 2040. Southern African countries can plan co-ordinated actions, such as the Africa Clean Energy Corridor (Box 3.2), to better attract investment into clean energy regional power pools.

Box 3.2. The Africa Clean Energy Corridor

The Africa Clean Energy Corridor (ACEC) is a regional initiative that aims to accelerate the development of renewable energy and cross-border trade of renewable power within the Eastern Africa Power Pool and Southern African Power Pool. The initiative was launched in 2014 by 19 African countries in Eastern and Southern Africa and has since involved more than 30 governments, regional organisations, development partners and financial institutions. Following the successes achieved in East and Southern Africa, the West Africa Clean Energy Corridor was initiated in 2016.

The ACEC spans five main pillars:

i) Zoning and Resource Assessment to identify sites for renewable power generation in areas with high resource potential and suitable transmission routes
ii) National and Regional Planning to fully consider cost-effective renewable power options
iii) Enabling Frameworks for Investment to open markets and reduce financing costs
iv) Capacity Building to plan, operate, maintain and govern power grids and markets with higher shares of renewable electricity generation
v) Public Information and Awareness Raising on how the corridor can provide secure, sustainable and affordable energy.

By creating a larger regional electricity market, the ACEC could attract investments of up to USD 25 billion per year in generation and USD 15 billion in grid infrastructure by 2030. The full operationalisation of the initiative could meet 40-50% of the power needs in East and Southern Africa by 2030, increase the electricity supply by 2.5 times and cut the annual CO_2 emission level by 310 megatonnes.

Sources: AU/IRENA (n.d.), "Africa Clean Energy Corridor / West Africa Clean Energy Corridor", *Working Document*, https://au.int/sites/default/files/newsevents/workingdocuments/33313-wd-africa_clean_energy_corridor_west_africa_clean_energy_corridor_e.pdf and UNEP (2020), "Clean Energy Corridors in Africa", https://climateinitiativesplatform.org/index.php/Clean_Energy_Corridors_in_Africa.

Public-private partnerships and development finance can help de-risk investments in renewable energies

Public-private partnerships can help mobilise the resources needed for renewable energy projects. The amount of funds needed to decarbonise the energy sector is beyond the financial capacity of governments in the region. For example, South Africa's energy transition requires about USD 250 billion in the next three decades (Reuters, 2022). This translates to USD 8.3 billion per year, which the South African government cannot raise on its own. Public-private partnerships can allow governments to access private sector finance, technology and skill expertise which can lead to a better allocation of risk between public and private entities (World Bank, 2022b). Joint ventures between government-owned public utilities and private players are emerging as effective solutions to finance renewable energy projects across the region. In November 2022, during COP27, SkyPower Global and the government of Zimbabwe signed an agreement on a 500-megawatt solar photovoltaic project worth USD 400 million. The project is expected to generate a USD 1.5 billion stimulus to Zimbabwe's GDP and 14 000 job years (Khaleej Times, 2022).

Countries can use various policy instruments to promote private investments in renewable energy. Examples from Southern Africa appear in Table 3.2.

Table 3.2. **Examples of policy instruments to promote private investments in renewable energy in Southern African countries**

Policy instrument	Brief description	Example
Renewable Energy Feed-in Tariffs (REFiTs)	Long-term contracts with renewable energy producers, typically based on the cost of generating the renewable energy technology (Couture et al., 2010)	In Namibia, an interim Feed-In Tariff programme was announced in September 2015 that aimed at increasing investment in non-hydro sources. Fourteen projects rated at 5 MW were awarded and reached commercial operation within 12 to 24 months (IRENA/AfDB, 2022).
Public tenders	A government power purchase agreement with the successful bidder of a call for tenders to install a certain capacity of renewable energy-based electricity. The final selection follows the evaluation of all offers on the basis of the price and other criteria (IRENA, 2013)	Established in 2010, South Africa's Renewable Energy Independent Power Producer Procurement Programme is a competitive, market-based tender procedure that expedites private sector investment into renewable energy production. As of 2021, the programme had procured and signed agreements with 93 independent power producers for 7.308 GW of total capacity (TaiyangNews, 2021).
Net metering	A billing mechanism that credits solar energy system owners for the electricity they add to the grid (SEIA, n.d.)	Zimbabwe's 2022 regulation on net metering allows households and corporations to feed back up to 5 MW of their excess electricity into the grid (RenewAfrica.Biz, 2022).
Investment incentives	Fiscal, financial and other incentives to promote private sector investment in renewable energies	In 2022, Angola introduced fiscal incentives for companies engaged in the production and sale of renewable energy. The incentives include a 35% reduction of the corporate income tax and a 60% reduction of the investment income tax (PLMJ, 2022).

Source: Authors' compilation based on desk research.

Procurement programmes from independent power producers[14] (IPPs) can promote investments in renewable energy but necessitate effective regulatory frameworks. IPPs are becoming Africa's fastest-growing solution to mobilise private investment in renewable energy. However, these procurement schemes require established regulatory and institutional frameworks and remain concentrated in a few countries. South Africa's Renewable Energy Independent Power Producer Procurement Programme is the headline renewable investment promotion strategy in Southern Africa, attracting 80% of the total IPP investments in the region in 2020 (IRENA/AfDB, 2022).

Shifting from Renewable Energy Feed-in Tariffs (REFiTs) to auctions can reduce the risk related to renewable energy investments for governments, but using both can be more beneficial in some cases. Many countries are shifting away from the use of REFiTs to auctions. REFiTs impose a higher risk to governments and may not reflect a true market price. While auctions are suited for established projects, they transfer most of the risk to investors (IRENA, 2018). South Africa has switched its focus from REFiTs to auctions with significant success (Eberhard and Kåberger, 2016). However, most of its peers in the region do not have the same financial, legal and regulatory environment nor the advantages stemming from the country's size that would give them similar results. Hence, most countries in Southern Africa would benefit from REFiTs as a complement to auctions rather than as a substitute for them.

Net metering can respond to the demand for small-scale renewable energy projects but requires clear regulations at the local level. The growing population and the increasing share of small to medium-sized enterprises in Southern Africa have amplified the demand for small-scale decentralised renewable energy projects. Net metering – which allows the owners of renewable energy systems to receive credit for the energy they add to the grid (SEIA, n.d.) – not only can boost investment in renewables but can also encourage energy efficiency. Namibia and South Africa were the first Southern African countries to use net metering as a renewable energy policy (IFC, 2020b). Research shows that clear national regulations are necessary to prevent challenges related to the management of net metering solutions at the local level (Roux and Shanker, 2018).

Development finance institutions can be instrumental in de-risking renewable energy investments. The COVID-19 pandemic has exacerbated Southern African countries' debt situation, thereby increasing the financial risk of renewable energy investments. Development finance institutions can serve to spearhead the mobilisation of private sector players and institutional investors into renewable energy investments. To address credit and currency risks, among many others, development finance institutions can offer financial instruments such as guarantees for renewable energy projects, co-investments, co-financing and subordinated debts (Masamba et al., 2022; OECD, 2021b). Furthermore, development finance institutions can provide technical support and capacity building to catalyse the development of less risky bankable projects. For example, the World Bank Group's Scaling Solar programme implemented in Zambia in 2015-16 offered a standardised and replicable solar photovoltaics procurement model with significant risk mitigation products that translated into low tariffs and rapid project implementation (IRENA/AfDB, 2022).

Collaborative relationships between institutional investors and development finance providers at the local level can help mobilise capital for investments in renewable energies. The successful mobilisation of private capital for sustainable investments – including from institutional investors – has mostly taken place through collaborative initiatives at the local level, often in the form of strategic investment funds and green banks (Halland et al., 2021). One example is the Climate Finance Facility (CFF) of the Development Bank of Southern Africa (DBSA), launched in 2019 as a specialised lending facility designed to increase private investment in climate-related infrastructure projects (including off-grid power, mini-grids and urban distributed solar systems, energy and water efficiency) in Eswatini, Lesotho, Namibia and South Africa. It is the first example of a green bank applied to an emerging market. The project raised an initial USD 110 million through the DBSA and the United Nations' Green Climate Fund. During its 20-year lifespan, the CFF is expected to generate a reduction of about 30 million tonnes of CO_2-equivalent, save approximately 23 000 jobs through the installation of efficient water systems and reach more than 400 000 indirect beneficiaries (Convergence, 2019).

Dedicated policies and financing solutions can increase access to clean energy in rural areas

Scaling up off-grid and mini-grid renewable energy solutions requires dedicated policies and regulations. Key regulatory issues to address off-grid renewable energy solutions include licensing and permitting requirements (including quality standards), tariff-setting frameworks and the implications of the arrival of the main grid (IRENA, 2016). A growing number of countries in Africa have introduced dedicated mini-grid policies (UNIDO, 2020). Specific policy initiatives have been less prevalent in Southern Africa (IRENA/AfDB, 2022), but some promising exceptions exist, such as in Mozambique (Box 3.3), and could be adapted to other countries in the region.

Box 3.3. **Policy initiatives to scale up off-grid renewable energy projects in Mozambique**

In 2021, only 40% of the population in Mozambique had access to electricity, 36% from the grid and 4% via off-grid projects (AfDB, 2021). The government's target is 100% access by 2030, with 68% of Mozambicans connected to the national grid and 32% accessing energy off-grid (Zitamar, 2022).

In September 2021, the Mozambican government approved a new policy regulating energy provision through off-grid solutions. The policy offers an improved regime

Box 3.3. Policy initiatives to scale up off-grid renewable energy projects in Mozambique *(continued)*

to attract private investments in solar home systems and other standalone energy solutions in rural areas. Besides promoting interest from the private sector, the policy aims to mobilise several existing incentive schemes from international partners (Laakso and Petric, 2022). Two examples of such schemes follow:

- Founded in 2019, BRILHO is a USD 35.5 million programme mandated to catalyse energy access through solar home systems, green mini-grids and improved cooking solutions, to benefit 1.9 million Mozambicans and 17 000 small businesses by 2024. In the first quarter of 2022, the BRILHO programme connected more than 80 000 homes in Mozambique to solar-powered systems (Zitamar, 2022).
- The Beyond the Grid Fund for Africa (BGFA) is an international multi-donor initiative to incentivise energy service providers to scale up innovative sustainable businesses and accelerate access to affordable and clean off-grid energy in peri-urban and rural areas. Launched in 2021, BGFA's second financing round will offer a total of EUR 6.7 million in results-based financing to private off-grid energy providers (Beyond the Grid, 2021).

Source: Authors' compilation.

Supportive policies can help scale up the use of sustainable and affordable biogas in rural areas. Biogas production relies on agricultural waste such as forest and crop residues, and animal manure from rural areas. It is one of the means to reduce the consumption of fossil fuels and contribute to the transition towards a net zero energy system (IEA, 2022c). At the end of 2019, 410 000 Africans were using biogas for residential cooking. Over the past decade, the annual growth rate of biogas production declined continuously until it became negative in 2019. The decline in growth has been attributed to a lack of maintenance, a shortage of feedstock or the upfront initial cost of installing a biodigester (IRENA/AfDB, 2022). Communicating and promoting the use of biogas through low-cost digesters, setting up appropriate policies and institutional frameworks, and offering financing solutions can facilitate the diffusion of biogas technologies and help increase energy security in Southern Africa (Kaifa and Parawira, 2019).

Flexible renewable energy policies can serve clean energy and rural development goals. Reducing the use of spatially blind incentives, introducing a flexible policy framework and taking into account the characteristics and specific needs of rural communities are key policy considerations to promote clean energy access and economic development in rural areas (OECD, 2012). For example, land-use conflicts can often slow down the uptake of renewable energies in rural areas (Groenendaal, 2018). Agrovoltaics – the simultaneous use of areas of land for both solar photovoltaic power generation and agriculture (Dinesh and Pearce, 2016) – can provide innovative solutions to address these conflicts and serve both clean energy and food security objectives. Since 2014, the SUNfarming Food and Energy (F&E) Plant in South Africa undertakes scientific research on food plants and herbs that grow underneath solar modules. Today, the plant facilities are also used to develop joint certified training programmes for local students and to produce healthy food (vegetables, fruit, medicinal herbs) for low-income communities in the area while generating carbon-neutral solar energy (Matich, 2022).

There is a strong case for developing the capacity of local investors and financial intermediaries to engage in much-needed off-grid renewable energy projects. Over the 2007-19 period, investments from developed countries accounted for 85% of commitments to off-grid renewable energy in most African countries (IRENA/CPI, 2020). Launched in June 2019, the Southern African Renewable Energy Investment and Growth Programme is implementing a prototype approach to enable small and medium-sized enterprises in rural areas that are leveraging solar energy to access climate finance, especially local currency financing: the programme is now supporting four participating local financing institutions in Tanzania and three in Zambia to deploy climate finance to green small and medium-sized enterprises (REEEP, n.d.).

Energy communities would benefit from policies that increase local ownership of energy projects. Energy communities are grassroots innovations that diffuse the local production and use of renewable energy at the community level (Hargreaves et al., 2013). A study on energy communities in 46 African countries shows that, overall, these communities are not sufficiently empowered to institute and manage their own energy projects. Currently, ownership of community energy projects is a challenge, as most projects are owned by the government solely or in partnership with elitist groups. Enabling policies are necessary to provide platforms for participatory stakeholder engagement that allow the involvement of citizens in the planning, implementation and management of energy communities (Ambole et al., 2021).

Notes

1. This refers to the geometric average of the 2020, 2021, and 2022 growth rates, or the annualised change between 2019 and 2022.
2. Authors' calculations based on UNCTADstats (2022).
3. Authors' calculations based on OECD (2022b).
4. Impact investing refers to "investments made with the intention to generate positive, measurable social and environmental impact alongside a financial return" (GIIN, 2023).
5. Authors' calculations based on OECD (2021a).
6. Authors' calculations based on fDi Intelligence (2022).
7. Authors' calculations based on Bureau van Dijk (2022). See Annex 1.B in Chapter 1 for methodological information.
8. Authors' calculations based on IRENA (2022a).
9. Authors' calculations based on IRENA (2022b).
10. Authors' calculations based on OECD (2022c).
11. Authors' calculations based on IEA (2022b). Non-combustion energy sources include energy sources reported as renewable within the *International Energy Agency* database but exclude energy sources relying on fuel combustion, such as biofuels and municipal waste. Data reported for Southern Africa do not include Lesotho and Malawi.
12. Authors' calculations based on fDi Intelligence (2022).
13. Authors' calculation based on Roy (forthcoming).
14. "An Independent Power Producer is an entity, which is not a public electricity utility, which owns and or operates facilities to generate electric power for sale to a utility, central government buyer and end users" (SAIPPA, n.d.).

References

AfDB (2021), *Country Priority Plan and Diagnostic of the Electricity Sector – Mozambique*, African Development Bank Group, www.afdb.org/sites/default/files/2021/11/22/mozambique.pdf.

Ambole, A. et al. (2021), "A review of energy communities in sub-Saharan Africa as a transition pathway to energy democracy", *Sustainability*, Vol. 13/4, https://doi.org/10.3390/su13042128.

AU/IRENA (n.d.), "Africa Clean Energy Corridor / West Africa Clean Energy Corridor", *Working Document*, https://au.int/sites/default/files/newsevents/workingdocuments/33313-wd-africa_clean_energy_corridor_west_africa_clean_energy_corridor_e.pdf (accessed 13 February 2023).

AUC/OECD (2022), *Africa's Development Dynamics 2022: Regional Value Chains for a Sustainable Recovery*, AUC, Addis Ababa/OECD Publishing, Paris, https://doi.org/10.1787/2e3b97fd-en.

Ayukegba, V. (14 April 2022), "Angola targets 60% electrification by 2025 driven by renewables", Energy Capital & Power, https://energycapitalpower.com/angola-targets-60-electrification-by-2025-driven-by-renewables/.

Bartz-Zuccala, W. et al. (2022), *Scaling Up Blended Finance in Developing Countries*, OECD, Paris, www.oecd.org/dac/scaling_up_blended_finance_in_developing_countries.pdf.

Beyond the Grid (8 July 2021), "Strong private sector interest in the calls in Mozambique and Uganda", article, https://beyondthegrid.africa/news/strong-private-sector-interest-in-the-calls-in-mozambique-and-uganda/.

Bhargav, A., K. Gumbi and A. Winning (26 January 2023), "South Africa trims rate hikes as power cuts slash growth prospects", *Reuters* article, www.reuters.com/world/africa/south-africas-central-bank-raises-main-lending-rate-725-percent-2023-01-26/.

Bureau van Dijk (2022), *Orbis* (database), www.bvdinfo.com/en-gb/our-products/data/international/orbis (accessed October 2022).

CCA (n.d.), "The Value of Clean Cooking", Clean Cooking Alliance webpage, https://cleancooking.org/the-value-of-clean-cooking/ (accessed 13 February 2023).

CCA (2022), "CleanStar Mozambique", Clean Cooking Alliance Sector Directory webpage, https://cleancooking.org/sector-directory/cleanstar-mozambique/ (accessed 28 November 2022).

CCA (8 January 2021), "Leveraging off-grid solar infrastructure for modern cooking", Clean Cooking Alliance, https://cleancooking.org/news/01-08-2021-leveraging-off-grid-solar-infrastructure-for-modern-cooking/.

COBENEFITS (2019), *Future Skills and Job Creation through Renewable Energy in South Africa: Assessing the Co-benefits of Decarbonising the Power Sector*, Figure 2, p. 12, www.cobenefits.info/wp-content/uploads/2019/03/COBENEFITS-Study-South-Africa-Employment.pdf.

Convergence (2019), *Case Study: Climate Finance Facility*, Green Bank Network, https://greenbanknetwork.org/wp-content/uploads/2019/07/Convergence_Climate_Finance_Facility_Case_Study_2019.pdf.

Couture, T. D. et al. (2010), *A Policymaker's Guide to Feed-in Tariff Policy Design*, NREL, www.nrel.gov/docs/fy10osti/44849.pdf.

De Jonghe, O. (7 September 2022), "The state of renewable energy in South Africa", The Borgen Project blog, https://borgenproject.org/renewable-energy-in-south-africa/.

Dinesh, H. and J. Pearce (2016), "The potential of agrivoltaic systems", *Renewable and Sustainable Energy Reviews*, Vol. 54, pp. 299-308, https://hal.science/hal-02113575/file/The_potential_of_agrivoltaic_systems.pdf.

Eberhard, A. and T. Kåberger (2016), "Renewable energy auctions in South Africa outshine feed-in tariffs", *Energy Science & Engineering*, Vol. 4, https://doi.org/10.1002/ese3.118.

Eckstein, D., V. Künzel and L. Schäfer (2021), *Global Climate Risk Index 2021*, Germanwatch, www.germanwatch.org/sites/default/files/Global%20Climate%20Risk%20Index%202021_2.pdf.

EEP Africa (2021), *Tier 4 Clean-Cooking with Paygo*, Energy and Environment Partnership Trust Fund, https://eepafrica.org/wp-content/uploads/2022/02/2021_EEP_ResultsBrochure_FINAL.pdf.

Engineering News (8 June 2022), "Is going off grid SA's biggest energy myth?", Media Statement, www.engineeringnews.co.za/article/is-going-off-grid-sas-biggest-energy-myth-2022-06-08.

Espoir, D. K., R. Sunge and F. Bannor (2023), "Renewable and non-renewable electricity consumption, economic growth and climate change: Evidence from a panel of selected African countries", *Energy Nexus*, Vol. 9, https://doi.org/10.1016/j.nexus.2022.100165

fDi Intelligence (2022), *fDi Markets* (database), www.fdiintelligence.com/fdi-markets (accessed August 2022).

Gbadamosi, N. (25 January 2023), "How South Africa's energy crisis became an economic crisis", *Foreign Policy*, https://foreignpolicy.com/2023/01/25/south-africa-energy-crisis-corruption-anc/.

GIIN (2023), Impact Investing website, https://thegiin.org/impact-investing/ (accessed 24 February 2023).

GIIN (2020), *Annual Impact Investor Survey*, Global Impact Investing Network, https://thegiin.org/assets/GIIN%20Annual%20Impact%20Investor%20Survey%202020.pdf.

GIIN (2016), *The Landscape for Impact Investing in Southern Africa*, Global Impact Investing Network, https://thegiin.org/assets/documents/pub/Southern%20Africa/GIIN_SouthernAfrica.pdf.

Goel, R. and K. Miyajima (2021), "Analyzing capital flow drivers using the 'at-risk' framework: South Africa's case", *IMF Working Paper*, No. 2021/253, www.imf.org/en/Publications/WP/Issues/2021/10/22/Analyzing-Capital-Flow-Drivers-Using-the-At-Risk-Framework-South-Africas-Case-497224.

GreenCape (2021), *The South African Renewable Energy Master Plan: Emerging Actions Discussion Document*, https://green-cape.co.za/assets/SAREM-Emerging-Actions-Discussion-Doc_20211103_ntt-1.pdf.

Groenendaal, B. (2018), "S.Africa: Land expropriation effects on renewable energy investment", ESI Africa, www.esi-africa.com/top-stories/s-africa-land-expropriation-effects-on-renewable-energy-investment/.

GWEC (2022), *Capturing Green Recovery Opportunities from Wind Power in Developing Economies*, Global Wind Energy Council, https://gwec.net/wp-content/uploads/2022/02/REPORT_Capturing-Green-Recovery-Opportunities-from-Wind-Power-in-Developing-Economies.pdf.

Halland, H. et al. (2021), "Mobilising institutional investor capital for climate-aligned development", *OECD Development Policy Papers*, No. 35, OECD Publishing, Paris, https://doi.org/10.1787/e72d7e89-en.

Hargreaves, T. et al. (2013), "Grassroots innovations in community energy: The role of intermediaries in niche development", *Global Environmental Change*, Vol. 23/5, www.sciencedirect.com/science/article/pii/S0959378013000381.

IEA (2022a), *Africa Energy Outlook 2022*, International Energy Agency, Paris, www.iea.org/reports/africa-energy-outlook-2022.

IEA (2022b), "Renewables Information", *International Energy Agency* (database), www.iea.org/data-and-statistics/data-product/renewables-information (accessed October 2022).

IEA (2022c), "The role of biogas and biomethane in pathway to net zero", *IEA Position Paper*, International Energy Agency, Paris, www.ieabioenergy.com/wp-content/uploads/2022/12/2022_12_12-IEA_Bioenergy_position-paper_Final2.pdf.

IEA (2021a), *World Energy Outlook – 2021*, International Energy Agency, Paris, www.iea.org/reports/world-energy-outlook-2021.

IEA (2021b), "World Energy Balances 2021", *International Energy Agency* (database), www.iea.org/data-and-statistics/data-product/world-energy-balances.

IEA (2020), *Climate Impacts on African Hydropower*, International Energy Agency, Paris, www.iea.org/reports/climate-impacts-on-african-hydropower.

IEA/CCFI (2021), *Clean Energy Investing: Global Comparison of Investment Returns*, International Energy Agency/Centre for Climate Finance & Investment, https://iea.blob.core.windows.net/assets/ef1d6b50-66a6-478c-990e-ee227e2dd89b/Clean_Energy_Investing_-_Global_Comparison_of_Investment_Returns.pdf.

IFC (2020a), *Sustainable Finance Practices in South African Retirement Funds: Opportunities to Unlock Investment in Green and Climate Finance and Support a Resilient Economy*, International Finance Corporation, Washington, DC, www.ifc.org/wps/wcm/connect/93d586c6-fe64-439e-907a-d067e640e8ec/South+AfricaRetirementFunds-SustainableFinance040221.pdf?MOD=AJPERES&CVID=nu3gl6v.

IFC (2020b), *Regulatory and Tariff Review for Distributed Generation in the Commercial and Industrial Sectors in Southern Africa*, International Finance Corporation, Washington, DC, www.ifc.org/wps/wcm/connect/090c58a2-2b98-482e-8c6d-b5931ed793e2/202006-Regulatory-Tariff-Review-Southern-Africa.pdf?MOD=AJPERES&CVID=nbDqlVa.

IMF (2023a), *World Economic Outlook Database*, April 2023 Edition, International Monetary Fund, www.imf.org/en/Publications/WEO/weo-database/2023/April (accessed April 2023).

IMF (2023b), "List of LIC DSAs for PRGT-eligible countries", International Monetary Fund, www.imf.org/external/pubs/ft/dsa/dsalist.pdf.

IMF (2022a), *World Economic Outlook Database*, October 2022 Edition, International Monetary Fund, www.imf.org/en/Publications/WEO/weo-database/2022/October (accessed October 2022).

IMF (2022b), *Balance of Payments and International Investment Position Statistics (BOP/IIP)* (database), International Monetary Fund, https://data.imf.org/?sk=7A51304B-6426-40C0-83DD-CA473CA1FD52 (accessed 22 November 2022).

IMF (2022c), *Investment and Capital Stock Dataset (ICSD) (database)*, https://data.imf.org/?sk=1CE8A55F-CFA7-4BC0-BCE2-256EE65AC0E4 (accessed October 2022).

IRENA (2022a), "Installed renewable electricity capacity (MW) by region/country/area, technology and year", *IRENASTAT* (database), https://pxweb.irena.org/pxweb/en/IRENASTAT/IRENASTAT__Power%20Capacity%20and%20Generation/RECAP_2022_cycle2.px/ (accessed October 2022).

IRENA (2022b), "Renewable Energy Employment by Country", *Statistics Data* (database), www.irena.org/Data/View-data-by-topic/Benefits/Renewable-Energy-Employment-by-Country (accessed February 2023).

IRENA (2021), *Renewable Power Generation Costs in 2020*, International Renewable Energy Agency, Abu Dhabi, www.irena.org/-/media/Files/IRENA/Agency/Publication/2021/Jun/IRENA_Power_Generation_Costs_2020.pdf?rev=c9e8dfcd1b2048e2b4d30fef671a5b84

IRENA (2020), *Mobilising Institutional Capital for Renewable Energy*, International Renewable Energy Agency, Abu Dhabi, www.irena.org/-/media/Files/IRENA/Agency/Publication/2020/Nov/IRENA_Mobilising_Institutional_Capital_2020.pdf.

IRENA (2018), *Renewable Energy Auctions: Cases from Sub-Saharan Africa*, International Renewable Energy Agency, Abu Dhabi, www.irena.org/-/media/Files/IRENA/Agency/Publication/2018/Apr/IRENA_Auctions_Sub-Saharan_Africa_2018.pdf.

IRENA (2016), *Policies and Regulations for Private Sector Renewable Energy Mini-grids*, International Renewable Energy Agency, Abu Dhabi, www.irena.org/-/media/Files/IRENA/Agency/Publication/2016/IRENA_Policies_Regulations_minigrids_2016.pdf?rev=1fbca1c70aad4b31b49cc7cd96f06e92.

IRENA (2013), *Renewable Energy Auctions in Developing Countries*, https://ppp.worldbank.org/public-private-partnership/library/renewable-energy-auctions-developing-countries-irena-2013.

IRENA/AfDB (2022), *Renewable Energy Market Analysis: Africa and Its Regions*, International Renewable Energy Agency and African Development Bank, Abu Dhabi and Abidjan, www.irena.org/-/media/Files/IRENA/Agency/Publication/2022/Jan/IRENA_Market_Africa_2022.pdf?rev=bb73e285a0974bc996a1f942635ca556.

IRENA/CPI (2020), *Global Landscape of Renewable Energy Finance 2020*, International Renewable Energy Agency, Abu Dhabi, www.irena.org/-/media/Files/IRENA/Agency/Publication/2020/Nov/IRENA_CPI_Global_finance_2020.pdf?rev=7b096feb04e7473abdd0f2425ee71036.

IRENA/ILO (2022), *Renewable Energy and Jobs: Annual Review 2022*, International Renewable Energy Agency/International Labour Organization, Abu Dhabi/Geneva, www.irena.org/publications/2022/Sep/Renewable-Energy-and-Jobs-Annual-Review-2022.

ITA (2022), "Angola Energy Transition", webpage, International Trade Administration, www.trade.gov/market-intelligence/angola-energy-transition (accessed 13 February 2023).

Kaifa, J. and W. Parawira (2019), "A study of the current state of biogas production in Zimbabwe: Lessons for Southern Africa", *Advances in Biotechnology & Microbiology*, Vol. 13/3, Juniper Publishers, Irvine, https://juniperpublishers.com/aibm/pdf/AIBM.MS.ID.555865.pdf.

Khaleej Times (17 November 2022), "SkyPower inks solar climate deal with Zimbabwe", article, www.khaleejtimes.com/business/skypower-inks-solar-climate-deal-with-zimbabwe.

Kozul-Wright, A. (19 February 2023), "Year of war in Ukraine left developing nations picking up pieces", *Al Jazeera* article, www.aljazeera.com/economy/2023/2/19/a-year-of-war-in-ukraine-has-left-developing-countries-picking-up-pieces.

Laakso, M. and S. Petric (23 May 2022), "An increased role for private sector: Mozambique's new regulatory policy in the off-grid energy sector", Brookings, www.brookings.edu/blog/africa-in-focus/2022/05/23/an-increased-role-for-private-sector-mozambiques-new-regulatory-policy-in-the-off-grid-energy-sector/.

Masamba, M. et al. (2022), *Renewable Energy Transitions in a Period of Debt Distress in Southern Africa: The Role of Development Finance Institutions*, SADC Development Finance Resource Centre, www.bu.edu/gdp/files/2022/06/GDP_SADC_Report_2022_EN_FIN.pdf.

Matich, B. (6 August 2022), "The long read: Farming the southern sun", PV Magazine, www.pv-magazine-india.com/2022/08/06/the-long-read-farming-the-southern-sun/.

Moreira da Silva, J. (3 November 2021), "Leapfrogging to green: The world's energy transition depends on support to developing countries", The Forum Network, www.oecd-forum.org/posts/leapfrogging-to-green-the-world-s-energy-transition-depends-on-support-to-developing-countries.

Muñoz Cabré M. et al. (2020), *Expanding Renewable Energy for Access and Development: The Role of Development Finance Institutions in Southern Africa*", Global Development Policy Center, Boston University, Boston, www.bu.edu/gdp/files/2020/11/GDP_SADC_Report_EN_Nov_16.pdf.

OECD (2022a), "Aid (ODA) disbursements to countries and regions", *OECD.Stat* (database), https://stats-1.oecd.org/Index.aspx?DataSetCode=TABLE2A (accessed October 2022).

OECD (2022b), "Mobilisation", *OECD.Stat* (dataset), https://stats.oecd.org/Index.aspx?DataSetCode=DV_DCD_MOBILISATION (accessed December 2022).

OECD (2022c), "GHG Emissions from fuel combustion (summary)", *IEA CO2 Emissions from Fuel Combustion Statistics: Greenhouse Gas Emissions from Energy* (database), https://doi.org/10.1787/445ec5dd-en (accessed 3 September 2022).

OECD (2021a), *OECD Global Pension Statistics* (database), https://doi.org/10.1787/pension-data-en (accessed October 2022).

OECD (2021b), "De-risking institutional investment in green infrastructure: 2021 progress update", *OECD Environment Policy Papers*, No. 28, OECD Publishing, Paris, https://doi.org/10.1787/357c027e-en.

OECD (2019), *Aligning Development Co-operation and Climate Action: The Only Way Forward*, The Development Dimension, OECD Publishing, Paris, https://doi.org/10.1787/5099ad91-en.

OECD (2012), *Linking Renewable Energy to Rural Development*, OECD Green Growth Studies, OECD Publishing, Paris, https://doi.org/10.1787/9789264180444-en.

PLMJ (2022), "Angola: Tax Benefits Code", News, www.plmj.com/xms/files/03_Novidades_legislativas/2022/04_abril/N_Colab_RVA-PLMJ_Tax_Benefits_Code.pdf.

REEEP (n.d.), "Southern African Renewable Energy Investment and Growth Programme (SOARING)", Renewable Energy and Energy Efficiency Partnership webpage, www.reeep.org/southern-african-renewable-energy-investment-and-growth-programme-soaring.

RenewAfrica.Biz (31 March 2022), "Zimbabwe: Up to 5MW can now be fed to the grid through net metering", article, https://renewafrica.biz/regional-news/southern-africa/zimbabwe-up-to-5mw-can-now-be-fed-to-the-grid-through-net-metering/.

Reuters (26 May 2022), "S.Africa needs $250 bln over three decades for clean energy transition – report", article, www.reuters.com/business/sustainable-business/safrica-needs-250-bln-over-three-decades-clean-energy-transition-report-2022-05-26/.

Roux, A. and A. Shanker (2018), *Net Metering and PV Self-consumption in Emerging Countries*, International Energy Agency, https://iea-pvps.org/wp-content/uploads/2020/01/T9_NetMeteringAndPVDevelopmentInEmergingCountries_EN_Report.pdf.

Roy, R. (forthcoming), "Africa's developmental path as a solution to the problem of air pollution in Africa", background paper for *Africa's Development Dynamics 2023*.

Rust, J. and L. Ossenbrink (12 February 2022), "Germany eyes Namibia's green hydrogen", *Deutsche Welle article*, https://p.dw.com/p/4KPay.

SACREEE (2019), "REEESAP – Southern Africa Renewable Energy and Energy Efficiency Strategy and Action Plan", SADC Centre for Renewable Energy and Energy Efficiency Publication, www.sacreee.org/document/reeesap-southern-africa-renewable-energy-and-energy-efficiency-strategy-and-action-plan.

SAIPPA (n.d.), "What does SAIPPA do?", South African Independent Power Producers Association webpage, www.saippa.org.za/ (accessed 13 February 2023).

SEIA (n.d.), "Net Metering", Solar Energy Industries Association webpage, www.seia.org/initiatives/net-metering (accessed 13 February 2023).

Stafford, W. H. L. et al. (2019), "Biofuels technology development in Southern Africa", *Development Southern Africa*, Vol. 36/2, Taylor & Francis Group, London, https://doi.org/10.1080/0376835X.2018.1481732.

Sy, A. N. R. (2017), *Leveraging African Pension Finds for Financing Infrastructure Development*, The Brookings Institute, www.brookings.edu/wp-content/uploads/2017/03/global_20170314_african-pension-funds.pdf.

TaiyangNews (29 October 2021), "2.6 GW renewable energy capacity for South African auction", article, https://taiyangnews.info/markets/south-africa-concludes-reipppp-round-5/.

Udeagha, M. and N. Ngepah (2021), "Disaggregating the environmental effects of renewable and non-renewable energy consumption in South Africa: Fresh evidence from the novel dynamic ARDL simulations approach", *Economic Change and Restructuring*, Vol. 55, https://doi.org/10.1007/s10644-021-09368-y.

UN DESA (2022), "World Population Prospects: The 2022 Revision", *United Nations* (database), United Nations Department of Economic and Social Affairs, New York, https://population.un.org/dataportal/data/indicators/67/locations/903/start/2000/end/2030/table/pivotbylocation (accessed October 2022).

UNCTAD (2022a), *World Investment Report 2022*, United Nations Publishing, New York, https://unctad.org/webflyer/world-investment-report-2022.

UNCTAD (2022b), *The Impact on Trade and Development of the War in Ukraine*, https://unctad.org/system/files/official-document/osginf2022d1_en.pdf.

UNCTAD (2021), *World Investment Report 2021*, United Nations Publishing, New York, https://unctad.org/webflyer/world-investment-report-2021.

UNCTADstats (2022), *Handbook of Statistics* (database), https://unctadstat.unctad.org/EN/ (accessed October 2022).

UNEP (2020), "Clean Energy Corridors in Africa", Climate Initiatives Platform webpage, United Nations Environment Programme, https://climateinitiativesplatform.org/index.php/Clean_Energy_Corridors_in_Africa.

UNIDO (2020), *Clean Energy Mini-Grid Policy: Development Guide*, United Nations Industrial Development Organisation, www.unido.org/sites/default/files/files/2021-03/CEMG_Development_Guide_EN.pdf.

Ver Angola (30 January 2023), "Fitch Solutions: withdrawal of fuel subsidies in Angola is the biggest risk to stability", article, www.verangola.net/va/en/012023/Energy/34233/Fitch-Solutions-withdrawal-of-fuel-subsidies-in-Angola-is-the-biggest-risk-to-stability.htm.

Wang, Q. et al. (2018), "Renewable energy and economic growth: New insight from country risks", *Energy*, Vol. 238, www.sciencedirect.com/science/article/pii/S0360544221022660.

WHO (2021), "Household Energy Database", *World Health Organisation* (database), www.who.int/data/gho/data/themes/air-pollution/who-household-energy-db.

World Bank (2022a), *World Development Indicators* (database), https://data.worldbank.org/products/wdi (accessed 12 April 2022).

World Bank (2022b), "Public-Private Partnerships – Overview", webpage, www.worldbank.org/en/topic/publicprivatepartnerships/overview (accessed 13 February 2023).

World Bank-KNOMAD (2022), *Remittances* (database), The Global Knowledge Partnership on Migration and Development (KNOMAD), World Bank, www.knomad.org/data/remittances (accessed 19 December 2022).

Zitamar (22 December 2022), "Mozambique looks to off-grid systems to provide energy for all", article, https://zitamar.com/mozambique-looks-to-off-grid-systems-to-provide-energy-for-all/#:~:text=In%20the%20first%20quarter%20of,energy%20to%20meet%20household%20needs.

Chapter 4

Investing in natural ecosystems for Central Africa's sustainable development

This chapter focuses on mobilising sustainable investment in Central Africa's nine countries [Burundi, Cameroon, the Central African Republic (CAR), Chad, the Republic of the Congo (Congo), the Democratic Republic of the Congo (DRC), Equatorial Guinea, Gabon and São Tomé and Príncipe]. It analyses the region's financial inflows and considers how they are allocated to sustainable activities that promote regional integration. It then proposes a case study on the potential monetisation of natural ecosystems to attract investment and help transform production in the region. It provides a baseline study of natural ecosystems and existing monetisation mechanisms, before analysing the main challenges facing their development. Finally, this chapter proposes public policies to quantitatively and qualitatively increase the monetisation of natural ecosystems in Central Africa.

IN BRIEF

The high potential of Central Africa's natural ecosystems should make it possible to increase sustainable investment in local economies. Monetising the ecosystem services they provide – such as carbon sequestration by forests, estimated at more than USD 344 trillion – could leverage more financing for sustainable development.

Despite this potential, Central African countries are struggling to extract value from their natural capital. In 2019-20, they received USD 1.5 billion, i.e. just 5.3% of the climate finance allocated to the continent and 0.2% of global climate finance. Technical constraints at the local level and weak institutional and governance frameworks are some of the factors hindering local governments' ability to establish effective mechanisms for monetising natural ecosystems.

National, regional and international actors should consider three priority actions to increase the monetisation of natural ecosystems: 1) improve natural capital accounting in Central Africa to better inform investors and stakeholders; 2) establish institutional frameworks adapted to the monetisation of ecosystems; and 3) promote innovative financing mechanisms in consultation with community, political and financial actors.

Central Africa

Central Africa attracts less sustainable investments than other African regions

Greenfield FDI inflows

-23%

2012-16 — 2017-22

due to a 67% decrease in flows in the extractive sector

In 2019-20, **Central African** *countries received USD* **1.5 billion** *in climate finance*

or 5.3% of climate finance towards **Africa**

Central Africa accounts for **35%** of the continent's forest area

or 5.5% of the world's forest area

61% of the continent's biomass carbon stock is in Central Africa

or 11% of the global stock

Multiple financial mechanisms enable natural ecosystems monetisation

Carbon credits

Value of the carbon currently sequestered in Central Africa = USD 344 trillion

or 29% of total world wealth in 2018

Ecotourism

950 000km² - roughly 18% of land and 8% of marine area in the region are protected

more than the African and world average

What's next?

- **Improve natural capital accounting** to better inform investors and stakeholders
- **Establish institutional frameworks** for the monetisation of natural ecosystems
- **Ensure local ownership** when developing innovative financing mechanisms

Central Africa regional profile

Figure 4.1. Components of economic growth and sources of financing in Central Africa

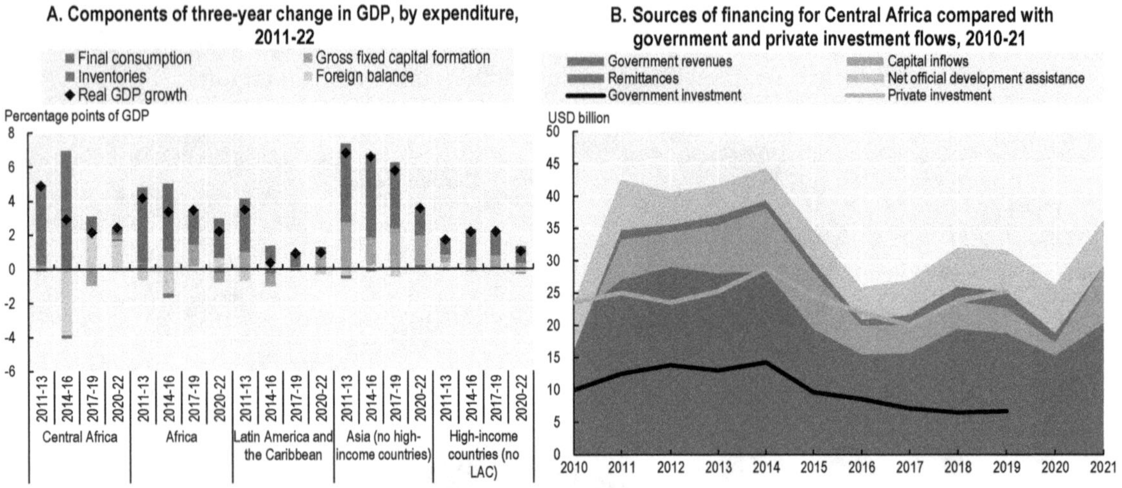

Note: The components of growth in gross domestic product (GDP) are calculated on an annual basis using real annual GDP growth to estimate the increase in real USD. Aggregate figures are calculated by taking the average of national figures weighted by GDP in PPP (purchasing power parity) dollars. The components of three-year change in GDP were calculated by taking the difference between the geometric average of real annual GDP growth over the period and real GDP growth when each component is set to zero for the individual years. Foreign balance is the difference between imports and exports. Imports make a negative contribution negatively to GDP. "High-income countries" refers to countries outside of Latin America and the Caribbean that are classified as "high-income" according to the World Bank's country and lending groups. Government revenues include all government tax and non-tax revenues, less debt service and grants received. Capital inflows include foreign direct investment (FDI), portfolio investment and other investment inflows reported by the International Monetary Fund (IMF) on an asset/liability basis. Capital inflows should be interpreted with caution as some of the figures for 2021 and for portfolio inflows may be missing.

Source: Authors' calculations based on IMF (2022a), *World Economic Outlook, October 2022* (database) www.imf.org/en/Publications/WEO/weo-database/2022/October; (OECD, 2022a), *OECD Development Assistance Committee* (database), https://stats-1.oecd.org/Index.aspx?DataSetCode=TABLE2A; World Bank (2022a), *World Development Indicators* (database), https://data.worldbank.org/products/wdi; IMF (2022b), *Balance of Payments and International Investment Position Statistics (BOP/IIP)* (database), https://data.imf.org/?sk=7A51304B-6426-40C0-83DD-CA473CA1FD52; IMF (2022c), *Investment and Capital Stock Dataset (ICSD)* (database), https://data.imf.org/?sk=1CE8A55F-CFA7-4BC0-BCE2-256EE65AC0E4; and World Bank-KNOMAD (2022), *Remittances* (database), www.knomad.org/data/remittances.

StatLink https://stat.link/dm75np

Figure 4.2. Greenfield foreign direct investment flows to Central Africa by activity, source and destination, 2017-22

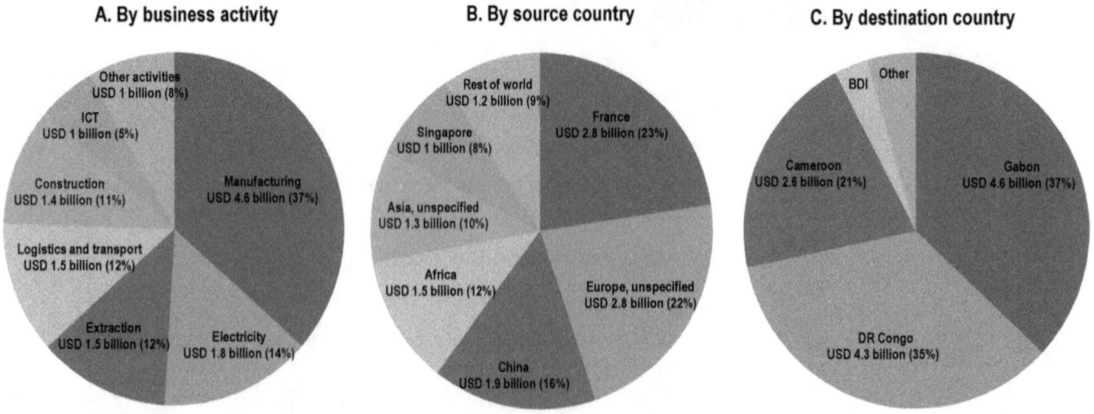

Note: The fDi Markets database is used only for comparative analysis. Actual investment amounts should not be inferred, as fDi Markets data are based on upfront announcements of investment projects, including a share of projects that do not actually materialise. ICT = information and communications technology. BDI = Burundi.

Source: Authors' calculations based on fDi Intelligence (2022), *fDi Markets* (database), www.fdiintelligence.com/fdi-markets.

StatLink https://stat.link/6k4eua

Despite its unique potential, Central Africa receives fewer sustainable investments than other African regions

Financial flows must be enhanced to ensure sustainable development in Central Africa

Investment has contributed little to Central Africa's growth since the 2010s. The region's strong population growth may in part explain the significant consumption-led growth over the 2011-13 and 2014-16 periods (Figure 4.1). However, between 2015 and 2016, falling oil prices upset the balance between these different components of growth. The trade balance had a negative effect on growth in 2015 when the value of Central Africa's oil exports fell suddenly, and then contributed positively when exports slowly bounced back. A 32% decline in public investment and 14% decline in private investment (the largest on the continent) also followed the 2015 price shock. Investment did not return to its previous levels until 2019 and, as a result, gross fixed capital formation had a negative effect on GDP growth during the 2017-19 period.

The declining extractive sector (due to lower oil prices) has been a major factor in reducing investment in the region. Total capital inflows (inflows of FDI, portfolio investments and other types of investment, Figure 4.1) averaged USD 7.5 billion between 2011 and 2015 but averaged only USD 3.8 billion between 2016 and 2020. Nevertheless, Central African economies remain heavily dependent on extractive industries, particularly oil production, whose 2015 price drop was followed not only by a decline in GDP growth, but also by a 59% decline in new investment projects between 2011-15 and 2016-21.

The COVID-19 pandemic has weakened public finances in most Central African countries. Prior to the COVID-19 pandemic, government revenue mobilisation remained relatively low following the 2015 shock (and subsequent 30% decline). According to an IMF and World Bank debt sustainability analysis in February 2023, most Central African countries were either experiencing debt distress (Congo and São Tomé and Príncipe) or at high risk of debt distress (Burundi, Cameroon, the Central African Republic and Chad) (IMF/World Bank, 2023). In 2020, the region's countries faced an average increase in general government gross debt of 5.5 percentage points of GDP (from 39.9% to 45.3%) as a result of the COVID-19 pandemic. In 2022, most Central African countries continued to be classified as "fragile" contexts, with the exception of Gabon and São Tomé and Príncipe (OECD, 2022b). According to the IMF, however, in 2023 total revenues for Central African countries are expected to increase by 41% from their 2019 level, which could help improve the situation.

The rise in oil prices is having a mixed impact on the region's economies. Oil prices reached a ten-year high in July 2022, increasing the value of oil exports by 6 percentage points of Central Africa's GDP. Oil prices are expected to remain high over the next few years, which could lead to an upturn in investment in Africa in the short to medium term (World Bank, 2022b). Reinvestment in fossil fuels, however, would have negative environmental consequences and hinder sustainable development in the region. Moreover, the effects of this price increase have been mixed. They had positive impacts for the majority of net oil-exporting Central African countries (Cameroon, Chad, Congo, Equatorial Guinea and Gabon), but negative effects on the economies of the other four countries.

Central Africa remains vulnerable to a number of other risks beyond oil prices. Recent international conflicts are disrupting food supply chains in the region. Burundi, Congo and the Democratic Republic of the Congo, for example, receive the majority of their wheat imports from Russia and Ukraine (UNCTAD, 2022). Climate change is also increasing instability and exacerbating conflict in a region whose development is already hampered by its fragility (National Intelligence Council, 2021).

Investment is inadequately allocated to sustainable activities

New investment projects have shifted away from extractive industries towards manufacturing, power and logistics, but the overall amounts have fallen sharply. The total value of new investment projects in Central Africa fell by 23% between 2012-16 and 2017-22, mainly due to a 67% decline in flows in the extractive sector (Figure 4.3). Much of this decline predated the COVID-19 crisis: total new investment project flows to Central Africa were 40% higher in 2020 and 2021 than in 2017-18. Investment-related job creation also declined, going from 2.6 to 2.3 jobs per million USD invested. Even in the manufacturing industry, the ratio of jobs dropped from 4.2 to 3.8 jobs per million USD invested.

Figure 4.3. **Job intensity of investment flows in new projects in Central Africa, by activity**

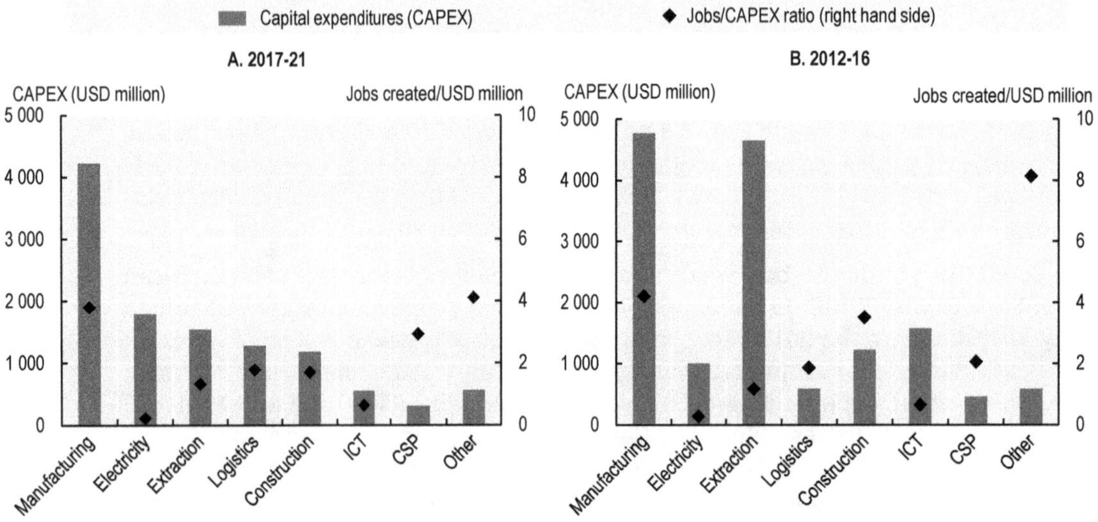

Note: CAPEX = Capital expenditure, ICT = Information and communication technologies, CSP = Corporate services provider.
Source: Authors' calculations based on fDi Intelligence (2022), *fDi Markets* (database), www.fdiintelligence.com/fdi-markets.
StatLink https://stat.link/cxme8f

Central Africa has the least carbon-intensive economies in Africa. In 2020, Central African countries produced 31 megatonnes of carbon dioxide-equivalent emissions ($MtCO_2e$), accounting for just 2.5% of Africa's emissions and 0.1% of global emissions. According to the International Energy Agency (IEA), Central Africa's share of greenhouse gas (GHG) emissions from residential sources exceeds its share from power generation, which is not the case in other regions of Africa or the world. Since 2000, however, GHG emissions from electricity generation have been on the rise, despite the region's total emissions having decreased since 2014 (Figure 4.4).

Figure 4.4. **GHG emissions in Central Africa, by sector**

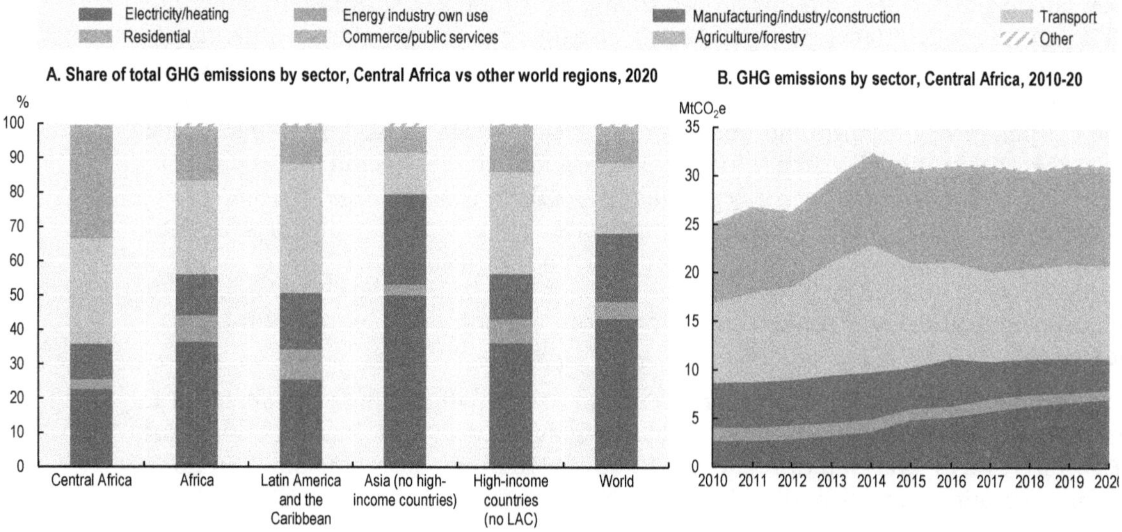

Source: IEA (2021), *GHG Emissions from Fuel Combustion (summary)* (database), http://dotstat.oecd.org/Index.aspx?DataSetCode=GHG#.

StatLink https://stat.link/eskf70

Central Africa depends less on fossil fuels to generate electricity than other African regions. Approximately 78% of electricity generation comes from hydroelectric power, with the remainder reliant on fossil fuels. However, Central Africa produces just 3% of the continent's electricity, leaving 72% of its population (118 million people) without access to electricity in 2020. In addition, renewable electricity meets only a small portion of the region's energy needs (heating, cooking, transport) (Figure 4.5).

Figure 4.5. **Non-combustion electricity and heat production in Central Africa and the world, 2020**

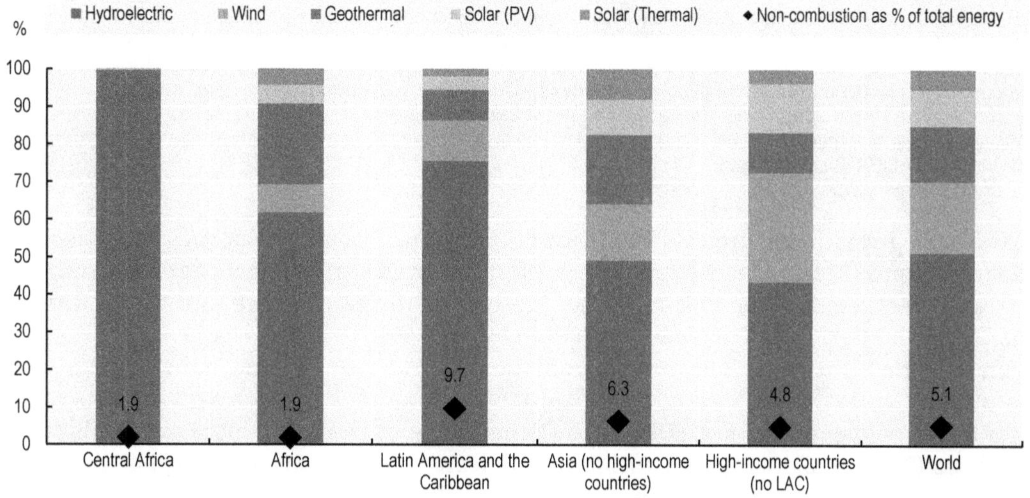

Note: Non-combustible energy sources include sources declared renewable by the IEA, but exclude energy sources based on fuel combustion, such as biofuels and waste. The IEA does not consider nuclear energy to be a renewable energy.

Source: IEA (2021), *GHG Emissions from Fuel Combustion (summary)* (database), http://dotstat.oecd.org/Index.aspx?DataSetCode=GHG#.

StatLink https://stat.link/cuais8

Investment in infrastructure and social services also remains limited in Central Africa. Public and private spending on health and education in Central Africa amounted to 3.7% and 2.3% of GDP, respectively, in 2019. These figures are lower than in other regions of the continent, with the exception of West Africa. Oil-rich countries, such as Congo, the Democratic Republic of the Congo, Equatorial Guinea and Gabon, have the lowest levels of spending on health and education as a percentage of GDP. However, official development assistance allocated to infrastructure and social services in 2020 represented 1.6% of GDP in Central Africa – a much higher proportion than in other African regions, but still insufficient to meet needs and compensate for the lack of public investment in these areas.

Regional integration will make the region more attractive to sustainable investment

Regional integration remains weak in Central Africa, which limits the potential for intra-regional investment development. Regional integration in the Economic Community of Central African States (ECCAS) remains lower than in other regional economic communities, with some disparities between countries (Table 4.1).

Table 4.1. **Regional integration indices in Central Africa in 2019**

Country	Trade integration	Infrastructure integration	Productive integration	Free movement of people	Macroeconomic integration	Average
Burundi	0.12	0.25	0.08	0.06	0.49	0.20
Cameroon	0.38	0.79	0.87	0.16	0.81	0.60
Congo Republic	0.90	0.43	0.43	0.54	0.77	0.61
Gabon	0.50	0.83	0.39	0.54	0.79	0.61
Equatorial Guinea	0.37	0.37	0.32	0.38	0.80	0.44
Central African Republic	0.31	0.15	0.17	0.63	0.75	0.40
DR Congo	0.08	0.11	0.27	0.47	0.60	0.30
São Tomé and Príncipe	0.31	0.15	0.17	0.63	0.75	0.40
Chad	0.41	0.18	0.54	0.78	0.00	0.38
ECCAS	**0.37**	**0.36**	**0.36**	**0.51**	**0.61**	**0.44**

Note: The Africa Regional Integration Index (ARII) measures the extent to which African countries are meeting their commitments to pan-African integration initiatives, such as Agenda 2063 or the Abuja Treaty. The ARII addresses the following five dimensions of regional integration: trade integration, productive integration, macroeconomic integration, infrastructure integration and free movement of people. The index ranges from 0 (minimum) to 1 (maximum).
Source: Adapted from African Union Commission (AUC)/African Development Bank/United Nations Economic Commission for Africa (2019), *Africa Regional Integration Index Report 2019 Edition*, www.integrate-africa.org/fileadmin/uploads/afdb/Documents/ARII-Report2019-FIN-R40-11jun20.pdf.

Most new investment projects in Central Africa are from high-income countries. Between 2017 and 2021, the main sources of new foreign investment projects (in descending order) were the People's Republic of China (hereafter "China"), France, Singapore, the Netherlands and Germany. Only one-tenth of inward investment flows came from other African countries. Outbound investments from the region are 50 times lower than inbound investments. Central Africa accounted for 0.06% of new outbound investment projects to the continent between 2017 and 2021, with Cameroon accounting for more than half of these flows (Figure 4.6). Compared with other African regions, Central Africa has fewer regional multinational companies investing in the region's countries.

Figure 4.6. **Greenfield foreign direct investment outflows from Central African countries, by destination regions, 2017-21, USD million**

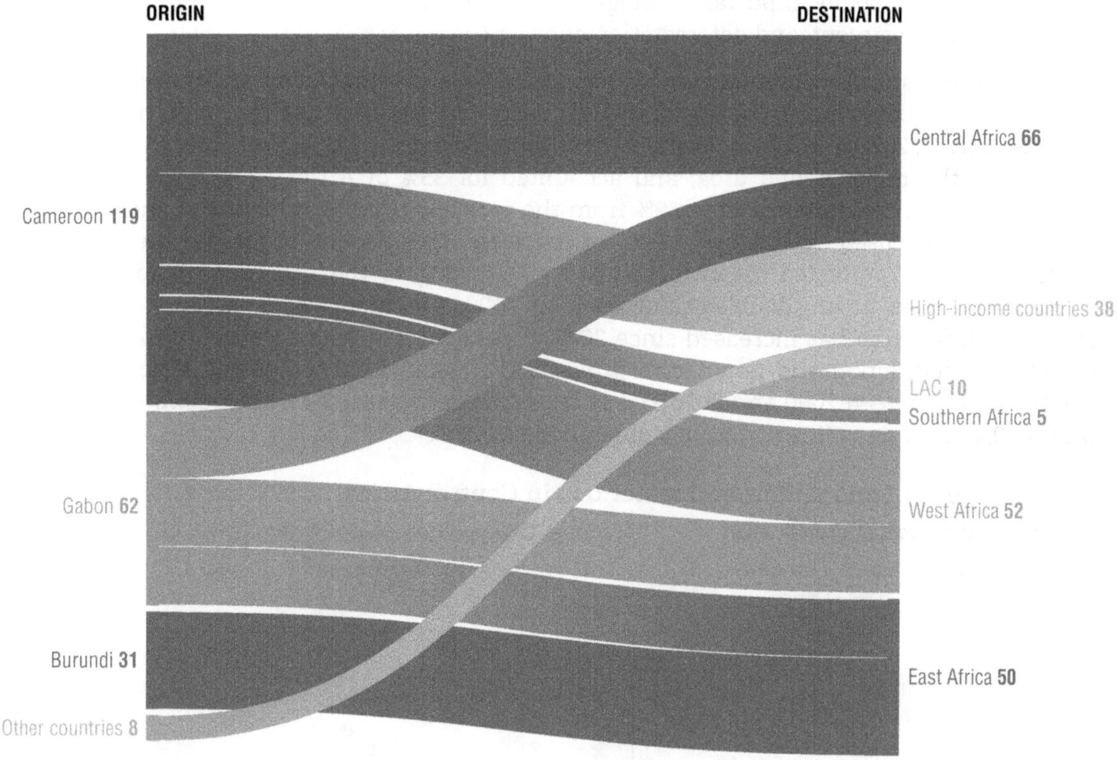

Note: "Other countries" includes the Congo Republic (USD 7 million) and Equatorial Guinea (USD 1 million). "High-income countries" refers to countries classified as "high-income" in the World Bank's classification of countries by income group, excluding Latin America and the Caribbean (LAC).

Source: Authors' calculations based on fDi Intelligence (2022), *fDi Markets* (database), www.fdiintelligence.com/fdi-markets.

StatLink https://stat.link/5nari8

Monetising natural ecosystems will attract more sustainable investment in Central Africa

To mobilise financing, policy makers must understand the economic potential of natural ecosystems. This is particularly true in Central Africa – home to one of the world's largest intact ecosystems, which is immensely valuable to both the Earth's biosphere and the global economy. However, despite these ecosystems requiring significant investment, sustainable investments in Central Africa remain lower than in the rest of the continent. Monetising ecosystems would therefore make it possible to leverage the financing necessary to protect them, while ensuring the economic development of the countries in the region – in particular by facilitating productive transformation, digitisation or participation in global value chains.

The exploitation of natural ecosystems in Central Africa is struggling to compete with more lucrative, environmentally destructive activities

Monetising natural ecosystems in Central Africa enables them to increase their contribution to sustainable economic development. Attributing monetary values to nature and the environment [sometimes called "monétarisation" in French literature: see, for example, Bouscasse et al. (2011)] may justify their protection and enable additional inputs to be mobilised. If Central African ecosystems do not produce financial returns for investors, they will be tempted to turn to activities that generate higher returns, such as agriculture or housing. Although Central Africa's tropical forests and rivers are recognised as having globally important ecological and economic value, they struggle to attract significant investment, and deforestation shows no signs of slowing.

Central African natural ecosystems are losing ground because other forms of land use have higher commercial value. According to the Food and Agriculture Organization of the United Nations (FAO, 2021a), in 2020, Central African forests covered 221 million hectares (ha), i.e. 41% of the region's land area, and accounted for 35% of Africa's forest land (Figure 4.7). However, this figure is down 9% from the year 2000, while agricultural and urban land have increased by 10% and 131%, respectively. This decline in forest cover has occurred despite protected areas in countries belonging to the Commission for Central African Forests[1] having doubled since the early 2000s (Doumenge et al., 2021). The rate of forest degradation has increased since 2017 in particular, driven by agriculture, infrastructure construction and population growth. The population of Central Africa increased by 87% between 2000 and 2020 and is expected to increase by 119% between 2020 and 2050, according to United Nations projections (2022a).

Figure 4.7. **Land and inland water use in Central Africa**

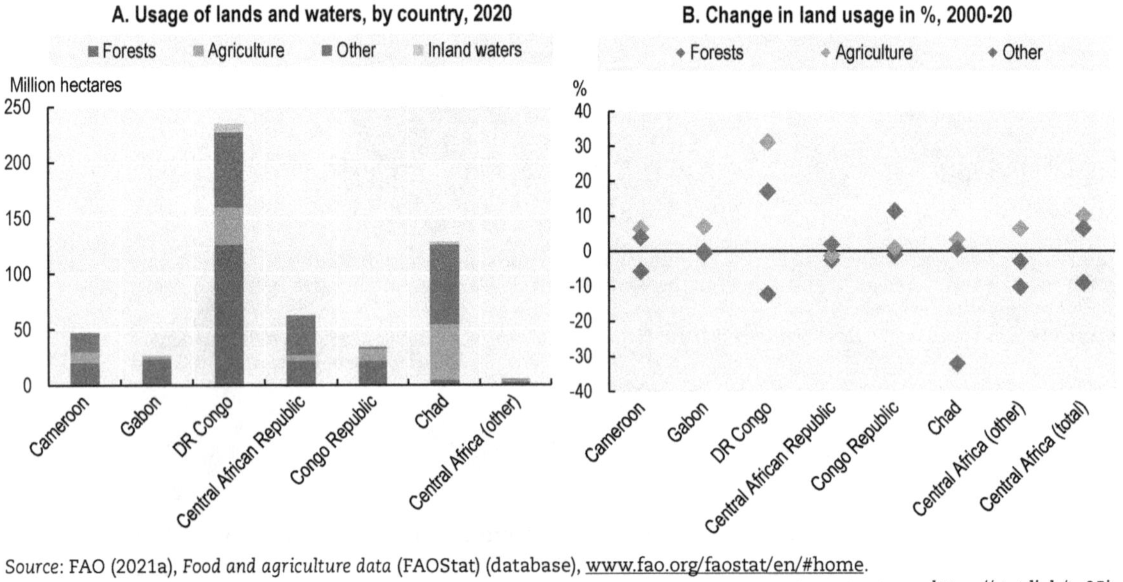

Source: FAO (2021a), *Food and agriculture data* (FAOStat) (database), www.fao.org/faostat/en/#home.

StatLink https://stat.link/tn95ir

Central Africa has major assets with which to monetise its natural ecosystems

More than in any other region of Africa or the world, forests hold a significant share of Central Africa's wealth. According to a World Bank estimate (2021) of the total value of human, physical and natural capital in the world's economies:

- The capital stored in Central African ecosystems was USD 394 billion in 2018, i.e. 26.6% of the region's GDP. This figure exceeds the USD 383 billion in regional value attributed to fishing, agriculture, fossil fuels and minerals combined.

- Central Africa's forests, protected areas and ecosystem services account for 19% of the region's total wealth, compared with 6% for Africa as a whole and around 1% for other regions of the world (Figure 4.8).
- Of the wealth attributed to Central African ecosystems in 2018, 58% comes from future timber production, 27% from ecosystem services (recreation, hunting and fishing, non-timber forest products, watershed protection – see Box 4.1) and 15% from protected natural resources.

However, these estimates do not include the value of carbon sequestration in Central African ecosystems. They also depend on socio-economic factors: higher incomes and larger populations near forests increase the value of ecosystem services.

Figure 4.8. **Distribution of natural capital as a percentage of national wealth (excluding external assets), 2018**

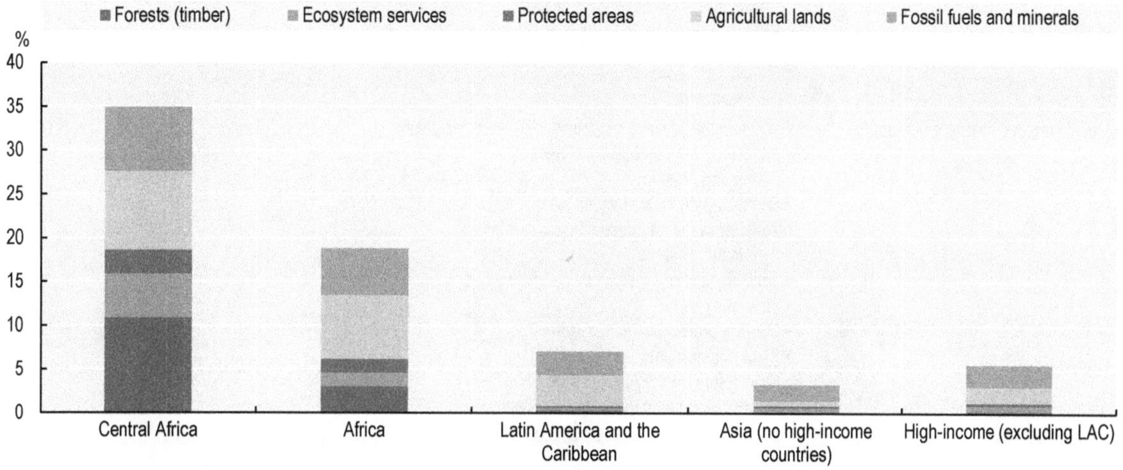

Note: The calculation excludes countries for which complete national wealth accounts were unavailable. This includes 11 African countries, including Equatorial Guinea from Central Africa. "High-income (excluding LAC)" refers to countries outside of Latin America and the Caribbean (LAC) classified by the World Bank as high-income for 2022 according to gross national income.

Source: World Bank (2021), *The Changing Wealth of Nations 2021: Managing Assets for the Future*, http://hdl.handle.net/10986/36400.

StatLink https://stat.link/01cyfx

Central African forests are particularly valuable as carbon reservoirs. Although Central Africa accounts for just 35% of Africa's forest area, it contains 62% of the continent's biomass carbon stock, or 11% of the global stock (Figure 4.9). These figures do not take into account the potential for carbon storage in the forests' topsoil, which would increase carbon stocks in West and Central African forests by around 41% (FAO, 2021b). Peatlands in the central Congo Basin account for an additional 30 gigatonnes of carbon stocks (Brown, 2017).

Box 4.1. Ecosystem services: Concept and method of economic evaluation

Ecosystem services refer to the benefits that natural ecosystems provide. These include tangible benefits, such as improved air and water quality, and intangible benefits, such as aesthetic value that can inspire art. The Common International Classification of Ecosystem Services lists three main categories of ecosystem services (Table 4.2).

Table 4.2. Ecosystem services listed in the Common International Classification of Ecosystem Services (CICES)

Ecosystem service category	Ecosystem goods and services
Provisioning services	• Food • Fresh water • Fuel • Fibre • Biochemicals and pharmaceuticals • Genetic resources • Ornamental resources
Regulating and maintenance services	• Maintain the gaseous composition of the atmosphere • Regulating local and global climate • Controlling erosion • Regulating the flow of water • Purifying water and decomposing waste • Regulating diseases • Controlling crop/livestock pests and diseases • Pollinating plants • Offering protection against storms • Recycling nutrients • Maintaining primary production • Oxygen production through photosynthesis
Cultural services	• Spiritual and religious experiences • Education and culture • Aesthetic value • Leisure • Tourism

Source: Authors' compilation based on Dasgupta (2021), *The Economics of Biodiversity: The Dasgupta Review*, https://assets.publishing.service.gov.uk/government/uploads/system/uploads/attachment_data/file/962785/The_Economics_of_Biodiversity_The_Dasgupta_Review_Full_Report.pdf.

Economic evaluation of ecosystem services makes it possible to quantify their value in monetary units. For example, it is possible to evaluate the economic contribution of ecosystems based on the costs of building replacement infrastructure following ecosystem loss. However, this approach is just one of many existing evaluation methods (United Nations, 2005). According to Dasgupta (2021), more and more countries are incorporating estimates of natural capital and ecosystem services into their economic evaluations. These evaluations can help establish systems of "payments for ecosystem services" based on compensation in exchange for environmental preservation.

Figure 4.9. **The world's two largest carbon sinks, in Central Africa and the Amazon rainforest, are in decline**

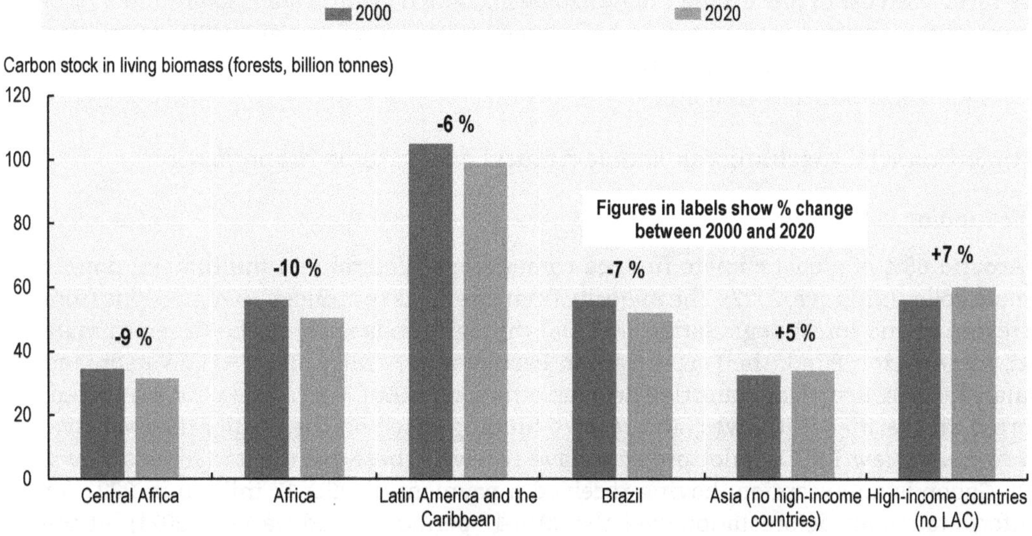

Note: "High-income (excluding LAC)" includes countries outside of Latin America and the Caribbean classified by the World Bank as high-income for 2022 according to gross national income.

Source: FAO (2021a), *Food and agriculture data* (FAOStat) (database), www.fao.org/faostat/en/#home.

StatLink *https://stat.link/kmx9u1*

Undegraded Central African forests have maintained strong carbon storage capacities (Hubau et al., 2020). Conversely, the carbon sink capacity of undisturbed Amazonian forests has been declining since the 1990s due to increased tree mortality, thought to be a result of climate change (Brienen et al., 2015).

The value of the carbon currently sequestered in Central Africa is estimated at over USD 344 trillion. However, the methods used to calculate this value change radically depending on the climate scenario under consideration.

- The social cost of carbon (in other words the projected cost to society of releasing additional carbon dioxide into the atmosphere) could be as high as USD 307 per tonne of carbon dioxide (tCO_2) (Kikstra et al., 2021). Releasing the 31.3 billion tonnes of carbon sequestered in Central African forests into the atmosphere would create global damages equivalent to USD 35.2 trillion.[2]
- Assuming the economic damage caused by the released carbon persisted, the social cost of carbon would exceed USD 3 000 per tonne, i.e. USD 344 trillion for the carbon sequestered in Central Africa.

Although the theoretical costs of carbon pollution are extremely high, market-determined carbon prices vary and can be much lower. The World Bank (2022c) identifies 67 carbon prices from around the world, with an average price of USD 30 per tonne of CO_2 equivalent (tCO_2e), but ranging from USD 0.08 tCO_2e to USD 137 tCO_2e. Gabon plans to sell 90 million tonnes of carbon credits, with prices ranging from USD 25 to USD 35 per tonne of sequestered CO_2 (Njoroge, 2022). At this price, Central Africa's total forest stock is estimated to be worth USD 2.8 trillion to 4 trillion, while the annual net reduction in Central African forest stock is worth between USD 17 billion and USD 24 billion per year.

In return for the monetary value associated with Central African ecosystems as carbon sinks, preserving their biodiversity is a global concern. The World Wide Fund for Nature (WWF) estimates that failure to prevent biodiversity destruction will cost USD 479 billion per year globally, i.e. USD 10 trillion by 2050 (Roxburgh et al., 2020). Meanwhile, it costs USD 1.7 billion to USD 2.8 billion per year to preserve the Amazon rainforest. Based on these rates, the cost of preserving the Congo Basin, which is equivalent to around 30% of the area of the Amazon forests, would be between USD 500 million and USD 800 million per year. The Central African Forest Initiative (CAFI) estimates the cost of preserving Gabon's forests at USD 150 million.

Multiple financial mechanisms enable natural ecosystems monetisation

Public funding

Around 68% of global climate finance comes from bilateral and multilateral donors (Climate Policy Initiative, 2022). The majority finance efforts to reduce GHG emissions from deforestation and forest degradation (REDD+) through funds such as the Green Climate Fund, the Amazon Fund, the Forest Carbon Partnership Facility and CAFI (Watson and Schalatek, 2020). Recipient countries develop a national REDD+ strategy with measured, reported and verified initiatives, and receive funding based on the results they achieve. However, very few REDD+ pilot projects have received these payments (Forests News, 2020). Gabon is an exception, having received a payment of USD 17 million in 2021 for its efforts to reduce deforestation over the 2016-17 period (United Nations, 2021). At the 26th Conference of the Parties to the United Nations Framework Convention on Climate Change (COP 26), collective funding of at least USD 1.5 billion for 2021-25 was pledged to support efforts to protect and maintain the Congo Basin's forests and peatlands.

Central African governments are beginning to allocate a portion of the revenue generated by environmentally damaging activities towards sustainable financing. In Gabon, for example, reallocated oil revenues account for 10% of the finance received by the Gabonese Fund for Strategic Investments (FGIS), which manages around USD 2 billion in assets and aims to achieve net-zero decarbonisation by 2050 (Box 4.2). In Equatorial Guinea, the government also allocates 0.5% of its oil revenues to the Fund for Future Generations (Yonga, 2014). Countries such as Cameroon, Chad and Equatorial Guinea have also introduced environmental taxes to raise additional revenue while discouraging polluting behaviours. However, the revenue mobilised was below 0.5% of their GDP in 2020 (OECD/ATAF/AUC, 2022).

Box 4.2. Gabon's forests in the Gabonese Fund for Strategic Investments (FGIS)

Established in 2019, FGIS has an ecological and economic purpose. It operates in three strategic sectors: infrastructure financing, support for small and medium-sized enterprises, and support for social sectors. Three core principles inform its approach: sustainable impact, innovation, and risk mitigation for its stakeholders. FGIS is the first African sovereign wealth fund to join the Net Zero Asset Owner Alliance convened by the United Nations. It has also joined the One Planet Sovereign Wealth Fund Coalition, the International Forum of Sovereign Wealth Funds and the Africa Sovereign Investors Forum. With its green commitments, and management of over USD 2 billion in assets, FGIS aims to achieve net-zero GHG emissions from its portfolio by 2050, set interim targets every five years and report annually.

Gabon's forests not only play a central role in its ecological objectives but also serve as a source of sustainable financing. Forests cover more than 88% of Gabon's territory, providing the largest forest cover in Central Africa. Despite the general decline in forest

Box 4.2. **Gabon's forests in the Gabonese Fund for Strategic Investments (FGIS)** ***(continued)***

cover in the region, Gabon is the only Central African country to demonstrate that its forests absorb more carbon than they emit. Gabon's forests are therefore a net carbon sink, absorbing more than 100 million tCO_2 per year according to the forest reference emission level it reported to the United Nations Framework Convention on Climate Change (Eba'a Atyi et al., 2022). Given this ecological importance, the first of the three strategic objectives of Gabon's "Plan Vert" [Green Plan] is to sustainably manage Gabon's forest and position the country as a world leader in certified tropical timber. The second strategic objective is to create value from Gabon's agricultural potential and ensure food security, while the third is to promote sustainable exploitation and development of fisheries resources.

Green bonds

Development projects are starting to include innovative financing mechanisms, such as green bonds. Africa's green bond market remains limited (Table 4.3) but is attracting the attention of policy makers in Central Africa. Between 2014 and 2022, 25 green bonds were issued in 9 African countries, raising USD 4.5 billion, or 0.2% of the global market (Climate Bonds Initiative, 2022). Gabon plans to issue a sovereign green bond through FGIS (worth between USD 100 million and USD 200 million) to finance hydroelectric plant construction (Afrimag, 2022). At the regional level, the Central African Financial Market Supervisory Commission (COSUMAF) has also indicated that it intends to introduce green, social and sustainable bonds on the Central African Securities Exchange in the coming years. These tools can be deployed more effectively by learning from the experiences of other countries that have issued green bonds, such as Morocco or Egypt in Africa (Chapter 6), and Colombia or Uruguay in Latin America (OECD et al., 2022).

Table 4.3. **Cumulative total of green bonds by region, in descending order of value, 2014-22**

Region	Green bond markets	Number of issuers	Number of transactions	Value (in USD billions)
Africa	**9**	**23**	**25**	**4.5**
North America	2	872	5 629	382.2
Latin America	14	107	195	32.8
Asia-Pacific	23	1 224	1 827	458.6
Europe	33	1 151	2 434	867.4
Total	79	3 377	10 110	1 745.5

Source: Climate Bonds Initiative (2022), *Climate Bonds Interactive Data Platform* (database), www.climatebonds.net/market/data/.

Carbon credits

Central Africa's large forest cover allows the region to monetise carbon-absorption ecosystem services by implementing carbon credits. In the Congo Basin, the forest's carbon removal services are estimated to be worth the equivalent of USD 55 billion per year, i.e. 36% of the GDP of the six forest-hosting countries (Cameroon, the Central African Republic, Congo, the Democratic Republic of the Congo, Equatorial Guinea and Gabon) (CGDEV, 2022). In the Democratic Republic of the Congo, for example, the Ibi Batéké agroforestry carbon sink project rewards sustainable forestry with a remuneration of USD 184 000 linked to carbon absorption, which is paid to local agroforestry cooperatives

(Eba'a Atyi, 2022). Gabon also hopes to mobilise USD 2 billion through the sale of carbon credits. The country plans to allocate 25% of these funds to forest management and rural communes, 25% to FGIS, 25% to service national debt, and 25% to the national budget for education, health, and climate resilience (Ngounou, 2022).

Sustainable resource management in the agricultural, forestry and mining sectors

Sustainable natural resource management can promote value chain integration while preserving ecosystems. Over the 2015-20 period, the agricultural sectors (agriculture, forestry and fisheries) contributed on average 17% to the region's GDP, while the extractive sector contributed 31%. Adopting regenerative agricultural practices would increase yields by at least 13%, and at the same time reduce soil erosion by 30% and increase the carbon in soils by 20% (Africa Regenerative Agriculture Study Group, 2021). This would sequester the equivalent of 4.4 $GtCO_2$ per year, as well as an additional 106 $MtCO_2e$ by restoring land degraded by forestry. Furthermore, the growing demand for rare metals represents an opportunity for some countries in the region, but social and environmental protection rules must be implemented (AUC/OECD, 2022).

Ecotourism

Ecotourism can support local communities and help diversify economic activities. In Congo, for example, revenue from ecotourism in the Odzala-Kokoua National Park contributes to the local economy through salaries, service provision and community projects, including agricultural diversification, livestock farming, infrastructure development and delivery of medical supplies to health centres (Doumenge et al., 2021).

Protected areas in the region have been extended but remain under stress. The Strategic Plan for Biodiversity 2011-2020 and the Aichi Biodiversity Targets (CBD, 2010) aimed to protect at least 17% of the world's land area and 10% of its marine and coastal area by 2020 through systems of internationally recognised protected areas. There are currently 206 protected areas in Central Africa, occupying more than 950 000 km², or about 18% of the region's land and 8% of its marine area – more than the African and global average of about 14% (Figure 4.10). Despite these efforts, 55% of the region's protected areas remain threatened by oil, gas and mining permits (Doumenge et al., 2021).

Figure 4.10. **Protected areas in Central Africa (percentage of national area), by country**

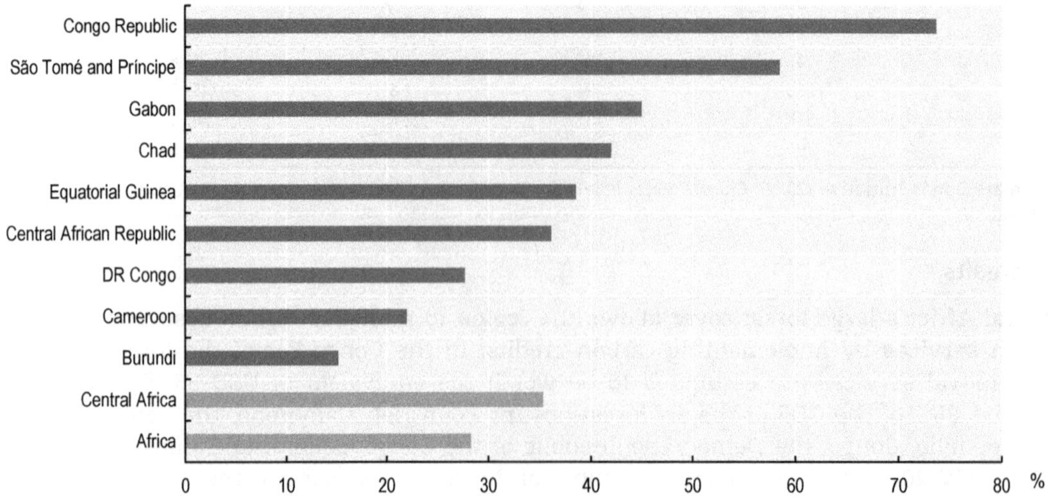

Note: National and international protected areas recognised by the World Database on Protected Areas.
Source: UNEP-WCMC/IUCN (2023), *World Database on Protected Areas* (database), https://doi.org/10.34892/6fwd-af11.
StatLink https://stat.link/8d6est

Challenges to monetising natural ecosystems

Central African countries receive only a small proportion of global climate finance. In 2019-20, they received USD 1.5 billion, i.e. just 5.3% of the climate finance allocated to the continent and 0.2% of global climate finance. The Democratic Republic of the Congo and Cameroon were the main beneficiaries (Figure 4.11). São Tomé and Príncipe received financing equivalent to 10% of its GDP over the period, which amounted to just USD 48 million, or about 3% of the financing received by the region. In contrast to other regions, more than half of the financing (54%) was for climate change adaptation projects, mostly in the agriculture, forestry, fisheries and land-use sectors (CPI, 2022).

Figure 4.11. **Climate-related financing received by Central Africa, 2019-20 average**

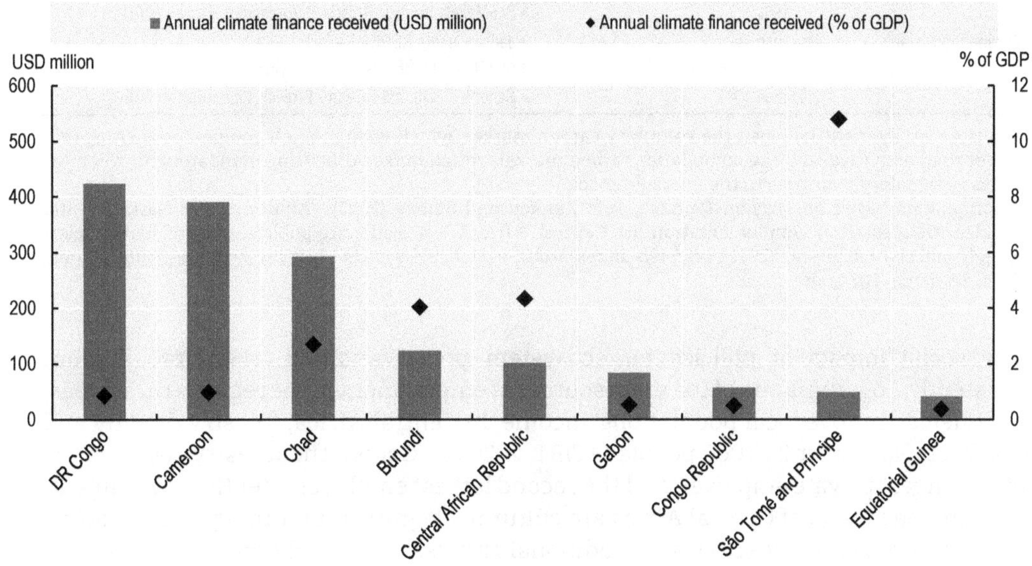

Source: Climate Policy Initiative (2022), *Landscape of Climate Finance in Africa*, www.climatepolicyinitiative.org/wp-content/uploads/2022/09/Landscape-of-Climate-Finance-in-Africa.pdf.

StatLink https://stat.link/wu3qrs

Corruption risks are a major constraint to natural ecosystem monetisation and climate investments in Central Africa. An evaluation of initiatives and mechanisms to monetise ecosystems highlights the governance issues affecting the region. For example, an evaluation of the implementation of the REDD+ initiative in Cameroon reveals the lack of an independent review mechanism to prevent falsification of data feeding into the environmental and social impact assessments required to validate of REDD+ projects (TI, 2016). In the Democratic Republic of the Congo, the national audit of industrial logging concessions by the General Inspectorate of Finances revealed that at least 18 illegal concessions had been awarded (Ligodi, 2022). At the regional level, CAFI has highlighted the fund's good practices in transparency and anti-corruption, but its implementation has been difficult due to the multiple actors involved in its governance (TI, 2020).

Local technical constraints and the large number of forest carbon certification standards complicate the implementation of a voluntary carbon market. Capacity to implement carbon certification remains low in the region, which affects the credibility of initiatives such as REDD+, particularly in terms of calculating reference scenarios on which payments for results are based (Brimont, 2016). In the Democratic Republic of the Congo, for example, the Ntsio agroforestry project covering 5 500 ha and 260 agroforestry farms has been unable to benefit from carbon certification due to the technical constraints that local producers face in managing carbon transactions (Eba'a Atyi, 2022). Different certification standards use different methods to measure results and evaluate carbon prices (Angelsen et al., 2019). For example, mitigation projects certified by the Verified Carbon Standard achieve an average price four times higher than that of the Gold Standard (Table 4.4).

Table 4.4. Sequestered carbon standards and certifications used in REDD+ project compensation

Standard	Voluntary-carbon-market share	Price per tCO_2e in USD	Examples of REDD+ projects in Central Africa
Verified Carbon Standard	81%	4.8	• North Pikounda REDD+ Project (Congo) • Mai N'dombe REDD+ Project (DRC)
Gold Standard	19%	12.2	• EcoMakala Virunga REDD+ Reforestation Project (DRC)
Climate, Community and Biodiversity Standards	less than 1%	5.4	• Jadora-Isangi REDD+ Project (DRC) • Mai N'dombe REDD+ Project (DRC)
Plan Vivo	less than 1%	7	• Sangha Trinational Forestry Project (Cameroon and CAR)

Note: A distinction is generally made between the voluntary carbon market, which is open to all companies wishing (but not obliged) to offset their activities, and the compliance carbon market, which makes offsetting mandatory for the most polluting companies in signatory countries to the Kyoto Protocol.
Source: Authors' compilation based on Tsayem Demaze, Sufo-Kankeu and Sonwa (2020), "Analysing the Narrative and Promises of 'Avoided Deforestation' Implementation in Central Africa", www.cifor.org/publications/pdf_files/articles/ASufoKankeu2001.pdf; and Eba'a Atyi et al. (2022), *Les forêts du bassin du Congo : état des forêts 2021*, www.cifor.org/publications/pdf_files/Books/Etat-des-forets-2021.pdf.

The social impact of policies for ecosystem preservation is taken into account inconsistently. Logging is one of the main sources of employment in the region's rural areas, where it helps improve local populations' income. In Central Africa, forestry directly and indirectly employs over 200 000 people (ATIBT, 2020). In Gabon, the forestry sector is the country's largest private employer, and the second largest employer after the government. In addition, the forests of Central Africa are culturally significant for indigenous peoples, who sometimes use forest species in traditional rituals. The establishment of protected areas may limit indigenous peoples' cultural practices, harming hunter-gatherers and transhumant and nomadic populations. Arbitration should be used to compensate local populations who have to give up some of their land-use rights in order to protect environmental services (Lescuyer et al., 2008).

The development of sustainable activities, such as ecotourism or regenerative agriculture, is limited by insecurity and the lack of infrastructure. The number of visitors to the region's protected reserves remains low due to poor infrastructure and a lack of skills in the tourism sector. In addition, security problems have had serious repercussions on tourist visits to Waza National Park in Cameroon and Virunga National Park in the Democratic Republic of the Congo (Doumenge et al., 2021).

Implementing regenerative agricultural practices requires support from governments, agribusinesses or non-governmental organisations (NGOs) to train local producers. The Nestlé Group has committed to investing USD 1.2 million over five years to promote regenerative agriculture throughout its supply chain by providing technical assistance, investment support and premiums for regenerative agriculture products. In Chad, Moët Hennessy Louis Vuitton (commonly known as LVMH) partnered with the Circular Bioeconomy Alliance (CBA) to launch a regenerative agroforestry project alongside 500 local cotton producers (CBA, 2022).

Central African governments have several policy levers to reconcile monetisation and natural ecosystem preservation

Improving evaluation of natural capital values to inform investors and stakeholders

Improving natural capital evaluation

National policies to mobilise sustainable investment will be more effective if they are based on reliable estimates of natural capital. A lot of data already exist on global ecosystems, but policy makers need to better understand their economic value for investors, both for their own planning and to promote these resources to partners. Developing and reporting reliable estimates of renewable resource wealth will help decision makers increase their transparency and credibility, while identifying gaps in the data that are most relevant to them.

Central African governments can build on existing international efforts to develop natural capital accounts. The World Bank includes estimates of renewable and non-renewable natural capital in its accounting published in *The Changing Wealth of Nations* 2021 (World Bank, 2021). However, systematic natural resource accounting at the national level is less common. Natural capital accounts for the United States date back to only 2016, while European countries have focused on ecosystem accounts in only the last decade (Bagstad et al., 2021). Gabon is one of ten countries to adhere to the Gaborone Declaration for Sustainability in Africa, one of the main commitments of which is to integrate the value of nature into national accounting and development (Gaborone Declaration for Sustainability in Africa, 2012). The System of Environmental Economic Accounting concept and methodology are based on the System of National Accounts. To date, only two Central African countries (Burundi and Cameroon) feature among the 92 countries from around the world that have implemented the System of Environmental Economic Accounting (UN, 2022b).

Better accounting of renewable natural capital leads to better evaluation of the value of ecosystem services and improved arbitrations on the impact of certain economic activities. Natural resource accounting also draws attention to environmental issues and can enhance efforts to identify greener investment opportunities, as well as helping investors estimate and promote the sustainable nature of their investments. It can also improve evaluation of the losses caused by illegal exploitation of natural resources (illegal mining, poaching, unregulated fishing and environmental degradation). In the Central African Republic, for example, a field survey revealed that over 95% of gold production is not officially documented (USAID, 2019).

Taking into account current climatic and biological knowledge

Evaluating the value of natural capital is largely dependent on scientific knowledge, which must be kept up to date. Climate scientists are constantly collecting new temperature and atmospheric readings that feed into climate models, while refining their understanding of the mechanisms behind global warming. In addition, approximately 18 000 species are discovered each year and most remain unknown to science. The value of an ecosystem therefore also depends on the evaluation's timing.

New discoveries in biology continue to have important implications for estimates of the value of natural capital. The Congo Basin's peatlands and their potential for carbon sequestration have been only internationally recognised since 2017 (Brown, 2017). Similarly, the carbon-sequestration services that elephants provide in African rainforests have only recently come to light: by promoting the growth of larger trees, they help increase forest biomass. In 2020, the IMF (Chami et al., 2020) estimated the total value of carbon-capture services provided by African forest elephants at over USD 150 billion (based on USD 25 per metric tonne of carbon). In other words, the services of a single forest elephant would be worth USD 1.75 million.

Leveraging new technologies and computer infrastructure to access and share data

To meet the growing demand for environmental data, new technologies are needed to increase data generation and analysis. The United Nations Conference on Trade and Development calls for a "data revolution" to improve the mobilisation and accreditation of unofficial sources that can complement traditional data sources (Africanews, 2022; IHSN, 2003). A recent survey of conservation-technology users highlighted the three most important new tools for conservation: artificial intelligence, environmental DNA and networked sensors (Speaker, 2021). Outside Africa, Uruguay provides an example of using new technologies in the context of Sovereign Sustainability-Linked Bonds to better assess natural capital, track sustainability efforts and mobilise sustainable financing, using satellite imagery and remote sensing mapping tools (Ministry of Economy and Finance of Uruguay, 2022).

Integrating the value of natural ecosystems into local, national and regional institutions

Developing a natural ecosystem co-management system, assigning appropriate roles to local, national and international actors

Isolated communities can participate in local natural ecosystem management and benefit financially as a result. This could mean obtaining a share of carbon credits or exclusive rights to certain forest products. For example, a REDD+ initiative in Mai N'dombe Province in the Democratic Republic of the Congo relies on local farmers to plant trees and set aside land to reverse local forest degradation. Over 15 000 locals were involved in the initial project consultations. Some 3 772 local farmers have received payments from international donors through the Forest Carbon Partnership Facility in exchange for their services to preserve ecosystems, including planting 1.3 million acacia trees and restoring over 4 000 ha of forest (World Bank, 2018). In 2018, the Nachtigal hydroelectric power plant construction project in Cameroon introduced compensation payments for populations who lost access to forest land due to flooding from the dam.

Special attention could be given to integrating indigenous interests into land ownership. The land rights of local populations remain a sensitive issue when it comes to preserving the ecological sustainability of forest cover. For example, local farmers reported losing access to their fields when Total established a 40 000 ha acacia plantation on the Batéké Plateau in Congo (Quashie-Idun and Howard, 2022). Implementing procedural manuals – including, for example, participatory mapping – can help identify indigenous peoples' lands. In addition, legal recognition of forced labour and land expropriation cases, as well as the imposition of dissuasive sanctions, should be strengthened in the region.

Central African governments are integrating local and indigenous interests into laws on natural ecosystem management. Act No. 2021/014 of 9 July 2021 to govern access to genetic resources in Cameroon guarantees "the involvement of indigenous people and local communities in the sharing of benefits arising from the use of genetic resources or associated traditional knowledge". The Central African Republic was the first African country to ratify International Labour Organization (ILO) Convention No. 169 in 2010 (ILO, 2023). This convention gives indigenous communities the right to be consulted prior to any natural resource exploration or exploitation being undertaken on their lands.

In 2010, this same country was also one of the first to pass a law protecting indigenous peoples' rights (IWGIA, 2011). The publication of regular reports by local institutions and NGOs could improve monitoring of the implementation of regulations and imposition of sanctions, if necessary.

Joining international efforts to create certifications for sustainable investments, while identifying cases of greenwashing

International institutions are taking steps to address fraudulent environmental claims that may dilute demand or erode support for sustainable investments. The United Nations Secretary-General has called for "zero tolerance" for greenwashing (UN, 2022). In 2021, the European Commission examined the environmental claims of a selection of websites and concluded that half made baseless claims (European Commission, 2021a). The OECD advises companies to avoid greenwashing, emphasising the importance of producing credible corporate transition plans (OECD, 2022c).

As certifications increase, standards will evolve. In 2022, Europe reached an agreement on a draft regulation prohibiting companies in the European Union (EU) from participating in value chains that may contribute to deforestation (Oeschger, 2022; European Commission, 2021b). As a result, more sustainability certifications will be required for Central African forest industries to participate in global value chains (AUC/OECD, 2022, Chapter 4). The EU's Forest Law Enforcement, Governance and Trade Action Plan sets out a stricter certification mechanism to discourage illegal logging (Eba'a Atyi et al., 2022). This programme promotes the legal timber trade by proposing that timber-producing countries outside the EU sign Voluntary Partnership Agreements, giving them privileged access to EU markets. It also prohibits operators in Europe from placing illegally harvested timber on the EU market. Five of the ten countries that have signed agreements with the EU are in Central Africa: Cameroon, the Central African Republic, Congo, the Democratic Republic of the Congo and Gabon (VPA Africa – Latin America Facility, 2023).

Promoting new financing mechanisms to monetise natural ecosystems

Central African governments can seek new opportunities in financial instruments. For example, the Bank for International Settlements has proposed adding mitigation outcome interests to green bonds (BIS Innovation Hub, 2022). This mechanism tracks and finances the environmental commitments attached to green bonds. When green bonds are purchased, mitigation outcome interests must be repaid in mitigation outcome units or carbon credits. Internationally recognised memoranda of understanding will need to be developed, based on real assets. Increased trade in these instruments may increase demand for Central African forests to be preserved.

Diaspora support programmes can increase flows and broaden the funding base for natural ecosystems. Migrant remittances represent a limited source of financing, accounting for around 1% of Central Africa's GDP over the 2015-20 period. However, they could be further mobilised towards productive and sustainable investments, particularly through information, co-financing and technical assistance programmes established by international partners and host countries. For example, France has created the MEET Africa platform, which provides technical assistance for diaspora business creation, co-financed by the EU and the French Development Agency (Meet Africa, 2022). In 2022, the government of Cameroon announced that it had established a fund to support entrepreneurship among young people in the diaspora (Investir au Cameroun, 2022).

Governments can encourage financial innovation by creating an enabling environment, providing seed funding and incorporating these innovations into their programmes and investments. Carbon footprint and biodiversity impact considerations can be integrated into national planning, pursuing synergies with private actors. Governments can mobilise catalytic finance to create demand by using green finance for their own budgets and by moving away from investments in environmentally harmful activities. Linking carbon credits to large infrastructure projects can add a green component to substantial investments or intra-regional projects, which can be certified through African mechanisms such as the Programme for Infrastructure Development in Africa quality label.

International co-operation can help local institutions benefit from carbon credits. For example, the Africa Carbon Markets Initiative (ACMI) launched at COP 27 aims to support the growth of voluntary carbon markets, mobilise USD 6 billion and create 30 million jobs by 2030. Gabon and Burundi are signatories (ACMI, 2022). At the regional level, COSUMAF joined the World Bank's Sustainable Banking and Finance Network in 2022, which proposes innovative and stable sustainable finance mechanisms, such as green and blue bond issuance (COSUMAF, 2022).

When debt renegotiations are necessary, future sustainable investments should be encouraged. Globally, the total nominal value of debt relieved through debt-for-nature swaps is about USD 3.7 billion, of which only USD 318 million is in Africa. In Central Africa, only Cameroon benefited from this type of initiative in 2006. The African Development Bank (AfDB, 2022) notes that implementing this type of initiative can be difficult – particularly in the Democratic Republic of the Congo – mainly because of governance problems. Directly allocating some resources to independent conservation funds – such as the Okapi Fund, the Democratic Republic of the Congo's first private conservation trust – may be an alternative.

Notes

1. The Commission for Central African Forests includes all Central African countries, as defined by the Abuja Treaty, with the addition of Rwanda.
2. Burning one tonne of carbon produces 44/12 tCO_2.

References

ACMI (2022), *Africa Carbon Markets Initiative (ACMI): Roadmap Report*, Sustainable Energy for All (SEforALL), Africa Carbon Markets Initiative, www.seforall.org/publications/africa-carbon-markets-initiative-roadmap-report.

AfDB (2022), *Debt-for-Nature-Swaps: Feasibility and Policy Significance in Africa's Natural Resources Sector*, African Development Bank, Abidjan, Côte d'Ivoire, www.afdb.org/en/documents/debt-nature-swaps-feasibility-and-policy-significance-africas-natural-resources-sector.

Africanews, "RDC's government confirms general census is going ahead", *Africanews*, www.africanews.com/2022/01/10/rdc-s-government-confirms-general-census-is-going-ahead/, (accessed 10 January 2022).

Africa Regenerative Agriculture Study Group (2021), *Regenerative Agriculture: An opportunity for businesses and society to restore degraded land in Africa*, International Union for Conservation of Nature (IUCN), Gland, www.iucn.org/sites/default/files/2022-06/regnererative_agriculture_in_africa_report_2021.pdf.

Afrimag (2022), *Le Gabon émettra des green bonds de 200 millions de dollars*, https://afrimag.net/le-gabon-emettra-des-green-bonds-de-200-millions-de-dollars/.

Angelsen, A. et al. (2019), *REDD+: la transformation. Enseignements et nouvelles directions*, Center for International Forestry Research (CIFOR), Bogor, www.cifor.org/knowledge/publication/7447.

ATIBT (2020), *Rapport d'activité 2020*, Association Technique Internationale des Bois Tropicaux, Nogent-sur-Marne, www.atibt.org/files/upload/Activity_report/ATIBT-RAPPORT-ACTIVITE-2020.pdf.

AUC/AfDB/ECA (2019), *Africa Regional Integration Index Report 2019*, African Union Commission, Addis-Ababa; African Development Bank, Abidjan; United Nations Economic Commission for Africa, Addis-Ababa, www.integrate-africa.org/fileadmin/afdb/Documents/ARII-FR-Report2019.pdf.

AUC/OECD (2022), *Africa's Development Dynamics 2022: Regional Value Chains for a Sustainable Recovery*, African Union Commission, Addis Ababa/OECD Publishing, Paris, https://doi.org/10.1787/f92ecd72-fr.

Bagstad, K. J. et al. (2021), "Lessons learned from development of natural capital accounts in the United States and European Union", *Ecosystem Services*, vol. 52, https://doi.org/10.1016/j.ecoser.2021.101359.

BIS Innovation Hub (2022), *Project Genesis 2.0: Smart Contract-based Carbon Credits attached to Green Bonds*, BIS Innovation Hub, Hong Kong, www.bis.org/publ/othp58.pdf.

Bouscasse et al. (2011), *Economic valuation of wetlands services - Methodological lessons*, « Études et documents » collection of the Service de l'Économie, de l'Évaluation et de l'Intégration du Développement Durable (SEEIDD) of the Commissariat Général au Développement Durable (CGDD), Paris, France, https://hal.inrae.fr/hal-02596502.

Brienen, R. et al. (2015), "Long-term decline of the Amazon carbon sink", *Nature*, vol. 519, pp. 344–348, https://doi.org/10.1038/nature14283.

Brimont, L. (2016), "La performance des projets REDD+ : prédire le pire et promettre le meilleur?", Institut du développement durable et des relations internationales (IDDRI), 28 September 2016, www.iddri.org/fr/publications-et-evenements/billet-de-blog/la-performance-des-projets-redd.

Brown, G. (2017), "World's largest tropical peatland found in Congo basin", *The Guardian*, 11 January 2017, www.theguardian.com/environment/2017/jan/11/worlds-largest-peatland-vast-carbon-storage-capacity-found-congo.

CBA (2022), "CBA and LVMH announce major new project", Circular Bioeconomy Alliance, 7 November 2022, https://circularbioeconomyalliance.org/sustainable-cotton-growing-in-africa/.

CDB (2010), *Plan stratégique pour la diversité biologique 2011-2020 et les Objectifs d'Aichi*, Convention sur la diversité biologique, Montreal, www.cbd.int/doc/strategic-plan/2011-2020/Aichi-Targets-FR.pdf.

Centre d'analyse stratégique (2009), *Rapport d'activité*, http://archives.strategie.gouv.fr/cas/system/files/rapport_annuel_d_activite_2009_0.pdf.

CGDEV (2022), *How Much Should the World Pay for the Congo Forest's Carbon Removal?* Center for Global Development, Washington, DC, www.cgdev.org/sites/default/files/how-much-world-pay-congo-forest-carbon-removal.pdf.

Chami, R. et al. (2020), "Le travail de l'ombre des éléphants", *Finance & Development, December 2020*, vol. 57, No. 004, International Monetary Fund (IMF), Washington, DC, www.imf.org/external/pubs/ft/fandd/fre/2020/12/pdf/how-african-elephants-fight-climate-change-ralph-chami.pdf.

Climate Bonds Initiative (2022), *Climate Bonds Interactive Data Platform* (database), www.climatebonds.net/market/data/.

COSUMAF (2022), "La Cosumaf rejoint le Réseau banque et finance durables du Groupe de la World Bank", Press release, Commission de surveillance du marché financier de l'Afrique centrale, https://cosumaf.org/actualite/la-cosumaf-rejoint-le-reseau-banque-et-finance-durables-du-groupe-de-la-banque-mondiale/.

CPI (2022), *Landscape of Climate Finance in Africa*, Climate Policy Initiative, San Francisco, www.climatepolicyinitiative.org/wp-content/uploads/2022/09/Landscape-of-Climate-Finance-in-Africa.pdf.

Dasgupta, P. (2021), *The Economics of Biodiversity: The Dasgupta Review*, HM Treasury, United Kingdom, www.gov.uk/government/publications/final-report-the-economics-of-biodiversity-the-dasgupta-review.

Doumenge, C. et al. (2021), "Ecotourism and protected areas in Central Africa: a future in common", in *State of protected areas 2020*, OFAC-COMIFAC and International Union for Conservation of Nature (IUCN), Gland and Yaoundé, www.observatoire-comifac.net/publications/edap.

Eba'a Atyi, R. et al. (2022), *Les forêts du bassin du Congo : état des forêts 2021*, Center for International Forestry Research (CIFOR), Bogor, www.cifor.org/publications/pdf_files/Books/Etat-des-forets-2021.pdf.

European Commission (2021a), "Screening of websites for 'greenwashing': half of green claims lack evidence", Press release, European Commission, https://ec.europa.eu/commission/presscorner/detail/en/ip_21_269.

European Commission (2021b), "Questions and Answers on new rules for deforestation-free products" European Commission, https://ec.europa.eu/commission/presscorner/detail/en/qanda_21_5919.

FAO (2021a), *Food and agriculture data* (FAOStat) (database), www.fao.org/faostat/en/#home (accessed 18 November 2021).

FAO (2021b), *Global Forest Resources Assessments 2020: Main Report*, Food and Agriculture Organization of the United Nations, Rome, https://doi.org/10.4060/ca9825fr.

fDi Intelligence (2022), *fDi Markets* (database), www.fdiintelligence.com/fdi-markets (accessed August 2022).

Forests News (2020), "Tracking REDD+: A story of remuneration and rewards for avoided deforestation in Central Africa?", Forests News, Center for International Forestry Research (CIFOR), https://forestsnews.cifor.org/REDD+.

Gaborone Declaration for Sustainability in Africa (2012), "Ecosystem Valuation and Natural Capital Accounting", Gaborone Declaration for Sustainability in Africa, www.gaboronedeclaration.com/nca.

Hubau, W. et al. (2020), "Asynchronous carbon sink saturation in African and Amazonian tropical forests", *Nature*, No. 579, pp. 80-87, https://doi.org/10.1038/s41586-020-2035-0.

IEA (2021), *GHG Emissions from fuel combustion (summary)* (database), International Energy Agency, Paris, http://dotstat.oecd.org/Index.aspx?DataSetCode=GHG# (accessed 23 September 2022).

IHSN (2003), "General Population and Housing Census 2003", International Household Survey Network, https://catalog.ihsn.org/catalog/4083/study-description.

ILO (2023), "Ratifications of C169 - The Indigenous and Tribal Peoples Convention (No. 169), 1989", *Normlex* (database), International Labour Organisation, Geneva, www.ilo.org/dyn/normlex/en/ (accessed 13 February 2023).

IMF (2022a), *World Economic Outlook, October* 2022 (database), International Monetary Fund, Washington, DC, www.imf.org/en/Publications/WEO/weo-database/2022/October.

IMF (2022b), *IMF Balance of Payments and International Investment Position Statistics (BOP/IIP)* (database), International Monetary Fund, Washington, DC, https://data.imf.org/?sk=7A51304B-6426-40C0-83DD-CA473CA1FD52.

IMF (2022c), *IMF Investment and Capital Stock Dataset (ICSD) (database)*, International Monetary Fund, Washington, DC, https://data.imf.org/?sk=1CE8A55F-CFA7-4BC0-BCE2-256EE65AC0E4.

IMF/World Bank (2023), *List of LIC DSAs for PRGT-Eligible Countries as of February 28, 2023*, International Monetary Fund, Washington, DC, www.imf.org/external/Pubs/ft/dsa/DSAlist.pdf.

Investir au Cameroun (2022), "Entrepreneuriat : le Cameroun lance des consultations pour la création d'un fonds d'appui aux jeunes de la diaspora", *Investir au Cameroun*, 14 October 2022, www.investiraucameroun.com/gestion-publique/1410-18579-entrepreneuriat.

IWGIA (2011), "Congolese Law on indigenous peoples' rights translated into English", International Work Group for Indigenous Affairs, 31 October 2011, www.iwgia.org/en/republic-of-congo/1452-congolese-law-on-indigenous-peoples-rights-transla.html.

Kikstra, J. S. et al. (2021), "The social cost of carbon dioxide under climate-economy feedbacks and temperature variability", *Environmental Research Letters*, vol. 16, n° 9, DOI: 10.1088/1748-9326/ac1d0b.

Lescuyer, G., A. Karsenty and R. Eba'a Atyi (2008), "A New Tool for Sustainable Forest Management in Central Africa: Payments for Environmental Services", in *The Forests of the Congo Basin – State of the Forest* 2008, Publications Office of the European Union, Luxembourg, pp. 127-139, https://data.europa.eu/doi/10.2788/32456.

Ligodi, P. (2022), "RDC: les ONG de défense de l'environnement demandent des sanctions après l'audit de l'IGF", Radio France internationale, 10 April 2022, www.rfi.fr/fr/afrique/rdc-ong-environnement-sanctions.

Meet Africa (2023), www.meetafrica.fr/en/ (accessed 13 February 2023).

Ministry of Economy and Finance of Uruguay (2022), *Uruguay's Sovereign Sustainability-Linked Bond (SSLB) Framework*, Ministry of Economy and Finance of Uruguay, Montevideo, http://sslburuguay.mef.gub.uy/innovaportal/file/30690/20/uruguay_sslb_framework__2.pdf.

National Intelligence Council (2021), *Climate Change and International Responses Increasing Challenges to US National Security Through 2040*, National Intelligence Council, Office of the Director of National Intelligence, Washington, DC, NIC-NIE-2021-10030-A, www.dni.gov/files/ODNI/documents/assessments/NIE_Climate_Change_and_National_Security.pdf.

Ngounou, B. (2022), "Gabon : le pays obtient la certification au crédit carbone de la CCNUCC", Afrika21, 1 November 2022, www.afrik21.africa/gabon-le-pays-obtient-la-certification-au-credit-carbone-de-la-ccnucc/.

Njoroge, J. (2022), "Gabon's Carbon Credit Sale - Silver Bullet for Economic Revival?", *The Exchange Africa*, 1 November 2022, https://allafrica.com/stories/202211020075.html.

OECD (2022a), "Aid (ODA) disbursements to countries and regions", *Development Assistance Committee* (database), https://stats.oecd.org/Index.aspx?DataSetCode=TABLE2A (accessed 10 September 2022).

OECD (2022b), *States of Fragility 2022*, OECD Publishing, Paris, https://doi.org/10.1787/c7fedf5e-en.

OECD (2022c), *OECD Guidance on Transition Finance: Ensuring Credibility of Corporate Climate Transition Plans*, Green Finance and Investment, OECD Publishing, Paris, https://doi.org/10.1787/7c68a1ee-en.

OECD et al. (2022), *Latin American Economic Outlook 2022: Towards a Green and Just Transition*, OECD Publishing, Paris, https://doi.org/10.1787/3d5554fc-en.

OECD/ATAF/AUC (2022), *Revenue Statistics in Africa 2022*, OECD Publishing, Paris, https://doi.org/10.1787/ea66fbde-en-fr.

Oeschger, A. (2022), "EU Paves Way for Landmark Deforestation-free Products Regulation", SDG Knowledge Hub - International Institute for Sustainable Development, 8 December 2022, https://sdg.iisd.org/news/eu-paves-way-for-landmark-deforestation-free-products-regulation/.

Quashie-Idun, S. et E. Howard (2022), "How are we going to live? Families dispossessed of their land to make way for Total's Congo offsetting project", *Unearthed*, 12 December 2022 https://unearthed.greenpeace.org/2022/12/12/total-congo-offsetting-land-dispossessed/.

Roxburgh, T. et al. (2020), *Global Futures: Assessing the Global Economic Impacts of Environmental Change to Support Policy-Making*, January 2020, www.wwf.org.uk/globalfutures.

Speaker, T. (2021), "A global community-sourced assessment of the state of conservation technology", *Conservation Biology*, vol. 36, No. 3, https://doi.org/10.1111/cobi.13871.

TI (2020), *Governance Assessment : Central African Forest Initiative (CAFI) & DRC's National REDD+ Fund (FONAREDD)*, Transparency International, Berlin, https://images.transparencycdn.org/images/2020_Report_GovernanceAssessmentCAFI_English.pdf.

TI (2016), *REDD+ and corruption risks for Africa's Forests: Case studies from Cameroon, Ghana, Zambia and Zimbabwe*, Transparency International, Berlin, https://images.transparencycdn.org/images/2016_REDDCorruptionRisksAfrica_EN.pdf.

Tsayem Demaze, M., R. Sufo-Kankeu and D.J. Sonwa (2020), "Analysing the Narrative and Promises of 'Avoided Deforestation' Implementation in Central Africa", *International Forestry Review*, vol. 22, Issue. 2, www.cifor.org/publications/pdf_files/articles/ASufoKankeu2001.pdf.

UN (2022a), *World Population Prospects 2022, Online Edition* (database), Department of Economic and Social Affairs United Nations, Population Division, United Nations, New York, https://population.un.org/wpp/Download/Standard/Population/.

UN (2022b), "2022 Global Assessment Results", *System of Environmental-Economic Accounting* (database), United Nations, New York, https://seea.un.org/content/2022-global-assessment-results-1.

UN (2022c), *Le SG réclame une « tolérance zéro » pour l'écoblanchiment*, www.un.org/fr/delegate/le-sg-r%C3%A9clame-une-%C2%AB-tol%C3%A9rance-z%C3%A9ro-%C2%BB-pour-l%E2%80%99%C3%A9coblanchiment.

UN (2021), "Gabon receives payment for reducing CO2 emissions", Office of the Special Adviser on Africa, United Nations, New York, www.un.org/osaa/news/gabon-receives-payment-reducing-co2-emissions.

UN (2005), "Global Assessment Reports", *Millennium Ecosystem Assessment*, United Nations, New York, www.millenniumassessment.org/fr/Global.html.

UNCTAD (2022), "The Impact on Trade and Development of the War in Ukraine: UNCTAD Rapid Assessment – 16 March 2022", United Nations Conference on Trade and Development, Genève, https://unctad.org/system/files/official-document/osginf2022d1_en.pdf.

UNEP-WCMC/IUCN (2023), *World Database on Protected Areas* (database), UN Environment Programme World Conservation Monitoring Centre (UNEP-WCMC), Cambridge, UK/International Union for Conservation of Nature (IUCN), Paris, France, https://doi.org/10.34892/6fwd-af11 (accessed February 13, 2023).

USAID (2019), "Key findings of research on the artisanal gold sector in the Central African Republic", The United States Agency for International Development, Washington, DC, www.land-links.org/wp-content/uploads/2020/05/USAID-AMPR-Summary-of-Gold-Sector-Findings_clean_FINAL.pdf.

VPA Africa-Latin America Facility (2023), https://flegtvpafacility.org/countries/ (accessed 13 February 2023).

Watson, C. et L. Schalatek (2020), "Climate Finance Thematic Briefing: REDD+ Finance", Heinrich-Böll-Stiftung Washington, DC and Overseas Development Institute, London, https://climatefundsupdate.org/wp-content/uploads/2020/03/CFF5-2019-ENG-DIGITAL.pdf.

World Bank (2022a), *World development indicators* (database), World Bank, Washington, DC, https://datatopics.worldbank.org/world-development-indicators/ (accessed 12 April 2022).

World Bank (2022b), *Commodity Markets Outlook: Pandemic, war, recession: Drivers of aluminum and copper prices (October)*, World Bank, Washington, DC, https://openknowledge.worldbank.org/handle/10986/38160?locale-attribute=fr.

World Bank (2022c), *Carbon Pricing Dashboard* (database), World Bank, Washington, DC, https://carbonpricingdashboard.worldbank.org/map_data.

World Bank (2021), *The Changing Wealth of Nations 2021: Managing Assets for the Future*, World Bank, Washington, DC, http://hdl.handle.net/10986/36400.

World Bank (2018), "Mai Ndombe Redd+ Initiative in DRC", Fact Sheet, World Bank, Washington, DC, www.banquemondiale.org/fr/country/drc/brief/fact-sheet-mai-ndombe-redd-initiative-in-drc.

World Bank-KNOMAD (2022), *Remittances* (database), The Global Knowledge Partnership on Migration and Development (KNOMAD), World Bank, www.knomad.org/data/remittances (accessed 19 December 2022).

Yonga, R. (2014), *Guide des Fonds Souverains Africains*, African Markets, www.african-markets.com/pdf/fr/Guide_des_Fonds_Souverains_Africains_FR.pdf.

Chapter 5

Investing in renewable energies for East Africa's sustainable development

This chapter analyses the investment trends and dynamics in East Africa (Comoros, Djibouti, Eritrea, Ethiopia, Kenya, Madagascar, Mauritius, Rwanda, Seychelles, Somalia, South Sudan, Sudan, Tanzania and Uganda), with a focus on the renewable energy sector. The chapter first shows that investments have been a major driver of East Africa's recent growth, but their allocation towards social and environmental sustainability remains insufficient. Second, it discusses East Africa's vast renewable energy potential while highlighting that current investments are insufficient to meet the region's energy access needs. It outlines major investment barriers hampering the growth of the renewable energy market and identifies the potential of innovative enterprises to both accelerate the uptake of renewable energies and contribute to productive transformation in the region. Finally, the chapter offers policy recommendations for mobilising greater renewable energy investments across East Africa.

IN BRIEF

Diverse public and private investments have contributed to strong economic growth in East Africa, and the region's sources of finance have been resilient during the COVID-19 pandemic. Foreign investments, development finance, export credits and regional lead firms have all been drivers of sustainable development but remain concentrated on the region's largest countries.

While East Africa's renewable energy sector has grown, most of its potential for sustainable investments has remained untapped. The sector is core to East Africa's goal to expand access to electricity and clean cooking, at the same time supporting entrepreneurship and the region's productive transformation; at the end of 2020, 49% of the population had access to electricity and only 14% to clean cooking. Despite East Africa's diverse renewable energy assets – encompassing vast hydro, wind, solar and geothermal energy resources – only 4% of greenfield foreign direct investment inflows into East Africa were directed at renewable energy projects during 2017-22, compared to 17% for Africa as a whole.

Ineffective energy regulation, poor energy infrastructures and unstable macroeconomic conditions, exacerbated by recent global shocks, weigh negatively on investor confidence in most East African countries. Nonetheless, innovative enterprises are growing across the region and offer the potential to catalyse more investments in renewable energies and support productive transformation.

Three priorities stand out for policy makers in East Africa to mobilise greater investments in renewable energies:

- enhancing regulatory frameworks and the capacity of energy utilities to improve investor confidence in the renewable energy sector
- strengthening local financial institutions and instruments to catalyse resources for renewable energy projects
- deepening regional integration through infrastructure projects to support the emergence and upscaling of innovative enterprises.

East Africa

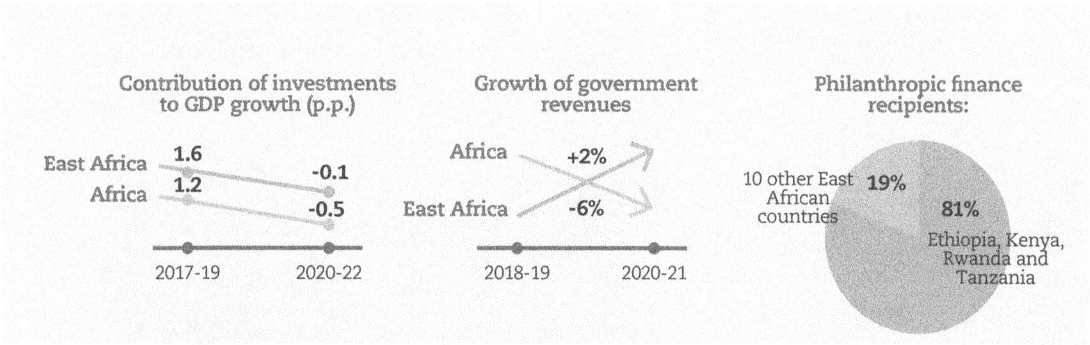

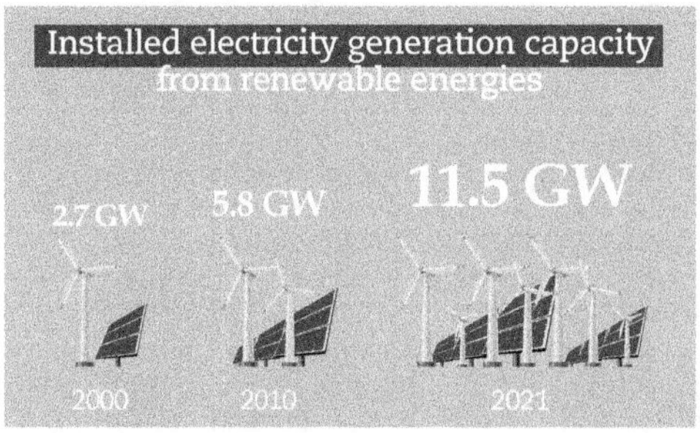

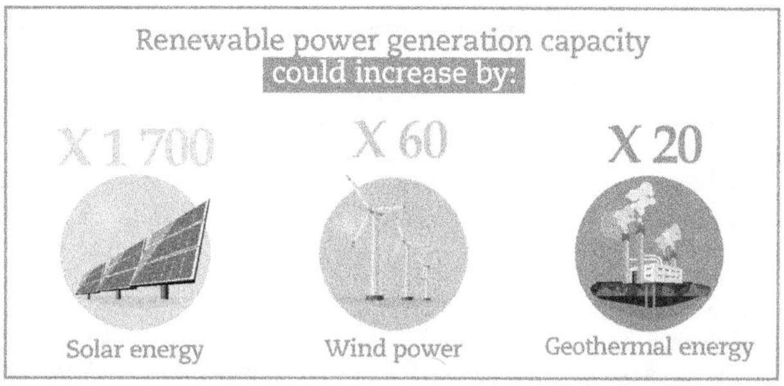

Investments in renewable energies can expand access to electricity and support entrepreneurship

Only **49%** of the population has access to **electricity**

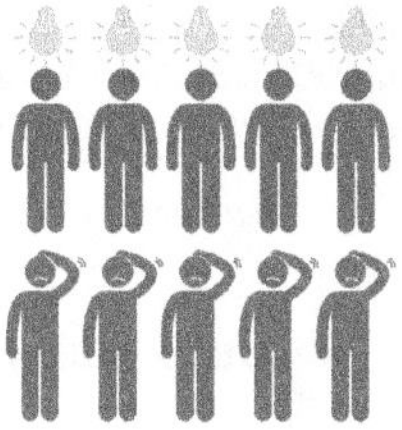

Only **14%** of the population has access to **clean cooking**

Public financial flows into renewable energy projects amounted to only **USD 900 million** per year from 2015 to 2020

East Africa needs about **USD 66 billion** per year to meet the goals of the Paris Agreement by 2030

What's next?

- **Enhance regulatory frameworks** and the capacity of energy utilities to improve investor confidence
- **Strengthen local financial institutions and instruments** to catalyse resources for renewable energy projects
- **Couple regional integration policies with programmes** to promote innovative enterprises

East Africa regional profile

Figure 5.1. Components of economic growth and sources of financing in East Africa

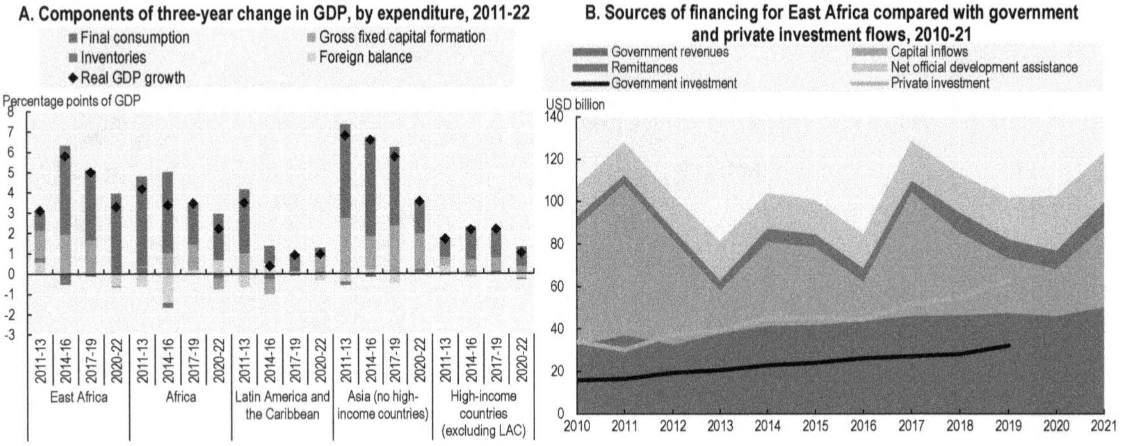

Note: The components of gross domestic product (GDP) growth are calculated on an annual basis by using real annual GDP growth to estimate the increase in real US dollars. Aggregate figures are calculated by taking the average of the national figures weighted by GDP in purchasing-power-parity dollars. The components of GDP growth over three-year periods were calculated by taking the difference between the geometric average of the annual real GDP growth over the period and the real GDP growth when setting each component to zero for individual years. Foreign balance is the difference between imports and exports. Imports contribute negatively to GDP. "High-income countries" refers to countries classified as "high-income" according to the World Bank Country and Lending Groups outside of Latin America and the Caribbean. Government revenues include all tax and non-tax government revenues minus debt service and grants received. Capital inflows include foreign direct investment, portfolio investment and other investment inflows reported by the International Monetary Fund under asset/liability accounting. Figures for capital inflows should be interpreted with some caution as some figures for 2021 and for portfolio inflows are missing.

Sources: Authors' calculations based on IMF (2022a), *World Economic Outlook Database*, www.imf.org/en/Publications/WEO/weo-database/2022/October; OECD (2022a), *OECD Development Assistance Committee* (database), https://stats-1.oecd.org/Index.aspx?DataSetCode=TABLE2A; World Bank (2022a), *World Development Indicators* (database), https://data.worldbank.org/products/wdi; IMF (2022b), *Balance of Payments and International Investment Position Statistics (BOP/IIP)* (database), https://data.imf.org/?sk=7A51304B-6426-40C0-83DD-CA473CA1FD52; IMF (2022c), *Investment and Capital Stock Dataset (ICSD)* (database), https://data.imf.org/?sk=1CE8A55F-CFA7-4BC0-BCE2-256EE65AC0E4; and World Bank-KNOMAD (2022), *Remittances* (database), www.knomad.org/data/remittances.

StatLink https://stat.link/o3p46w

Figure 5.2. Greenfield foreign direct investment flows into East Africa, by activity, source and destination, 2017-22

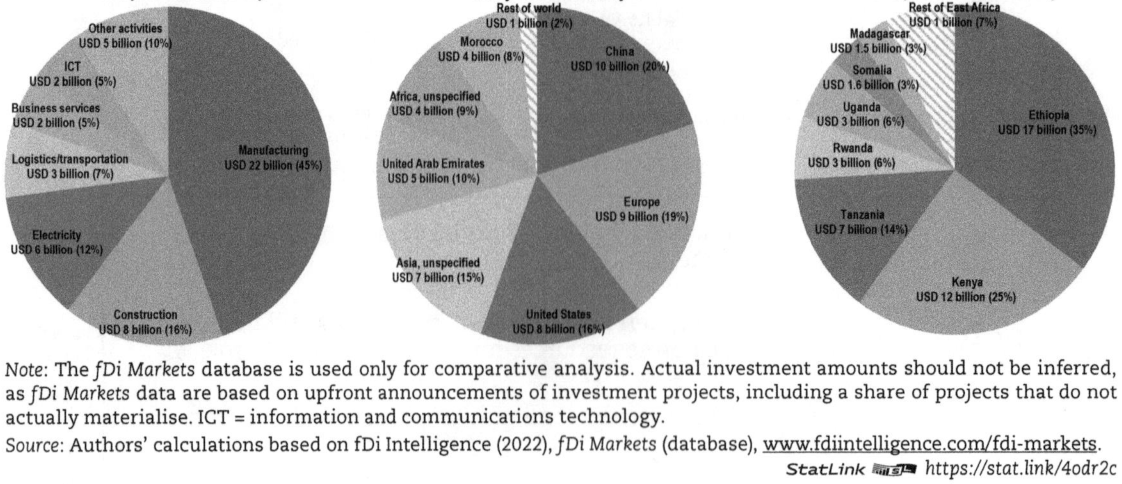

Note: The *fDi Markets* database is used only for comparative analysis. Actual investment amounts should not be inferred, as *fDi Markets* data are based on upfront announcements of investment projects, including a share of projects that do not actually materialise. ICT = information and communications technology.

Source: Authors' calculations based on fDi Intelligence (2022), *fDi Markets* (database), www.fdiintelligence.com/fdi-markets.

StatLink https://stat.link/4odr2c

Diverse investment flows are a major driver of East Africa's growth and sustainable development but focus on only a few countries

Investments have contributed to strong economic growth in East Africa

Compared to Africa as a whole, East Africa has experienced higher gross domestic product (GDP) growth, with investments being a more important driver. The trend that East Africa consistently achieves higher growth than other African regions has been sustained during the COVID-19 pandemic, with GDP growth reaching 0.7% in 2020, 5.4% in 2021 and 4.3% in 2022, compared to -1.7%, 4.9% and 3.8% for Africa (IMF, 2023a). Investments (gross fixed capital formation) have been on an upward trend in the last decade and have contributed to recent GDP growth far more in East Africa (1.6 percentage points in 2017-19 and -0.1 percentage points in 2020-22) than in the whole of Africa (1.2 and -0.5 percentage points in the same periods) (Figure 5.1, Panel A).

Except for capital inflows, sources of financing have been stable in East Africa, with government revenues showing more resilience than in other African regions. During the COVID-19 pandemic, government revenues have been more stable in East Africa (+2% between 2018-19 and 2020-21) than in Africa as a whole (-6% over the same period). In line with trends at the continental level, official development assistance (ODA) and remittances have increased during the pandemic (by 30% and 6% respectively), thereby partially compensating for the drop in capital inflows (-7%) (Figure 5.1, Panel B).

Global inflows of foreign direct investment (FDI) come from diverse destinations, with Chinese and Emirati investments playing a more significant role than in other African regions. The People's Republic of China (hereafter "China") (USD 10 billion), Europe (USD 9 billion) and the United States (USD 8 billion) have accounted for the highest greenfield FDI inflows into East Africa in 2017-22. Notably, 10% (USD 5 billion) of the region's FDI has come from the United Arab Emirates – which represents more than half of FDI from all African countries outside the region combined (Figure 5.2, Panel B). As of February 2023, the International Monetary Fund considers two East African countries to be in debt distress (Somalia and Sudan), with five other countries (Comoros, Djibouti, Ethiopia, Kenya and South Sudan) facing a high risk of moving to this status (IMF, 2023b).

Private and public investment sources concentrate on a range of sectors but mostly in the region's largest countries

Manufacturing is the largest recipient of greenfield FDI, and business services rank relatively high. Between 2017 and 2021, the manufacturing sector (including the processing of coal, oil and gas) attracted more greenfield FDI than the next four sectors combined (USD 16.4 billion vs. USD 14.9 billion). Absolute investment amounts are well aligned with sectoral job/capital expenditure ratios. East Africa is the only African region where business services rank among the top five sectors targeted by FDI (Figure 5.3).

Figure 5.3. **Greenfield foreign direct investment to East Africa, capital expenditures and job creation, by business activity, 2017-21**

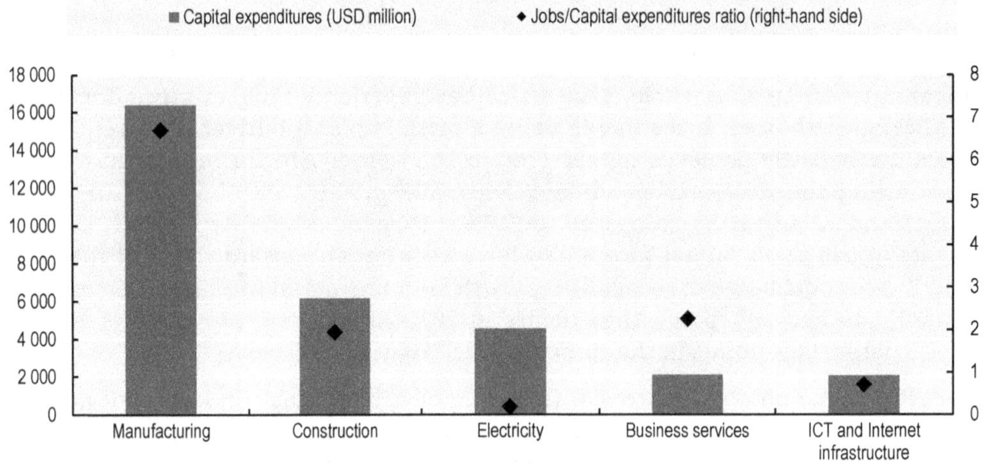

Note: The figure shows the top five business activities by capital expenditures. It covers the period from 2017 to 2021 and therefore shows a different total capital expenditure for electricity compared to Figure 5.2. ICT = information and communications technology.

Source: Authors' calculations based on fDi Intelligence (2022), *fDi Markets* (database), www.fdiintelligence.com/fdi-markets.

StatLink https://stat.link/1javyn

Private finance mobilised through development finance and export credits target different sectors, but both focus on the region's four largest countries. In 2012-20, USD 8.3 billion of private finance were mobilised by development finance in the region; the energy sector attracted the highest share (40%), followed by banking and financial services (20%). By far, the most private finance was mobilised by development finance in Kenya (USD 3.9 billion), followed by Uganda (USD 1.5 billion), Ethiopia (USD 0.6 billion) and Tanzania (USD 0.6 billion) (Figure 5.4). According to the OECD Export Credits Group, export credits from OECD countries to East Africa amounted to a total of USD 6.64 billion from 2012 to 2021, focusing mostly on construction (47%), transport and storage (23%), health (7%) and industry (7%), with Tanzania attracting the largest amount (USD 2.1 billion), followed by Kenya (USD 1.9 billion), Ethiopia (USD 1.6 billion) and Uganda (USD 0.5 billion).

Figure 5.4. **Private finance mobilised through official development finance in East Africa, 2012-20**

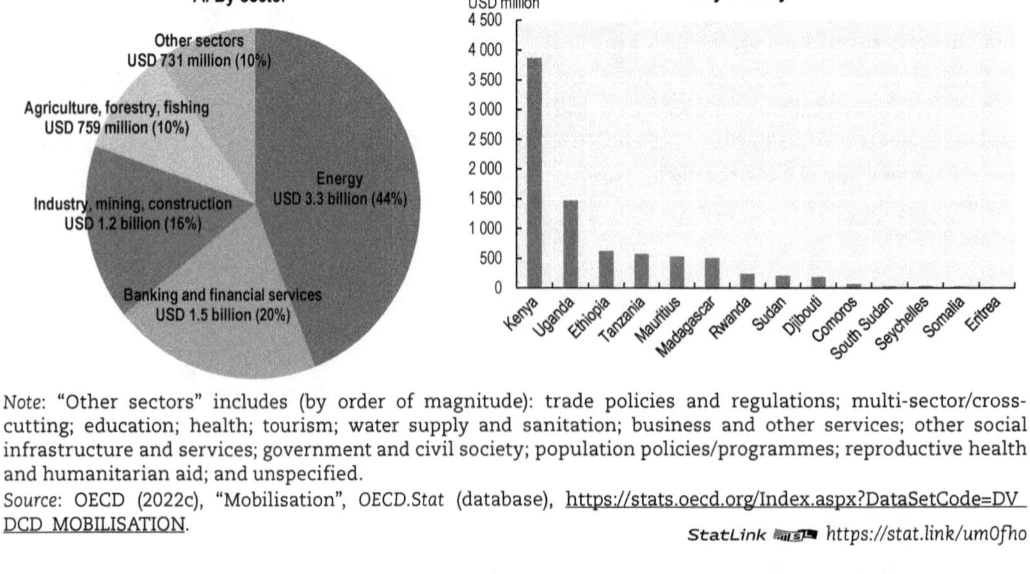

Note: "Other sectors" includes (by order of magnitude): trade policies and regulations; multi-sector/cross-cutting; education; health; tourism; water supply and sanitation; business and other services; other social infrastructure and services; government and civil society; population policies/programmes; reproductive health and humanitarian aid; and unspecified.

Source: OECD (2022c), "Mobilisation", *OECD.Stat* (database), https://stats.oecd.org/Index.aspx?DataSetCode=DV_DCD_MOBILISATION.

StatLink https://stat.link/um0fho

ODA and philanthropy inflows focus on social sectors, mainly targeting education, health, agriculture and humanitarian efforts. These funds complement the more limited government spending in these domains. For instance, in 2019, public healthcare expenditures reached 1.4% of GDP in East Africa, less than in North Africa (2.2%) and Southern Africa (3.8%). ODA and philanthropy were concentrated in Ethiopia, Kenya, Rwanda and Tanzania. The four countries account for 62% of the region's population and received 55% of ODA and 81% of philanthropic flows.

East Africa is more integrated into intra-African investment flows than other African regions, supported by large multinational enterprises in the finance and insurance sector in Mauritius and Kenya. Greenfield FDI outflows from East African countries are dominated by transactions from Mauritius (USD 5.5 billion), mostly targeting Southern Africa, followed by West Africa and other East African countries. Outward greenfield FDI from Kenya (USD 1.6 billion) is more evenly distributed, with similar amounts reaching other East African countries (USD 397 million), developing Asia (USD 422 million) and West Africa (USD 436 million) (Figure 5.5). Finance and insurance companies with headquarters in Kenya and Mauritius also dominate the region's leading companies. Consumer-facing firms with strong regional footprints (such as the Kenya Commercial Bank) employ the largest number of people, albeit remaining far behind retailers that have headquarters outside the region (such as South African Shoprite operating in East Africa). Kenya also stands out as the country with the largest institutional investors in the region: Kenyan pension fund assets under management amounted to 12% of GDP in 2015-20, the fourth highest share in Africa after Namibia (98%), South Africa (84%) and Botswana (53%).[1]

Figure 5.5. **Greenfield foreign direct investment outflows from East African countries, by destination region, 2017-21, USD million**

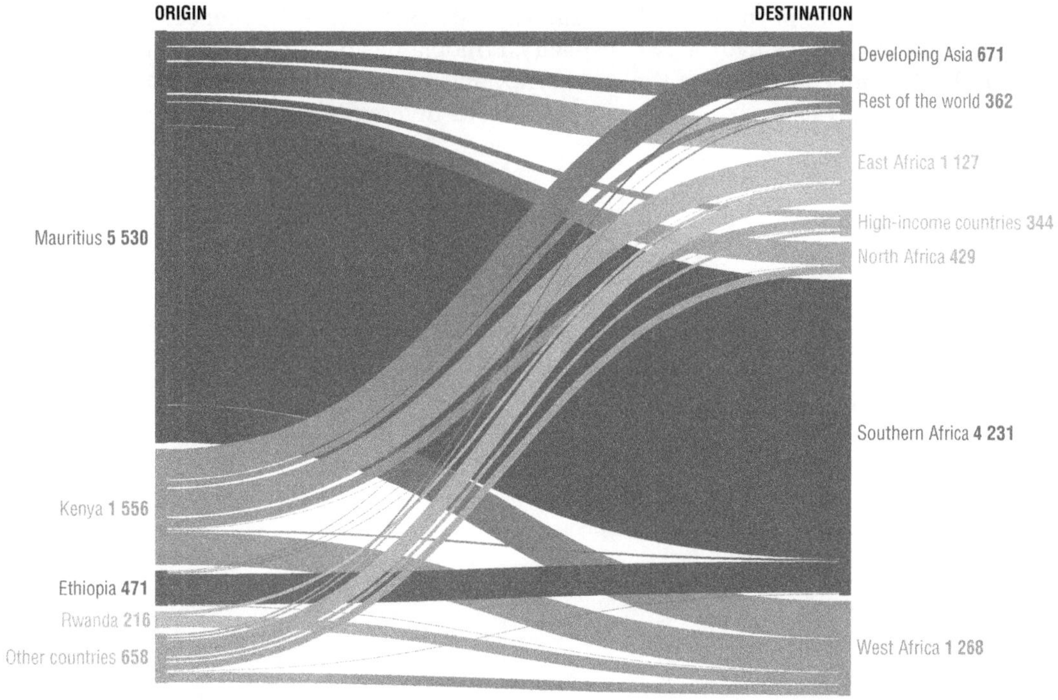

Note: "Other countries" includes Madagascar (USD 160 million), Seychelles (USD 150 million), Djibouti (USD 146 million), Sudan (USD 105 million), Tanzania (USD 87 million) and South Sudan (USD 2 million). "Rest of the world" includes countries from Central Africa (USD 276 million), Latin America and the Caribbean (LAC) (USD 33 million) other regions not specified in the chart (USD 52 million). "High-income countries" refers to countries classified as "high-income" in the World Bank's classification of countries by income group, excluding LAC.

Source: Authors' calculations based on fDi Intelligence (2022), *fDi Markets* (database), www.fdiintelligence.com/fdi-markets.

StatLink https://stat.link/nmk926

Mobilising investments in East Africa's renewable energy sector can increase access to clean energy and support productive transformation

Despite East Africa's vast renewable energy potential, current investments are insufficient to meet the region's energy access needs

East Africa holds unique potential for renewable energies, as its countries benefit from a range of energy reserves. The region's untapped renewable energy reserves cut across hydro, wind, solar and geothermal power (IEA, 2022). The region has an average annual solar irradiation of 2 100 kilowatt hours (KWh) per square metre and wind speeds averaging 5.5 metres per second – and up to 8 metres per second in Ethiopia, Kenya and Somalia. Based on a mere 1% utilisation of land suitable for energy project development, technically installable capacities amount to 1 067 gigawatts for solar power and 47.2 for wind power (IRENA/AfDB, 2022). The Great Lakes area and Nile Basin offer further potential for hydropower, while the Rift Valley holds the richest geothermal potential on the continent (IRENA, 2022a). The region is currently using less than 5% of its geothermal capacity, mostly in Kenya and Ethiopia (Kincer, 2021).

The renewable energy market in East Africa has seen fast growth, but solar and wind power account for only a small share of electricity generation. The region's electricity generation capacity from renewable energies amounted to 11.5 gigawatts (GW) in 2021, a more than fourfold increase from 2000 (2.7 GW) and a nearly doubling since 2010 (5.8 GW). In 2021, renewable energy thus accounted for 65% of East Africa's total electricity capacity. This growth was primarily driven by the expansion of hydropower in the early 2000s, which was later complemented by geothermal, bioenergy, wind and solar power. Despite their vast potential, solar and wind energy have only recently begun to be exploited and still represent a small share of the region's overall capacity (3.5% and 4.5% respectively) (Figure 5.6). Thanks to its large hydropower capacity, Ethiopia has become an electricity exporter and the African country with the most renewable energy jobs (about 57 800 in 2021 [IRENA, 2022b]). Kenya stands out in the region for its diversified renewable energy mix (Figure 5.7).

Figure 5.6. **Installed electricity capacity and access to electricity in East Africa by source, 2000-22**

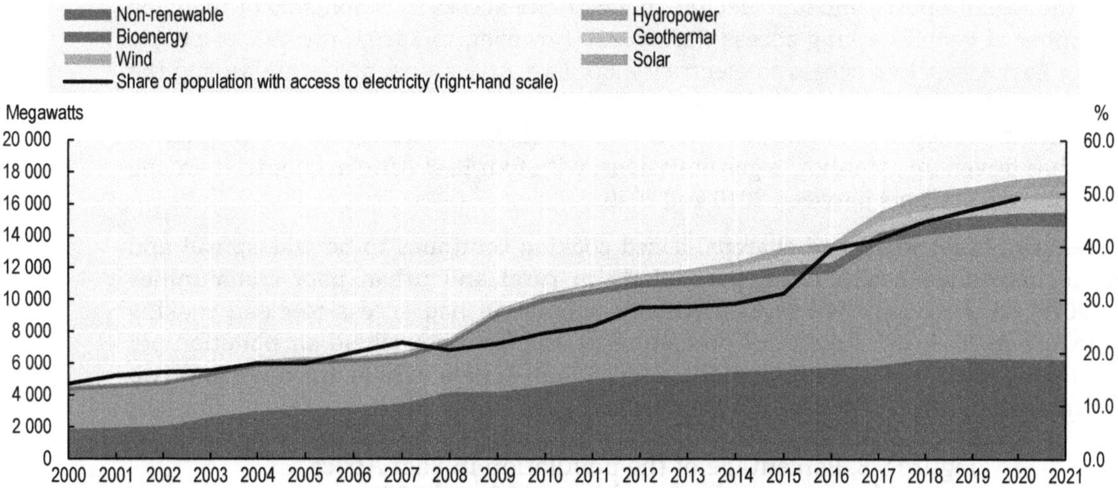

Note: "Solar" includes photovoltaic and concentrated solar power. "Wind" includes onshore and offshore wind. "Bioenergy" includes solid biofuels, liquid biofuels and biogas. "Hydropower" includes renewable hydropower and pumped storage. "Non-renewable" includes coal and peat, oil, natural gas, fossil fuels not elsewhere specified, nuclear, non-renewable municipal waste and other non-renewable energy.

Source: Authors' compilation based on IRENA (2022a), *IRENASTAT* (database), https://pxweb.irena.org/pxweb/en/IRENASTAT?gl=1*fltysn*_ga*MTA3NTM0NzYxLjE2NjE3NzAyNzQ.*_ga_7W6ZEF19K4*MTY3ODI4NTgxNC40NC4xLjE2NzgyODU4MzguMzYuMC4w and World Bank (2022a), *World Development Indicators* (database), https://data.worldbank.org/products/wdi.

StatLink https://stat.link/4kfwb3

Figure 5.7. **Installed electricity capacity from renewable energy sources in 2021, by country**

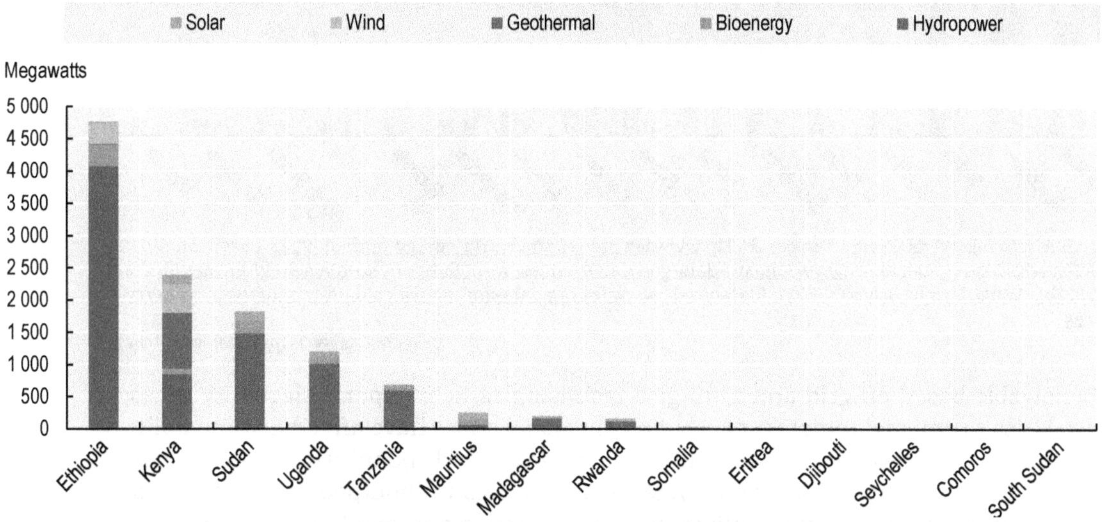

Note: "Solar" includes photovoltaic and concentrated solar power. "Wind" includes onshore and offshore wind. "Bioenergy" includes solid biofuels, liquid biofuels and biogas. "Hydropower" includes renewable hydropower and pumped storage.

Source: Authors' compilation based on IRENA (2022a), *IRENASTAT* (database), https://pxweb.irena.org/pxweb/en/IRENASTAT?gl=1*fltysn*_ga*MTA3NTM0NzYxLjE2NjE3NzAyNzQ.*_ga_7W6ZEF19K4*MTY3ODI4NTgxNC40NC4xLjE2NzgyODU4MzguMzYuMC4w.

StatLink https://stat.link/0ld3j6

Despite significant progress, half of East Africa's population – around 200 million people – lack access to electricity, while pollution from non-renewable energy sources remains problematic. In part driven by the growth of renewable energies, the region's electricity access rates increased considerably between 2000 and 2020 (Figure 5.6). Kenya and Rwanda have been among the world's fastest-electrifying countries; in 2022, they defied the region's post-pandemic decline in electricity access by stabilising or reducing the number of people lacking access (IEA, 2022). However, in 2020, only 49% of people living in East Africa had access to electricity. Six East African countries are among the world's 20 countries with the lowest access rates. While electricity generation has become predominantly renewable-based, the use of fossil fuels in the transport and residential sectors has driven up greenhouse gas emissions, with four East African countries among Africa's top ten emitters between 2010 and 2020.[2]

The use of fuel wood and charcoal-based cooking continues to be widespread and leads to immediate health risks, particularly in rural and urban poor communities (IEA, 2022). In 2020, only 14% of East Africa's population had access to clean cooking (Figure 5.8). In 2019, the number of premature deaths from household air pollution per million population was 1 724 in Somalia and 1 124 in Eritrea, which are three and two times more than Africa's average (Roy, forthcoming).

Figure 5.8. **Percentage of the population in East Africa with access to clean cooking, 2000 and 2020**

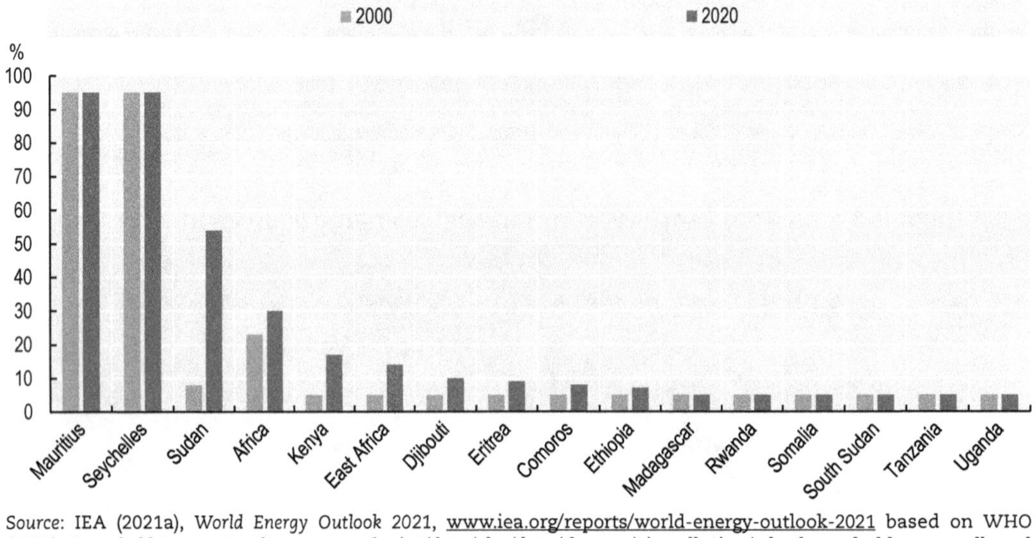

Source: IEA (2021a), *World Energy Outlook 2021*, www.iea.org/reports/world-energy-outlook-2021 based on WHO (2021), *Household Energy Database*, www.who.int/data/gho/data/themes/air-pollution/who-household-energy-db and IEA (2021b), *World Energy Balances 2021* (database), www.iea.org/data-and-statistics/data-product/world-energy-balances.

StatLink https://stat.link/j4nla0

Renewable-based off-grid and mini-grid technologies help expand electricity access in East Africa's rural and remote areas, but recent global crises have affected affordability. In 2019, decentralised energy access solutions, such as off-grid and mini-grid technologies including standalone and solar home systems, served 38.5 million people, as the region recorded four times as many installations as West Africa and eight times as many as Southern Africa (IRENA/AfDB, 2022). Ethiopia and Kenya boast the most attractive markets for off-grid solutions in the region, accounting for close to 30% of the world's off-grid solar market in 2021, with 19 million people in Kenya and 8 million people in Ethiopia connected to off-grid solar solutions (IEA, 2022). In Rwanda, solar-based off-grid solutions provide electricity to 15% of households and 7% of the total population, the highest off-grid electricity access rate in Africa and the third highest in the world (GIZ/IRENA, 2020). While off-grid and mini-grid technologies offer potential, especially in rural areas, affordability continues to be a major obstacle. As a result of supply chain disruptions and inflation caused by the COVID-19 pandemic and international conflicts, off-grid devices have become unaffordable for many consumers, slowing down their adoption (IEA, 2022).

Investments in East Africa's renewable energy production do not match the potential to widen access to electricity and reduce pollution. Both private and public investments have remained comparatively small. Only 4% of greenfield FDI capital expenditures into East Africa was directed at renewable energy projects in 2017-22 compared to 17% for the African continent.[3] Public financial flows into renewable energy projects are even less significant, amounting to USD 5.6 billion from 2015 to 2020, or USD 900 million per year, with an annual low of USD 334 million in 2020[4], the first year of the pandemic. Public financing particularly under exploits wind and solar energy, with only Ethiopia and Kenya having made significant investments in these technologies in recent years (Figure 5.9). For comparison, East Africa's combined nationally determined contributions to meet the Paris Agreement's goal to keep global warming below 1.5°C by 2030 amount to USD 65.96 billion per year from 2020 to 2030 (AfDB, 2022).

Figure 5.9. **Top six East African countries with public investments in renewable energy sources, 2001-20, USD million**

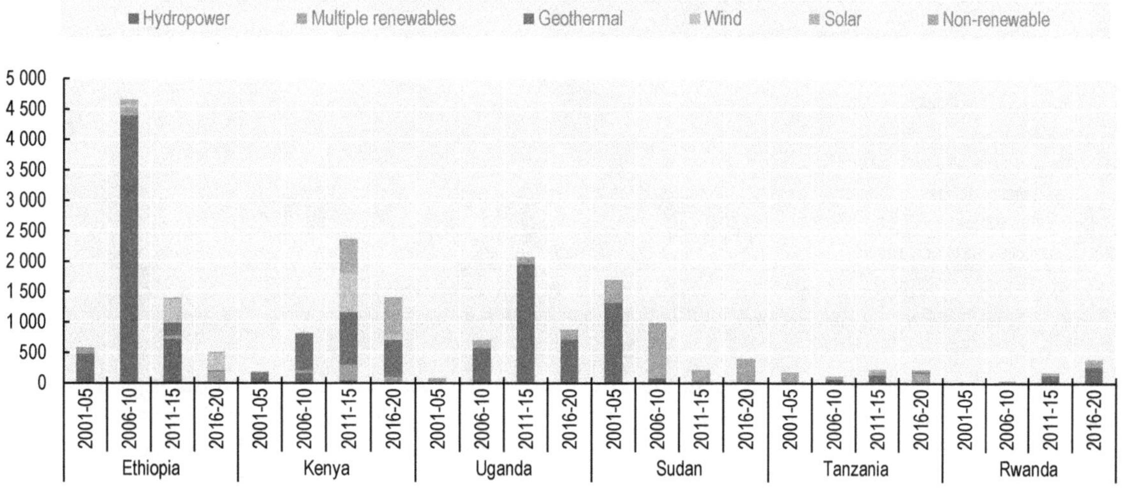

Note: "Solar" includes photovoltaic and concentrated solar power. "Hydropower" includes renewable hydropower and pumped storage. "Wind" includes onshore and offshore wind. "Non-renewable" includes coal and peat, oil, natural gas, fossil fuels not elsewhere specified, nuclear, non-renewable municipal waste and other non-renewable energy. "Multiple renewables" include public investments in more than one renewable energy technology.

Source: Authors' compilation based on IRENA (2022a), *IRENASTAT* (database), https://pxweb.irena.org/pxweb/en/IRENASTAT?_gl=1*fltysn*_ga*MTA3NTM0NzYxLjE2NjE3NzAyNzQ.*_ga_7W6ZEF19K4*MTY3ODI4NTgxNC40NC4xLjE2NzgyODU4MzguMzYuMC4w.

StatLink https://stat.link/bsnc6r

Structural barriers and recent crises hinder renewable energy investments in East African countries

Insufficient regulations, a lack of bankable projects, difficult financing conditions and poor energy infrastructures represent major structural barriers to most private and international investments. Interviews with multinational enterprises and a comprehensive literature review identified a range of investment barriers that consistently hamper investments in renewable energies (Table 5.1; see also Chapter 1). Investors and industry sources mentioned the following as barriers to FDI and other forms of private investments: regulatory restrictions on private participation and inadequately implemented reforms (e.g. in Ethiopia and Kenya), monopsonist behaviour by utilities, high off-taker risk and other vested interests (e.g. in Tanzania and Uganda), a deteriorating or opaque sovereign credit profile (e.g. in Ethiopia), and a lack of bankable projects (e.g. in Seychelles and Tanzania). With some exceptions, domestic, other African and non-African private investors face similar barriers. Philanthropic and international development finance institutions are generally less affected by many barriers, but the implementation of reforms, political stability, and project-specific governance and capacity issues affect their investment decisions.

Table 5.1. **Barriers to renewable energy investments in East Africa for different types of investors**

Investment barrier		Non-African private investors	African private investors	Domestic private investors	Philanthropic institutions	International development finance institutions
Unfavourable regulatory and institutional environments	Restrictions to private and market-based energy production and distribution	x	x	x		
	Poor and inconsistent implementation of reforms	x	x	x		x
	Monopsonist activities of utilities and state-owned enterprises, off-taker risk	x	x	x		
	Political conflict and security concerns	x	x	x	x	
	Land rights disputes	x	x	x	x	
Lack of bankable projects	Governance concerns	x	x	x		x
	Project capacity limitations	x			x	x
	Skills shortages	x	x	x		
Difficult financing conditions	Weak domestic financing system	x	x	x		x
	Sovereign credit risk	x	x			
	High upfront cost			x		
Poor infrastructure	Inadequate grid infrastructure	x	x	x		

Note: "Private investors" refer to multinational enterprises, banks, and institutional and portfolio investors.
Source: Authors' assessment based on interviews with multinational energy producers and a desk review of grey and academic literature.

Recent crises have stalled investments in projects across the region, reducing access to electricity and clean cooking. Deteriorating macroeconomic conditions, due to recent global crises, have had ripple effects on overall investor confidence, the financial stability of utilities, equipment suppliers and off-grid technology providers, thereby stalling infrastructure and energy access projects across East Africa (IEA, 2022; see also Chapter 1). Only a few countries, most notably Kenya, were able to add new on-grid electricity connections in 2020-21, mainly by completing projects initiated prior to the COVID-19 pandemic. Electricity and clean cooking access rates have thus declined, particularly where population growth has outpaced the number of new connections, such as in Ethiopia, Madagascar, Tanzania and Uganda (IEA, 2022).

Renewable energy investment barriers and opportunities differ greatly across countries, depending on market size, energy access levels and energy independence. All East African countries face significant barriers to attracting investments in renewable energies. Yet, based on the above analysis, East African countries can be divided into three clusters based on the different investment barriers and opportunities they face:

- **Cluster 1: Expanding and diversifying renewable energy markets.** Ethiopia, Kenya, Rwanda, Tanzania and Uganda have seen the most significant growth in renewable energy production in the region (AfDB, 2022). Kenya, Ethiopia and Uganda received 66% of greenfield FDI capital expenditures for renewable energy projects in all of East Africa over 2017-22.[5] Kenya in particular has been able to diversify its renewable energy production and was recognised as one of the top five global destinations for clean energy investments in 2019 (Business Daily, 2019). Despite a much lower GDP, Rwanda is included within Cluster 1 due to its investment in renewable energies as a percentage of GDP ranking in the top five globally (IEA, 2022). Cluster 1 countries have established national energy strategies, updated regulations and engaged in regional energy trade (AfDB, 2021). Their challenge will be to expand and diversify renewable energy production more quickly, supported by targeted public investments and a reduction of barriers for private investors.

- **Cluster 2: Widening energy access.** Comoros, Djibouti, Eritrea, Madagascar, Somalia, Sudan and South Sudan offer fewer opportunities for private investments. For instance, only Djibouti and Madagascar attracted any greenfield FDI projects for renewable energy projects from 2017 to 2022, according to the *fDi Markets* database, together receiving 9% of East Africa's total FDI inflows.[6] Cluster 2 countries focus on expanding energy access and replacing polluting energy sources with clean ones wherever this is cost-effective and affordable; however, they continue to rely on combustible renewable energy (biofuels) and even fossil fuels where necessary to increase energy access. These countries mostly concentrate on regulatory fundamentals such as transparent and predictable tariff regimes (AfDB, 2021).
- **Cluster 3: Achieving renewable-based energy independence.** Mauritius and Seychelles are small island states and, as high-income countries, they are attractive destinations for private investments. They received 25% of East Africa's greenfield FDI capital expenditures in renewable energies over 2017-22.[7] They have high electricity and clean cooking access rates, and their energy regulation systems are well developed. These countries can focus on attracting private investments for renewable energy projects to reduce their dependence on fossil fuel imports and increase their resilience. For instance, innovative projects such as floating solar power plants make use of these countries' natural and financial assets (Largue, 2020).

Emerging innovative enterprises are spurring the regional renewable energy sector, thus benefiting productive transformation

Innovative enterprises and their business models have begun to enhance and expand renewable energy production and distribution in East Africa. Following the success of start-ups such as Kenya's M-Kopa Solar, local private businesses have taken advantage of opportunities across renewable energy value chains, covering the manufacturing of devices and components, infrastructure development, the direct distribution and access to electricity and clean cooking, and transportation (Table 5.2). Common are manufacturers and assemblers of solar panels (e.g. Kenya's Strauss Energy and Solinc), wind turbines (e.g. Uganda's Millennium Engineers), clean cookstoves (e.g. Kenya's Acacia Innovations) and electricity distributors (e.g. Tanzania's Juabar). Notably, enterprises have created innovative business models in response to existing energy system challenges (e.g. pay-as-you-go electricity and subscription cookstove models) focused on specific target groups (e.g. agricultural value chains), thereby achieving productive transformation and environmental sustainability goals at the same time. Market-based innovative business models have almost exclusively come from Cluster 1 countries, due to their market sizes, efforts to liberalise energy systems and existing entrepreneurial talent. In Cluster 2 countries, grant-funded innovative projects contribute to sustainable development (see Box 5.1).

Table 5.2. Examples of innovative enterprises and their business models in East Africa's renewable energy sector

Value chain focus	Enterprise	Business model	Target group	Market reach	Industri-alisation	Job creation	Innovation	Digitalisation
Manufacturing and assembly	Strauss Energy, a Kenyan start-up and manufacturer of innovative solar energy-generating roofing tiles (Building Integrated Photovoltaics)	Three-year cost-recovery via surplus power sale back	H, I+C	N	x	x	x	
	Solinc, Kenya's and East Africa's first solar panel manufacturer, assembler and distributor	Pay-as-you-go via dealers and firms	C	R	x	x	x	
Infrastructure provision	Group Filatex, Madagascar's leading producer of mini-grids and renewable energy infrastructure (a provider of over 10 000 jobs)	Servicing of industrial zones' rooftops	H, I+C	C	x	x	x	
	PowerGen, Kenya's provider of clean renewable energy and leading global mini-grid developer	10 000 grid connections	H, I+C	C	x	x	x	x
	Power Point Systems, Kenya's Infrastructure (grid and mini-grid) developer and power systems provider	Diversified provider	I+C, O	C	x	x	x	x
	CrossBoundary Energy, Kenya-based award-winning financier of over USD 100 million in renewable energy infrastructure projects.	Project financing	I+C	C	x	x	x	
Distribution and access	M-KOPA Solar, Kenya's provider of solar-powered home systems	Pay-as-you-go	H	R		x	x	
	Juabar, Tanzania's provider of solar-powered kiosks for mobile phone charging in off-grid communities	Franchise	C	N		x	x	
	Acacia Innovations, Kenya's SDG7 award-winning provider of clean cookstoves to schools	Subscription service	O	N			x	
	Solagen Power Ltd, Kenya's provider of solar energy	B2C+B2B	H, C, O	R	x	x		
	Energy Systems Ltd, Uganda's provider of solar energy, including to off-grid areas	B2C+B2B	H, I+C, O	N	x	x		
	Empower Renewable Energy, Sudan's renewable energy access provider	Diversified provider	H, I+C, O	C	x	x	x	
	SunCulture, Kenya's provider of solar-powered irrigation and ancillary services to smallholder farmers	Customised provision	I+C	R		x	x	x
	Power OffGrid, Somalia's provider of smart solar solutions to farmers and others in off-grid communities	PayGo asset financing platform, Goat4kWh	H, C	N		x	x	x
Transportation	Ampersand, Rwanda's electric mobility operator	Rideshare	C	R		x		
	BasiGo, Kenya's assembler and provider of renewable energy-powered e-buses	Pay-as-you-drive	C	C	x	x	x	x

Notes: SDG7 = Sustainable Development Goal 7: Affordable and clean energy. B2C+B2B = business to consumer and business to business. Target group: H = households; I+C = industrial and commercial; O = organisational. Market reach: N = national; R = regional; C = continental.
Source: Authors' compilation based on a literature review.

Box 5.1. Solar energy and clean cooking programmes targeting rural areas

Solar energy and clean cooking programmes have a range of benefits for rural communities across East Africa. They offer solutions directly to schools, hospitals, dispensaries, refugee camps or night-time markets.

Power OffGrid Somalia provides solar solutions and clean energy for rural off-grid and hard-to-reach communities in Jowhar, Somalia. Its innovative and affordable hybrid smart renewable energy services and PayGo asset financing platform for unbanked communities, Goat4kWh, allows pastoralists and farmers to use their livestock as capital to finance their electrification. The firm thereby increases access to electricity, adequate clean water, and clean cooking for thousands of Somalian households (Impakter, 2019).

Women in rural Africa can act as community leaders, entrepreneurs and trainers championing access to solar-powered electricity and emission-reducing clean cookstoves. The Maasai Stoves and Solar Project has, for example, been training Tanzanian women for jobs as distributors and installers of solar panels and cookstoves for traditional mud houses. In addition to reducing emissions and indoor pollution deaths, according to Ligami (2017), such clean energy transition initiatives can help alleviate poverty.

Digital technologies have allowed for more renewable energy, through new business models and data sharing. Digital technologies have enhanced renewable energy generation (e.g. digital wind farms and hydropower digitisation), distribution (e.g. smart grid and e-shops) and energy usage (e.g. smart metering, mobile platforms and energy efficiency applications) (Table 5.2). The declining costs of digital components such as sensors and of data storage technologies have enabled the creation of new business models in data analytics and cybersecurity, operational efficiency, and controls for distributed renewable energy and storage (GE, 2018). Kenya's Plexus Energy, Somalia's Power OffGrid and Uganda's Energy Monitoring Ltd exemplify East Africa's renewable energy-focused digital solution providers (Wilson, 2021). At a larger scale, synthetic weather models such as the Renewable Energy Space Analytics Tool (RE-SAT) and Small Islands Developing States' Digital Toolkit, developed through collaboration between the Seychelles government, the International Energy Agency, the Commonwealth Secretariat and other international partners, provide data and additional information as a public good (The Commonwealth, 2021).

Some East African energy infrastructure providers are emerging as lead firms, while established regional multinational enterprises act as investors. Large grid infrastructure firms (e.g. PowerGen and Group Filatex), infrastructure finance providers (e.g. CrossBoundary Energy), and regional and continental renewable energy producers (e.g. Power Point Systems and Group Filatex) are beginning to establish a region-wide footprint (Table 5.2). The diversification of Kenya's Safaricom into solar and wind power generation and the Mauritius Commercial Bank's financing of renewable energy electrification projects indicate that the region's largest multinational enterprises seek investment opportunities in the sector (International Finance, 2022).

Increasing demand by commercial energy users and by green development projects is supporting larger-scale, customised renewable energy generation and distribution projects. As a result of the high costs of deployment and of commercial customers, such as retailers and hospitality businesses, seeking alternatives to grid-based energy access, business models that offer renewable energy-based solutions have become increasingly viable in East Africa. For instance, the retailer SunCulture in Kenya provides solar-powered irrigation solutions to farmers (BII, n.d.). In addition, industrial parks and newly established "green cities" now have opportunities to integrate on-site renewable energy sources into their energy provision. Rwanda's Green City in Kigali, spearheaded by the Rwanda Green Fund (FONERWA), with financial support from Germany's KfW Development Bank, seeks to use renewable energy investments to generate positive knock-on effects for social and environmental sustainability (Nkurunziza, 2021).

Public policies can improve East Africa's renewable energy sector and help mobilise investments

To mobilise investments in East Africa's renewable energy sector, policy makers must improve energy regulation, strengthen public investments and support regional integration and lead firms (Table 5.3). As a first priority, large and small-scale private investments will continue to be required to better exploit the potential of East Africa's renewable energy generation, and policy makers can focus on improving regulatory reforms and developing the region's renewable energy sector. Second, scarce public funds need to be invested in more strategic and innovative ways, which requires capable financial and public institutions. Third, regional integration can be further enhanced by promoting large-scale government-led projects and by encouraging investments from regional lead firms and innovative enterprises.

Table 5.3. **Priority policy recommendations for clusters of East African countries**

Policy domain	Recommendation	Cluster 1: Ethiopia Kenya Rwanda Tanzania Uganda	Cluster 2: Comoros Djibouti Eritrea Madagascar Somalia South Sudan Sudan	Cluster 3: Mauritius Seychelles
Regulatory frameworks and capacity	Develop a regulatory framework with credible sector plans and incentives, based on learning from regional peers		X	
	Implement reforms robustly and consistently	X		
	Regularly evaluate the regulatory framework, drawing pertinent lessons and redress investor concerns	X	X	X
Public investments and innovative financial mechanisms	Create long-term financial commitments and instruments for public and institutional investments	X		X
	Establish a sovereign green bond to support domestic investments	X		X
	Resolve conflicts and offer political risk insurance and other de-risking tools	X	X	
	Enhance institutional governance and capacity to support the development of bankable proposals and access to financing opportunities	X	X	X
Regional integration, lead firms and entrepre-neurial innovation	Deepen regional infrastructure projects to facilitate cross-border energy transport and trade	X	X	X
	Harmonise regulations to encourage cross-border market development and value chains	X		
	Facilitate the emergence of more renewable energy enterprises and strengthen local entrepreneurship and community-based financing	X		
	Promote the transformation of utilities and state-owned enterprises into lead firms and reliable partners for enterprises	X	X	X
	Increase investment in grid infrastructure and partner with private investors and development finance institutions to promote decentralised energy access	X	X	

Source: Authors' compilation based on a literature review.

Enhancing regulatory frameworks and the capacity of energy utilities will expand the region's renewable energy sector

Most East African countries have embraced foundational regulatory reforms and institutional pilot projects in favour of renewable energies, while their full implementation is still pending. A range of promising policy initiatives has emerged across the region, especially in Cluster 1 countries (Table 5.4). This group of countries also has more complete regulatory frameworks than their Cluster 2 counterparts (Table 5.5).

Table 5.4. Examples of policies to enhance institutional capacity and regulatory frameworks in renewable energies in East Africa

Policy example	Policy goal	Impact
Kenya's regulatory reforms and tax incentives for private investors	Enhance the legal framework for the renewable energy sector	Kenya jumped 52 places over 5 years in the World Bank's Ease of Doing Business Index and has grown into a regional renewable energy powerhouse (RES4Africa and PWC, 2021).
Uganda's Global Energy Transfer Feed-in-Tariff (GET FiT) Premium Payment Mechanism	Improve market access for independent power producers (IPPs)	The additional payments that GET FiT receives make small-scale private renewable energy generation projects more financially viable and have contributed to 17 competed IPPs and have produced a total of 158 megawatts, or 760 GW/hour per annum (KFW and Multiconsult, 2021).
Madagascar's USD 40 million Off-Grid Market Development Fund	Accelerate and achieve sustainable electrifica-tion through off-grid solar technologies	The Fund, with the World Bank's support, has provided debt financing to solar distributors and to institutions that finance end users or distributors (World Bank, 2018), following regional examples, notably from Kenya and Rwanda.
Madagascar's Electricity Sector Operations and Governance Improvement Project (ESOGIP)	Promote innovations among utilities and state-owned enterprises to enhance their operations and financial viability	This World Bank-financed project introduced a transparent international bidding process, digitalisation of state agencies' work processes and legal frameworks for grid connections (World Bank, 2018).
Uganda's Twaake pilot project	Combine centralised and decentralised technologies to achieve universal electrification	Utilities 2.0 *Twaake*, the energy integration pilot project of Uganda's main power utility, Umeme, has resulted in an intelligent and interactive smart network, which delivers clean energy solutions, revenue management and cost efficiencies (Wilson, 2021).

Source: Authors' compilation based on a literature review.

Table 5.5. Regulatory frameworks in East Africa's renewable energy sector

Regulatory feature	Cluster 1					Cluster 2							Cluster 3	
	Ethiopia	Kenya	Rwanda	Tanzania	Uganda	Comoros	Djibouti	Eritrea	Madagascar	Somalia	Sudan	South Sudan	Mauritius	Seychelles
Electrification/energy masterplan or roadmap covering rural areas			x	x	x		x	x	x					x
Nationally determined contributions commitment	x	x	x	x	x	x	x	x	x	x	x	x	x	x
Renewable energy targets and a diversified mix of energy sources	x	x	x	x		x			x	x	x		x	x
Private participation reforms completed		x		x		x			x					x
Transparent auction-based energy licensing and procurement		x			x								x	
Unbundled user access provided by utilities	x	x		x										x
Independent regulator	x	x		x		x	x							
Tax incentives and subsidies for renewable energies	x		x	x									x	x
Differentiation in feed-in tariffs by technology and plant size		X											x	

Source: Authors' compilation based on AfDB (2021) and desk research.

East African governments need to regularly evaluate the effectiveness of existing renewable energy regulatory frameworks, including through investor feedback. Such regular policy self-evaluations can help reveal the outcomes of implemented policies and highlight those aspects requiring further reform. Following investor feedback, Uganda replaced its original feed-in-tariff (FiT) policy with a more attractive Global Energy Transfer Feed-in-Tariff (GET FiT) Premium Payment Mechanism (KFW and Multiconsult, 2021). Seeking input, dialogue and active buy-in from investors can help clarify risk perceptions and lead to more impactful and relevant policies (RES4Africa and PWC, 2021).

East African countries can learn from and emulate each other's successful regulatory efforts. In particular, Cluster 2 countries with incomplete renewable energy policies (Table 5.5) can adapt regulations and laws from Cluster 1 countries to their contexts, notably, national electrification and clean cooking plans that define roles for distribution (e.g. grid and decentralised) and clean cooking technologies (e.g. e-cooking and biomass pellets). Cluster 1 countries can learn from each other about novel and technically ambitious initiatives, such as green, sustainability and sustainability-linked bonds (Dembele, Schwarz and Horrocks, 2021; see also Chapter 2). For example, Kenya's denomination of its feed-in tariff in United States dollars could potentially serve Ethiopia's policy makers who have encountered difficulties arising from their Ethiopian Birr-denominated feed-in tariff policy, including the loss of the International Finance Corporation's backing for the Scaling Solar project (RES4Africa and PWC, 2021).

East Africa's utilities could be reformed to become facilitators of market access for renewable energy providers and embrace smart grid technologies. Reforms that mandate utilities to unbundle end-user access and allow for private participation in electricity generation and distribution (such as power wheeling, net metering and a direct-to-customer selling option for independent power producers) could be advanced and deepened. Policy makers can also encourage utilities to adopt smart grid technologies that facilitate the seamless and efficient integration of centralised and decentralised sources of energy into intelligent and interactive networks (Blankers, 2022; ESI Africa, 2022;). The Utilities 2.0 Twaake pilot project of Uganda's main power utility, Umeme, in collaboration with Power for All and the Rockefeller Foundation, recently reinforced the revenue management, efficiency and decarbonisation benefits of its digital grids (Smith, 2021).

Strengthening local financial institutions and instruments can catalyse resources for renewable energy projects

East Africa's policy makers can increase financing for renewable energy by prioritising long-term public investments, establishing green bonds and improving institutional capacity for the development of bankable projects. High-upfront costs, the costs of capital and investment risks need to be effectively mitigated to raise financing conditions to viable levels. Budgetary commitments, green funds and project preparation toolkits offer solutions (Table 5.6).

Table 5.6. **Examples of policies to strengthen local financial systems to mobilise and channel resources for renewable energy projects in East Africa**

Policy example	Policy goal	Impact
Uganda's ten-year budgetary commitment	Sustain public investments in renewable energy and de-risk private investments	USD 5.4 billion is allocated over ten years to finance 2 471 megawatts of renewable energy from hydro, solar, biomass and geothermal sources (AfDB, 2022).
Rwanda Green Fund	Deploy new innovative financing, notably green funding, to mitigate upfront costs and catalyse domestic investments	The Fund has facilitated investments of USD 40 billion in 35 projects, created over 137 500 green jobs and extended off-grid clean energy access to 57 500 households (UN, 2022).
Seychelles' SIDS Toolkit	Drive the development of internal capacity for preparing compelling project proposals	This digital toolkit for Small Island Developing States effectively supports the preparation of investment-grade business cases (Wilson, 2021).

Source: Authors' compilation based on a literature review.

Well-tailored financial instruments and long-term financial commitments by East African governments and institutional investors can expand access to finance and reassure investors. Mitigating the effects of high upfront costs, inflationary pressures and currency depreciation on domestic renewable energy investments by deploying financial instruments tailored to countries' needs can unlock and mobilise additional local funding (AfDB, 2022). Dedicated facilities and blended finance institutions – such as national climate funds, green banks and regional institutions like the Facility for Energy Inclusion, incubated by the African Development Bank, and the Sustainable Energy Fund for Africa – can help to manage these funds. Long-term commitments can provide security for investors' decision-making. Rwanda has committed to sustained public investments to boost renewable energy generation, distribution and access through a USD 40 billion Green Bond and Renewable Energy Fund, while Uganda has made a ten-year budgetary commitment of USD 5.4 billion to finance renewable energy projects (AfDB, 2022). Institutional investors can also play an important role: in 2021, Kenya's Retirement Benefits Authority committed to allocating USD 229 billion to infrastructure assets for the local renewable sector over 2021-26 (US Embassy Kenya, 2020).

New financial instruments can be leveraged for investments in renewable energies. Innovative financing instruments dedicated to climate resilience and the just energy transition are often available for renewable energy projects; they include green, social, sustainability and sustainability-linked bonds, debt-for-climate swaps, and climate-linked debt. Governments can increase their eligibility for financial instruments by strengthening the internal capacity and technical expertise of financial institutions, regulators and utilities. Generating revenue through carbon credits can, for example, support further investment in renewable energy projects as well as co-finance or subsidise upfront investment costs, such as for clean cooking appliances for end users (AfDB, 2022).

Local financial institutions can improve collaboration with development finance institutions and international partners to develop bankable projects, adjusted to the local market size. Local financial institutions, such as development banks, can help co-ordinate funding and support mechanisms from development finance institutions and other international partners (Chapter 2). Particularly in Cluster 2 countries, enhancing the capacities of local institutions to effectively access and channel international support will be essential, since bankable projects will remain scarce due to the small size of their markets. Technical assistance grants, funded internships and personnel exchanges, and project preparation grants from development partners – for instance, the Sustainable Energy Fund for Africa – can support this process (SEFA, 2021). The African Rift Geothermal Development Facility (ARGeo) provides an example of a high-impact project. Launched by the United Nations Environment Program in 2010, ARGeo aimed to develop the untapped potential of geothermal resources and reduce greenhouse gas emissions in several East African countries. Through technical assistance for surface exploration studies, the project lowered risks associated with resource exploration and catalysed USD 300 million of investment in Ethiopia, Kenya, Tanzania and Uganda, while also boosting regional networks and establishing the Africa Geothermal Center of Excellence (GEF, 2021).

Regional integration policies can facilitate the emergence and upscaling of innovative enterprises

East African policy makers can deepen regional integration and support the growth of regional enterprises. The small size of many of the region's renewable energy markets makes regional integration paramount. East Africa's vibrant emerging renewable energy sector presents a unique opportunity for the region to complement large-scale regional integration projects with dedicated enterprise promotion programmes (Table 5.7).

Table 5.7. **Examples of policies to facilitate the emergence and regional upscaling of innovative enterprises in East Africa's renewable energy sector**

Policy example	Policy goal	Impact
Zambia-Tanzania-Kenya Transmission Line Project	Increase regional and pan-African energy trade	Through the Zambia-Tanzania-Kenya Transmission Line Project, more than 2 200 km of a bi-directional 400-megawatt power transmission line from Kabwe in Zambia to Isinya in Kenya will be established by 2026, enhancing regional power transmission capacity by 2 550 megawatts and increasing co-operation with Southern African Power Pool countries (World Bank, 2022b).
Enhancement of a Sustainable Regional Energy Market project	Harmonise the regional regulatory framework and market conditions	This project involving the Eastern Africa, Southern Africa and Indian Ocean (EA-SA-IO) Region developed 12 regional guidelines to promote renewable energy and energy efficiency initiatives and trained 363 regional officials on aligning member states' national legislations with the harmonised regional regulatory framework they adopted (Osemo, 2022).
Rwanda's Renewable Energy Fund	Stimulate greater entrepreneurship to optimise renewable energy opportunities	This fund managed by the Rwanda Development Bank has provided low-cost loans, direct equity and grants to companies, commercial banks and solar companies to purchase off-grid solar home systems, develop mini-grids and support clean cooking technologies (Nkurunziza, 2021).
Africa Adaptation Initiative	Enhance continental and cross-sector collaboration on climate change adaptation	The investment led by this public-private partnership enables African countries to achieve their resilience objectives, facilitating the energy transition (UNEP, 2021).
Uganda's renewable energy policy principle 8: "Stakeholder Participation and the Poor"	Promote universal renewable energy access to foster social transformation	The Rural and Urban-Poor Electrification Access Programme expressly mandates future projects to be extended to the poor and women at subsidised connection costs (World Bank, 2021).

Source: Authors' compilation.

East African governments and regional institutions can intensify the promotion of cross-border energy trade, including through infrastructure projects (see also Box 3.2 in Chapter 3). The Eastern Africa Power Pool (EAPP), established in 2005, aims to enhance cross-border energy trade and ensures the operation of the interconnected power grid for several East African and other African countries (EAPP, n.d.). The EAPP could reduce energy trade costs by USD 18.6 billion if a tight integration scenario is achieved, including substantial new interconnection projects that support renewable energy plans optimised at the regional level. Under this scenario, the region's reliance on gas would decrease from 63% to 58% (Remy and Chattopadhyay, 2020), while a lower levelled cost of energy could generate savings of 10% for end users in East Africa (Castellano et al., 2015). Cross-border infrastructure projects, such as the Kenya-Ethiopia Electricity Highway Project or the Zambia-Tanzania-Kenya Transmission Line Project (Table 5.7), underpin this effort.

Regional integration initiatives present opportunities to further harmonise regulatory frameworks and market rules for power producers and organised private sector groups. The EAPP established the basic rules to regulate and govern the regional energy market (Deloitte, 2015). The African Continental Free Trade Area can improve the harmonisation of energy and business regulations, thereby stimulating both supply of and demand for renewables (Yavarhoussen, 2020), including accelerating the interconnectivity of grids. Certain regional institutions can implement market integration and regulatory harmonisation. One such institution is the East African Community's East African Centre for Renewable Energy and Efficiency, which can provide technical assistance and ensure a more active mobilisation of the region's organised private sector groups.

Supporting innovative enterprises can have many benefits for sustainable development. Targeted measures to instigate the emergence of new ventures, enterprise scaling and job creation across renewable energy value chains include financial incentives, partial risk guarantees and blended finance for scale-up funding. For instance, the Scaling Solar programme supported by the International Finance Corporation assists governments with project preparation and structuring and provides project developers with documentation and de-risking services (IFC, 2023). Entrepreneurial initiatives in the renewable energies sector can serve to expand access to electricity and clean cooking, foster the energy transition and create high-quality jobs, thereby increasing sustainable development (Tiedeman, 2022).[8]

Notes

1. Authors' calculation based on OECD (2021).
2. Authors' calculation based on OECD (2022b).
3. Authors' calculation based on fDi Intelligence (2022). Data for 2022 is available only until May 2022.
4. Authors' calculation based on IRENA (2022a).
5. Authors' calculation based on fDi Intelligence (2022). Data for 2022 is available only until May 2022.
6. Authors' calculation based on fDi Intelligence (2022). Data for 2022 is available only until May 2022.
7. Authors' calculation based on fDi Intelligence (2022). Data for 2022 is available only until May 2022.
8. While estimates for East Africa are missing, off-grid or decentralised renewables could create 3.4 million new jobs in India alone by 2030 (IRENA/ILO, 2022).

References

AfDB (2022), *African Economic Outlook 2022: Supporting Climate Resilience and a Just Energy Transition in Africa*, African Development Bank, Abidjan, www.afdb.org/en/documents/african-economic-outlook-2022.

AfDB (2021), *Electricity Regulatory Index for Africa 2021*, African Development Bank Group, Abidjan, https://africa-energy-portal.org/sites/default/files/2021-12/08122021%20ERI%20report%202021.pdf.

BII (n.d.), "How a Kenyan Company is helping farmers with irrigation", British International Investment, www.bii.co.uk/en/sustainable-investing/solar-powered-irrigation-kenya/.

Blankers, C. (14 July 2022), "Can we build net-zero data centres in Africa?", Bizcommunity, www.bizcommunity.africa/Article/410/640/229679.html.

Business Daily (8 December 2019), "Kenya rises to the top five in global clean energy ranking", *Business Daily Africa*, www.businessdailyafrica.com/bd/economy/kenya-rises-to-the-top-five-in-global-clean-energy-ranking-2273126.

Castellano, A. et al. (2015), *Brighter Africa: The Growth Potential of the Sub-Saharan Electricity Sector*, McKinsey, www.icafrica.org/fileadmin/documents/Knowledge/Energy/McKensey-Brighter_Africa_The_growth_potential_of_the_sub-Saharan_electricity_sector.pdf.

The Commonwealth (10 November 2021), "New toolkit to boost clean energy investments in small island nations", The Commonwealth, https://thecommonwealth.org/press-release/new-toolkit-boost-clean-energy-investments-small-island-nations.

Deloitte (2015), "The roadmap to a fully integrated and operational East African Power Pool", Deloitte, www2.deloitte.com/content/dam/Deloitte/ke/Documents/energy-resources/ER_Power%20TL.pdf.

Dembele, F., R. Schwarz and P. Horrocks (2021), *Scaling up Green, Social, Sustainability and Sustainability-linked Bond Issuances in Developing Countries*, OECD Publishing, Paris, www.oecd.org/dac/financing-sustainable-development/blended-finance-principles/documents/scaling-up-green-social-sustainability-sustainability-linked-bond-issuances-developing-countries.pdf.

EAPP (n.d.), "Facilitating longterm development of electricity market in the region", East African Power Pool website, https://eappool.org/.

ESI Africa (2 August 2022), "Why the digital grid is key to RE integration", ESI Africa, www.esi-africa.com/renewable-energy/why-the-digital-grid-is-key-to-re-integration/.

fDi Intelligence (2022), *fDi Markets* (database), www.fdiintelligence.com/fdi-markets (accessed August 2022).

GE (2018), *Digitization of Energy Transmission & Distribution in Africa: The Future of Energy in Sub-Saharan Countries*, Frost & Sullivan, www.gegridsolutions.com/press/gepress/2018/wp-digitization.pdf.

GEF (2021), "African Rift Geothermal Development Facility (ARGeo)", webpage, United Nations Environment Program, www.thegef.org/projects-operations/projects/2119.

IEA (2022), *Africa Energy Outlook 2022*, International Energy Agency, Paris, www.iea.org/reports/Africa-energy-outlook-2022.

IEA (2021a), *World Energy Outlook 2021*, International Energy Agency, Paris, www.iea.org/reports/world-energy-outlook-2021.

IEA (2021b), "World Energy Balances 2021", *International Energy Agency* (database), www.iea.org/data-and-statistics/data-product/world-energy-balances.

IFC (2023), "Scaling solar", webpage, International Finance Corporation, www.ifc.org/wps/wcm/connect/news_ext_content/ifc_external_corporate_site/news+and+events/news/scaling-solar (accessed 17 March 2023).

International Finance (2020), "Safaricom to diversify into energy, to supply power to the national grid", International Finance, https://internationalfinance.com/safaricom-diversify-energy-supply-power-national-grid/.

IMF (2023a), *World Economic Outlook Database*, April 2023 Edition, International Monetary Fund, www.imf.org/en/Publications/WEO/weo-database/2022/April (accessed April 2023).

IMF (2023b), "List of LIC DSAs for PRGT-eligible countries", International Monetary Fund, www.imf.org/external/pubs/ft/dsa/dsalist.pdf.

IMF (2022a), *World Economic Outlook Database*, October 2022 Edition, International Monetary Fund, www.imf.org/en/Publications/WEO/weo-database/2022/October (accessed October 2022).

IMF (2022b), *Balance of Payments and International Investment Position Statistics (BOP/IIP)* (database), International Monetary Fund, https://data.imf.org/?sk=7A51304B-6426-40C0-83DD-CA473CA1FD52 (accessed 22 November 2022).

IMF (2022c), *Investment and Capital Stock Dataset (ICSD)* (database), https://data.imf.org/?sk=1CE8A55F-CFA7-4BC0-BCE2-256EE65AC0E4 (accessed October 2022).

Impakter (26 April 2019), "Power offgrid: Innovating the energy market in Somalia", Medium, https://medium.com/@impakter.com/power-offgrid-innovating-the-energy-market-in-somalia-cc3bc502cf1a.

IRENA (2022a), *IRENASTAT* (database), https://pxweb.irena.org/pxweb/en/IRENASTAT?_gl=1*fltysn*_ga*MTA3NTM0NzYxLjE2NjE3NzAyNzQ.*_ga_7W6ZEF19K4*MTY3ODI4NTgxNC40NC4xLjE2NzgyODU4MzguMzYuMC4w (accessed October 2022).

IRENA (2022b), "Renewable Energy Employment by Country", *Statistics Data* (database), www.irena.org/Data/View-data-by-topic/Benefits/Renewable-Energy-Employment-by-Country (accessed March 2023).

IRENA/AfDB (2022), *Renewable Energy Market Analysis: Africa and Its Regions*, International Renewable Energy Agency and African Development Bank, Abu Dhabi and Abidjan, www.irena.org/-/media/Files/IRENA/Agency/Publication/2022/Jan/IRENA_Market_Africa_2022.pdf?rev=bb73e285a0974bc996a1f942635ca556.

IRENA/ILO (2022), *Renewable Energy and Jobs: Annual Review 2022*, International Renewable Energy Agency/International Labour Organization, Abu Dhabi/Geneva, www.irena.org/publications/2022/Sep/Renewable-Energy-and-Jobs-Annual-Review-2022.

KfW and Multiconsult (2021), *Get FiT Uganda Annual Report 2021*, KfW Group, www.getfit-uganda.org/annual-reports/annual-report-2021/.

Kincer, J. (July 2021), "What's the status of East Africa's geothermal market?", Energy for Growth Hub, www.energyforgrowth.org/wp-content/uploads/2021/07/Whats-the-status-of-East-Africas-geothermal-market_-.pdf.

Largue, P. (4 July 2020), "Seychelles to build world's largest floating solar plant", Renewable Energy World, www.renewableenergyworld.com/solar/seychelles-to-build-worlds-largest-floating-solar-plant/?topic=245866.

Ligami, C. (2017), "Renewable energy projects are uplifting Maasai women", *Earth Island Journal*, www.earthisland.org/journal/index.php/articles/entry/renewable_energy_projects_uplifting_maasai_women.

Nkurunziza, M. (1 November 2021), "How can Rwanda make the most of the global clean energy investment platform?", *The New Times*, www.newtimes.co.rw/article/190795/News/how-can-rwanda-make-the-most-of-the-global-clean-energy-investment-platform.

OECD (2022a), "Aid (ODA) disbursements to countries and regions", *OECD.Stat* (database), https://stats-1.oecd.org/Index.aspx?DataSetCode=TABLE2A (accessed October 2022).

OECD (2022b), "GHG Emissions from fuel combustion (summary)", *IEA CO2 Emissions from Fuel Combustion Statistics: Greenhouse Gas Emissions from Energy* (database), https://doi.org/10.1787/445ec5dd-en (accessed 3 September 2022).

OECD (2022c), "Mobilisation", *OECD.Stat* (database), https://stats.oecd.org/Index.aspx?DataSetCode=DV_DCD_MOBILISATION (accessed February 2023).

OECD (2021), *OECD Global Pension Statistics* (database), https://doi.org/10.1787/pension-data-en.

Osemo, W. (8 June 2022), "Comoros to have a national energy regulation board", Common Market for Eastern and Southern Africa, www.comesa.int/comoros-to-have-a-national-energy-regulation-board/.

Remy, T. and D. Chattopadhyay (2020), "Promoting better economics, renewables and CO2 reduction through trade: A case study for the Eastern Africa Power Pool", *Energy for Sustainable Development*, Vol. 57, 2020, pp. 81-97, https://doi.org/10.1016/j.esd.2020.05.006.

RES4Africa/PwC Italy (2021), *Investor Survey on Sub Saharan Africa*, RES4Africa and PricewaterhouseCoopers Italy, https://static1.squarespace.com/static/609a53264723031eccc12e99/t/6180ffb91e351d4c7fcdd981/1635844031170/Investor+survey+on+Sub+Saharan+Africa_RES4Africa+PwC+%281%29.pdf.

Roy, R. (forthcoming), "Africa's developmental path as a solution to the problem of air pollution in Africa", background paper for *Africa's Development Dynamics 2023*.

SEFA (2021), *Sustainable Energy Fund for Africa (SEFA) - Annual Report 2021*, Sustainable Energy Fund for Africa, www.afdb.org/en/documents/sustainable-energy-fund-africa-sefa-annual-report-2021.

Smith, T. (29 June 2021), "Uganda: Integrated energy and approach to create energy for all", ESI Africa, www.esi-africa.com/business-and-markets/uganda-integrated-energy-approach-to-create-energy-for-all/.

Tiedeman, M. (27 June 2022), "Harnessing renewable energy for climate-friendly development", RTI International, www.rti.org/insights/harnessing-renewable-energy-for-climate-friendly-development.

UN (2022), "Rwanda Green Fund – FONERWA", webpage, United Nations, https://unfccc.int/climate-action/momentum-for-change/financing-for-climate-friendly-investment/rwanda-green-fund-fonerwa.

UNEP (2021), "African Adaptation Initiative (AAI)", webpage, United Nations Environment Programme, 22 September 2021, https://climateinitiativesplatform.org/index.php/African_Adaptation_Initiative_(AAI)

US Embassy Kenya (2020), "U.S. announces new Kenyan pension consortium to mobilize investment in large scale infrastructure projects", US Embassy Kenya, https://ke.usembassy.gov/united-states-announces-new-kenyan-pension-consortium-to-mobilize-investment-in-large-scale-infrastructure-projects/.

WHO (2021), "Household Energy Database", *World Health Organisation* (database), www.who.int/data/gho/data/themes/air-pollution/who-household-energy-db.

Wilson, C. (3 November 2021), "Seychelles: Mobilising the 'Tools' for renewable energy investment in the Seychelles", AllAfrica, https://allafrica.com/stories/202111050484.html.

World Bank (2022a), *World Development Indicators* (database), https://data.worldbank.org/products/wdi (accessed April 2022).

World Bank (2022b), "AFR RI-3A Tanzania-Zambia Transmission Interconnector (P163752)", https://documents1.worldbank.org/curated/en/099074001312362436/pdf/P1637520d5d2ff0f0090cd0ce7da89154d2.pdf.

World Bank (2021), *The Renewable Energy Policy for Uganda*, World Bank, Washington, DC, https://ppp.worldbank.org/public-private-partnership/library/renewable-energy-policy-uganda.

World Bank (14 June 2018), "Madagascar - Electricity Sector Operations and Governance Improvement Project – Additional financing", World Bank Group, Washington, DC, www.worldbank.org/en/news/loans-credits/2018/06/14/madagascar-electricity-sector-operations-and-governance-improvement-project-additional-financing.

World Bank-KNOMAD (2022), *Remittances* (database), Global Knowledge Partnership on Migration and Development and World Bank, www.knomad.org/data/remittances (accessed 19 December 2022).

Yavarhoussen, H. (15 September 2020), "Innovation is imperative for Africa's renewable energy", *Energy Voice*, www.energyvoice.com/opinion/265093/madagascar-africa-solar-demand/.

Chapter 6

Investing in climate action for North Africa's sustainable development

This chapter focuses on mobilising sustainable investment in North Africa's six countries (Algeria, Egypt, Libya, Mauritania, Morocco and Tunisia). It analyses the region's financial inflows and considers in particular how they are allocated to sustainable activities that promote regional integration. Next it explores the potential of sustainable finance markets to attract investment for climate action in North Africa. It examines the vulnerability of the region's economies to climate change and identifies their sustainable development financing needs. Finally, this chapter suggests public policies that would allow sustainable finance markets to be developed and integrated into North Africa.

IN BRIEF

Climate change is having a significant socio-economic impact on North African countries, reducing per capita gross domestic product (GDP) growth by between 5% and 15% each year. In particular, the region is more exposed than the rest of the continent to risks associated with temperature increases, which lead to droughts, water stress and fires. It does, however, have the assets to encourage energy transition, such as its potential capacity to generate solar and wind power – which is about 3 times greater than Europe's total installed capacity in 2021.

However, North African countries are struggling to attract climate finance. Over 2019-20, they received an annual average of USD 5.8 billion – well below the over USD 39 billion per year needed by 2030 to address climate change. Developing innovative financial mechanisms, such as green bonds, nevertheless enabled Egypt and Morocco to mobilise USD 1.1 billion between 2016 and 2021. However, weak institutional co-ordination and the lack of regulatory frameworks adapted to sustainable finance are limiting the development of this type of instrument in the region.

Policy makers can use three levers to mobilise investment for climate action: 1) improving the identification and allocation of financing needs according to national priorities; 2) developing inclusive and supportive regulatory frameworks for sustainable finance; and 3) supporting the development of the sustainable finance market through regional co-operation.

North Africa

An unequal allocation of investments

Greenfield FDI allocation

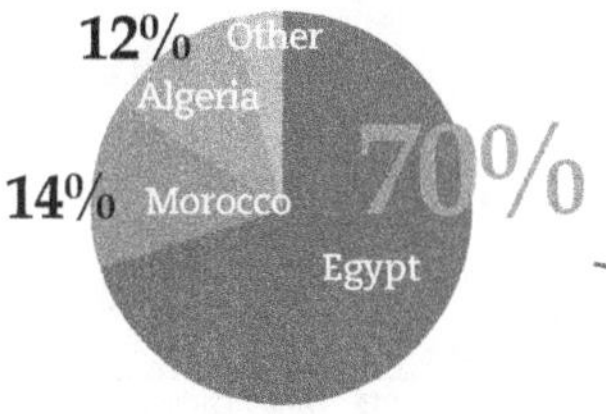

(in 2017-22)

75% of greenfield FDI targeted:

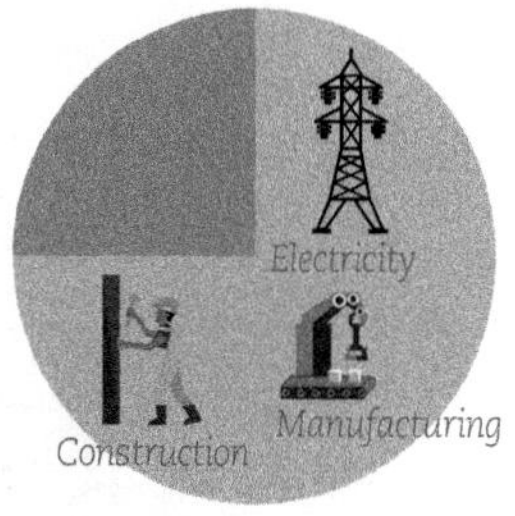

Only 1/4 of FDI in the energy sector went to renewables

despite a potential 3 times greater than Europe's total installed energy capacity in 2021

Climate finance is lagging behind

USD 38.9 billion

the annual amount required
for the implementation over 2020-30 of Nationally Determined Contributions (NDCs) under the Paris Agreement by North African countries

USD 5.8 billion

the annual amount received
on average by North African countries over 2019-20

Green bonds issuance in Egypt and Morocco between 2016-21 mobilised

USD 1.1 billion

=

25% of the total amount mobilised by the entire continent

Blended finance allocated to climate action in North Africa

What's next?

- **Improve assessment of financing needs** based on national and multi-sectorial priorities
- **Adopt and implement inclusive regulatory frameworks** on sustainable finance
- Encourage the **development of sustainable finance markets**

North Africa regional profile

Figure 6.1. **Components of economic growth and sources of financing in North Africa**

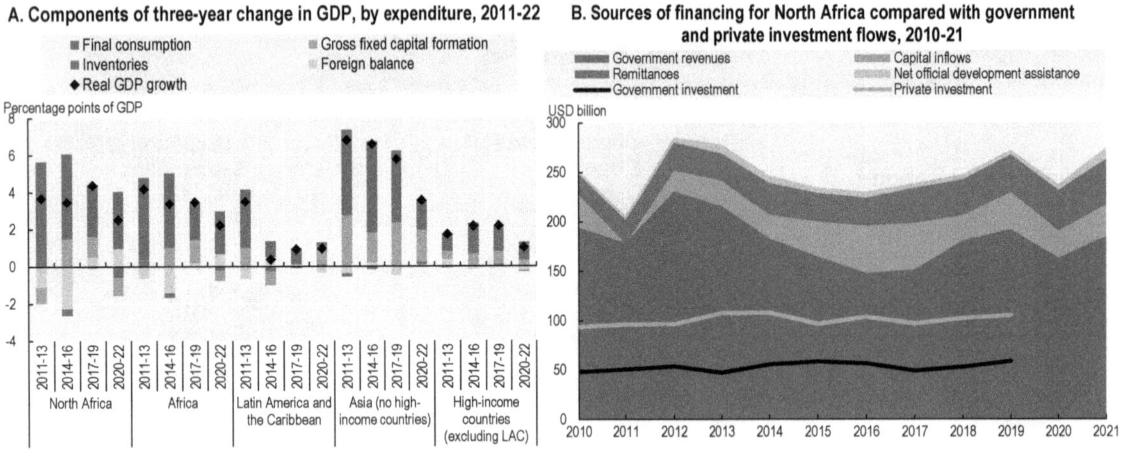

Note: The components of GDP growth are calculated on an annual basis by using real annual GDP growth to estimate the increase in real US dollars. Aggregate figures are calculated by taking the average of the national figures weighted by GDP in purchasing-power-parity dollars. The components of GDP growth over three-year periods were calculated by taking the difference between the geometric average of the annual real GDP growth over the period and the real GDP growth when setting each component to zero for individual years. Foreign balance is the difference between imports and exports. Imports contribute negatively to GDP. "High-income countries" refers to countries classified as "high-income" according to the World Bank Country and Lending Groups outside of Latin America and the Caribbean. Government revenues include all tax and non-tax government revenues minus debt service and grants received. Capital inflows include foreign direct investment (FDI), portfolio investment and other investment inflows reported by the International Monetary Fund under asset/liability accounting. Figures for capital inflows should be interpreted with some caution as some figures for 2021 and for portfolio inflows are missing.

Source: Authors' calculations based on IMF (2022a), *World Economic Outlook Database, October 2022* (database), www.imf.org/en/Publications/WEO/weo-database/2022/October; (OECD, 2022a), *Development Assistance Committee* (database), https://stats-1.oecd.org/Index.aspx?DataSetCode=TABLE2A; World Bank (2022a), *World Development Indicators* (database), https://data.worldbank.org/products/wdi; IMF (2022b), *Balance of Payments and International Investment Position Statistics (BOP/IIP)* (database), https://data.imf.org/?sk=7A51304B-6426-40C0-83DD-CA473CA1FD52; IMF (2022c), *Investment and Capital Stock Dataset (ICSD)* (database), https://data.imf.org/?sk=1CE8A55F-CFA7-4BC0-BCE2-256EE65AC0E4; and World Bank-KNOMAD (2022), *Remittances* (database), www.knomad.org/data/remittances.

StatLink https://stat.link/120xdy

Figure 6.2. **Greenfield foreign direct investment flows to North Africa, by activity, source and destination, 2017-22**

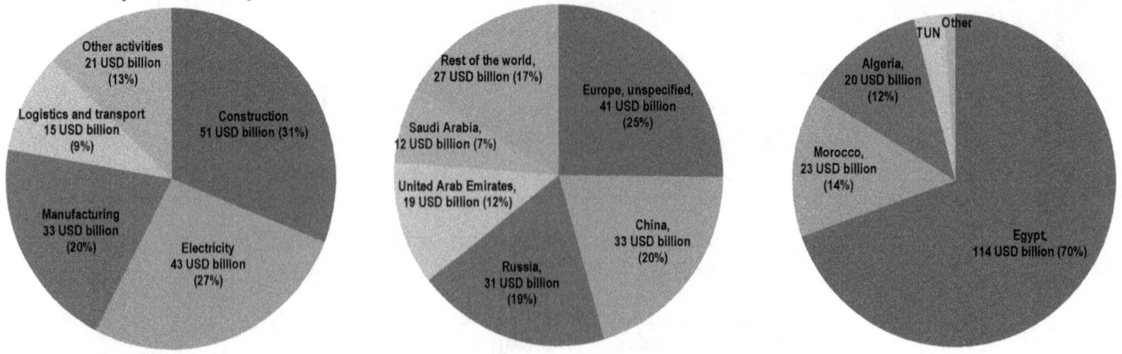

Note: The fDi Markets database is used only for comparative analysis. Actual investment amounts should not be inferred, as fDi Markets data are based on upfront announcements of investment projects, including a share of projects that do not actually materialise. TUN = Tunisia.

Source: Authors' calculations based on fDi Intelligence (2022), *fDi Markets* (database), www.fdiintelligence.com/fdi-markets.

StatLink https://stat.link/zidqs6

Sustainable investments remain unevenly distributed in North Africa

Development finance in North Africa has suffered from recent crises

The contribution of investment to North Africa's GDP growth has declined, despite buoyant regional demand. The COVID-19 pandemic had a negative effect on the contribution of public and private investment (gross fixed capital formation or GFCF) to GDP growth in North Africa, which decreased from a positive contribution of 1.1 percentage points per year over the 2017-19 period to a negative contribution of -1 percentage point in 2020-22 (Figure 6.1). Private consumption, however, continued to have a positive effect on GDP growth, rising from 2.8 percentage points in 2017-19 to 3.1 percentage points in 2020-22. This resilient consumption illustrates the significant potential that regional demand holds for local businesses.

Domestic revenue declined due to the COVID-19 pandemic, amid rising debt levels. From 2016 to 2019, governments mobilised additional revenue through comprehensive tax reform and oil price recovery following the 2015 fall. However, government revenue contracted in 2020 because of measures put in place to reduce the economic, health and social impact of the pandemic. Debt levels have increased in most countries, leading Mauritania, for example, to participate in the G20 Debt Service Suspension Initiative from June to December 2020 and to bilaterally restructure its debt. Several rating agencies progressively downgraded Tunisia's sovereign rating between 2020 and 2023, while Moody's recently downgraded Egypt's rating in 2023 (AfDB, 2022a; Moody's, 2023a, 2023b). Although the increased price of raw materials is benefiting the region's exporting countries, rising global inflation and the interest rate crisis could exacerbate North Africa's debt burden.

External financial inflows declined in 2020, with the exception of remittances (Figure 6.1). Remittances remain the largest source of external financial flows into the region, accounting for over 5% of GDP in Egypt, Morocco and Tunisia in 2020. In contrast, other financial flows continue to fluctuate and remain limited. Greenfield FDI inflows have declined since 2018. They accounted for just 1.3% of North Africa's GDP in 2020-21 compared with over 2% previously. Moreover, portfolio investments have remained volatile, declining from 7% of the region's GDP in 2017 to just 1% in 2020-21. This is partly due to political instability in some countries, global macroeconomic risks, and global supply disruptions and contractions in demand.

Investment allocation in sustainable sectors remains inconsistent

The distribution of foreign private financing in the region is geographically unbalanced. North Africa is the second-largest recipient of greenfield FDI on the continent, after Southern Africa. Between 2017 and 2022, Egypt received more than 70% of the region's FDI inflows, followed by Morocco (14%) and Algeria (12%) (Figure 6.2). The private finance mobilised by development banks and development finance institutions is allocated in much the same way as FDI across the region, with a focus on Egypt and Morocco. Blended finance increased nearly tenfold over the 2012-20 period (Figure 6.3, Panel A). Around half was allocated to banking and financial services, a promising sector for the region. The remainder went mostly to industry and renewable energy production (Figure 6.3, Panel B).

Figure 6.3. **Private finance mobilised by public development finance interventions in North Africa, 2012-20 (USD million)**

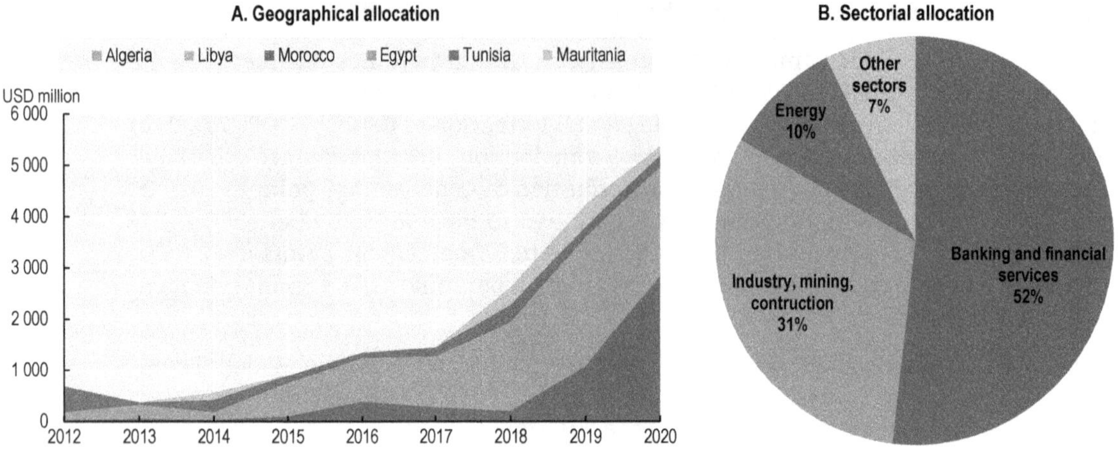

Note: "Other sectors" includes (in size order): multisectoral/cross-cutting; other infrastructure and social services; education; agriculture, forestry and fishing; health; water supply and sanitation; trade policies and regulations; unspecified allocation; tourism; corporate and other services; government and civil society; and population and reproductive health policies/programmes.

Source: OECD (2022b), "Mobilisation", *OECD.Stat* (database), https://stats.oecd.org/Index.aspx?DataSetCode=DV_DCD_MOBILISATION.

StatLink https://stat.link/hu3ogi

Foreign investment in North Africa has produced mixed results in terms of job creation. Around three-quarters (78%) of greenfield FDI received in 2017-22 targeted the construction, electricity and manufacturing sectors (Figure 6.2). In contrast to other sectors, the manufacturing industry offers the highest jobs-capital expenditure ratio, with more than four jobs created per million dollars invested (Figure 6.4). Greater investment in renewable energy could also create more jobs, particularly as part of the transition away from fossil fuels (Chapter 1; AUC/OECD, 2022). Compared with a business-as-usual scenario, limiting global warming to 1.5°C could increase the number of jobs in North Africa by 3% by 2030, despite job losses in the fossil fuel sector, and by 1.4% by 2050 (IRENA/AfDB, 2022).

Figure 6.4. **Greenfield FDI in North Africa, capital expenditure, and job creation by business activity, 2017-21**

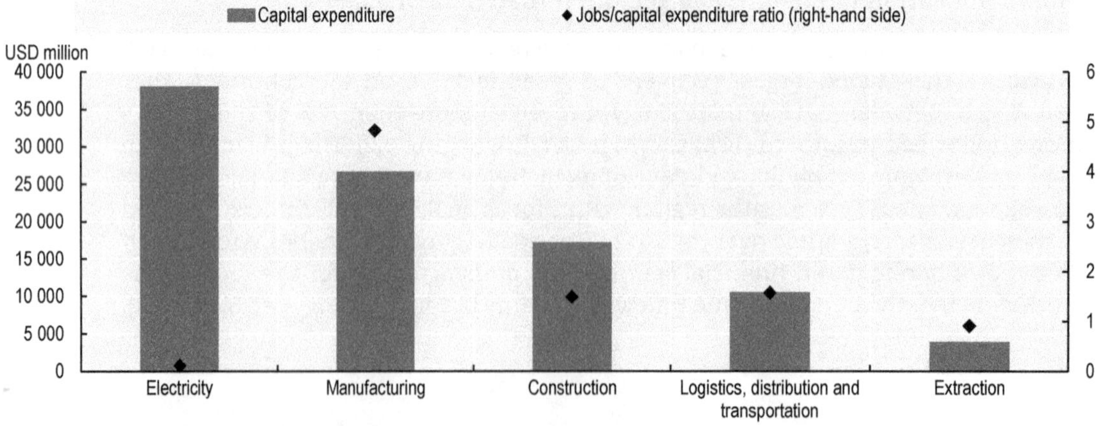

Note: The figure shows the main commercial activities by capital expenditure in 2017-21.

Source: Authors' calculations based on fDi Intelligence (2022), *fDi Markets* (database), www.fdiintelligence.com/fdi-markets.

StatLink https://stat.link/xcu7tw

Until now, most foreign investment has targeted sectors that negatively affect the environment. At present, North Africa accounts for only 1.5% of global carbon dioxide (CO_2) emissions and the region's per capita emission levels are similar to those of southern Africa and Latin America and the Caribbean. More than half of total emissions come from power generation and transport, both of which attract significant private financing. For example, more than half of the USD 14 billion allocated through OECD export credit agencies over the 2012-21 period went to the energy sector, followed by industry (27%), then transport and storage (19%). Given Algeria, Libya and Mauritania's significant resource endowments, around three-quarters of FDI in the energy sector targeted coal, oil and gas projects over the past decade (Figure 6.5). However, most countries in the region have placed renewable energy among their priority sectors for investment and are implementing policies to attract investment in sustainable energy production (OECD, 2021a).

Figure 6.5. **CO_2 emissions and investments in the energy sector in North Africa**

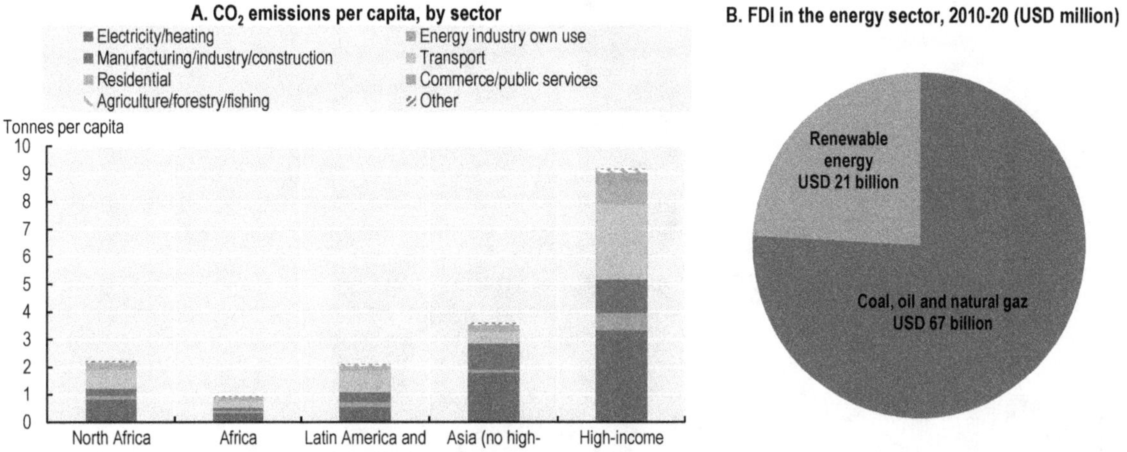

Source: IEA (2022), *Data and Statistics* (database), www.iea.org/data-and-statistics/data-tools/greenhouse-gas-emissions-from-energy-data-explorer; fDi Intelligence (2022), *fDi Markets* (database), www.fdiintelligence.com/fdi-markets.

StatLink https://stat.link/np8vgj

Official development assistance (ODA) and philanthropy are aimed at more-sustainable sectors, but are limited sources of funding. In 2020, ODA accounted for less than 1% of GDP in North Africa, which is made up almost entirely of middle-income countries (which receive proportionately less aid than less-advanced economies). Morocco and Egypt received the highest amounts of ODA in 2020, yet this still accounted for just 0.4% and 1.6% of their respective GDPs. In contrast, ODA made up 7% of GDP in Mauritania in 2020, the only low-income country in North Africa. Over the 2011-20 period, most ODA targeted socio-economic services, such as education (18%), health (15%) and energy (13%) (OECD, 2022a). Philanthropic flows remain limited (at around USD 150 million) and are directed mainly towards government and civil society, such as local non-governmental organisations, followed by environmental protection (OECD, 2021b).

North Africa has significant potential to boost intra-African investment

North Africa's outward FDI highlights the potential for increased continental integration. Inbound investment for new projects comes mostly from Europe, the People's Republic of China (hereafter "China"), Russia and the Middle East (by order of magnitude), while intra-African FDI accounted for only 1.3% of the total over the 2017-22 period (Figure 6.2). In contrast, most outward flows from North Africa for new investment projects targeted other African countries over the same period (Figure 6.6). Morocco accounted for more than 50% of outbound investments and had the largest continental reach (larger than South Africa), targeting mainly West African countries but also Central and East African countries. Egypt, the second-largest investor, targeted high-income countries and southern Africa, while Tunisia invested mainly at the regional level. Algerian investment flows targeted non-African destination countries in the Middle East and other high-income countries.

Figure 6.6. **Greenfield foreign direct investment outflows from North African countries, by destination regions, 2017-21, USD million**

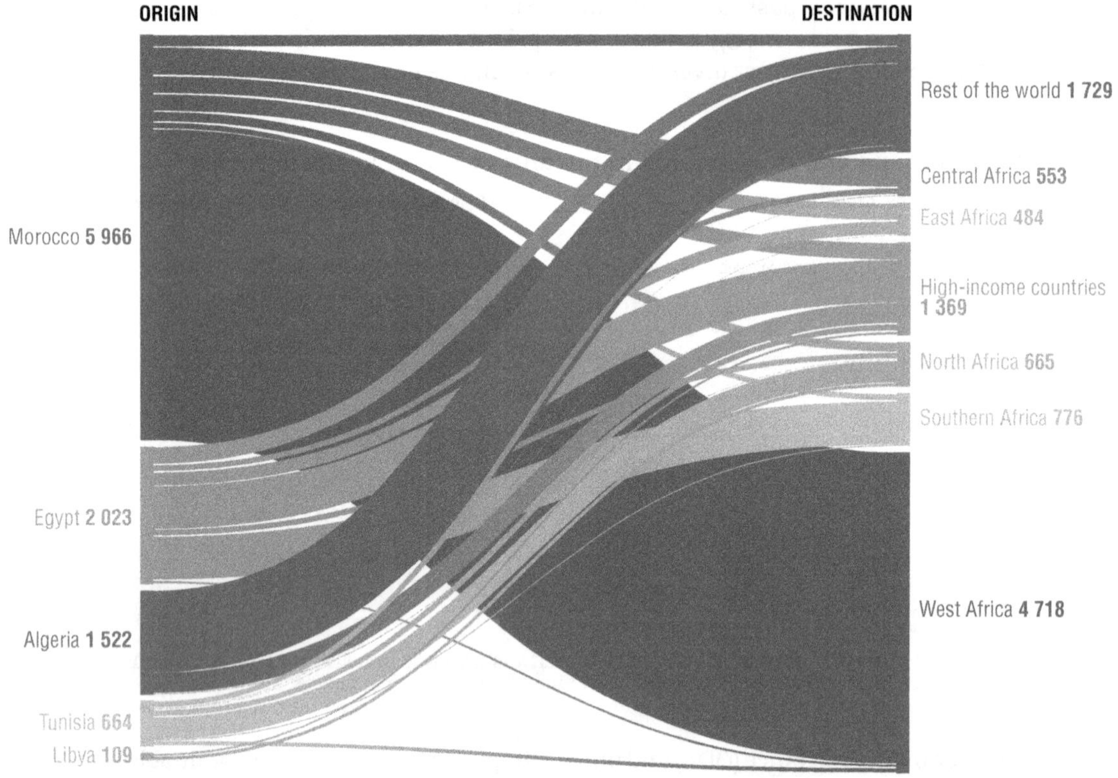

Note: "Rest of the World" includes developing countries in Asia (USD 370 million), Latin America and the Caribbean (USD 131 million) and other regions not included in the figure (USD 1 228 million).

Source: Authors' calculations based on fDi Intelligence (2022), *fDi Markets* (database), www.fdiintelligence.com/fdi-markets.

StatLink https://stat.link/fjt3xb

The leading regional companies could expand into manufacturing and financial services in Africa. Of the 147 North African private companies with subsidiaries in Africa listed in the Orbis database, 89 are based in Egypt, 35 in Tunisia, 22 in Morocco and 1 in Algeria (Bureau van Dijk, 2022). More than half of these companies operate in the manufacturing (28%) and financial services (26%) sectors, followed by real estate, information and communication technologies, and retail – sectors with great potential to develop regional value chains. North Africa also has many state-owned enterprises. While most of them have high levels of debt (IMF, 2021), some offer additional sources of sustainable investment in the region and the continent. The Moroccan OCP Group, for example, partners with West African governments to provide capacity-building programmes for local farmers and to make agricultural ecosystems more resilient (OCP Group, n.d.).

The financing gap hinders North Africa's response to the urgent climate crisis

Most North African countries have submitted their nationally determined contributions (NDCs) for climate action

The region's countries are relatively better prepared for climate change than the rest of the continent, but they remain vulnerable. North African countries can be divided into three groups based on their resilience to climate change (particularly in terms of the intensity of temperature variations) and their level of preparedness for its negative effects. The first group, comprising Mauritania, is the most vulnerable and least prepared to face the consequences of climate change in the region. The second, less vulnerable, group comprises Algeria, Egypt and Libya. The final group, the best prepared to deal with climate change, comprises Morocco and Tunisia (University of Notre Dame, 2020). Most North African countries are classified as "low vulnerability, high preparedness". However, the region remains extremely vulnerable to the impacts of climate change due to its high exposure to temperature increases, resulting in droughts, water stress and fires (AfDB, 2022a; Cos et al., 2022). The Physical Vulnerability to Climate Change Index (PVCCI), which measures the exposure of countries to climate shocks, confirms this trend (Table 6.1).

Table 6.1. **Classification of North African countries according to the Physical Vulnerability to Climate Change Index, 1950-2016**

	PVCCI	Risks related to progressive shocks linked to climate change		Risks related to intensifying recurrent shocks linked to climate change		
		Flooding	Aridity	Rainfall	Temperature	Storms
Algeria	61.2	0.6	82.5	84.9	68.6	0.1
Egypt	61.7	5.0	81.9	85.4	71.0	0.0
Libya	62.6	1.1	83.0	85.4	73.7	0.0
Morocco	58.7	0.9	82.9	81.1	61.2	4.8
Mauritania	64.7	1.0	83.1	84.5	83.1	0.0
Tunisia	61.1	3.6	86.5	81.9	66.8	0.0
North Africa (average)	**61.7**	**2.0**	**83.3**	**83.9**	**70.7**	**0.8**
Rest of Africa (average)	**54.7**	**2.4**	**55.4**	**70.5**	**78.3**	**7.5**

Note: The PVCCI is a composite indicator that measures both exposure to climate shocks and the size of the shocks for 191 countries. It comprises five dimensions, which refer to the risks of flooding, aridity, temperature shocks, rainfall shocks and cyclones. For each risk, the degree of exposure to these shocks and their likely magnitude was measured. The PVCCI components were then normalised on a scale of 0 (minimum) to 100 (maximum). Morocco has the lowest index score in the region (58.7), making it the least vulnerable country in North Africa. Mauritania has the highest score in the region, making it the most vulnerable country in North Africa (ranked tenth in terms of physical vulnerability to climate change globally).
Source: Cornier et al. (2018), *Physical Vulnerability to Climate Change Index* (database), https://ferdi-indicators.shinyapps.io/PVCCI/.

Climate change will have a serious socio-economic impact in North Africa. The annual loss in per capita GDP growth due to climate change is estimated at between 5% and 15% over the 1986-2015 period (AfDB, 2022a). Climate change affects the productive sectors. For example, in Egypt, where the agrifood sector accounts for around 20% of exports and one-third of employment, production could fall by 5.7% by 2050 – a greater drop than the 4.4% forecast for the rest of the world. Egypt's poorest populations will likely be the most affected, as climate change impacts on agriculture and health could increase the population living on less than USD 4 a day by 0.8% by 2030 (World Bank, 2022b). Fishing-related activities are also likely to be affected by global warming, which alters the availability of micronutrients and oxygen levels in the water, affecting the livelihoods of an estimated 300 000 people in Mauritania (ITA, 2022). Meanwhile, droughts could displace around 2 million of Morocco's poorest rural inhabitants by 2050 (World Bank, 2022b, c, d).

The transition to carbon neutrality in North Africa could contribute to post-COVID-19 economic recovery and make the region more resilient to crises. In 2022, global conflicts and periods of drought exacerbated North Africa's economic fragility, jeopardising food security in the region. This situation demonstrated some countries' reliance on global food supply chains. Egypt, for example, relied on Ukraine and Russia for more than 80% of its wheat imports (UNDP, 2022). Making the region's countries more resilient to climatic and external shocks offers opportunities. In Morocco, international restrictions on fertiliser exports boosted the OCP Group's profits from fertiliser sales by 83% between 2021 and 2022 (reaching USD 3.6 billion), and spurred investment, particularly in green fertiliser production (Les inspirations Éco, 2023; Mousjid, 2022). In addition, investment in renewable energies could help alleviate the energy crisis that is particularly affecting European countries(El-Katiri, 2023).

Most North African countries have submitted their NDCs in the context of the Paris Agreement. These contributions include adaptation and mitigation measures to reduce climate change impacts and greenhouse gas (GHG) emissions, with the aim of limiting global warming to below 1.5°C. To date, all North African countries apart from Libya have submitted their NDCs. They estimate their financing needs at USD 389 billion for implementation over the 2020-30 period. For most countries in the region, achieving these commitments remains largely conditional on financial support from the international community (Table 6.2).

Table 6.2. **NDCs from North African countries**

Country	Submission date	Estimated financing needs (USD billion)	Commitment to reducing greenhouse gas (GHG) emissions and adapting to climate change
Algeria	2017	N/A	Reduce its GHG emissions by 7% on its own, and by 22% with international financial and technological support.
Egypt	2017 and 2022	246 • Adaptation: 50 • Mitigation: 196	Reduce its GHG emissions by 33% in the electricity sector, 65% in the oil and gas sector, and 7% in the transport sector.
Morocco	2016 and 2021	78.8 • Adaptation: 40 • Mitigation: 38.8	Reduce its GHG emissions by 18.3% on its own, and by 45.5% with international financial and technological support.
Mauritania	2017 and 2021	46.6 • Adaptation: 10.6 • Mitigation: 34.3 • Other activities: 1.7	Reduce its GHG emissions by 22.3% by 2030, and by up to 92% with the support of the international community.
Tunisia	2017 and 2021	19.4 • Adaptation: 4.3 • Mitigation: 14.4 • Other activities: 0.7	Reduce its GHG emissions by 45% by 2030 compared with its 2010 level.

Note: Libya has not submitted an NDC.
Source: Authors' compilation based on UNFCCC (n.d), *Nationally Determined Contributions Registry* (database), https://unfccc.int/NDCREG.

North African countries have also put national and sectoral strategies in place to achieve these objectives.

- **Algeria** has developed a National Climate Plan 2020-30, which includes 155 projects, in addition to other plans, such as the National Action Plan for the Environment and Sustainable Development, the National Biodiversity Strategy and Action Plan, and the National Strategy for Integrated Waste Management by 2035 (People's Democratic Republic of Algeria, 2015, 2019).
- In 2022, **Egypt** adopted the National Climate Change Strategy 2050, which aims to: 1) improve governance and management of climate change mitigation and adaptation projects; 2) improve the regulatory framework for green finance by

promoting national green banks and credit lines that prioritise adaptation measures; 3) promote scientific research, technology transfer, knowledge management and awareness-raising to tackle climate change; and 4) facilitate the dissemination of information among government institutions and citizens (Arab Republic of Egypt, 2022).

- **Morocco** has developed its National Climate Plan 2020-30, as well as Regional Climate Plans. It devised a strategic framework that includes the National Charter for the Environment and Sustainable Development, the National Sustainable Development Strategy, and the National Water Plan. In 2021, Morocco published its Low-Carbon Development Strategy 2050 to achieve an integrated and shared vision, setting out the main directions for the Moroccan economy and society between 2020 and 2050, and envisioning profound economic and social transformations in a carbon-neutral world (Kingdom of Morocco, 2021a, b).
- **Mauritania** established its National Adaptation Programme in 2020, which covers ecosystem protection and conservation; sustainable rangeland management; biodiversity conservation; fishing and aquaculture; housing and urban planning; agriculture and food security (including genetic improvement, health, water, coastal management, prevention of extreme climate events, infrastructure and education) (Islamic Republic of Mauritania, 2021).
- In 2022, **Tunisia** published its Strategy for Carbon-Neutral and Climate-Resilient Development 2050, which includes the National Low-Carbon Strategy and the National Climate Change Resilience Strategy. The latter encompasses all sectors and areas of intervention, paying particular attention to water, agriculture, ecosystems and natural resources, coastal development, health, tourism, land-use and urban planning, and gender issues (Republic of Tunisia, 2021a, b, 2022).

North African countries are directing their mitigation strategies mainly towards the renewable energy sector (AUC/OECD, 2022). Algeria aims to achieve a 27% share of renewables in national electricity production by 2030, while Morocco is aiming to reach 52%. Egypt has set its objective at 42% by 2035. Given their strategic location and environments that are conducive to solar and wind energy, North African countries could provide developed countries with climate change mitigation solutions. In 2021, revenue from Moroccan electricity exports to developed countries increased by nearly 700% in a single year, reaching around MAD 565 million (Moroccan dirhams). Assuming a land-utilisation factor of 1% for renewables, North Africa has an electricity generation potential of 2 792 gigawatts for solar and 223 gigawatts for wind, which is over 12 times Africa's installed electricity generation capacity and about 3 times Europe's total installed capacity in 2021 (IRENA/AfDB, 2022). Other opportunities could strengthen the region's exportable renewable energy offer, including green hydrogen (AU/ISA/EIB, 2022). However, such strategies require careful evaluation, taking into account local energy needs and the technological dependencies they may create (CEO/TNI, 2022).

Financing needs for climate change adaptation projects are nevertheless likely to be underestimated. Despite their vulnerability to the consequences of climate change, North African countries estimate that 73% of financing needs come from mitigation projects and that only 27% of funding is reserved for investment in adaptation actions (Table 6.2). In addition to human and productivity challenges, it is crucial to consider climate change adaption needs, in order to ensure the financial stability of these countries. In Morocco, for example, the direct and indirect exposure of banks to drought and flood risks is estimated at 35% of total assets, mostly in the agricultural, tourism and real estate sectors (World Bank, 2022c).

The climate finance gap hinders the achievement of climate change mitigation and adaptation goals in North Africa

North African countries face a significant climate finance gap. Over the 2019-20 period, they received an average of USD 5.8 billion per year in climate finance, well below the over USD 39 billion needed annually by 2030 according to their NDCs. The amount received is equivalent to 19% of the finance mobilised by the African continent and only 1% of global finance (IPC, 2022). Egypt, Morocco and Tunisia received the majority of climate project financing in North Africa. The other countries in the region each received less than 2% (Figure 6.7, Panel A). Of the total, 36% went to the energy sector, compared with 19% for transport, 11% for waste, 7% for buildings and infrastructure, and 6% for agriculture, forestry and fishing (Figure 6.7, Panel B). Most of the financing was spent on mitigation measures (Figure 6.7, Panel C).

Figure 6.7. **Climate finance received by North Africa, 2019-20 average**

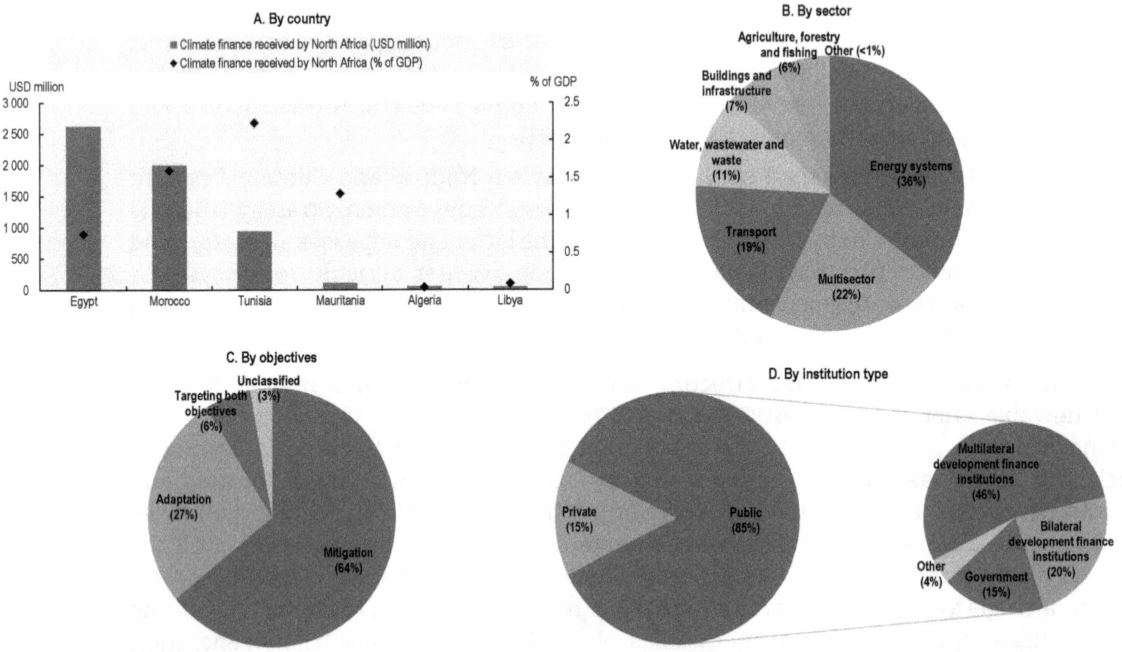

Note: The "Other" category in Panel B includes the information and communications technology and industrial sectors. The "Other" category in Panel D covers state-owned enterprises, export credit agencies, multilateral climate funds and domestic development finance institutions.

Source: Adapted by the authors from CPI (2022), *Landscape of Climate Finance in Africa* (database), www.climatepolicyinitiative.org/publication/landscape-of-climate-finance-in-africa/.

StatLink https://stat.link/wf59j6

Given the finance gap, diversifying climate finance sources remains crucial. Approximately 85% of the climate finance received in 2019-20 came from the public sector, including bilateral and multilateral development finance institutions, as well as multilateral climate funds (Figure 6.7, Panel D). The region benefits from large investment programmes, such as the Great Green Wall Initiative, which includes Mauritania and plans to regreen 100 million hectares in the Sahel and southern Sahara to combat desertification. This project was launched in 2007 and supported by many donors. However, it has encountered implementation difficulties due to the lack of steering and funding. In 2021, the international community committed to reviving the project by investing USD 12 billion over the next five years (One Planet Summit, 2021).

Achieving the international community's commitments, including those made at the United Nations Climate Change Conferences (COP, Box 6.1), will be crucial to sustaining climate change action.

Box 6.1. **Comparing the results of the United Nations Climate Change Conferences (COP) held in North Africa**

North Africa has hosted two editions of the COP, which have enabled some progress but have not achieved their more ambitious goals:

- COP22, held in Morocco in 2016, was marked by the official ratification of the Paris Agreement, in which developed countries committed to allocating USD 100 billion per year to developing countries by 2020. However, no agreement was reached on how these funds would be distributed between adaptation and mitigation projects.
- COP27, held in Egypt in 2022, reaffirmed the commitment to the Paris Agreement, but failed to achieve a concrete commitment to reducing fossil fuels from the world's major GHG emitters. An agreement between China, the European Union, India and the United States would cover 64% of future global CO_2 emissions, while the expansion of such an agreement to include all G20 members would cover 85% (IMF, 2021). COP27 ended with a decisive agreement to establish a dedicated global fund for loss and damage, intended to compensate the most vulnerable countries for the irreversible damage caused by global warming (UNFCCC, 2022).

COP22 and 27 enabled initiatives to be put in place to mobilise financial flows and develop green financial markets at the continental level. At the national level, COP22 was an opportunity for Morocco to develop a regulatory framework conducive to mobilising climate finance, with the establishment of a road map to link the Moroccan financial sector to sustainable development. At the regional level, COP22 enabled 25 countries to ratify the Marrakech Pledge for Fostering Green Capital Markets in Africa. COP27 was marked by the launch of continental initiatives, including the Alliance for Green Infrastructure in Africa and the African Carbon Markets Initiative, which could provide a basis for strengthening the mobilisation of sustainable investments in the region.

North African countries could mobilise more financing for climate action by developing their sustainable finance markets

Sustainable financing can be mobilised through multiple financial mechanisms. Sustainable financing brings together all financial processes, management methods and regulations that connect the community's economic, social and environmental interests in the medium and long term. Sustainable finance therefore aims to achieve the Sustainable Development Goals (SDGs) through various financial mechanisms (Table 6.3). Green finance refers to all financial activities and operations geared towards investments that explicitly aim to preserve the environment by working towards the energy transition and tackling global warming.

Table 6.3. **Selection of financial instruments to mobilise sustainable financing**

Financial mechanism	Definition	Examples in North Africa
Blended finance	The strategic allocation of public funding to channel private capital flows towards achieving the SDGs through risk-mitigation mechanisms (credit lines, guarantees, hedging, syndicated loans, insurance products, and subordinated shares, etc.).	Private finance mobilised through public development finance allocated to climate action increased from an average of USD 91 million over the period 2012-16 to USD 447 million over 2017-21 (OECD, 2022b).
Performance- or results-based funding	Payments to a government, organisation or individual that are conditional on achieving predetermined and measurable objectives.	In Morocco, the Results-Based Financing Employment Programme targets populations experiencing barriers to entering the job market. This programme is part of Compact II, a co-operation programme concluded between Morocco and the United States and implemented by the Millennium Challenge Account-Morocco Agency.
Sustainable bonds (green, blue and social)	Bonds where the interest rate applied is linked to contributions towards the SDGs (climate and/or social objectives).	North Africa mobilised 25% of the cumulative volume of green bonds in Africa during the 2014-21 period.
Green sukuk	Bonds that comply with Islamic law and remunerate the investor based on the project's environmental performance, progressively repaying the capital invested.	In 2018, Morocco launched a sovereign sukuk, worth USD 104.2 million, which was 3.6 times oversubscribed. In 2020, Egypt issued the first private-sector sukuks worth USD 127 million for real estate development (UNEP, 2021).

Source: Compiled by the authors.

Focus on green bonds in North Africa

Some North African countries have recently started participating in the green bond market. The international green bond market has grown significantly since 2014, increasing from a cumulative USD 37 billion to USD 1.7 trillion in 2022. By region, Europe is the top issuer, with a share of approximately 50% of cumulative volume over the 2014-22 period, followed by Asia-Pacific and North America, with shares of 26% and 21%, respectively. Although Africa's share remains marginal (0.3% of the total issued on the international market), North Africa stands out, having issued green bonds worth USD 1.1 billion, i.e. 25% of the continent's cumulative amount over the same period (Figure 6.8).

Figure 6.8. **Green bond issuance in Africa, 2014-21 (USD million)**

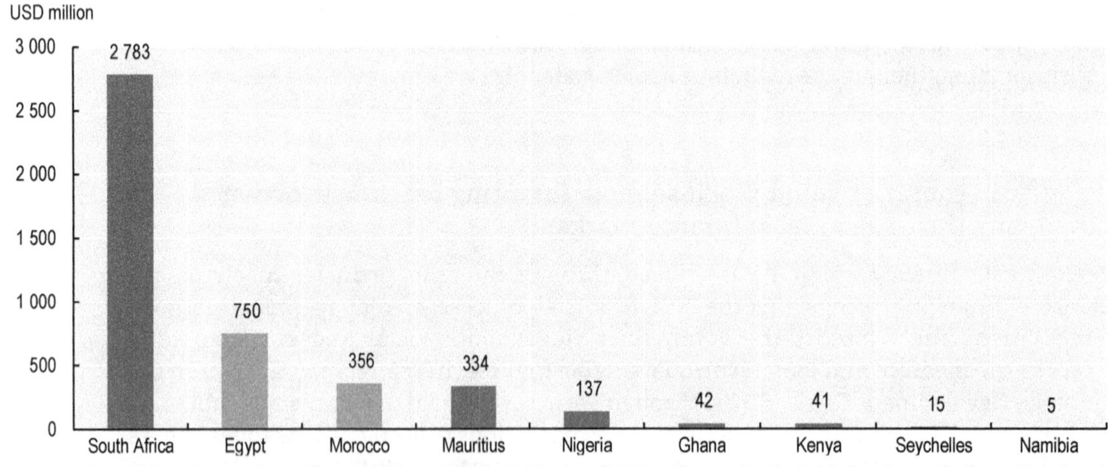

Source: Adapted by the authors from Climate Bonds Initiative (2022), *Climate Bonds Initiative Data Platform* (database), www.climatebonds.net/market/data/.

StatLink https://stat.link/jl7gt5

The reforms initiated at COP22 have allowed Morocco to lead the way by issuing two green bonds (Box 6.1). The Moroccan Agency for Sustainable Energy issued the first bond in 2016, with national stakeholders (including the Moroccan Pension Fund and the Central Reinsurance Company) and commercial banks (Al Barid Bank and Attijariwafa

Bank), to provide MAD 1.15 billion in co-financing for the Noor solar power project. Also in 2016, the Moroccan Bank for Foreign Trade (now Bank of Africa) issued green bonds for renewable energy projects worth MAD 500 million (USD 50 million). In 2017, the People's Central Bank, supported by the International Finance Corporation (IFC) and Proparco, issued the country's first foreign-currency green bond (EUR 135 million) to refinance investments in energy efficiency. Since 2018, five green bonds have been issued by public companies (National Railways Office), the private sector (Al Ormane, Casablanca Finance City Authority) and municipal actors (City of Agadir) to finance projects for issues such as energy efficiency, renewable energy, and sustainable transport and buildings.

In 2020, Egypt issued the region's first foreign-currency sovereign green bond. The Egyptian Financial Regulatory Authority approved the legal framework for issuing green bonds in 2018, allowing the government to develop its first sovereign bond in 2020, with the support of the World Bank. This USD 750 million bond is aimed at financing projects in the transport sector (46% of the funds mobilised) and sustainable water and wastewater management sectors (54%) (Ministry of Finance of the Arab Republic of Egypt, 2021). In 2021, Commercial International Bank – also supported by the IFC – launched the first private-sector green bond, worth USD 100 million, to develop energy-efficient industrial transformation projects (IFC/HSBC, 2022). Green bonds issued by private companies are more likely to provide additional private financing for investment (UNEP, 2022). In 2022, the Norwegian group Scatec Solar, in partnership with Africa50, committed to refinancing six Egyptian solar power plants, issuing a green bond worth USD 334.5 million.

However, there are obstacles to mobilising sustainable financing in the rest of the region. The lack of information and data on investment opportunities and climate risks is a major constraint to investment in the region, particularly for climate change adaptation projects (AfDB, 2022a). A clear institutional and regulatory framework, such as that established in Egypt and Morocco, could enable other countries in the region to take advantage of innovative financial mechanisms to attract greater sustainable investment. Adequate public finance management and support from the international community will also be essential to ensure that blended financing mechanisms are established in the most vulnerable countries, such as Mauritania.

Policy levers to support the development of sustainable finance markets in North Africa

Improve the identification and allocation of financing needs according to national priorities

A green transition requires better institutional co-ordination to assess financing needs and establish allocation priorities. Many countries have adopted a sectoral approach in their climate change action strategies, making it difficult to identify priorities and allocate financing effectively. In Morocco, for example, the National Water Plan does not take into account the water needs of the National Road Map for Green Hydrogen. Similarly, water desalination solutions should be developed alongside renewable energy deployment, taking into account demand from other sectors (such as transport and industry) (World Bank, 2022c).

Reforming public finance management and monitoring the implementation of national strategies will strengthen their credibility and improve funding allocation. Most governments in the region have not introduced legal or regulatory requirements to integrate climate change into public finance management instruments. It is therefore difficult to assess the extent to which unconditional commitments made as part of NDCs are also reflected in national budgets. A green taxonomy would allow public authorities to ascertain whether economic activities are sustainable and to limit the risk of greenwashing through green labelling. This would enable public resources to be prioritised for interventions that include a climate dimension, thereby sending a strong and credible signal to market players about the authorities' commitment to advancing the green transition.

Tax reforms and voluntary carbon markets could also provide financing for climate change adaptation.

- An environmental tax could raise additional revenue to finance the green transition and climate change adaptation for the countries in the region, while discouraging polluting behaviour. Egypt, Mauritania, Morocco and Tunisia, for example, have introduced environmental taxes in recent years, mainly in the energy and transport sectors. However, the revenue mobilised did not exceed 1.5% of their GDP in 2020 and could be extended to other sectors (OECD/ATAF/AUC, 2022).
- Introducing a carbon tax or a carbon credit market could also be considered. Reforming the use of fossil fuel subsidies and introducing a carbon tax on fossil fuels equivalent to EUR 30 per tonne of CO_2 (a low estimate of the climate damage currently caused by 1 tonne of CO_2 emitted) could generate additional revenue estimated at 4.6% of GDP in Egypt and 1.7% in Morocco (OECD, 2021c). North African governments could build on the African Carbon Markets Initiative established at COP27 to create a credible continent-wide carbon credit certification system (ACMI, 2022).

A just energy transition must be strategically sequenced to limit the negative effects on local economies. The implementation of tax reforms and energy subsidies must be carefully designed and sequenced to avoid unintended side effects such as energy affordability problems or job losses in the fossil fuel sector. As such, the Equitable Framework and Finance for Extractive-Based Countries in Transition (EFFECT) provides a toolkit for policy makers in fossil-fuel-producing and mineral-rich developing countries to chart low-carbon transition pathways in line with their national development priorities. EFFECT identifies ways of mitigating the transition's impacts on fossil fuel industries and poor workers and households, and of preventing the risks of high-carbon lock-in and stranded assets. This initiative is structured around three interrelated pillars: i) decarbonising extractive industries and managing uncertainties; ii) planning for a sustainable exit from fossil energy; and iii) achieving systemic change and economy-wide decarbonisation (OECD, 2023).

Leveraging local institutions for climate change will better align the funding received with national needs. Local institutions are ideally placed to channel funding to the projects with the greatest needs, while offering risk-minimisation mechanisms and services (such as information on local market conditions). Tunisia, for example, could expand the mandate of its Energy Transition Fund, which is currently limited to providing grants (AfDB, 2021). Local institutions can benefit from initiatives such as the Green Climate Fund (GCF) Readiness Programme, which provides countries with grants and technical assistance for developing strategies and receiving the accreditation necessary to secure international funding. For example, the GFC supported Mauritania to develop its National Adaptation Plan in 2018 (GCF, 2018).

Regional and international partners can help develop bankable projects to attract more investment to the region. For example, the Mediterranean Solar Plan offered all countries in the region (except Mauritania) a technical assistance system to help them prepare renewable-energy and energy-efficiency projects, and to mobilise funding from European institutions (EIB, 2015). In 2023, the African Development Bank (AfDB) also plans to launch the USD 1.5 billion African Green Finance Facility Fund (AG3F), which will provide technical assistance grants to help local governments and financial institutions design green finance facilities and develop sustainable project portfolios in line with the Paris Agreement (AfDB, 2022b).

Facilitate the implementation of inclusive and supportive regulatory frameworks for sustainable finance

Central banks and financial regulators can co-ordinate to establish a regulatory framework to integrate climate change into the national financial system. Morocco and Egypt's experience can provide examples. Thanks to the publication of national road maps, green bonds have been issued in both these countries. These reforms included inclusive consultation processes (UNEP, 2021). In Morocco, for example, the central bank mobilised the association of banks and five other national financial regulators to draft its Road Map for Aligning the Moroccan Financial Sector with Sustainable Development (Banque Al-Maghrib et al., 2016). In addition, in 2022, the Financial Market Council of Tunisia partnered with the World Bank's IFC to establish its *Guide d'émission d'obligations vertes, socialement responsables et durables en Tunisie* [Guide to Issuing Green, Social and Sustainability Bonds in Tunisia] (FMC/IFC, 2022), thus ensuring a framework for project assessment and financing.

Financial regulators could also require publication of environmental, social and governance (ESG) criteria. In 2010, the Egyptian stock exchange became the second stock exchange in the world to adopt an ESG sustainability index. As early as 2012, it was one of four stock exchanges to implement the United Nations Sustainable Stock Exchanges initiative, designed to improve transparency and increase listed companies' engagement on ESG issues (UNEP, 2021). Since 2022, the regulator has also required companies listed on the Egyptian stock exchange and those operating in non-banking financial activities to provide quarterly compliance reports containing ESG information (Ashraf Atef, 2022). In Morocco, the central bank introduced ESG and climate disclosure requirements in 2021. Banks must estimate their exposure to physical and transitional climate risks under different climate change scenarios. These risks relate to the direct impact of climate change and the economic implications of the low-carbon transition (UNEP, 2021).

Stronger financial inclusion would increase access to sustainable finance among the poorest populations. The populations most exposed to climate risks, especially in rural areas, are also the most excluded from access to financing. According to the Global Findex, about 70% of the poorest people in North Africa did not have a bank account in 2021 (World Bank, 2021). Adapting financial inclusion policies to these populations will therefore be crucial if climate change adaptation strategies are to be effective. In Morocco, for example, the National Strategy for Financial Inclusion aims to improve access to finance, particularly among young people, women and rural populations, while promoting green financing solutions. It also aims to develop alternative financing mechanisms, such as mobile payments, microfinance and inclusive insurance (UNEP, 2021). In addition, digital microfinance solutions used by local start-ups could help reduce financial exclusion among these populations. Regulatory sandboxes (or regulatory frameworks for testing) allow new digital solutions to facilitate access to finance to be tested, as has been done in Tunisia, for example (AUC/OECD, 2021).

Support the development of the sustainable finance market through regional co-operation

Regional co-operation can support capacity-building for regulators and financial service providers. In 2021, Egypt launched the Regional Centre for Sustainable Finance to build capacity and raise awareness of sustainable finance among financial institutions in the Middle East and North Africa region. The centre provides technical assistance on topics related to integrating ESG, implementing the recommendations of the G20 Task Force on Climate-related Financial Disclosures, and considering climate risks. It also encourages redirecting of private capital flows to finance the SDGs (Ashraf Atef, 2022). At the international level, Egypt, Mauritania, Morocco and Tunisia participate in the Network of Central Banks and Supervisors for Greening the Financial System, a platform for sharing best practices in climate risk management and implementing a regulatory framework that supports green finance.

Integrating financial markets could also allow sustainable finance to be developed in other countries in the region. Financial market integration, within the broader framework of continental integration (Jedlane et al., 2012), would offset underdeveloped financial systems in some countries in the region. For example, linking national stock exchanges would diversify the financial instruments available, while reducing the costs of cross-border investments. In 2022, the Egyptian and Moroccan stock exchanges, alongside others, joined the African Exchanges Linkage Project, launched by the African Securities Exchanges Association and the AfDB to facilitate cross-border trading between African stock exchanges and selected brokerage firms (AfDB, 2022c).

References

ACMI (2022), *Africa Carbon Markets Initiative (ACMI): Roadmap Report*, Sustainable Energy for All (SEforALL), Africa Carbon Markets Initiative, www.seforall.org/publications/africa-carbon-markets-initiative-roadmap-report.

AfDB (2022a), *North Africa Economic Outlook 2022*, African Development Bank, Abidjan, https://www.afdb.org/en/documents/north-africa-economic-outlook-2022.

AfDB (2022b), "African Development Bank launches model for deploying green financing across the continent", African Development Bank, Abidjan, www.afdb.org/en/news-and-events/african-development-bank-launches-model-deploying-green-financing-across-continent-56903.

AfDB (2022c), "African Development Bank, African Securities Exchange Association launch AELP E-Platform linking seven African capital markets with $1.5 trillion market capitalization", African Development Bank, Abidjan, www.afdb.org/en/news-and-events/press-releases/african-development-bank-african-securities-exchange-association-launch-aelp-e-platform-linking-seven-african-capital-markets-15-trillion-market-capitalization-57245.

AfDB (2021), *Potential for Green Banks & National Climate Change Funds in Africa – Scoping Report*, African Development Bank, Abidjan, www.afdb.org/en/documents/potential-green-banks-national-climate-change-funds-africa-scoping-report.

Arab Republic of Egypt (2022), *Egypt's First Updated Nationally Determined Contributions*, NDC Registry, United Nations Framework Convention on Climate Change (UNFCCC), https://unfccc.int/sites/default/files/NDC/2022-07/EgyptUpdatedNDC.pdf.

Ashraf Atef, N. (2022), "Scaling up sustainable finance and investment in the Middle East and North Africa", in *Scaling Up Sustainable Finance and Investment in the Global South*, Centre for Economic Policy Research (CEPR) Press, London, https://cepr.org/system/files/publication-files/175477-scaling_up_sustainable_finance_and_investment_in_the_global_south.pdf.

AU/ISA/EIB (2022), *Africa's extraordinary green hydrogen potential*, African Union, Addis-Ababa, International Solar Alliance, European Investment Bank, Luxembourg, www.eib.org/attachments/press/africa-green-hydrogen-flyer.pdf.

AUC/OECD (2022), *Africa's Development Dynamics 2022: Regional Value Chains for a Sustainable Recovery*, African Union Commission, Addis Ababa/OECD Publishing, Paris, https://doi.org/10.1787/f92ecd72-fr.

AUC/OECD (2021), *Africa's Development Dynamics 2021: Digital Transformation for Quality Jobs*, African Union Commission, Addis Ababa/OECD Publishing, Paris, https://doi.org/10.1787/cd08eac8-fr.

Banque Al-Maghrib et al. (2016), *Feuille de route pour l'alignement du secteur financier marocain sur le développement durable – Feuille de route du secteur financier marocain pour l'émergence de la finance durable en Afrique*, Bank Al-Maghrib, Rabat, www.acaps.ma/sites/default/files/feuille-de-route-globale.pdf.

Bureau van Dijk (2022), *Orbis* (database), www.bvdinfo.com/en-gb/our-products/data/international/orbis (accessed October 2022).

CEO/TNI (2022), *Hydrogen from North Africa – a neocolonial resource grab: The reality of EU green hydrogen import plans*, Corporate European Observatory and Transnational Institute, https://corporateeurope.org/en/2022/05/hydrogen-north-africa-neocolonial-resource-grab.

Climate Bonds Initiative (2022), *Climate Bonds Interactive Data Platform* (database), www.climatebonds.net/market/data/ (accessed January 2023).

CMF/IFC (2022), "Guide d'émission d'obligations vertes, socialement responsables et durables en Tunisie", Conseil du Marché Financier and International Finance Corporation, Tunis and Washington, DC, www.cmf.tn/?q=publication-par-le-cmf-du-guide-d-emission-d-obligations-vertes-socialement-responsables-et-durables.

Cornier, A. et al. (2018), *Indicateur de vulnérabilité physique au changement climatique* (database), Fondation pour les études et recherches sur le développement international (Ferdi), https://ferdi-indicators.shinyapps.io/PVCCI/ (accessed February 2023).

Cos, J. et al. (2022), "The Mediterranean climate change hotspot in the CMIP5 and CMIP6 projections", *Earth System Dynamics*, vol. 13, n° 1, European Geosciences Union, Munich, pp. 321-340, https://doi.org/10.5194/esd-13-321-2022.

CPI (2022), *Landscape of Climate Finance in Africa* (database), Climate Policy Initiative, www.climatepolicyinitiative.org/publication/landscape-of-climate-finance-in-africa/ (accessed 7 February 2023).

EIB (2015), *Mediterranean Solar Plan – Project Preparation Initiative (MSP-PPI)*, European Investment Bank, Luxembourg, https://www.eib.org/attachments/country/femip_msp_ppi_en.pdf.

El-Katiri, L. (2023), "Sunny side up: Maximising the European Green Deal's potential for North Africa and Europe", website of the European Council on Foreign Relations (ECFR), Paris, https://ecfr.eu/publication/sunny-side-up-maximising-the-european-green-deals-potential-for-north-africa-and-europe/.

fDi Intelligence (2022), *fDi Markets* (database), www.fdiintelligence.com/fdi-markets (accessed 7 February 2023).

GCF (2018), *Readiness grant agreement – with the Islamic Republic of Mauritania*, Green Climate Fund (GCF), www.greenclimate.fund/document/readiness-grant-agreement-mauritania-mrt-rs-001.

IEA (2022), "Greenhouse Gas Emissions from Energy Data Explorer", *Data and Statistics* (database), International Energy Agency, Paris, www.iea.org/data-and-statistics/data-tools/greenhouse-gas-emissions-from-energy-data-explorer (accessed October 2022).

IFC/HSBC (2022), *Emerging Market Real Economy Sustainable Bonds – current and potential issuance*, International Finance Corporation, World Bank Group, Washington, DC, www.environmental-finance.com/assets/files/IFC/emerging-market-real-economy-sustainable-bonds.pdf.

IMF (2022a), *World Economic Outlook, October 2022* (database), International Monetary Fund, Washington, DC, www.imf.org/en/Publications/WEO/weo-database/2022/October (accessed 7 February 2023).

IMF (2022b), *Balance of Payments and International Investment Position Statistics (BOP/IIP)* (database), International Monetary Fund, Washington, DC, https://data.imf.org/?sk=7A51304B-6426-40C0-83DD-CA473CA1FD52 (accessed 7 February 2023).

IMF (2022c), *Investment and Capital Stock Dataset (ICSD)* (database), International Monetary Fund, Washington, DC, https://data.imf.org/?sk=1CE8A55F-CFA7-4BC0-BCE2-256EE65AC0E4 (accessed 7 February 2023).

IMF (2021), *Finance & Development*, vol. 58, n° 3, International Monetary Fund, Washington, DC, www.imf.org/fr/Publications/fandd/issues/2021/09.

IRENA/AfDB (2022), *Renewable Energy Market Analysis: Africa and Its Regions*, International Renewable Energy Agency (IRENA) and African Development Bank, Abu Dhabi and Abidjan, www.irena.org/-/media/Files/IRENA/Agency/Publication/2022/Jan/IRENA_Market_Africa_2022.pdf.

Islamic Republic of Mauritania, (2021), *Mauritania First NDC (Updated submission)*, NDC Registry, United Nations Framework Convention on Climate Change (UNFCCC), https://unfccc.int/sites/default/files/NDC/2022-06/CDN-Mauritania.pdf.

ITA (2022), "Fisheries", *Mauritania Country Commercial Guide*, International Trade Agency (ITA), Washington, DC, www.trade.gov/country-commercial-guides/mauritania-fisheries.

Jedlane N. and D. Saidane (2012), "Intégration financière et gouvernance régionale en Afrique du Nord", United Nations Economic Commission for Africa (CEA), Casablanca, http://dx.doi.org/10.13140/RG.2.2.32661.73440.

Kingdom of Morocco (2021a), *Morocco First NDC (Updated submission)*, NDC Registry, United Nations Framework Convention on Climate Change (UNFCCC), https://unfccc.int/sites/default/files/NDC/2022-06/Moroccan_updated_NDC_Fr.pdf.

Kingdom of Morocco (2021b), *Stratégie Bas Carbone à Long Terme Maroc 2050*, Ministry of Energy Transition and Sustainable Development, https://unfccc.int/sites/default/files/reSource/MAR_LTS_Dec2021.pdf.

Kingdom of Morocco (2020), *Plan Climat National à horizon 2030*, Secretariat of State to the Minister of Energy, Mines and Sustainable Development, Casablanca, www.environnement.gov.ma/images/Climat/PCN1-min.pdf.

Les inspirations Éco (2023), "Sustainability : la stratégie gagnante d'OCP", *Les Inspirations Éco*, Horizon Press S.A., Casablanca, https://leseco.ma/maroc/sustainibility-la-strategie-gagnante-docp.html.

Ministry of Finance of the Arab Republic of Egypt (2021), *Egypt Sovereign Green Bond Allocation & Impact Report*, https://assets.mof.gov.eg/files/a3362b50-574c-11ec-9145-6f33c8bd6a26.pdf.

Moody's (2023a), "Moody's downgrades Tunisia's ratings to Caa2 with a negative outlook, concluding its review", Moody's Investors Service, New York, https://ratings.moodys.com/ratings-news/398103.

Moody's (2023b), "Moody's downgrades Egypt's ratings to B3, changes outlook to stable", Moody's Investors Service, New York, https://ratings.moodys.com/ratings-news/398535

Mousjid, B. (2022), "Engrais : Covid-19, guerre en Ukraine… une "aubaine" pour OCP", *Jeune Afrique*, Paris, www.jeuneafrique.com/1348134/economie/engraisaf-covid-19-guerre-en-ukraine-une-aubaine-pour-ocp/

OCP (n.d), "In-Country Partnerships", OCP Africa, Casablanca, Morocco, www.ocpafrica.com/fr/partenariats-nationaux

OECD (2023), *Equitable Framework and Finance for Extractive-based Countries in Transition (EFFECT)*, OECD Development Policy Tools, OECD Publishing, Paris, https://doi.org/10.1787/7871c0ad-en.

OECD (2022a), *OECD Development Assistance Committee* (database), https://stats-1.oecd.org/Index.aspx?DataSetCode=TABLE2A

OECD (2022b), "Mobilisation", *OECD.stat* (database), OECD Publishing, Paris, https://stats.oecd.org/Index.aspx?DataSetCode=DV_DCD_MOBILISATION (accessed 7 February 2023).

OECD (2021a), Middle East and North Africa Investment Policy Perspectives, OECD Publishing, Paris, https://doi.org/10.1787/6d84ee94-en.

OECD (2021b), *Private Philanthropy for Development: Data for Action*, OECD Publishing, Paris, https://oecd-main.shinyapps.io/philanthropy4development/ (accessed February 2023).

OECD (2021c), *Taxing Energy Use for Sustainable Development: Opportunities for energy tax and subsidy reform in selected developing and emerging economies*, OECD Publishing, Paris, www.oecd.org/tax/tax-policy/taxing-energy-use-for-sustainable-development.pdf.

OECD/ATAF/AUC (2022), *Revenue Statistics in Africa 2022*, OECD Publishing, Paris, https://doi.org/10.1787/ea66fbde-en-fr.

One Planet Summit (2021), "Accélérateur de la Grande muraille verte", www.oneplanetsummit.fr/les-coalitions-82/accelerateur-de-la-grande-muraille-verte-193.

People's Democratic Republic of Algeria (2019), *Plan National Climat*, Comité National Climat (CNC), www.me.gov.dz/telechargement/plan-national-climat/.

People's Democratic Republic of Algeria (2015), *Algeria First NDC*, NDC Registry, United Nations Framework Convention on Climate Change (UNFCCC), https://unfccc.int/sites/default/files/NDC/2022-06/AlgerieNDC2015.pdf.

Republic of Tunisia (2022), *Stratégie de Développement Neutre en Carbone et Résilient aux Changements Climatiques à l'horizon 2050*, United Nations Framework Convention on Climate Change (UNFCCC), https://unfccc.int/sites/default/files/reSource/StratTunisie.pdf.

Republic of Tunisia (2021a), *Tunisia First NDC (Updated submission)*, NDC Registry, United Nations Framework Convention on Climate Change (UNFCCC), https://unfccc.int/sites/default/files/NDC/2022-06/Tunisia%20Update%20NDC-french.pdf.

Republic of Tunisia (2021b), *Update of the Nationally Determined Contribution of Tunisia : Executive Summary*, NDC Registry, United Nations Framework Convention on Climate Change (UNFCCC), https://unfccc.int/sites/default/files/NDC/2022-08/CDN.pdf.

UNDP (2022), *The impact of the war in Ukraine on sustainable development in Africa*, United Nations Development Programme, New York, www.undp.org/africa/publications/impact-war-ukraine-sustainable-development-africa.

UNEP (2022), *A New Approach to Unlocking Private Finance for Climate and the SDGs in Egypt & Morocco*, UN Environment Programme Finance Initiative (UNEP FI), www.unepfi.org/wordpress/wp-content/uploads/2022/03/Unlocking-Private-Finance-for-Climate-FR.pdf.

UNEP (2021), *Promoting Sustainable Finance and Climate Finance in the Arab Region*, UN Environment Programme Finance Initiative (UNEP FI), www.unepfi.org/themes/climate-change/promoting-sustainable-finance-and-climate-finance-in-the-arab-region-2/.

UNFCCC (2022), "COP27 Reaches Breakthrough Agreement on New "Loss and Damage" Fund for Vulnerable Countries", Press release, United Nations Framework Convention on Climate Change, https://unfccc.int/news/cop27-reaches-breakthrough-agreement-on-new-loss-and-damage-fund-for-vulnerable-countries.

UNFCCC (n.d.), *Nationally Determined Contributions (NDCs)* (database), United Nations Framework Convention on Climate Change, https://unfccc.int/fr/NDCREG.

University of Notre Dame, (2020) "ND-GAIN Matrix", *Notre Dame-Global Adaptation Initiative Country Index* (database), https://gain.nd.edu/our-work/country-index/matrix/ (accessed 7 February 2023).

World Bank (2022a), *International Debt Statistics* (database), World Bank, Washington, DC, https://databank.worldbank.org/source/international-debt-statistics (accessed January 2023).

World Bank (2022b), *Egypt Country Climate and Development Report*, CCDR Series, World Bank, Washington, DC, https://openknowledge.worldbank.org/handle/10986/38245.

World Bank (2022c), *Morocco Country Climate and Development Report*, CCDR Series, World Bank, Washington, DC, https://openknowledge.worldbank.org/bitstream/handle/10986/38240/Morocco CCDR.pdf .

World Bank (2022d), *G5 Sahel Country Climate Development Report*, CCDR Series, World Bank, Washington, DC, https://openknowledge.worldbank.org/handle/10986/37620.

World Bank (2021), *The Global Findex Database 2021: Financial Inclusion, Digital Payments, and Resilience in the Age of COVID-19*, World Bank, Washington, DC, https://www.worldbank.org/en/publication/globalfindex

World Bank-KNOMAD (2022), *Remittances* (database), The Global Knowledge Partnership on Migration and Development (KNOMAD) and World Bank, Washington, DC, www.knomad.org/data/remittances (accessed 19 December 2022).

Chapter 7

Investing in agri-food value chains for West Africa's sustainable development

This chapter identifies policy options to strengthen sustainable investments in West Africa's agri-food sector. The sector is chosen due to its large contribution to employment and economic growth in West Africa. The chapter first discusses how investments flow into and out of the region and how they are distributed across sectors and countries (Benin, Burkina Faso, Cabo Verde, Côte d'Ivoire, Gambia, Ghana, Guinea, Guinea-Bissau, Liberia, Mali, Niger, Nigeria, Senegal, Sierra Leone and Togo). It then analyses in detail the potentials and limitations of West Africa's agri-food sector. The chapter concludes with concrete suggestions for West African policy makers on how to attract more sustainable investment.

IN BRIEF

Recent global crises have slowed down growth, increased debt and dampened investment in West African countries. These developments have also reduced sustainable investments in the region's agri-food sector (covering agriculture, food processing, packaging, transportation, distribution and retail) despite its vast potential for employment creation, poverty reduction and productive transformation.

Growing domestic and intra-regional demand for processed food products continues to offer the potential to develop West Africa's agri-food value chains. However, funding from domestic credit, development finance institutions and governments for the region's agricultural sector has stagnated, totalling USD 10.3 billion in 2021 and thus remaining below the pre-COVID-19 level of USD 10.8 billion in 2018. Foreign direct investment into agribusinesses, despite their importance for capital-intensive investments, amounted to less than USD 1.8 billion per year between 2017 and 2022. Between 2010 and 2020, only 4% of development finance for the agricultural sector went to agro-industrial activities and 12% to environmental protection. Compared with other African regions, informal private investments play a more significant role in West Africa; yet these have limited productivity effects and can introduce risks and vulnerabilities for informal suppliers. The agri-food sector's vast potential to drive industrialisation and contribute to job creation, livelihoods, food security and enhanced regional value chains remains vastly underexploited.

Policy makers can prioritise three sets of actions. First, public financial institutions can improve smallholder farmers' access to productivity- and sustainability-focused financial products. Second, regional integration policies and place-based programmes can fulfil complementary roles in strengthening agri-food value chains. Third, agro-poles, support organisations, international funders and technical partners that directly improve the capacities of small and informal businesses and strengthen linkages in agri-food value chains can be expanded.

West Africa

Contribution of investments to GDP growth (p.p.)

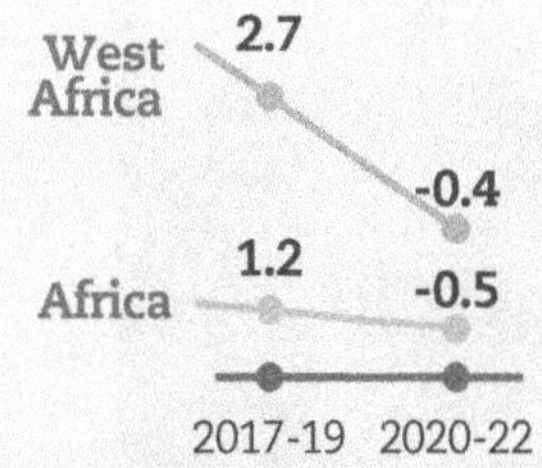

Share of greenfield FDI (2017-22)

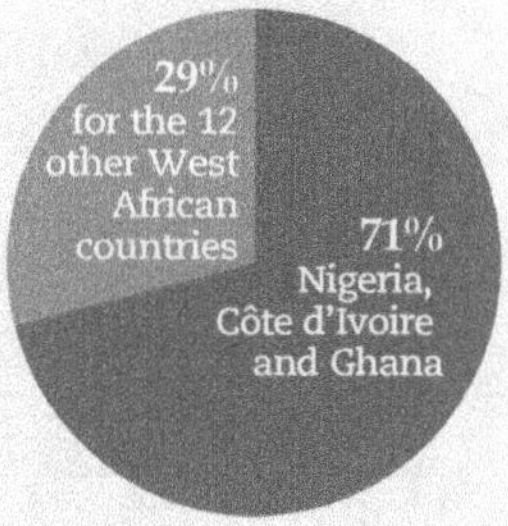

West Africa's export of food products in 2021 (USD billion)

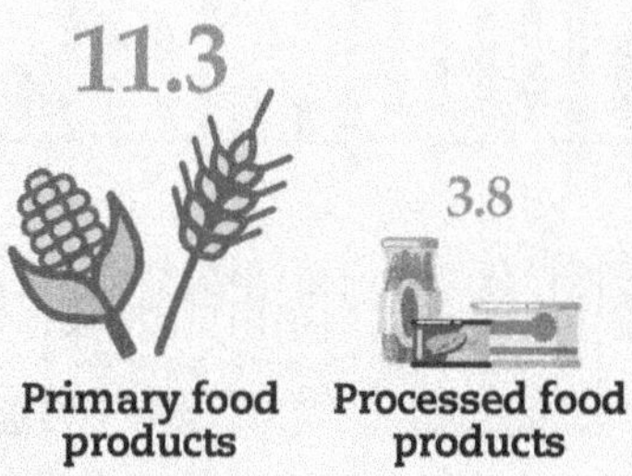

Agri-food industries accounts for the bulk of employment in West Africa

% of total employment

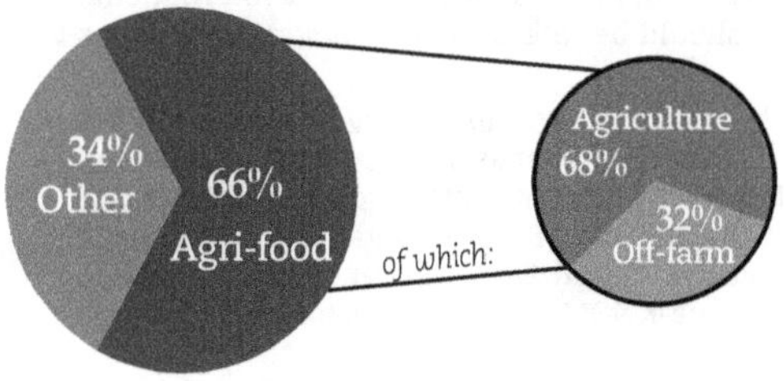

The region's growing off-farm food economy employs

82 million people

of the region's food economy workers are **women**

Investments in West Africa's agriculture, forestry and fishing sector amounted to only

USD 23.1 billion

in 2020

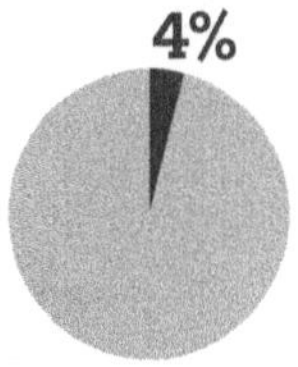

Agro-industrial activities received only 4% of total development finance in 2010-20

What's next?

- **Improve smallholder farmers' access to financial products** that include support for improving productivity and social or ecological sustainability
- **Strengthen regional agricultural policies** and place-based programmes, such as agro-industrial parks
- **Build agro-poles and incubators**, to enhance food security and agricultural practices

West Africa regional profile

Figure 7.1. Components of economic growth and sources of financing in West Africa

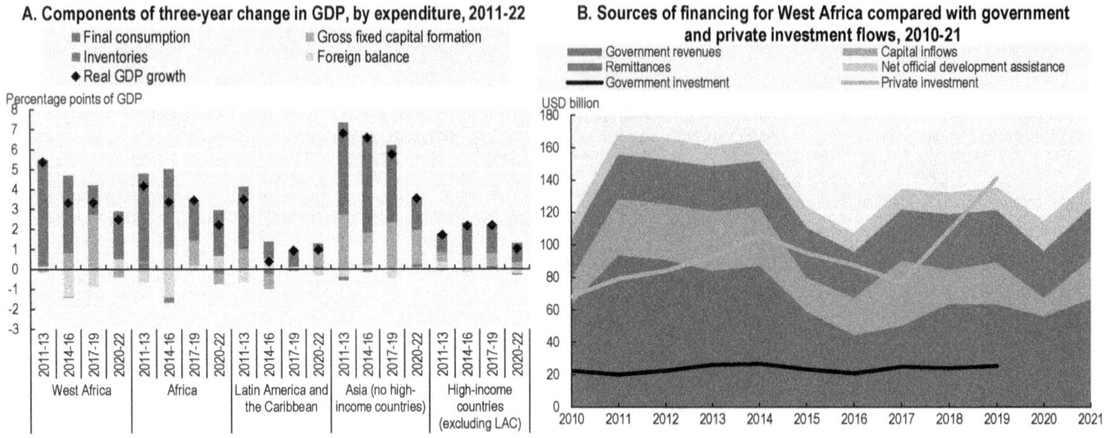

Note: The components of gross domestic product (GDP) growth are calculated on an annual basis by using real annual GDP growth to estimate the increase in real US dollars. Aggregate figures are calculated by taking the average of the national figures weighted by GDP in purchasing-power-parity dollars. The components of GDP growth over three-year periods were calculated by taking the difference between the geometric average of the annual real GDP growth over the period and the real GDP growth when setting each component to zero for individual years. Foreign balance is the difference between imports and exports. Imports contribute negatively to GDP. "High-income countries" refers to countries classified as "high-income" according to the World Bank Country and Lending Groups outside of Latin America and the Caribbean. Government revenues include all tax and non-tax government revenues minus debt service and grants received. Capital inflows include foreign direct investment, portfolio investment and other investment inflows reported by the International Monetary Fund under asset/liability accounting. Figures for capital inflows should be interpreted with some caution as some figures for 2021 and for portfolio inflows are missing.

Source: Authors' calculations based on IMF (2022a), *World Economic Outlook Database*, www.imf.org/en/Publications/WEO/weo-database/2022/October; OECD (2022a), *OECD Development Assistance Committee* (database), https://stats-1.oecd.org/Index.aspx?DataSetCode=TABLE2A; World Bank (2022a), *World Development Indicators* (database), https://data.worldbank.org/products/wdi; IMF (2022b), *Balance of Payments and International Investment Position Statistics (BOP/IIP)* (database), https://data.imf.org/?sk=7A51304B-6426-40C0-83DD-CA473CA1FD52; IMF (2022c), *Investment and Capital Stock Dataset (ICSD)* (database), https://data.imf.org/?sk=1CE8A55F-CFA7-4BC0-BCE2-256EE65AC0E4; and World Bank-KNOMAD (2022), *Remittances* (database), www.knomad.org/data/remittances.

StatLink https://stat.link/tnkj96

Figure 7.2. Greenfield foreign direct investment flows into West Africa, by activity, source and destination, 2017-22

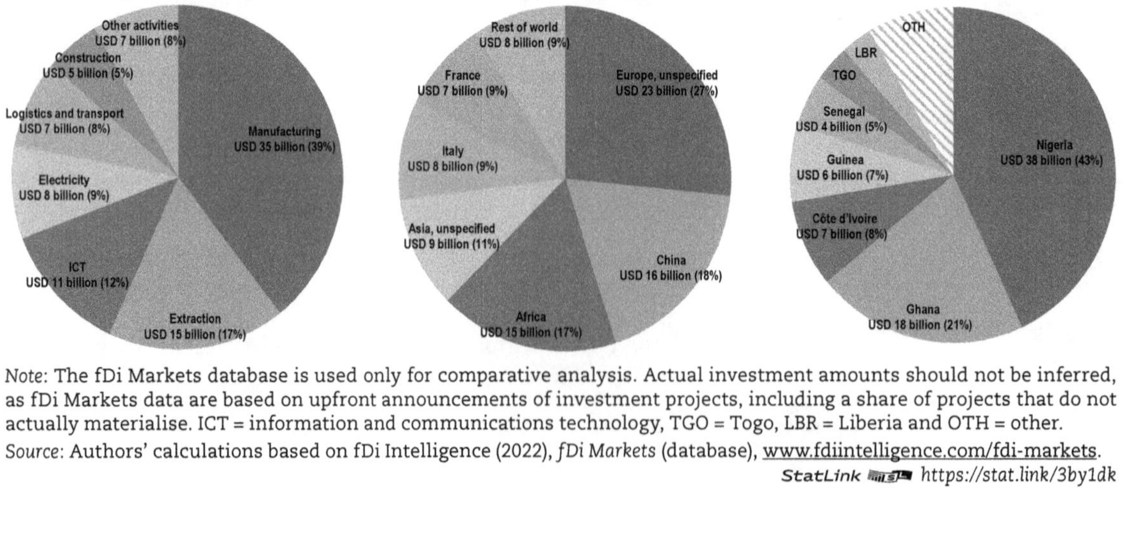

Note: The fDi Markets database is used only for comparative analysis. Actual investment amounts should not be inferred, as fDi Markets data are based on upfront announcements of investment projects, including a share of projects that do not actually materialise. ICT = information and communications technology, TGO = Togo, LBR = Liberia and OTH = other.

Source: Authors' calculations based on fDi Intelligence (2022), *fDi Markets* (database), www.fdiintelligence.com/fdi-markets.

StatLink https://stat.link/3by1dk

Recent crises have dampened investment into West Africa, and sustainable investments target few countries and sectors

COVID-19 temporarily thwarted investments and growth while increasing sovereign debt

The COVID-19 pandemic slowed down investments and growth in West African countries, and the recovery has yet to stabilise. In 2020, at the onset of the COVID-19 pandemic, West Africa's gross domestic product (GDP) shrunk by 0.6%, before rebounding to 4.4% in 2021 when the initial economic shock subsided. In 2022 – while disruptions in international trade, food and energy price inflation, and tightening fiscal conditions slowed the recovery – growth was still projected to remain robust at 3.9% (IMF, 2023a). Before the pandemic, private investments had surged, almost doubling from USD 76.8 billion in 2017 (7.9% of GDP) to USD 141.1 billion (9.6% of GDP) in 2019 (Figure 7.1, Panel B). Accordingly, investment (gross fixed capital formation) became the dominant driver of GDP growth during the 2017-19 period, contributing 2.7 percentage points. However, during the pandemic, disinvestments negatively affected the region's GDP, lowering it by 0.4 percentage points from 2020 to 2022 (Figure 7.1, Panel A).

In 2020, all external financial flows except official development assistance (ODA) contracted, but in 2021, flows rebounded to pre-crisis levels. External financial inflows to West Africa fell from USD 72 billion in 2019 to USD 60 billion in 2020. In contrast, ODA increased by 29% to USD 18.4 billion (2.8% of GDP), its highest level since 2011 (Figure 7.1, Panel B). In a reversal, all external flows rebounded in 2021, with foreign direct investment (FDI) reaching a nine-year peak of USD 13.8 billion in 2021 and portfolio investment climbing to USD 9.1 billion, matching the level of 2017 (Figure 7.1, Panel B).

Fiscal deficits and sovereign debt pressures are increasing in West Africa. In response to the COVID-19 pandemic, many governments implemented policies such as tax relief or social assistance programmes to support vulnerable populations and economic activities during and after lockdowns. Domestic revenue mobilisation in 2021 increased slightly from 10% to 11% of GDP, while expenditures increased by 4%, bringing the fiscal deficit to 47% of GDP for the region. Concerns over sovereign debt permeate West Africa, though less so than in other African regions. According to the International Monetary Fund (IMF, 2023b), 4 out of 15 countries – Gambia, Ghana, Guinea-Bissau and Sierra Leone – are at a high risk of debt distress. In particular, Ghana faces significant debt pressure, with the country engaging in negotiations with the IMF to obtain financial support in early 2023 (AfricaNews, 2023).

The allocation of sustainable investments is skewed towards a few countries and sectors

Greenfield FDI offers opportunities for job creation but targets sectors with mixed environmental outcomes. Nigeria, Côte d'Ivoire and Ghana received 71% of greenfield FDI to the region between 2017 and 2022 (Figure 7.2, Panel C). Thirty-nine per cent went to the manufacturing sector, a significant driver of employment, creating about four jobs per USD thousand invested, a higher ratio than any other sector (Figure 7.3, Panel A). Extraction and mining activities attracted the second-most FDI within the same period. Over the last decade, the transport sector received an important share of FDI but contributed more than any other sector to the overall increase in greenhouse gas emissions. Nigeria, the largest recipient of West Africa's FDI in 2017-22, contributed 68% to the region's total emissions (Figure 7.3, Panel B).

Figure 7.3. **Sectoral job creation of greenfield foreign direct investment and greenhouse gas emissions for economic activities in West Africa**

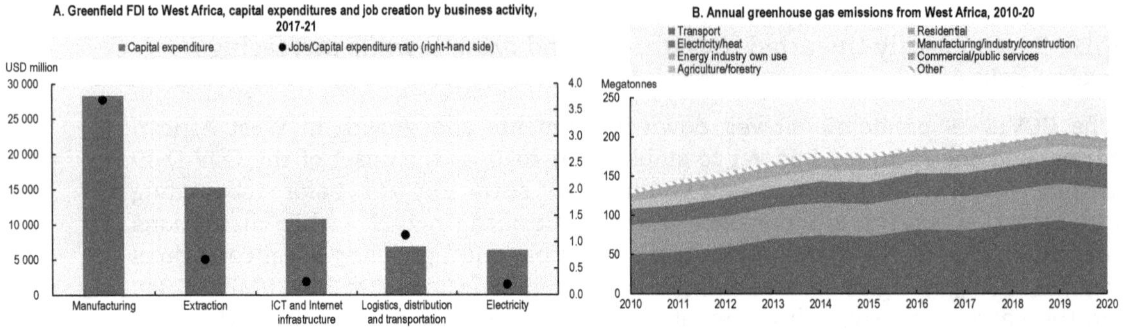

Note: ICT = information and communications technology.

Source: Authors' calculations based on fDi Intelligence (2022), *fDi Markets* (database), www.fdiintelligence.com/fdi-markets and IEA (2022), *Data and Statistics* (database), www.iea.org/data-and-statistics/data-tools/greenhouse-gas-emissions-from-energy-data-explorer.

StatLink https://stat.link/cs9txw

The majority of greenfield FDI in West Africa comes from outside the region and continent. Fifty-six per cent of greenfield FDI between 2017 and 2021 originated from high-income countries, followed by Asia (21%), mostly due to significant investments from the People's Republic of China (hereafter "China"). Investment from other African regions accounted for 17% of total greenfield FDI, mainly from Southern and North Africa, with a large share going to Nigeria. Togo received the largest share of intra-regional investments, most of which flowed from Nigeria (Figure 7.6).

ODA and philanthropic inflows complement limited public investment in social sectors but concentrate in one country. Public health expenditures accounted for only 0.8% of GDP in 2019, lower than in any other African region except Central Africa. Similarly, public investment in education represented only 1.6% of GDP, lower than in any other African region. In contrast, 46% of the USD 72 billion ODA over the 2011-20 period went to social infrastructure and services (health, education, civil society, and water supply and sanitation) (Figure 7.4, Panel A). About 48% of philanthropic flows allocated between 2016 and 2019 targeted the health and reproductive sector (Figure 7.4, Panel B). However, ODA and philanthropy remained heavily focused on Nigeria.

Figure 7.4. **Allocation of official development assistance and philanthropic inflows to West Africa**

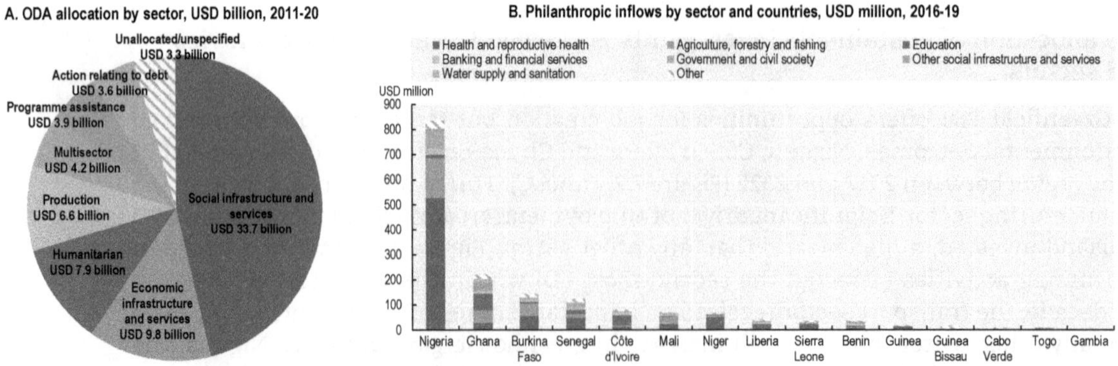

Note: The eight largest sectors are displayed. "Other" captures the remaining sectors.

Source: Authors' calculations based on OECD (2022a), *OECD Development Assistance Committee* (database), https://stats-1.oecd.org/Index.aspx?DataSetCode=TABLE2A; and OECD (2021a), *Private Philanthropy for Development: Data for Action Dashboard* (database), https://oecd-main.shinyapps.io/philanthropy4development/.

StatLink https://stat.link/ex42ps

Additional sources of private finance such as impact investments and domestic institutional investors are growing in West Africa. Interventions by development finance institutions accounted for about 97% of impact investment in the region between 2005 and 2015 (GIIN, 2015). Regulatory changes in Nigeria, such as the Regulation of Pension Fund Assets in 2006, have allowed pension funds to increase assets under management (Juvonen et al., 2019; National Pension Commission, 2006), reaching USD 32.3 billion in 2020 (OECD, 2021b). Ghanaian pension funds have also grown steadily, accumulating USD 4.7 billion as of 2021, making Ghana the second-largest pension fund market in the region (Nyang`oro and Njenga, 2022; OECD, 2021b). The Nigerian Sovereign Wealth Authority had USD 3 billion in assets under management in 2021, the highest amount of any sovereign wealth fund in West Africa. This was followed by the Senegalese Sovereign Wealth Fund for Strategic Investments (FONSIS) and the Ghana Heritage Fund, with assets under management of USD 0.8 and USD 0.7 billion respectively (SWFI, n.d.).

West Africa mobilised large amounts of blended finance, targeting sectors with both high and low sustainability potential. Over the 2012-20 period, on average USD 2.4 billion per year of private finance were mobilised through development finance institutions or development banks, more than in any other African region other than Southern Africa. Mirroring the allocation of greenfield FDI, most blended finance went to Nigeria (37%), Ghana (24%) and Côte d'Ivoire (15%), followed by Senegal (7%) and Guinea (6%). While significant shares went to sectors with high overall sustainability potential (e.g. energy, banking and financial services and agriculture, forestry and fishing), a sector with a poor environmental and social sustainability record – industry, mining and construction – attracted the second-highest amount (Figure 7.5; see Chapter 1).

Figure 7.5. **Private finance in West Africa mobilised through official development finance by sector, USD billion, 2012-20**

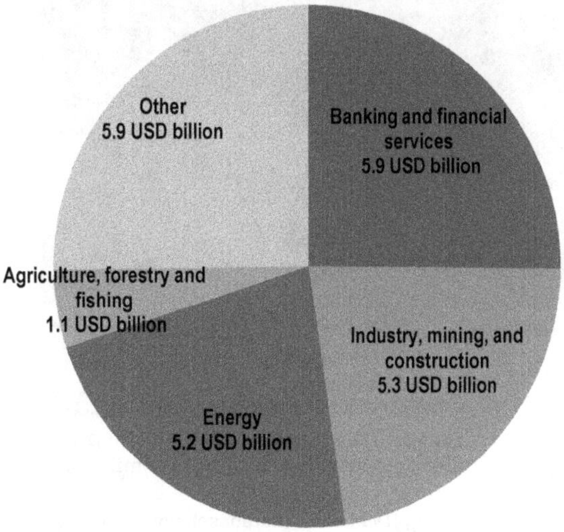

Note: "Other" includes (by order of magnitude): government and civil society; trade policies and regulations; multi-sector/cross-cutting; water supply and sanitation; education; health; business and other services; tourism; other social infrastructure and services; unspecified allocation; population policies/programmes and reproductive health and humanitarian aid.

Source: Authors' calculations based on OECD (2022b), "Mobilisation", *OECD.Stat* (database), https://stats.oecd.org/Index.aspx?DataSetCode=DV_DCD_MOBILISATION.

StatLink https://stat.link/wktxjn

West Africa is less integrated into intra-African investments and exports than other African regions

Intra-regional and intra-African exports are less significant in West Africa than in Southern Africa. About 57% of total formal exports from West African countries to other

African countries remained within the region between 2014 and 2016. For comparison, intra-regional exports constituted about 85% of the total exports from Southern African Development Community (SADC) countries to other African countries in the same period. Before the COVID-19 pandemic, Senegal was the only West African country among the top ten intra-African exporters, while three West African countries were among the bottom ten (UNCTAD, 2019).

Nigeria dominates intra-regional investments and has the most listed companies in the region. Greenfield FDI outflows from West African countries mostly target other West African countries (40%), followed by high-income countries (29%) and East Africa (14%). Nigeria accounts for 86% of the region's outward FDI (Figure 7.6). Nigeria is also home to 15 of the top 20 publicly listed private companies by market capitalisation in West Africa, 8 of which are in the finance and insurance sector.

Figure 7.6. **Greenfield foreign direct investment outflows from West African countries, by destination regions, 2017-21, USD million**

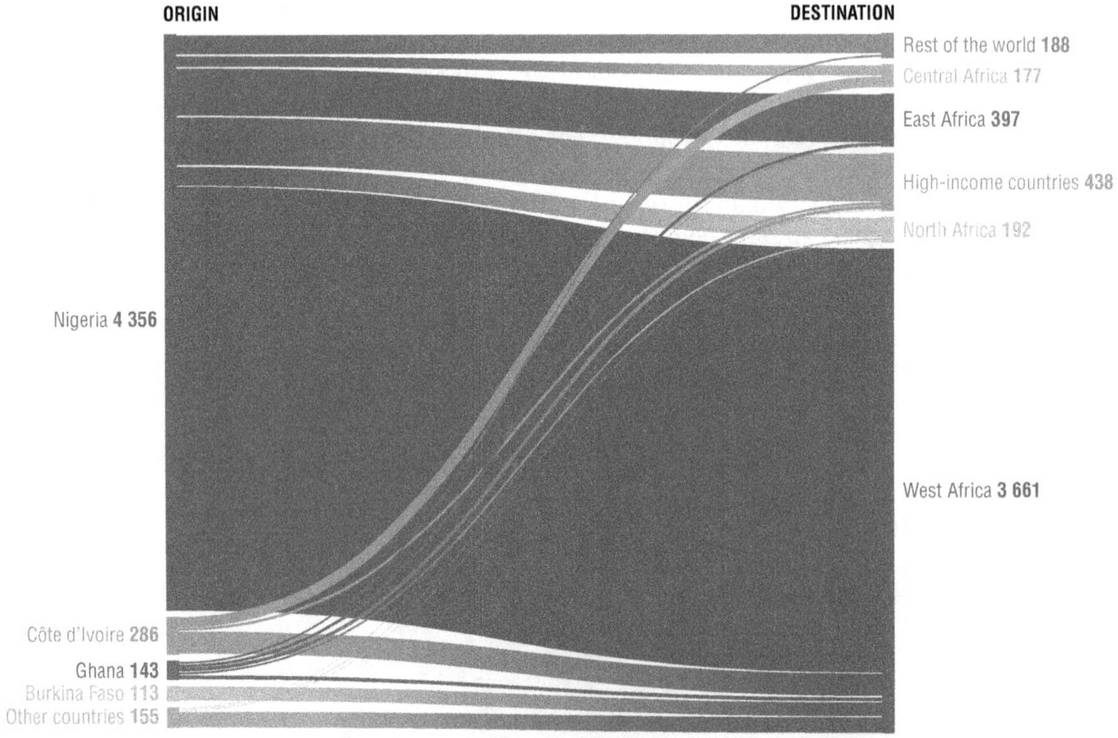

Note: "Other countries" includes Togo (USD 76 million), Senegal (USD 46 million) and Mali (USD 34 million) while "Rest of the world" includes countries in Southern Africa (USD 50 million), Developing Asia (USD 137 million) and Latin America and the Caribbean (USD 1 million).

Source: Authors' calculations based on fDi Intelligence (2022), *fDi Markets* (database), www.fdiintelligence.com/fdi-markets.

StatLink https://stat.link/xwuzj0

Sustainable investments into the agri-food sector can drive West Africa's productive transformation

West Africa's agri-food sector supports employment and livelihoods across the region, especially for rural populations, suggesting that it should be prioritised for sustainable investment. Average agriculture, forestry and fishing value-added was 24.4% of GDP in 2021, compared to 16.5% for Africa and 4.3% for the world (World Bank, 2021). At the end of 2020, the agricultural sector accounted for around 25% of the region's GDP and 45%

of employment. The agri-food sector as a whole (i.e. agriculture plus food processing, packaging, transportation, distribution and retail) accounts for around 66% of the region's total employment. The off-farm food economy employs 82 million people, mostly in retail and wholesale (68%), followed by food processing (22%), a segment projected to keep growing (Allen, Heinrigs and Heo, 2018). Investments in the agri-food sector and its workforce offer West African countries the opportunity to achieve long-term synergies between economic, social and environmental sustainability and resilience (Ali et al., 2020). Around 53% of the West African population lives in rural areas where most agricultural activities take place. Sixty-eight per cent of all employed women work in the food economy, and women make up 88% of employment in food-away-from-home services, 83% in food processing and 72% in food marketing (Allen, Heinrigs and Heo, 2018).

West Africa leads the world in primary agricultural production across a range of products, while export rates remain low. Since the 1980s, the value of agricultural production in West African countries has consistently grown, mostly driven by non-cereal agricultural products (Figure 7.7). In 2020, the total value of agricultural production in Africa reached about USD 319 billion. West Africa contributed almost USD 125 billion to this total (39%).[1] Several West African countries rank among the world's top producers of agricultural products (AUC/OECD, 2019). Over 2019-21, the bulk of the world's yams (95%) and cowpeas (85%) were produced in West Africa, and seven of the region's top 15 agricultural products accounted for 50% of Africa's total production. However, for most of West Africa's food products, only a fraction (less than 1%) is exported, with the notable exception of cocoa beans at 73% (Table 7.1).

Trade of food and beverage products between West African and other countries has stagnated since 2010, while imports of processed products from non-African countries have recently increased. Between 2010 and 2020, West African countries' imports and exports of food and beverage products remained at` a constant level, and far more of that trade was with non-African than with other African countries. Even though West Africa is a major exporter of primary food products to non-African countries, the region imports a large share of processed products from them (Figure 7.7). Between 2016 and 2020, West African countries imported close to USD 60 billion worth of food products, about 67% of which was semi-processed or processed (Badiane et al., 2022). The top imported products include cereal and cereal-based products, meat and dairy products, processed sugar and non-alcoholic beverages.

Figure 7.7. **Imports and exports of primary and processed food and beverage products for West African countries, 2010-21, USD million**

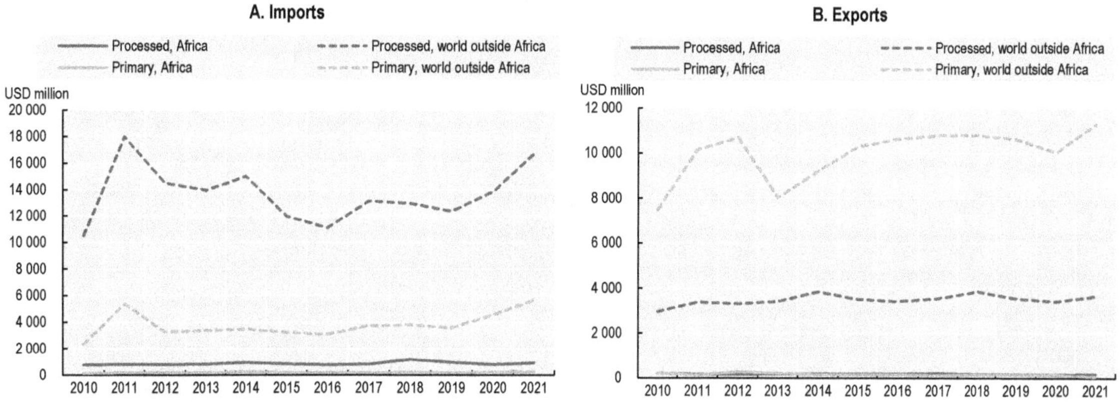

Source: Authors' calculations based on CEPII (2023), *BACI: International Trade Database at the Product-Level* (database), www.cepii.fr/CEPII/en/bdd_modele/bdd_modele_item.asp?id=37.

StatLink https://stat.link/i4uhds

West African agri-food output for some products is falling, while staple food prices are increasing globally. Recent crises have foregrounded West Africa's dependence on imports of some agri-food products and inputs, especially cereals (Figure 7.8). For instance, in some parts of the rural Sahel, cereal production fell by roughly one-third in 2022, in part due to fertiliser shortages (Oxfam, 2022), while international conflicts induced supply chain shocks that sent wheat prices soaring, jumping 60% in June 2022 compared to January 2021 (World Bank, 2022b).

Figure 7.8. **Gross value of agricultural and cereal production in West Africa, 1985-2020, constant 2014-16 USD**

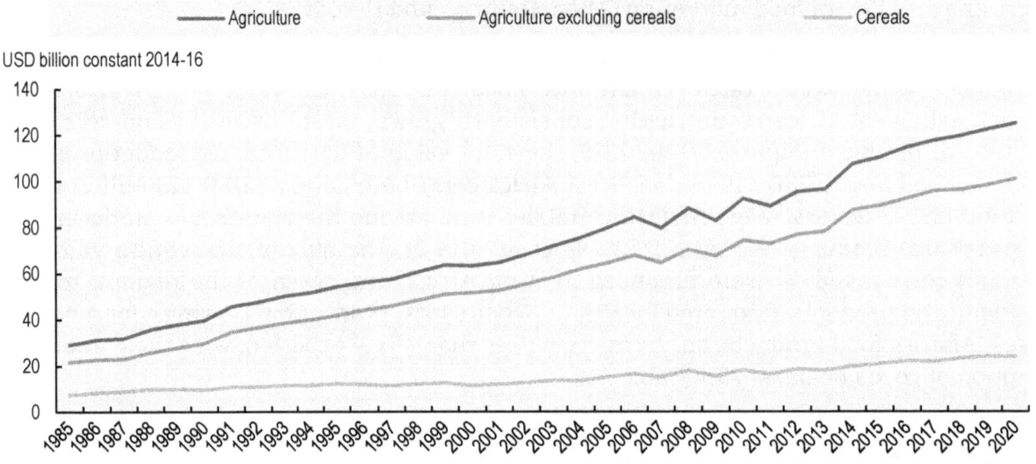

Source: Authors' calculations based on data from FAOSTAT (2022a), *Production* (database), www.fao.org/faostat/en/#data/QV.

StatLink https://stat.link/5mrfyq

Table 7.1. **Top 15 agricultural products in West Africa by production volume, 2019-21**

Agricultural product	Total production in 2019-21 (million tonnes)	Share in Africa's production	Share in global production	Country with highest production volume (share of the region's production)	Percentage exported	Share in Africa's exports	Share in global exports
Cassava, fresh	303	52%	33%	Nigeria (59%)	0%	0%	0%
Yams	215	97%	95%	Nigeria (71%)	0.1%	100%	37%
Maize (corn)	79	29%	2%	Nigeria (48%)	1%	5%	0%
Fresh eggs	70	29%	1%	Nigeria (66%)	0.002%	3%	0%
Rice	62	56%	3%	Nigeria (40%)	0.01%	13%	0%
Oil palm fruit	53	77%	4%	Nigeria (56%)	n.a.	n.a.	n.a.
Sorghum	39	47%	22%	Nigeria (51%)	0%	11%	0%
Plantains and cooking bananas	32	33%	24%	Ghana (45%)	1%	55%	3%
Other fresh vegetables, n.e.c.	29	46%	3%	Nigeria (70%)	0.3%	14%	1%
Groundnuts, excluding shelled	28	57%	18%	Nigeria (48%)	1%	76%	15%
Millet	28	70%	31%	Niger (32%)	0.2%	67%	4%
Dry cowpeas	23	88%	85%	Nigeria (48%)	0.03%	8%	2%
Sugar cane	22	8%	0%	Côte d'Ivoire (28%)	0.01%	2%	0%
Sweet potatoes	17	20%	6%	Nigeria (70%)	0.3%	18%	2%
Tomatoes	16	25%	3%	Nigeria (68%)	0.2%	1%	0%

Note: n.a. = not available. n.e.c. = not elsewhere classified.
Source: Authors' calculations based on data from FAOSTAT (2022b), *Trade* (database), www.fao.org/faostat/en/#data/TCL and FAOSTAT (2022c), *Production* (database), www.fao.org/faostat/en/#data/QCL.

West Africa is experiencing population growth, high food expenditure and an increasing demand for processed foods

The region's population is growing, and household expenditure on food is significant. West Africa's working-age population has grown at an annual average of 2.8%, compared to 1.2% in Southeast Asia and 1.3% in Latin America and the Caribbean. By 2030, West Africa will be home to 520 million people. Household food expenditures in West Africa remain high: in 2021, 59% of Nigerian and 39% of Ghanaian and Ivorian consumers' expenditures went to food, compared to 56% in Kenya, 50% in Angola, 45% in Cameroon, 44% in Uganda, 41% in Ethiopia, 27% in Tanzania and 20% in South Africa (USDA ERS, 2021).

West Africa's rising urban middle class increases the demand for processed and industrially produced food products, many of which are currently imported. In 2020, the region's 75 large urban agglomerations (i.e. cities with at least 300 000 inhabitants) had a total of over 93 million inhabitants, the largest of any African region (OECD/UN ECA/AfDB, 2022). Higher purchasing power in the urban middle class creates a large demand for processed foods which are relatively easier to transport, store and prepare (Allen and Heinrigs, 2016). For instance, focus group discussions held in Lagos (Nigeria) and Accra (Ghana) revealed that urban consumers prefer local foods but take issue with the packaging, presentation, food safety and quality of locally processed food items, ultimately choosing imported products that are more convenient to prepare (Badiane et al., 2022; Hollinger and Staatz, 2015; Box 7.1).

Box 7.1. The promise of the infant food value chain in Africa

Africa's demand for infant food is poised to keep expanding across the continent, while the dependence on imports remains high. African countries currently import ten times more food for infants under three years of age than they export. Current imports are valued at EUR 570 million and are expected to exceed EUR 1.1 billion by 2026. A study conducted between 2021 and 2022 showed that 16% of surveyed firms along the infant food value chain received inputs from African producers (ITC, 2022a).

With environmentally friendly packaging, African producers would be more competitive. Although products by African infant food producers are often better suited to local consumers' preferences and more affordable than imported brands, lower-quality processing and packaging can limit their attractiveness. Biodegradable packaging and refund schemes for packaging (such as bottles) represent an untapped opportunity for infant food production. An International Trade Centre survey shows the infant food value chain to be the only one of the four value chains it examined for which business clients and consumers are willing to pay a premium for more environmentally friendly products (ITC, 2022a).

Access to credit, transport logistics and difficulties in retaining skilled professionals constitute key bottlenecks for African infant food producers to scale. Local actors are beginning to challenge the dominant market position of multinational enterprises such as Nestlé, which currently accounts for 52-55% of the infant food market in West Africa. For instance, Nigeria's BabyGrubz, a female-led company, offers products for premature and malnourished babies. While 100% of its sourcing and processing takes place within Nigeria, the company plans to export to neighbouring countries in the near future. However, in Nigeria as elsewhere on the continent, infant food producers struggle with talent retention, the absence of robust food safety assessments, and fragmented regulations for labelling, packaging and shelf life (ITC, 2022a).

Formal investments in the agri-food sector have stagnated and insufficiently target downstream activities

Financing from domestic credit, development finance disbursements and government expenditure for West Africa's agricultural sector has remained largely unchanged. Albeit volatile, domestic credit (i.e. loans provided by local banks) represents by far the largest formal source of finance for the agriculture, forestry and fishing sector in West Africa (USD 6.7 billion in 2020). Development finance disbursements and government expenditure are smaller (USD 1.7 billion and USD 1.1 billion in 2020) (Figure 7.9).

Figure 7.9. **Financing provided to West Africa's agriculture, forestry and fishing sector through various formal channels, compared to gross fixed capital formation, 2010-21**

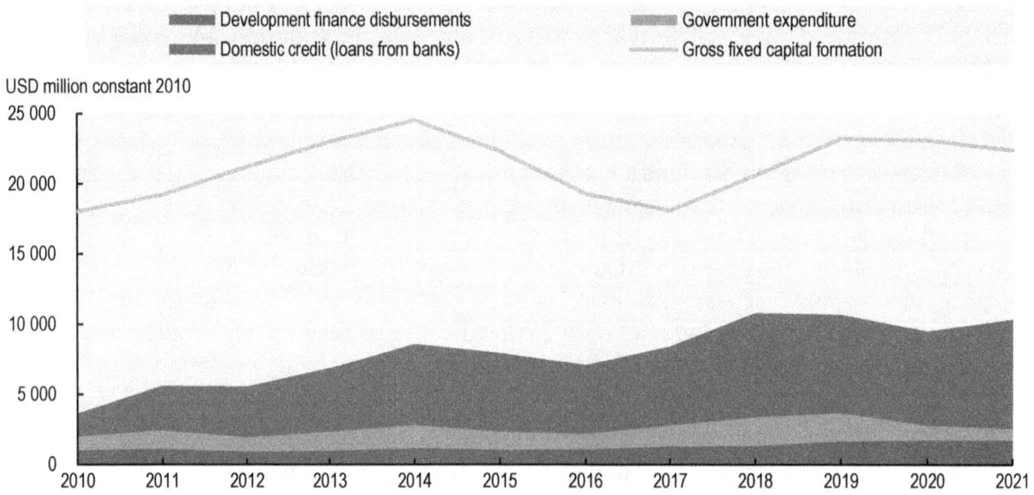

Note: 2021 figures for development finance disbursements are unavailable; 2020 values are used.
Source: FAOSTAT (2022d), *Investment* (database), www.fao.org/faostat/en/#data/CISP.
StatLink https://stat.link/5u1q69

Public investment in the agricultural sector has not grown and has been volatile. According to the monitoring of the Comprehensive Africa Agriculture Development Programme (CAADP) by the African Union Development Agency-New Partnership for Africa's Development, West Africa scores 3.47 out of 10, indicating that the region is not on track in implementing the CAADP's goal of allocating 10% of public budgets to agriculture, as it was reconfirmed in the Malabo Declaration on Agriculture transformation in Africa (AU/AUDA-NEPAD, 2020; AUC/OECD, 2022).[2] Across most countries of West Africa, the share of government budgets allocated to agriculture has been unstable or declining since 2001. Only Senegal and Burkina Faso have surpassed the 10% target, allocating 11% and 10.5% respectively (AUDA-NEPAD, 2017). Côte d'Ivoire (1.9%), Nigeria (2.2%) and Sierra Leone (4.9%) rank lowest in public spending on agriculture, while Benin stands at 9.3% (AUDA-NEPAD, 2017).

Compared with other African regions, informal private investments play a more significant role than credit or development finance in West Africa, limiting productivity and introducing risks for informal suppliers. Gross fixed capital formation (GFCF) – a measure of the total fixed assets that overall investments have financed – in the region's agriculture, forestry and fishing sector was more than double the amounts of domestic credit, development finance disbursements and government expenditure combined in 2020 (USD 23.1 billion vs. USD 9.5 billion; Figure 7.9). This suggests that informal private investments are the single largest source of financing for agricultural production in the region. GFCF has also grown much faster in West Africa than elsewhere on the continent, and West Africa's share of Africa's total GFCF is far greater than its shares of credit and development finance for agricultural production (Table 7.2). Most private domestic investments are mobilised by farmers' organisations, concentrating largely on the upstream (production) end of agri-food value chains. While informal private financing is an important channel for smallholder farmers, it does not typically support productivity upgrades and can create risks, for instance, through excessive interest rates or low financial accountability.

Table 7.2. **Domestic credit, development finance disbursements and gross fixed capital formation in the agriculture, forestry and fishing sector, Africa and West Africa, 2010-20**

	Africa	West Africa (share of Africa total)
Domestic credit		
Total (USD billion)	186.2	55.9 (30.0%)
Average annual growth rate	7.5%	14.9%
Development finance disbursements		
Total (USD billion)	49.6	13.5 (27.3%)
Average annual growth rate	6.9%	18.2%
Gross fixed capital formation		
Total (USD billion)	411.9	232.8 (56.5%)
Average annual growth rate	3.9%	6.5%

Source: Authors' calculations based on data from FAOSTAT (2022d), *Investment* (database), https://www.fao.org/faostat/en/#data/CISP.

FDI and blended finance are volatile and focus on large West African economies, suggesting a widespread shortage of financing for capital-intensive investments in agricultural productivity and downstream activities, such as processing. Large-scale and formal private sector investments are typically needed to establish downstream activities (transportation, processing, logistics, retail) but remain scarce in West Africa (Box 7.2). For instance, FDI to agribusinesses in West Africa is smaller than government expenditure for agricultural production, with announced capital expenditures for FDI projects amounting to USD 9 billion from 2017-22, or USD 1.8 billion per year on average. Over that same period, FDI to West Africa went almost entirely to agribusinesses in Nigeria (52%), Togo (22%), Côte d'Ivoire (15%) and Ghana (10%), with less than 1% going to all other countries in the region combined.[3] The role of blended finance is increasing but remains small as a share of overall investment amounts: an average of USD 228.8 million per year of private finance for the agriculture, forestry and fishing sector was mobilised through development finance from 2017 to 2020.[4]

Box 7.2. Poultry production and processing in West Africa

Poultry is a staple source of protein in West Africa, but its production and consumption are concentrated in only a few countries. Poultry meat accounts for over 70% of West Africa's total meat consumption, while demand is increasing with population growth. The top three producers in 2021 (Côte d'Ivoire, Nigeria and Senegal) accounted for 58% of production volumes; three countries (Benin, Ghana and Nigeria) accounted for 52% of consumption. In the past, Nigeria produced 68% of egg tonnage in the entire Sahel and West Africa region (SWAC-OECD/ECOWAS, 2008).

Demand for value-added poultry products in West Africa is rising, but production cannot match domestic demand. Across the region, consumer spending is shifting from basic towards higher-value poultry products. However, small-scale farmers dominating the poultry sector lack access to inputs, equipment and infrastructure (Adeyonu et al., 2021). The livestock sector receives little support in the form of public investment in processing and packaging infrastructure and lacks policies to stimulate regional trade in animal products (Amadou et al., 2012). The sector struggles with high production costs, capacity constraints and low productivity (Boimah et al., 2022). Investments can upgrade the poultry value chain by addressing gaps in production, processing, commercialisation and equipment/input (Salla, 2017). As a result, West African countries rely on imports to fulfil their domestic demand for poultry products (SWAC-OECD/ECOWAS, 2008).

Box 7.2. **Poultry production and processing in West Africa *(continued)***

Solutions exist to raise the productivity and competitiveness and to lower the production costs of West Africa's poultry sector. Removing infrastructural bottlenecks and enhancing input supply will increase productivity. Developing value-added poultry products, such as processed meats, can help to improve the sector's competitiveness (Eeswaran et al., 2022). The West African region imports a large amount of poultry inputs, such as feed and day-old chicks, to meet its demand. Developing these inputs' local production can also help to improve competitiveness. Increasing access to other quality inputs, such as feed, hatching eggs and vaccines, will help to reduce production costs (Boimah et al., 2022).

Large-scale investments are often missing, especially in the downstream segments of the value chain. Investments in the West African poultry sector are often local, small-scale and informal. Large-scale investments, where present, typically focus on upstream input supply. For instance, the Rearing for Food and Jobs (RFJ) programme in Ghana provided 729 smallholder farmers with a total of 72 967 cockerels at a 50% subsidised price. In a related intervention, the RFJ supplied an additional 25 poultry farmers with 43 183-day-old chicks at a 50% subsidised price (Boimah et al., 2022).

Development finance for agriculture is heavily skewed towards primary agricultural production and neglects downstream activities and environmental protection. West Africa's agro-industrial activities, such as processing, dairy production and fertiliser plants, received only USD 546 million in development finance from 2010-20, equivalent to 4% of the region's total development flows to agriculture. Over the same period, environmental protection received close to USD 1.7 billion (or 12%) of such development funding.[5] While fertiliser production has recently been bolstered, development funding for processing and other agro-industrial activities has stagnated. Environmental activities have mostly focused on research and administration rather than on direct interventions in supply chains (Figure 7.10).

Figure 7.10. **Development flows into West Africa's agro-industry and general environmental protection, 2010-20, USD million constant 2020**

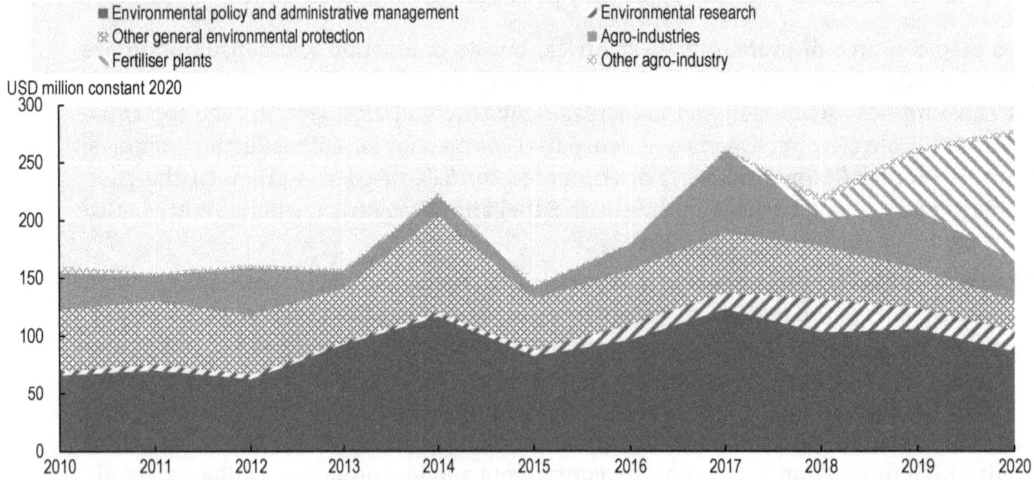

Note: "Agro-industries" refers to staple food processing, dairy products, slaughterhouses and equipment, meat and fish processing and preserving, oils/fats, sugar refineries, beverages/tobacco, and animal feed production. "Other agro-industry" includes cottage industries and handicrafts, textiles, leather and substitutes, forest industries, and fertiliser minerals. "Other general environmental protection" includes bio-diversity, biosphere protection, environmental education/training and site protection.

Source: Authors' calculations based on FAOSTAT (2022e), *Investment* (database), www.fao.org/faostat/en/#data/EA.

StatLink https://stat.link/dykh26

Current investments often remain inaccessible to smallholder farmers and are hampered by informality, fragmentation and land rights

Smallholder farmers face significant barriers to accessing financing that would allow them to improve their productivity and product quality. Physical distance is no longer the main barrier separating small-scale producers from urban consumption centres. Rather, the main constraint is the degree of sophistication demanded by a growing share of consumers – more ready-to-cook or ready-to-eat products (Badiane et al., 2022). However, smallholder farmers – mostly informal enterprises – face a number of barriers in accessing the financing necessary for them to upgrade production value (Box 7.3). The impact of mitigating those barriers can be substantial: in Nigeria, over 80% of farmers are classed as smallholders (Mgbenka and Mbah, 2016). Barriers include:

- **High collateral requirements for loans lock out smallholder farmers and agri-food entrepreneurs, preventing them from investing in improved farming practices and technologies.** Smallholder farmers and agri-food entrepreneurs often struggle to find adequate collateral to secure loans (e.g. lack of clarity on land rights can be an obstacle, in particular for women when they face discriminatory social norms [OECD, 2021c]). Consequently, bank financing for increasing productivity and innovation remains low (IFC, 2019). In Burkina Faso, where smallholders dominate the agri-food industry, less than 4% of loans provided by banks target the agricultural sector, despite agriculture comprising 27% of the country's GDP (IFC, 2019).
- **Shortages and increased prices of inputs, such as fertiliser, affect smallholder farmers.** The ripple effects of international conflicts in 2022 have tripled the cost of fertiliser (World Bank, 2022b). West Africa depends on fertiliser imports, with Russia having supplied over 50% of potash to Côte d'Ivoire, Mali, Niger, Senegal and Sierra Leone in 2021. As of April 2022, just 46% of fertiliser needs were met in West Africa and the Sahel (WFP, 2022). The high cost and fertiliser shortages risk decreasing fertiliser use, hence lowering yields (WFP, 2022; World Bank, 2022b). Smallholder farmers, rural communities and family farms, that struggle to access finance and are located far from major urban areas, are particularly vulnerable (Oxfam, 2022).
- **Limited information on financial products and market research hamstrings small actors in the agri-food value chains' ability to transform production.** Language barriers hinder the utilisation of available sustainable financing. Information related to green funds is often provided solely in English, hampering the dissemination of information on available financing (Lipton, 2022). Small and medium-sized enterprises (SMEs) often lack the investments they would need to scale up data and market research on food consumption trends, preventing them from designing strategies to capture demand (FAO, 2015).

Box 7.3. West Africa's cassava value chain

West Africa is a major cassava producer, and the crop plays an essential role in the region's food security. Cassava is a staple food crop in West Africa that can mitigate food security risks because of its resilience to drought and to poor soil conditions (Hershey et al., 2000; Howeler et al., 2013). Accordingly, cassava production in the region mainly focuses on capturing domestic food demand. In Nigeria's Niger Delta area, for example, roughly 80% of cassava demand is domestic (PIND, 2011). In Ghana, cassava is the most consumed food crop, with a per capita annual consumption of 152 kg (Acheampong et al., 2021). West Africa's cassava production represented 33% and 52% of global and African production volumes in 2020, respectively (AUC/OECD, 2022). Nigeria is the world's largest producer, accounting for 23.5% of global production. Despite high output, the region struggles to capture international demand, in part coming from the diaspora. West African cassava represents just 0.33% of global cassava exports (ITC, 2022b).

A lack of affordable credit prevents the realisation of cassava's yield potential. In Sierra Leone, for example, just 2% of farmers can access credit, even through informal means. Moreover, 80% of farmers who can access credit are delayed by complicated administrative processes (Coulibaly et al., 2014). Overcoming financing difficulties, through the expansion of microfinance institutions and development finance, can help fund the adoption of higher-yield cassava varieties and fertiliser, pesticides and other farming equipment (Coulibaly et al., 2014; MoFA of Ghana, 2019). For example, Ghana has the highest productivity rates in the region, with an average yield of 21 metric tonnes per hectare (Mt/ha) (Acheampong et al., 2021). However, despite its regional proficiency, productivity remains below the estimated yield potential of 45 Mt/ha (MoFA of Ghana, 2019). Developing credit access to farmers could increase production and support food security.

Increased regional production of value-added cassava derivatives can replace imports. Cassava cannot only be used as an input in many food products (including noodles, traditional desserts and sweeteners) but also in non-food industries. Yet, most of the starch for industrial use in West Africa is imported, totalling USD 51.3 million in 2020 (OECD, 2020). High-quality cassava flour (HQCF) can act as a replacement for wheat flour, which is largely imported to the region (CABRI, 2019; ITC, 2022b). Similarly, while ethanol for the beverage, food, manufacturing and pharmaceutical sectors is largely imported, cassava-based ethanol has been successfully integrated into processing by Allied Atlantic distilleries in Nigeria and the YUEN alcohol factory in Benin (ITC, 2022b).

Investment in agricultural equipment, post-harvest facilities and transport services along the cassava value chain can help alleviate price uncertainty and supply disruptions. Market price volatility, low access to financing for equipment, and a lack of disease and pest control services are major obstacles for smallholder farmers to upscale production (Adebayo and Silberberge, 2020; Coulibaly et al., 2014). Market price volatility, in particular, amplifies producers' needs for storage facilities to store the crop until favourable prices return. The induced volatility in domestic supply forces the import of derivatives, hindering the emergence of new, industrial processing centres (Adebayo and Silberberge, 2020). Underinvestment in road infrastructure can result in transportation delays that cause cassava to perish, as it is often harvested in the wet season (CABRI, 2019). Furthermore, the cost of transporting fresh cassava accounts for 5-10% of the total variable cost of processing (ITC, 2022b). Solving transport issues by upgrading roads to better withstand difficult seasonal weather and locating producers and processors close to markets would help in moving cassava along the value chain. Programmes such as the Root and Tuber Improvement and Marketing Programme in Ghana have achieved some success in working with cassava producer groups to improve productivity-enhancing practices, despite challenges related to financing and effectiveness (MoFA of Ghana, n.d.).

Firms in food processing and distribution are mostly small, informal and fragmented and do not represent attractive targets for investments. Africa's food processing sector is characterised by a small number of large firms with high labour productivity and a large number of lower-productivity informal micro and small firms (ReSAKSS, 2022). For instance, in Ghana, over 70% of agro-processing is done by small informal enterprises: 85% of the country's agro-processing firms are micro-enterprises, 7% are very small firms, 5% are small and only 3% are medium-sized. Also West Africa's informal distribution networks are ill-equipped to handle growing demand and supply. Informal market players dominate food distribution – such as vendors in small shops, street markets and food stalls, hawkers, and street food sellers (Allen, Heinrigs and Heo, 2018). These informal firms and microenterprises do not represent viable investment opportunities in themselves, and they limit capacity increases further up the chain.

Informal enterprises mostly have limited market experience and formal expertise, which lowers profits and hinders product innovation. The pervasiveness of informal enterprises limits technical innovations, knowledge transfer, quality control, value addition and linkages along agri-food value chains (Owoo and Lambon-Quayefio, 2018). While co-operatives offer one means to organise informal firms, they cannot achieve the same economies of scale and efficient application of technologies as larger, formal firms. Most staple food processing value chains in West Africa are currently in the initiation phase or about to enter a phase of expansion. Without innovation in production technology and improved business practices, the number of enterprises continues to rise and profits decline. A critical mass of firms with capabilities in product innovation, production methods, internal management, sales and marketing has yet to emerge (Badiane et al., 2022).

West Africa suffers from gender inequality in land rights, including agricultural land. Three of the eight African countries (Côte d'Ivoire, Equatorial Guinea and Guinea-Bissau) where, by law, the husband as the family head has control and ownership over the management of assets and properties, including agricultural plots and land, are located in West Africa (OECD, 2021c).

Irrigation projects offer a large potential for sustainable investments. For a long time, only large-scale irrigation projects in Africa were deemed viable to provide high returns on investment and drive agricultural productivity growth. However, recent estimates show that, in large parts of Africa, the internal rate of returns of investment for large-scale irrigation projects ranges from only 7% to 17%, while that for small-scale projects is 26-28% (Abebrese, 2017).

Good interactions between leading supermarkets and local producers can increase productivity and sustainability in West Africa's agri-food value chains

Supermarkets can contribute to transforming West Africa's agri-food value chains, but the right components must be present. Agri-food value chains are the interface between agricultural producers in rural areas and the increasing population of urban food consumers whose demand for food products is continuously evolving (Barret et al., 2022). Four central market actors are required for the transformation of agri-food value chains: producer organisations, the public sector, agribusiness and finance (Elbehri, 2013). Sophisticated retailers, particularly supermarkets, occupy a strategic position while also acting as a financing intermediary. Reardon, Liverpool-Tasie and Minten (2021) highlight the lead role that supermarkets, alongside large agribusinesses, played in transforming the agri-food sector in Latin America, Central and Eastern Europe, and Asia. While market opportunities for supermarkets exist in abundance in West Africa, two components – a stable macroeconomic environment and reliable contract enforcement – are often missing.

Supermarkets can orchestrate local value chains, thereby reducing fragmentation and driving supply chain efficiency. West Africa's agri-food value chains are fragmented, causing inefficiencies that limit labour productivity. For instance, although Ghana's wholesale and retail trade sector increased its employment share from 17% in 2000 to 25% in 2010, this did not create a corresponding rise in economic output (AfDB/OECD/UNDP, 2016). Supermarkets often create backward linkages with agricultural producers, which can remove intermediary costs and connect them directly to urban markets (Barrett et al., 2022; Reardon, Liverpool-Tasie and Minten, 2021). Supermarkets buy products in bulk directly from the primary producers (farmers) and make them available in their outlets at a relatively affordable price, while reducing transportation costs, which can contribute to reducing the ecological footprint of the agri-food value chain. They also sometimes directly invest in processing. The Dairy Development programme of Friesland Campina WAMCO, a multinational subsidiary in Nigeria, illustrates this point. The large dairy manufacturer provides technological interventions directly to local farmers to improve yield per cow, raw milk quality and hygiene as well as feeding, breeding and farm management.

The interaction of supermarkets with local producers can result in enhanced quality. Supermarkets typically have quality requirements. This is connected to the visibility of supermarket chains to regulators and quality standards agencies. Some supermarkets act as export intermediaries for local raw foods, such as yam and cassava, that are demanded globally but only grow in limited areas, including West Africa. Consequently, local producers are incentivised to meet higher quality standards, in order to satisfy the standards of the domestic procurement systems of supermarkets and the product requirements of export markets. While the quality requirements for different segments of the domestic market may vary, the safety certification is common for all the items of a given type (AfDB/OECD/UNDP, 2014; Weatherspoon and Reardon, 2003).

Supermarkets may pose risks for sustainability, in particular for social inclusion, but mitigation strategies are available.

- **Exclusion of producers that lack efficient scale:** As supermarkets engage in bulk buying, they may expect discounted prices and scale efficiencies that small-scale producers and input suppliers cannot deliver. Tailored policy solutions are required to disincentivise the liability of size and to ensure that agri-food value chains are inclusive of vulnerable smallholder farmers. One policy option is to set benchmarks for supermarkets' backward integration (i.e. the inclusion of producers into the supermarkets' operations, for example through combined stock management). Benchmarks may be calibrated according to the size of supermarkets and would help to minimise supermarkets' passing costs to producers once they have a stake in their success. Co-ordinated market and tax regulations by West African governments could boost the investments in and patronage of local producers by large supermarkets, some of which may prefer to import products from outside West Africa.
- **Crowding-out effects of quality standards:** As supermarkets introduce more stringent quality standards, small producers risk being excluded, as they often cannot meet the costs of compliance with standards without external help. Public-private alliances can support capacity building among small actors in the agri-food value chain to help mitigate this risk. Investments are less effective in the absence of knowledge, skills and capabilities. Thus, targeted interventions are required to develop the skills of farmers, strengthen formal educational programmes linked to agriculture (such as agricultural engineering, food preservation and nutrition) and invest in agricultural research and development.

- **Productivity pressure:** As supermarkets demand more volume from small-scale producers, some may be suppressed from the more developed downstream end of the agri-food value chains if they are unable to meet required production levels. Network-oriented policies will help to mitigate the risk of smallholder exclusion. First, such policies will incentivise smallholders to pool output in order to meet production targets. Second, they will discourage supermarkets from monopsony behaviour (i.e. exploiting the fact that they are the only buyer) by encouraging them to become embedded with their suppliers. Small neighbourhood or district-level markets are a common place for daily commercial business in many West African countries. Implementing policies that aggregate these fragmented markets would raise the standards, quantity and quality of products and would create more efficient markets.
- **Environmental footprint:** Estimates suggest that supermarkets are a major source of certain environmental hazards. They indicate extremely high per capita consumption rates of single-use plastics in West Africa, arising mainly from packaging in retail outlets (Jambeck et al., 2018; Miezah et al., 2015). Against this background, policies must incentivise supermarkets to rally investments in environmental sustainability. For instance, by investing in waste management systems and working with other value chain actors, including financiers, supermarkets can make agri-food value chains more environmentally friendly (Adam et al., 2020). Such a transformation would require not only waste management but also other aspects in which agri-food value chains have an environmental footprint. The Shoprite Group is an example: in August 2022, it obtained sustainability-linked loans totalling approximately USD 208 million to invest in its broad-based sustainability strategy. The strategy includes the increase of energy from renewable sources as a share of total electricity consumption, the recycling of cardboard and plastic, sustainable packaging, and energy efficiency.

Policies supporting the productive transformation of West Africa's agri-food sector can catalyse sustainable investment

The vast and growing local and regional demand for high-quality food products offers a unique policy opportunity to drive the sustainable transformation of West Africa's agri-food sector. It allows countries to focus on improving efficiency and sustainability standards of production and supply chains and to strengthen West Africa's resilience towards global shocks through regional integration (AUC/OECD, 2022). The region's agri-food sector provides a unique setting for achieving synergies between economic, social and environmental sustainability goals.

To transform agri-food value chains in West Africa's diverse economies, customised and co-ordinated policy approaches will be required. Countries will need to mobilise private investments where possible while using development and public finance where necessary. This chapter has shown stark intra-regional differences in production capacity (e.g. Table 7.1), which should inform how to tailor policy approaches. The suitable emphasis on private versus public investments will vary by country:

- Currently, private investment flows largely to agribusinesses in the economies of Côte d'Ivoire, Ghana, Nigeria and Togo, which attract the lion's share of the FDI flowing to the region. These countries can pursue public-private co-financing and risk sharing, as well as scale-oriented measures benefiting from their larger markets and attractiveness for FDI.

- Benin, Burkina Faso, Gambia, Guinea, Guinea-Bissau, Liberia, Mali, Niger, Senegal and Sierra Leone represent the Least Developed Countries with mostly smaller domestic markets. These economies will need to pursue product specialisation and integration with larger countries' markets and value chains (for example through Mali's dry mango value chain in Koulikoro and Sikasso). They can be supported by preferential access to development assistance, strategic public investments and partnerships with the Economic Community of West African States (ECOWAS) and larger economies in the region (for instance, for skill exchange programmes).
- The island nation of Cabo Verde can make use of its marine endowments.

Domestic financial institutions can improve smallholders' access to financing for downstream activities and insurance

Despite governance challenges, public financial institutions remain important sources of financing for agricultural producers. State-financed agricultural development banks and agricultural credit guarantee schemes became popular in the 1970s, though many underperformed and had to close. The factors that account for their poor performance include preferential treatment given to large-scale farmers and politically connected persons, embezzlement, poor loan repayment rates, and heavily skewed spending towards the purchase of agricultural inputs and outputs (Domke, 2022; Salami and Arawomo, 2013). Nonetheless, governments implemented reforms to ensure that agricultural development banks are viable and sustainable providers of financial services to all segments of the rural populations. National, regional, continental and global financial institutions – such as Ghana's Agricultural Development Bank, the West African Development Bank, the African Development Bank (AfDB) and the International Fund for Agricultural Development (IFAD) – continue to provide essential financial services to agricultural producers whom commercial banks often consider as not creditworthy.

Examples of agricultural financing programmes in West Africa that couple credit with productivity training and sustainability requirements include:

- IFAD co-financed the Shared-risk Agricultural Financing Incentive Mechanism Support project (ProMIFA) in Togo, which offers agricultural financing for SMEs and smallholder farmers between 2019 and 2025. Starting with key agropastoral value chains (including rice, market gardening, maize and poultry raising), the project seeks to improve financial literacy and business plan drafting among its beneficiaries, mainly women and youth. It is aligned with the country's Five-year National Development Plan for 2018-22 and implements one of the strategic pillars of the Ministry of Agriculture's 2025 roadmap: acceleration of the agricultural financing mechanism (IFAD, 2018).
- NSIA Banque Côte d'Ivoire and the Development Bank Ghana offer examples of attaching sustainability criteria to agricultural financing. They integrate credit with social and environmental criteria assessments at all stages of lending, including in the agricultural sector (Anesvad Foundation, 2020; MoF of Ghana, 2022).
- The West African Initiative for Climate-Smart Agriculture (WAICSA) is a unique example of a West Africa-led blended finance fund focusing on climate-smart agriculture (CSA). It has encouraged smallholder farmers to employ CSA practices. The fund pools public and concessional capital to offer loans of up to USD 1 million at subsidised interest rates to farmers' organisations and agribusinesses. WAICSA has been estimated to improve the food security of up to 90 000 farming households across the region (Climate Finance Lab, n.d.).

Financing instruments that provide comprehensive support for downstream activities along agri-food value chains should be strengthened. To address value chain gaps comprehensively, large amounts of funding and extensive co-ordination between funders and recipients can be necessary (Box 7.4). Here are three current financing instruments:

- The Africa Food Security Fund (AFSF) was launched to address the needs of agricultural SMEs that are outside of the scope of larger private equity funds and commercial banks. It focuses primarily on processing, distribution and provision of agricultural inputs such as fertiliser and agronomic services. AFSF invests in potential high-growth SMEs operating in the agri-food value chains with a view to enhancing food security in Africa. The fund's USD 100 million portfolio is managed by Zebu Investment Partners and supported by investments from the African Development Bank, British International Investment and the European Investment Bank. Much of AFSF's interventions take place in West Africa – given the size of its population relative to the rest of the continent – particularly in underserved countries such as Mali and Senegal. At least 20 direct jobs are expected to be created for each USD 1 million invested, benefiting over 14 000 small-scale farmers, mainly women (AfDB, 2019; BII, n.d.).
- In Ghana, the Outgrower and Value Chain Fund, effective since 2011, provides affordable credit for medium- and long-term investments through the banking sector, involving an outgrower association, a technical operator or buyer, and a participating bank. Outgrower schemes refer to contractual agreements between individual or collectives of farmers and firms that require a stable supply of agricultural products (Felgenhauer and Wolter, 2009). These co-ordinated commercial relations between producers, processors and traders allow integration into the agricultural value chain.
- In 2022, the AfDB approved a USD 127 million package to improve transport links to areas with potential for agriculture, forestry and livestock farming in Niger's Eastern region. The project includes support to farming value chains through farmers' centres and the installation of dairy units (AfDB, 2022).

Agriculture insurance can improve farmers' resilience to weather shocks and natural disasters while improving their access to credit. Insurance can help producers expand and upgrade their businesses, as financial institutions are more willing to lend to farmers who are insured. Africa represents a mere 0.5% of the world's agricultural insurance industry. By way of comparison, North America (55%), Europe and Asia (20% each) account for nearly the totality of the world's agricultural insurance premiums (Fonta et al., 2018). Instead of being based on claimed losses, weather index insurance payouts are based on predetermined rates against extended periods of droughts, floods, hurricanes, etc. Although the uptake is low on the continent – due to the poor involvement of farm households in the early stages of pilot initiatives – the reach of such products is increasing in West Africa. For example, OKO Mali was established in 2019 as a maize and cotton index insurance for unbanked smallholder farmers. Accessible via a mobile interface, it provides affordable insurance to farmers in Côte d'Ivoire, Mali and Uganda and delivers instant claim settlements (OKO, n.d.).

Digital avenues offer new pathways to make agricultural credit accessible for smallholder farmers. Given relatively high digital access rates among smallholder farmers, digital solutions offer untapped potential for financial institutions to reach informal agricultural producers and agro-processors with credit and insurance products. National efforts to incorporate digital channels include Sterling Bank's SABEX in Nigeria, a blockchain solution that allows farmers to use their produce as collateral, store harvested crops in dedicated facilities and trade agricultural commodities (Sterling, n.d.). Partnerships with digital platforms such as Thriv'Afric in Nigeria, which collect comprehensive credit-relevant transaction data, can improve farmers' credit scores and avoid the need for collateral.

Box 7.4. The role of public-private alliances in improving value addition in Senegal's rice production

By combining policy and practical support, public-private alliances can be effective in achieving competitive and inclusive agri-food value chains. One example is the rice value chain. Local rice production covers only around 60% of local demand in the 15 ECOWAS member countries. In 2021, drained foreign reserves with rice imports cost West Africa around USD 3.7 billion (Dione and Toto, 2022).

Supporting local production is essential, especially in countries where local demand is high, like Senegal. The country's average annual consumption of rice per capita is 85 kg (CFC, 2022). The government supported the founding of a consortium-led private processing and distribution company of local rice. The consortium includes a network of import marketers, producer organisations and processors. Improved rice quality and processing capacity were two of the short-term results of investments (Elbehri, 2013). Complementing investments in processing, Senegal's Common Fund for Commodities (CFC) offers USD 1.46 million in financial support to local rice millers and their smallholder suppliers while also building irrigation channels and modernising equipment (CFC, 2022).

Regional integration policies and place-based programmes can fulfil complementary roles in strengthening agri-food value chains

The gradual elimination of intra-African trade tariffs through the African Continental Free Trade Area offers an opportunity for West African countries not only to trade more but also to encourage more investment in the downstream segments of agri-food value chains. Overall, West Africa exhibits a higher level of forward integration in agri-food value chains for exports outside than within the region. This means that a higher share of its exports functions as inputs for non-West African countries' exports, reflecting the predominant role of agricultural commodities in West Africa's exports (AUC/OECD, 2022). Returns on strategic investments in specialised national agri-food value chains (including in processing) stand to increase as a result of reduced intra- and extra-regional trade barriers.

The ECOWAS provides a regional agricultural policy framework. Initially adopted in 2005, the Economic Community of West Africa Agricultural Policy (ECOWAP) supports the development of agricultural programmes in the region. It features a web-based monitoring and evaluation system that eases data collection, analysis and knowledge-sharing. The implementation of ECOWAP relies on three complementary mechanisms: i) the formulation of national agricultural investment plans; ii) a regional agriculture investment plan that puts in place regional programmes focused on issues such as the management of shared natural resources, and iii) specific regional policies and policy instruments (ECOWAS, n.d.). Assessments during the ECOWAP+10 review process questioned the coherence and co-ordination of agricultural policy implementation and called for greater emphasis on the post-harvest and commercialisation segments of the agricultural value chains (Oxfam, 2015; SWAC/OECD, 2015).

Countries can co-ordinate their agro-industrial strategies via ECOWAP. Countries have pursued export-oriented industrial strategies in various ways. Cash crops targeting exports, such as the cotton industry in Burkina Faso, have proven useful to generate foreign earnings in poorer economies but have had limited impact in reducing poverty, owing to insufficient local transformation. Senegal provides an example of how a Least

Developed Country can establish resilient food value chains (such as rice and fresh vegetables), catering to both local consumer needs and growing regional demand for agricultural exports. The country has employed policies targeting local entrepreneurs and developed public-private alliances and centres of intensive agricultural services. At the same time, duplicating strategies can come with risks. For instance, through the 2000s, most West African countries relied on cheap poultry imports from the European Union, which destabilised their national production capacity. Using ECOWAP can help the region's countries avoid trade conflicts and enable scaling and specialisation.

Place-based programmes to encourage sustainable investments in downstream agri-food value chain activities should be at the core of national development plans and regional strategies. Place-based programmes offer policy makers a toolbox to support the industrialisation of agri-food value chains through economies of scale and specialisation (e.g. large-scale production infrastructure and knowledge exchange) and multi-sectorial synergies (e.g. through the creation of shared infrastructure) (Table 7.3). Such programmes should be embedded in regional and continental strategies, such as the African Union's Common African Agro-Parks Programme (CAAPs). The CAAPs is one of the concrete initiatives to implement the Comprehensive Africa Agriculture Development Programme in support of Agenda 2063 and the Malabo commitment to triple intra-African trade in the agriculture and services sectors (AU, 2021).

Table 7.3. **Investment promotion tools in the agricultural sector**

Investment promotion tool	Overall objective	Geographic focus	Roles for public investment	Profile of target group
Agro-clusters	- Network linkages	Regional or provincial, close to production area	Growth of agglomeration economies and promotion of collective action	Multinational and domestic agribusiness/agro-industry firms and construction companies
Agro-industrial parks (including agro-techno parks, science parks and agro-eco-industrial parks)	- Value addition - Green agro-processing - Research and innovation	Urban, easily accessible to production area	Common infrastructure, logistics facilities and dedicated services	Agribusiness/agro-industry firms, specialised service providers and logistics companies
Special agro-industrial processing zone	- Processing - Export and FDI promotion	Urban, often near port area	Advantageous economic and regulatory frameworks, common infrastructure and services	Agribusiness/agro-industry firms, specialised service providers and logistics firms
Agro-incubators	- Entrepreneurship and innovation	Urban	Common infrastructure and dedicated services to create and coach new agribusiness firms	Agribusiness/agro-industry startups, venture capital and angel investors
Agro-corridors	- Integrated planning of infrastructure and agribusiness interventions.	Regional, national or supranational; linear agglomeration spanning across hundreds or thousands of kilometres	Infrastructure investments, trade and regulatory policy reforms, and sectoral development plans	Multinational and domestic agribusiness/agro-industry firms, construction companies, etc.

Source: Authors' compilation based on FAO (2017), *Territorial Tools for Agro-industry Development: A Sourcebook*, www.fao.org/3/i6862e/i6862e.pdf.

National strategies in West Africa can further develop special agro-industrial processing zones. Such zones offer an opportunity for countries to produce higher value-added exports. Efficiency and productivity can be bolstered by improving linkages between post-harvest production and value addition in the agro-cluster. The SKBo Triangle cross-border zone, launched in 2018, comprises the areas of Bobo Dioulasso (Burkina Faso), Korhogo (Côte d'Ivoire) and Sikasso (Mali). The zone is set to attract private investment in agro-industry and the mineral industry, across more than 6 million ha of land (AUC/OECD, 2019; UNCTAD, 2021). The USD 538 million Special Agro-Industrial Processing Zone programme and the Lekki Free Trade Zone in Nigeria are further examples.

Addressing infrastructure constraints is foundational to improving intra-regional trade within agri-food value chains (AUC/OECD, 2022). Infrastructure gaps in West African countries are large, and they vary widely (PPIAF, 2022). Agricultural investment promotion tools (Table 7.3) can be a viable approach to fill agri-food-specific infrastructure gaps, as they serve different value chains by providing centrally managed infrastructure and supporting services. For example, the Northern Agro-Industrial Pole Project in Côte d'Ivoire is designed to establish five sites to operate as storage, secondary packaging and primary processing centres for agricultural products; the project also includes dams, rural roads, healthcare centres and schools, and infrastructure for fisheries and livestock production (AfDB, 2023; OPEC Fund, 2021).

National agricultural investment plans (NAIPs) can increase focus on agro-processing and rural-urban supply chains, especially through distribution and logistics networks in intermediary cities. NAIPs that follow ECOWAS frameworks are currently in their second iteration (they expire around 2025-26). Forthcoming iterations could better target investments in downstream activities of agri-food value chains. Connecting the rural-urban supply chains via the NAIPs could transform value-added sectors such as agro-processing, branding and marketing. For instance, in its second generation NAIP (2018-21), Ghana's target was to increase domestic secondary and tertiary processing of cocoa beans to 50% of the annual output, from 30% in 2017-18 (MoFA of Ghana, 2018). Within NAIPs, strategically located intermediary cities can be destined as logistics hubs (e.g. storage facilities for perishable rural goods). The cities can increase the productivity of industrial and agricultural value chains by providing infrastructure such as roads and transportation networks (AfDB/OECD/UNDP, 2015; OECD/PSI, 2020).

Agro-poles, support organisations, international funders and technical partners can help improve food security and agricultural practices

Agro-poles can be a viable means to support food security, as shown in Benin. Since the early 2000s, roughly 40 agro-poles have been established across Africa both to ensure food security and accelerate the shift from subsistence farming to agro-industrial development. A success story emerges from agro-poles in Benin. As part of the Government of Benin's strategy to transform its agricultural sector, the country has designated 13 priority agricultural products. Since 2016, the country's *Programme National de Développement de la Filière Ananas* has promoted the sustainable production and competitiveness of pineapple in agro-poles to value its local potential (Jones, 2021). In 2021, Pain de Sucre pineapple from Benin's Allada Plateau became the country's first protected geographical indication by the African Intellectual Property Organization. Although this is an achievement, most countries in the region either have no dedicated food safety agency that provides oversight to the pineapple processing industry or lag behind in product certification (e.g. International Organization for Standardization [ISO]) (Schreinemachers et al., 2022).

With additional funding, support organisations such as agricultural research, agro-incubators and interprofessional associations could refocus support for smallholder farmers towards productivity and sustainability-related practices. Agricultural research could play a critical role in enhancing the product development of agro-processors (Owoo and Lambon-Quayefio, 2018). Agro-incubators can promote product quality: they are conducive to agricultural innovation given their combination of entrepreneurs and multidisciplinary, experienced teams of experts and mentors, together with knowledge and research organisations and investors (FAO, 2017). Interprofessional associations in West Africa's francophone countries can help to pool resources and information for SMEs, but they face financing issues (Shepherd et al., 2009). These interprofessional associations would benefit from public support, which in turn could aid SMEs in scaling up. Programmes such as the Fertilizer and Seed Recommendation Map for West Africa, an online platform that provides information on seeds of improved varieties, appropriate fertiliser recommendations and good agricultural practices specific to an agro-ecological zone (FeSeRWAM, n.d.), can help disseminate to West African farmers the most up-to-date farming practices.

A well-known case is the Shonga Farms in Nigeria's Kwara State. They invited 13 commercial farmers from Zimbabwe to develop dairy, poultry farming and commercial crops, with financial resources from five Nigerian banks through the Special Purpose Vehicle Shonga Farms Holding Limited (SFH). Its success mainly owes to the efficient balance between public support and majority private investment. The farms employ up to 4 500 workers in off-peak agricultural periods and 7 000 workers in peak periods. They process 40 000 chickens and 50 000 litres of milk per day, mainly for the regional Kwara market. Shonga Farms boast one of the continent's highest cassava yields, which they process for export outside of Africa (AUC/OECD, 2019; Mickiewicz and Olarewaju, 2020).

International funders and technical partners can support programmes that ensure food security and upgrade agricultural practices, but local ownership needs to be ensured. The New Alliance for Food Security and Nutrition (NAFSAN), established in 2012 under the auspices of the G8, aimed to encourage food security initiatives by catalysing private investment and accelerating private capital flows to African agriculture. However, evaluation assessments conducted at the national level pointed to mixed results due to lack of co-ordination, lack of ownership and leadership, and poor NAFSAN management and governance (Badiane et al., 2018). The case illustrates the importance of local ownership which can transform financial resources into local assets and skills. A collaboration between international funders and local technical partners has increased food security and improved agricultural practices at a shrimp farm in Cabo Verde (Box 7.5).

Box 7.5. **Shrimp farms in Cabo Verde**

In the late 2000s, aquaculture was introduced in Calhau (São Vicente Island) to help meet the local demand for shrimp consumption. At the time, all shrimp consumed in the country was imported (PSI, 2009).

The initial project deployed funding from a national banking institution and co-financing from the Dutch Privat Sector Investment programme. Current stakeholders include the local partner SUCLA, known for its canned tuna; Brazil's Universo, a company specialised in the wholesale and retail market of seafood; and Germany's SINN Power, which focuses on renewable energy solutions.

In 2022, one shrimp farm, the Fazenda do Camarão, produced approximately 40 tonnes of shrimp, aiming to double production by 2023. The total consumption of shrimp in Cabo Verde is roughly 115 tonnes per year. While there is a potential for export, the intention is to prioritise the domestic market.

The farm has been certified with quality and environmental labels such as Global GAP, HACCP and BAP, as it operates mostly on wind and solar energies. It also promotes a circular economy approach and is self-sufficient in the production of larvae. The shrimps are fed corn flour and fish meal from the neighbouring island of São Nicolau. With nearly 40 employees – mostly women – the farm is the largest employer in the village of Calhau.

Notes

1. Authors' calculations based on FAOSTAT (2022a).
2. See https://www.nepad.org/caadp (accessed 2 March 2023).
3. Authors' calculations based on fDi Intelligence (2022). Due to the low number of FDI projects for agribusinesses, annual values are highly volatile, and only the total amount for 2017-22 is presented.
4. Authors' calculations based on OECD (2022b).
5. Authors' calculations based on FAOSTAT (2022d).

References

Abebrese, F. K. A. (2017), "Investing in irrigation for agriculture productivity in Africa", Africa Up Close blog, Wilson Center, 4 October, https://africaupclose.wilsoncenter.org/investing-in-irrigation-for-agriculture-productivity-in-africa/.

Acheampong, P. P. et al. (2021), "Research and development for improved cassava varieties in Ghana: Farmers' adoption and effects on livelihoods", *Cassava – Biology, Production and Use*, IntechOpen, www.intechopen.com/chapters/76626.

Adam, I. et al. (2020), "Policies to reduce single-use plastic marine pollution in West Africa", *Marine Policy*, Vol. 116, www.sciencedirect.com/science/article/pii/S0308597X19304865#bib35.

Adebayo, W. G. and M. Silberberge (2020), "Poverty reduction, sustainable agricultural development, and the cassava value chain in Nigeria", in *The Palgrave Handbook of Agricultural and Rural Development in Africa*, Palgrave Macmillan, Cham, https://doi.org/10.1007/978-3-030-41513-6_24.

Adeyonu, A. G. et al. (2021), "An assessment of broiler value chain in Nigeria", *Open Agriculture*, Vol. 6/1, pp. 296-307, www.degruyter.com/document/doi/10.1515/opag-2020-0168/html.

AfDB (2023), "Côte d'Ivoire - Agro-Industrial Pole Project in the North (2PAI-NORD)", Project Summary, African Development Bank, https://projectsportal.afdb.org/dataportal/VProject/show/P-CI-AA0-030 (accessed 20 February 2023).

AfDB (2022), "Niger: African Development Bank Group approves $127 million package to open up eastern agricultural areas", Press Release, 17 March, www.afdb.org/en/news-and-events/press-releases/niger-african-development-bank-group-approves-127-million-package-open-eastern-agricultural-areas-50108.

AfDB (2019), "Project Summary Note - Africa Food Security Fund", African Development Bank Group, www.afdb.org/en/documents/document/project-summary-note-africa-food-security-fund-107391.

AfDB/OECD/UNDP (2016), *African Economic Outlook 2016: Sustainable Cities and Structural Transformation*, OECD Publishing, Paris, https://doi.org/10.1787/aeo-2016-en.

AfDB/OECD/UNDP (2015), *African Economic Outlook 2015: Regional Development and Spatial Inclusion*, OECD Publishing, Paris, https://doi.org/10.1787/aeo-2015-en.

AfDB/OECD/UNDP (2014), *African Economic Outlook 2014: Global Value Chains and Africa's Industrialisation*, OECD Publishing, Paris, https://doi.org/10.1787/aeo-2014-en.

AfricaNews (2023), "Ghana to conclude IMF deal in March - Akufo-Addo hopes", 7 February, www.africanews.com/2023/02/07.

Ali, Z. et al. (2020), "Long-term impact of West African food system responses to COVID-19", *Nature Food*, Vol. 1, pp. 768-770, www.nature.com/articles/s43016-020-00191-8.

Allen, T. and P. Heinrigs (2016), "Emerging opportunities in the West African food economy", *West African Papers*, No. 1, OECD Publishing, Paris, https://doi.org/10.1787/5jlvfj4968jb-en.

Allen, T., P. Heinrigs and I. Heo (2018), "Agriculture, food and jobs in West Africa", *West African Papers*, No. 14, OECD Publishing, Paris, https://doi.org/10.1787/dc152bc0-en.

Amadou, H. et al. (2012), "A comparison between urban livestock production strategies in Burkina Faso, Mali and Nigeria in West Africa", *Tropical Animal Health and Production*, Vol 44, pp. 1631-1642, https://doi.org/10.1007/s11250-012-0118-0.

Anesvad Foundation (2020), *2020 Impact Investment Report: Socially Responsible Investment*, www.anesvad.org/wp-content/uploads/2022/02/ANESVAD-IMPACT-REPORT-2020.pdf.

AU (2021), "AU- Common African Agro-Parks Programme (CAAPs) proposed as an Agenda 2063 Flagship Programme for the next 10 Years Implementation Plan", Press Release, 2 December, African Union, https://au.int/en/pressreleases/20211202/au-common-african-agro-parks-programme-caaps-proposed-agenda-2063-flagship.

AU/AUDA-NEPAD (2020), *CAADP: Synthesis of Lessons Learned from NAIPs and RAIPs Formulation and Implementation*, African Union/African Union Development Agency-New Economic Partnership for Africa's Development, www.nepad.org/caadp/publication/caadp-synthesis-of-lessons-learned-naips-and-raips-formulation-and-implementation.

AUC/OECD (2022), *Africa's Development Dynamics 2022: Regional Value Chains for a Sustainable Recovery*, AUC, Addis Ababa/OECD Publishing, Paris, https://doi.org/10.1787/2e3b97fd-en.

AUC/OECD (2019), *Africa's Development Dynamics 2019: Achieving Productive Transformation*, AUC, Addis Ababa/OECD Publishing, Paris, https://doi.org/10.1787/c1cd7de0-en.

AUDA-NEPAD (2017), "CAADP – Country Progress", webpage, African Union Development Agency-New Economic Partnership for Africa's Development, www.nepad.org/caadp/country-progress.

Badiane, O. et al. (2022), "The rise of Africa's processing sector and commercialization of smallholder agriculture", in *2022 ReSAKSS Annual Trends and Outlook Report*, Regional Strategic Analysis and Knowledge Support System, www.resakss.org/sites/default/files/2022_ator_individual_chapters/Chapter%202_ReSAKSS_AW_ATOR_2022.pdf.

Badiane, O. et al. (2018), *An Assessment of the New Alliance for Food Security and Nutrition: Synthesis Report*, Regional Strategic Analysis and Knowledge Support System/African Growth and Development Policy Modeling Consortium, https://au.int/sites/default/files/documents/34472-doc-nafsn20full20report20with20annexes.pdf.

Barrett, C. B. et al. (2022), "Agri-food value chain revolutions in low- and middle-income countries", *Journal of Economic Literature*, Vol. 60/4, pp. 1316-1377, https://pubs.aeaweb.org/doi/pdfplus/10.1257/jel.20201539.

BII (n.d.), "Africa Food Security Fund I", British International Investment, www.bii.co.uk/en/our-impact/fund/africa-food-security-fund-i/#:~:text=AFSF%20will%20invest%20in%20businesses,as%20fertiliser%20and%20agronomic%20services (accessed 20 January 2023).

Boimah, M. et al. (2022), "Doing it right to alleviate poverty: Application of the sustainable food value chain development framework to Ghana's poultry sector", *International Journal of Agricultural Sustainability*, Vol. 20/7, pp. 1454-1469, www.tandfonline.com/doi/full/10.1080/14735903.2022.2152605.

CABRI (2019), *The Role of Governments in Developing Agriculture Value Chains: Case Study 2: Rice and Cassava Value Chains*, Policy Dialogue, Collaborative Africa Budget Reform Initiative, South Africa, www.cabri-sbo.org/uploads/files/Documents/Case-Study-2_Rice-and-Cassava-ENG.pdf.

CEPII (2023), *BACI: International Trade Database at the Product-Level* (database), www.cepii.fr/CEPII/en/bdd_modele/bdd_modele_item.asp?id=37 (accessed 1 February 2023).

CFC (2022), "Turning Senegal's rice self-sufficiency vision into reality", Common Fund for Commodities, 25 November, www.common-fund.org/turning-senegals-rice-self-sufficiency-vision-reality.

Climate Finance Lab (n.d.), "The West African Initiative for Climate Smart Agriculture", webpage, www.climatefinancelab.org/project/africa-climate-smart-agriculture/ (accessed 6 March 2023).

Coulibaly, O. et al. (2014), *Regional Cassava Value Chains analysis in West Africa: A Case Study of Nigeria*, CORAF/WECARD, https://doi.org/10.13140/2.1.3421.6001.

Dione, N. and E. Toto (2022), "Senegal hones its home-grown rice to cut dependence on Asian imports", Reuters, 20 October, www.reuters.com/markets/commodities/senegal-hones-its-home-grown-rice-cut-dependence-asian-imports-2022-10-20/.

Domke, B. (2022), "Towards a renaissance of agricultural development banks in sub-Saharan Africa?", *Rural 21*, 19 December, www.rural21.com/english/current-issue/detail/article/towards-a-renaissance-of-agricultural-development-banks-in-sub-saharan-africa.html.

ECOWAS (n.d.), "About ECOWAP", Economic Community of West African States, https://ecowap.ecowas.int/about-ecowap (accessed 6 March 2023).

Eeswaran, R. et al. (2022), "Current and future challenges and opportunities for livestock farming in West Africa: Perspectives from the case of Senegal", *Agronomy*, Vol. 12/8, www.mdpi.com/2073-4395/12/8/1818.

Elbehri, A. (2013), *Rebuilding West Africa's Food Potential: Policies and Market Incentives for Smallholder-Inclusive Food Value Chains*, Food and Agriculture Organization of the United Nations and International Fund for Agriculture Development, https://reliefweb.int/report/mali/rebuilding-west-africas-food-potential-policies-and-market-incentives-smallholder.

FAO (2017), *Territorial Tools for Agro-industry Development: A Sourcebook*, Food and Agriculture Organisation of the United Nations, Rome, www.fao.org/3/i6862e/i6862e.pdf.

FAO (2015), *Agricultural Growth in West Africa*, Food and Agricultural Organisation of the United Nations, Rome, www.afdb.org/fileadmin/uploads/afdb/Documents/Publications/Agricultural_Growth_in_West_Africa_-_Market_and_policy_drivers_-_OSAN.pdf.

FAOSTAT (2022a), "Value of Agricultural Production", *Production* (database), www.fao.org/faostat/en/#data/QV (accessed 27 February 2023).

FAOSTAT (2022b), "Crops and Livestock Products", *Trade* (database), www.fao.org/faostat/en/#data/TCL (accessed 27 February 2023).

FAOSTAT (2022c), "Crops and Livestock Products", *Production* (database), www.fao.org/faostat/en/#data/QCL (accessed 27 February 2023).

FAOSTAT (2022d), "Country Investment Statistics Profile", *Investment* (database), www.fao.org/faostat/en/#data/CISP (accessed 27 February 2023).

FAOSTAT (2022e), "Development Flows to Agriculture", *Investment* (database), www.fao.org/faostat/en/#data/EA (accessed 27 February 2023).

fDi Intelligence (2022), *fDi Markets* (database), www.fdiintelligence.com/fdi-markets (accessed 19 August 2022).

Felgenhauer K. and D. Wolter (2009), "Outgrower schemes – Why big multinationals link up with African smallholders", OECD, Paris, www.oecd.org/dev/41302136.pdf.

FeSeRWAM (n.d.), "About FeSeRWAM", Fertilizer and Seed Recommendations Map for West Africa, https://feserwam.org/ (accessed 6 March 2023).

Fonta, W. M. et al. (2018), "Estimating farmers' willingness to pay for weather index-based crop insurance uptake in West Africa: Insight from a pilot initiative in Southwestern Burkina Faso", *Agricultural and Food Economics*, Vol. 6/11, https://agrifoodecon.springeropen.com/articles/10.1186/s40100-018-0104-6.

GIIN (2015), *The Landscape for Impact Investing in West Africa*, Global Impact Investing Network, https://thegiin.org/research/publication/westafricareport/.

Hershey, C. et al. (2000), "Expanding the competitive edge in diversified markets", in *FAO: A Review of Cassava in Asia with Country Case Studies on Thailand and Viet Nam (Vol. 3)*, Food and Agricultural Organization of the United Nations, Rome, www.fao.org/3/y1177e/y1177e.pdf.

Hollinger, F. and J. Staatz (2015), *Agricultural Growth in West Africa: Market and Policy Drivers – Chapter 7*, FAO, African Development Bank and ECOWAS, Rome, www.fao.org/3/i4337e/i4337e.pdf.

Howeler, R. et al. (2013), *Save and Grow: Cassava: A Guide to Sustainable Production Intensification*, Food and Agricultural Organization of the United Nations, Rome, www.fao.org/3/a-i3278e.pdf.

IEA (2022), "Greenhouse gas emissions from Energy Data Explorer", *Data and Statistics* (database), International Energy Agency, www.iea.org/data-and-statistics/data-tools/greenhouse-gas-emissions-from-energy-data-explorer (accessed October 2022).

IFAD (2018), *Proposed Loan and Grant under the Debt Sustainability Framework to the Togolese Republic for the Shared-risk Agricultural Financing Incentive Mechanism Support Project*, International Fund for Agricultural Development, https://webapps.ifad.org/members/lapse-of-time/docs/english/EB-2018-LOT-P-25.pdf?attach=1.

IFC (2019), *Creating Markets in Burkina Faso*, International Finance Cooperation, www.ifc.org/wps/wcm/connect/f45fd7a3-f8be-430b-bd9f-eb958ebe2d89/201907-CPSD-Burkina-Faso-EN.pdf?MOD=AJPERES&CVID=mNf5Bxk.

IMF (2023a), *World Economic Outlook Database*, April 2023 Edition, International Monetary Fund, www.imf.org/en/Publications/WEO/weo-database/2022/April (accessed April 2023).

IMF (2023b), "List of LIC DSAs for PRGT-Eligible Countries", IMF DSA Publication, International Monetary Fund, www.imf.org/external/Pubs/ft/dsa/DSAlist.pdf.

IMF (2022a), *World Economic Outlook Database*, October 2022 Edition, International Monetary Fund, www.imf.org/en/Publications/WEO/weo-database/2022/October (accessed October 2022).

IMF (2022b), *Balance of Payments and International Investment Position Statistics (BOP/IIP)* (database), International Monetary Fund, https://data.imf.org/?sk=7A51304B-6426-40C0-83DD-CA473CA1FD52 (accessed 22 November 2022).

IMF (2022c), *Investment and Capital Stock Dataset (ICSD)* (database), https://data.imf.org/?sk=1CE8A55F-CFA7-4BC0-BCE2-256EE65AC0E4 (accessed October 2022).

ITC (2022a), *Made by Africa: Creating value through integration*, International Trade Centre, Geneva, https://intracen.org/media/file/13012.

ITC (2022b), *West Africa Competitiveness Programme Regional Investment Profile – Summary: Cassava Value Chain*, International Trade Centre, Geneva, https://intracen.org/media/file/12415.

Jambeck, J. et al. (2018), "Challenges and emerging solutions to the land-based plastic waste issue in Africa", *Marine Policy*, Vol. 96, pp. 256-263, www.sciencedirect.com/science/article/pii/S0308597X17305286.

Jones, S. (21 September 2021), "Value Chain Analysis for Development (VCA4D) - Benin // Pineapple", Europa, https://europa.eu/capacity4dev/value-chain-analysis-for-development-vca4d-/wiki/222-benin-pineapple.

Juvonen, K. et al. (2019), "Unleashing the potential of institutional investors in Africa", *AfDB Working Papers*, No. 325, African Development Bank, Abidjan, www.afdb.org/sites/default/files/documents/publications/wps_no_325_unleashing_the_potential_of_institutional_investors_in_africa_c_rv1.pdf.

Lipton, G. (2022), "Investing time: The growth of green finance in West Africa", *Landscape News*, 26 May, https://news.globallandscapesforum.org/57332/investing-time-the-growth-of-green-finance-in-west-africa/.

Mgbenka, R. N. and E. N. Mbah (2016), "A review of smallholder farming in Nigeria: Need for transformation", *International Journal of Agricultural Extension and Rural Development*, Vol. 3/2, www.eajournals.org/wp-content/uploads/A-Review-of-Smallholder-Farming-In-Nigeria.pdf.

Mickiewicz, T. and T. Olarewaju (2020). "New venture evolution of migrants under institutional voids: Lessons from Shonga Farms in Nigeria", *International Small Business Journal*, Vol. 38/5, pp. 404-423. https://doi.org/10.1177/0266242619896266 (accessed 6 March 2023).

Miezah, K. et al. (2015), "Municipal solid waste characterization and quantification as a measure towards effective waste management in Ghana", *Waste Management*, Vol. 46, pp. 15-27, www.sciencedirect.com/science/article/pii/S0956053X15301185.

MoF of Ghana (2022), "Summary of Environmental and Social Management System (ESMS) - Development Bank Ghana", Ministry of Finance of Ghana, 2 March, https://mofep.gov.gh/news-and-events/2022-03-02/summary-of-environmental-and-social-management-system-development-bank-ghana.

MoFA of Ghana (2019), *Medium Term Expenditure Framework (MTEF) for 2019-2022*, Ministry of Food and Agriculture of Ghana, https://mofep.gov.gh/sites/default/files/pbb-estimates/2019/2019-PBB-MoFA.pdf.

MoFA of Ghana (2018), *Investing for Food and Jobs (IFJ): An Agenda for Transforming Ghana's Agriculture (2018–2021)*, Ministry of Food and Agriculture of Ghana, https://mofa.gov.gh/site/images/pdf/National%20Agriculture%20Investment%20Plan_IFJ.pdf.

MoFA of Ghana (n.d.), "Root & Tuber Improvement & Marketing Programme (RTIMP)", webpage, Ministry of Food and Agriculture of Ghana, https://mofa.gov.gh/site/programmes/42-root-tuber-improvement-marketing-programme-rtimp (accessed 6 March 2023).

National Pension Commission (2006), *Regulation of Investment of Pension Fund Assets*, www.pencom.gov.ng/wp-content/uploads/2017/04/1448884140_Regulation_on_Investment_of_Pension_Funds31.pdf.

Nyang`oro O. and G. Njenga (2022), "Pension funds in sub-Saharan Africa", *WIDER Working Paper 2022/95*, www.wider.unu.edu/sites/default/files/Publications/Working-paper/PDF/wp2022-95-pension-funds-in-sub-saharan-africa.pdf.

OEC (2020), "ECOWAS", *Observatory of Economic Complexity* (database), https://oec.world/en (accessed January 2023).

OECD (2022a), "Aid (ODA) disbursements to countries and regions", *OECD Development Assistance Committee* (database), https://stats-1.oecd.org/Index.aspx?DataSetCode=TABLE2A (accessed 15 December 2022).

OECD (2022b), "Mobilisation", *OECD.Stat* (database), https://stats.oecd.org/Index.aspx?DataSetCode=DV_DCD_MOBILISATION (accessed February 2023).

OECD (2021a), *Private Philanthropy for Development: Data for Action Dashboard* (database), OECD Publishing, Paris, https://oecd-main.shinyapps.io/philanthropy4development/ (accessed November 2022).

OECD (2021b), *Pension Fund Assets* (database), https://data.oecd.org/pension/pension-funds-assets.htm (accessed September 2022).

OECD (2021c), *SIGI 2021 Regional Report for Africa*, Social Institutions and Gender Index, OECD Publishing, Paris, https://doi.org/10.1787/a6d95d90-en.

OECD/PSI (2020), *Rural Development Strategy Review of Ethiopia: Reaping the Benefits of Urbanisation*, OECD Development Pathways, OECD Publishing, Paris, https://doi.org/10.1787/a325a658-en.

OECD/UN ECA/AfDB (2022), *Africa's Urbanisation Dynamics 2022: The Economic Power of Africa's Cities*, West African Studies, OECD Publishing, Paris, https://doi.org/10.1787/3834ed5b-en.

OKO (n.d.), "Qui êtes-vous?", webpage, https://fr.oko.finance/ (accessed 6 March 2023).

OPEC Fund (2021), "The Northern Agro-Industrial Pole Project", webpage, https://opecfund.org/operations/list/the-northern-agro-industrial-pole-project (accessed 28 January 2023).

Owoo, N. S. and M. P. Lambon-Quayefio (2018), "The agro-processing industry and its potential for structural transformation of the Ghanaian economy", in *Industries without Smokestacks: Industrialisation in Africa Reconsidered*, Oxford, https://academic.oup.com/book/12695/chapter/162725066.

Oxfam (2022), "Investing in family farming to end hunger crises in West Africa", article, 10 May, https://westafrica.oxfam.org/en/latest/press-release/investing-family-farming-end-hunger-crises-west-africa.

Oxfam (2015), "ECOWAP: A Fragmented Policy. Development partners and regional institutions should address leadership and coordination issues in order to build a common agricultural policy for West Africa", *Oxfam Briefing Paper*, www-cdn.oxfam.org/s3fs-public/file_attachments/bp-ecowap-fragmented-policy-131115-en.pdf.

PIND (2011), *A Report on Cassava Value Chain Analysis in the Niger Delta*, Foundation for Partnership Initiatives in the Niger Delta, Abuja, https://ndpifoundation.org/wp-content/uploads/2018/09/Cassava-Value-Chain-Analysis.pdf.

PPIAF (2022), "West Africa: PPIAF supports the region's first PPP framework", Feature Story, 13 April, Public-Private Infrastructure Advisory Facility, https://ppiaf.org/feature_story/west-africa-ppiaf-supports-region%E2%80%99s-first-ppp-framework.

PSI (2009), *Project Overview 2009*, Private Sector Investment programme, The Hague, https://english.rvo.nl/sites/default/files/2013/12/PSI%20project%20overview%202009_1.pdf.

Reardon, T., L. S. O. Liverpool-Tasie and B. Minten (2021), "Quiet revolution by SMEs in the midstream of value chains in developing regions: Wholesale markets, wholesalers, logistics, and processing", *Food Security*, https://link.springer.com/content/pdf/10.1007/s12571-021-01224-1.pdf.

ReSAKSS (2022), *Annual Trends and Outlook Report: Agrifood Processing Strategies for Successful Food Systems Transformation in Africa*, Regional Strategic Analysis and Knowledge Support System, www.resakss.org/node/6863.

Salami, A. and D. F. Arawomo (2013), "Empirical analysis of agricultural credit in Africa: Any role for institutional factors", *African Development Bank Group Working Paper*, No. 192, www.afdb.org/fileadmin/uploads/afdb/Documents/Publications/Working_Paper_192_-_Empirical_Analysis_of_Agricultural_Credit_in_Africa-_Any_Role_for_Institutional_Factors.pdf.

Salla, A. (2017), *Review of the Livestock/Meat and Milk Value Chains and Policy Influencing Them in West Africa*, Food and Agriculture Organization of the United Nations and Economic Community of West African States, www.fao.org/3/i5275e/i5275e.pdf.

Schreinemachers, P. et al. (2022), "The dynamics of Africa's fruit and vegetable processing sectors", in *2022 Annual Trends and Outlook Report*, ReSWAKSS, www.resakss.org/node/6863.

Shepherd, A. W. et al. (2009), *Commodity Associations: A tool for Supply Chain Management*, Food and Agriculture Organisation of the United Nations, Rome, https://cgspace.cgiar.org/handle/10568/24936.

Sterling (n.d.), "SABEX", webpage, https://sterling.ng/sabex/ (accessed 6 March 2023).

SWAC/OECD (2015), *ECOWAP+10 : Mutations de l'économie agro-alimentaire et implications*, Sahel and West Africa Club/OECD, www.oecd.org/swac/publications/ECOWAP10.pdf

SWFI (n.d.), "Top 100 Largest Sovereign Wealth Fund Rankings by Total Assets", webpage, Sovereign Wealth Fund Institute, www.swfinstitute.org/fund-rankings/sovereign-wealth-fund (accessed February 2023).

UNCTAD (2021), *Handbook on Special Economic Zones in Africa: Towards Economic Diversification across the Continent*, United Nations Conference on Trade and Development, Geneva, https://unctad.org/system/files/official-document/diaeia2021d3_en.pdf.

UNCTAD (2019), *Economic Development in Africa Report 2019: Made in Africa - Rules of Origin for Enhanced Intra-African Trade*, United Nations Conference on Trade and Development, Geneva, https://unctad.org/system/files/official-document/aldcafrica2019_en.pdf.

USDA ERS (2021), "Data on expenditures on food and alcoholic beverages in selected countries", *United States Department of Agriculture (USDA) Economic Research Service* (database), www.ers.usda.gov/topics/international-markets-u-s-trade/international-consumer-and-food-industry-trends/#data (accessed 28 January 2023).

Weatherspoon, D. D. and T. Reardon (2003), "The rise of supermarkets in Africa: Implications for agrifood systems and the rural poor", *Development Policy Review*, Vol. 21/3, pp. 333-355, https://doi.org/10.1111/1467-7679.00214.

WFP (2022), *Assessment of the Risks and Impact of the Russian-Ukrainian Agricultural Production on the ECOWAS Region*, ECOWAS, Food and Agricultural Organisation of the United Nations and World Food Programme, https://docs.wfp.org/api/documents/WFP-0000139841/download/.

World Bank (2022a), *World Development Indicators* (database), https://data.worldbank.org/products/wdi (accessed 12 January 2023).

World Bank (2022b), "West Africa food insecurity demands climate-smart response amid multiple crises", Featured Story, 8 September, www.worldbank.org/en/news/feature/2022/09/08/west-africa-food-insecurity-demands-climate-smart-response-amid-multiple-crises.

World Bank (2021), "Agriculture, forestry, and fishing, value added (% of GDP)", *World Bank Databank*, https://data.worldbank.org/indicator/NV.AGR.TOTL.ZS (accessed 28 January 2023).

World Bank-KNOMAD (2022), *Remittances* (database), Global Knowledge Partnership on Migration and Development and World Bank, www.knomad.org/data/remittances (accessed 19 December 2022).

Annex A. Statistical annex

Data used in this edition of *Africa's Development Dynamics* have been compiled and presented in tables available for free download on the Development Centre's website (https://oe.cd/AFDD-2023) along with some additional social and economic indicators that add context to the report's analysis.

All indicators that were chosen for the annex provide national data figures for all or nearly all African countries, as well as most countries in the rest of the world. These choices were made in order to allow for both comparisons between African countries and comparisons with groups of similar countries outside of Africa that could serve as benchmarks. These data give context to the analyses presented in the report and allow readers to investigate the underlying data in more depth.

Data were obtained from various sources, including harmonised data sets of annual national data from reputable international institutions, as well as some indicators that were calculated by researchers working on the publication. Figures will get updated as new data come available so that readers can always track the latest versions of key indicators. Therefore some differences between figures in the statistical annex and figures reported in the publication may reflect changes to the data tables made after the publication of the written report.

Access the online Africa's Development Dynamics statistical annex here: https://oe.cd/AFDD-2023.

Data tables available for free download on line

		Download it here
Table 1	Indicators of growth, employment and inequality	https://rb.gy/nbvyy
Table 2	Annual real GDP growth rate, 1990-2028	https://rb.gy/ad0nb
Table 3	Annual population growth rate, 1990-2028	https://rb.gy/n7u22
Table 4	Annual real GDP growth per capita, 1990-2028	https://rb.gy/cxevh
Table 5	Demographic estimates	https://rb.gy/r0s5x
Table 6	Basic education indicators	https://rb.gy/4z5zj
Table 7	Labour force characteristics	https://rb.gy/f5cnh
Table 8	Sectoral breakdown of the economy	https://rb.gy/tnc5g
Table 9	Indicators of inequality and poverty	https://rb.gy/vyu71
Table 10	Gender indicators	https://rb.gy/wbkc4
Table 11	Communications infrastructure	https://rb.gy/rmtpq
Table 12	Digitalisation	https://rb.gy/oqxy6
Table 13	Basic health indicators	https://rb.gy/23en6
Table 14	Subjective well-being	https://rb.gy/mn6ha
Table 15	Growth decomposition by expenditure	https://rb.gy/kuagg
Table 16	Public finances	https://rb.gy/panoi
Table 17	Trade by manufacturing intensity	https://rb.gy/yuwln
Table 18	Export diversification	https://rb.gy/2k574
Table 19	Global and regional trade	https://rb.gy/t077o
Table 20	External financial inflows	https://rb.gy/l0hvf
Table 21	Investment and capital stock	https://rb.gy/aiee9
Table 22	Returns on direct investments	https://rb.gy/nm68y
Table 23	Ecological sustainability	https://rb.gy/22ykf
Table 24	Sustainable public investments and adjusted net savings	https://rb.gy/9c0yq
Table 25	GHG emissions by sector	https://rb.gy/hel4e
Table 26	Electricity and sustainable energy	https://rb.gy/g3ztg
Table 27	Origin and destination of added value	https://rb.gy/68ta7
Table 28	International trade costs	https://rb.gy/et3vg
Table 29	National wealth	https://rb.gy/r4ig4
Table 30	Environmental causes of premature deaths	https://rb.gy/lf2h9
Table 31	Informal economies and informal employment	https://rb.gy/71rhy

Download a table of country groupings here: https://rb.gy/pr8ji (see below).

Download the data dictionary for the variables in these tables here: https://rb.gy/3ujvj.

Download all annex tables in a single Excel file here: https://rb.gy/g87k4.

More extensive data, including time series for all variables back to 2000, are also available on line

The figures presented in these statistical tables, with the exception of Tables 2-4, represent the most recent years for which data are available. However, a complete dataset containing all these indicators for the years 2000-present in one Excel file can be downloaded from the following link: https://rb.gy/1m1n8. Otherwise, the same indicators can be found online through the OECD's online statistical portal at https://stats.oecd.org/ and clicking on "Development", followed by "Africa's Development Dynamics" on the menu.

The online statistical annex includes interactive data analysis

In addition to allowing users to download all data listed above, the online statistical annex at the *Africa's Development Dynamics 2023* web page (https://oe.cd/AFDD-2023) features the interactive *Compare Your Country* data analysis tool. Users can use this tool to create visualisations of the full time series of certain key variables interactively, selecting which countries can be placed in comparison, the type of chart, and other parameters.

The data in the statistical annex are also available for key country groupings

The statistical annex reports statistics for nearly all world countries, and also aggregations of indicators over country groups developed for benchmarking and analysis. The table (https://rb.gy/pr8ji) indicating the countries that belong to each group is among the files available in the statistical annex. The country groups featured in the analysis are the following:

- **The five regions of the African Union** (Central Africa, East Africa, North Africa, Southern Africa, and West Africa, as defined by the Abuja Treaty).
- **Africa and benchmark country groupings** (Africa, Asian countries excluding high-income countries, Latin America and Caribbean countries, and the World).
- **Resource-rich countries.** Countries that obtain a significant fraction of their GDP from underground natural-resource extraction are referred to as "resource-rich". These resource endowments can have major implications for economic, political, and social development. In this report, countries are identified as resource-rich based on whether, over the previous decade, the estimated contribution of the extraction of hydrocarbons, coal and minerals to economic output exceeds 10% of GDP in at least five years.
- **Income level.** The World Bank divides the countries of the world into four categories based on GNI per capita, using their Atlas Method:[1] low-income countries, lower middle-income countries, upper middle-income countries, and high-income countries.
- **Geographic access.** The report provides a breakdown between countries that are landlocked, countries that have a portion of coastline, and island nations. Gaining access to world trade can be complicated by a country's access to the ocean or lack thereof, while island nations have been shown to have different development patterns than other coastal nations. In addition to this three-way breakdown of countries, this report provides data on countries deemed "Landlocked Developing Countries (LLDC)" and "Small Island Developing States (SIDS)" by the UN Office of the High Representative for the Least Developed Countries, Landlocked Developing Countries and Small Island Developing States (UN-OHRLLS).[2]

- **Least developed countries.**[3] The UN-OHRLLS classifies some countries as "Least Developed Countries (LDC)". This categorisation of countries was officially established in 1971, by the UN General Assembly, and represents countries that face low levels of socio-economic development. Countries are designated as LDC countries based on income criteria, the health and education of their populations, and their economic vulnerability.
- **Fragile states.**[4] The OECD studies fragility as a multi-dimensional concept of risks that could pose a critical challenge to the ability of countries to achieve their development aspirations, in particular the goals outlined by the UN's 2030 Agenda for Sustainable Development. Based on the results of this research, presented in the OECD *States of Fragility* report, countries are categorised as being "fragile" or "extremely fragile".
- **Regional Economic Communities and other intergovernmental organisations.** Partnerships of countries formed for the purposes of regional integration or co-operation that have economic or political significance and that are particularly relevant to an analysis of African economic performance are included here. This includes the 8 Regional Economic Communities (REC) recognised by the African Union, as well as other regional and international organisations, such as the Association of Southeast Asian Nations (ASEAN), Mercado Común del Sur (MERCOSUR), the European Union (EU) and the OECD that serve as benchmarks. Aggregate figures for PALOP (Países Africanos de Língua Oficial Portuguesa, the Portuguese-speaking African countries) were included in response to a request from members of this country grouping.

Notes

1. Please see http://datahelpdesk.worldbank.org/knowledgebase/articles/378832-what-is-theworld-bank-atlas-method.
2. Please see www.un.org/ohrlls/.
3. Please see www.un.org/ohrlls/content/least-developed-countries.
4. Please see www.oecd.org/dac/conflict-fragility-resilience/listofstateoffragilityreports.htm.

www.ingramcontent.com/pod-product-compliance
Lightning Source LLC
Chambersburg PA
CBHW061207240926
51846CB00006B/1133
* 9 7 8 9 2 6 4 4 2 5 0 1 9 *